WHO KILLED JANE STANFORD?

Selected Books by
RICHARD WHITE

CALIFORNIA EXPOSURES
Envisioning Myth and History
(photographs by Jesse Amble White)

THE REPUBLIC FOR WHICH IT STANDS
The United States During the Gilded Age and Reconstruction

RAILROADED
The Transcontinentals and the Making of Modern America

REMEMBERING AHANAGRAN
Storytelling in a Family's Past

THE ORGANIC MACHINE
The Remaking of the Columbia River

THE MIDDLE GROUND
*Indians, Empires, and Republics in the Great Lakes Region,
1650–1815*

"IT'S YOUR MISFORTUNE AND NONE OF MY OWN"
A New History of the American West

THE ROOTS OF DEPENDENCY
*Subsistence, Environment, and Social Change Among the
Choctaws, Pawnees, and Navajos*

LAND USE, ENVIRONMENT, AND SOCIAL CHANGE
The Shaping of Island County, Washington, 1790–1940

WHO KILLED
JANE STANFORD?

A Gilded Age Tale

of Murder, Deceit, Spirits, and

the Birth of a University

RICHARD WHITE

W. W. NORTON & COMPANY
Independent Publishers Since 1923

Frontispiece: Jane Lathrop Stanford, 1900; Stanford Family Photograph Collection
(PC0001), Stanford University, Department of Special Collections and University
Archives, Stanford, California; courtesy of Stanford University Archives

For information about permission to reproduce selections from this book,
write to Permissions, W. W. Norton & Company, Inc.,
500 Fifth Avenue, New York, NY 10110

For information about special discounts for bulk purchases, please contact
W. W. Norton Special Sales at specialsales@wwnorton.com or 800-233-4830

Manufacturing by Lake Book Manufacturing
Book design by Marysarah Quinn
Production manager: Lauren Abbate

ISBN 978-1-324-00433-2

W. W. Norton & Company, Inc., 500 Fifth Avenue, New York, N.Y. 10110
www.wwnorton.com

W. W. Norton & Company Ltd., 15 Carlisle Street, London W1D 3BS

1 2 3 4 5 6 7 8 9 0

TO MY BROTHER,
STEPHEN

CONTENTS

Illustrations follow page 192

PREFACE

FOR YEARS a visit to Stanford University has involved crossing paths with tours led by undergraduates who, walking backward, face a trailing audience of prospective students and their families. Those in the tours crave admission to one of the wealthiest and most exclusive universities in the world.

The tour guides convey an origin story of the university: a beloved child of a rich couple dies tragically; the grieving parents vow to devote their fortune to the creation of a college for the children of California, and Leland Stanford Junior University opens in 1891. The story is true as far as it goes, but it leaves out critical details that change the story's meaning. The full story involves a dubious and insecure fortune laundered into a monument to the founding family, and a school rejuvenated through the blood of one of its founders.

It is a Gilded Age story, and this book tells that story.

Who Killed Jane Stanford? originated from another tour, one I gave for years as part of a class I taught on the nineteenth century. I walked my students back into the past—into the Gilded Age—to get them to decipher what was hidden in front of their eyes. My tour covered the oldest parts of Stanford— the Quad, the Memorial Church, the museum, the mausoleum, and remnants of the Memorial Arch—that date from the late nineteenth and early twentieth centuries. In their original form, these monuments to the Stanfords were so grandiose and brazen—so lacking in subtlety—that the immediate instinct was to accept them at face value and never consider what they might conceal.

But Leland Stanford Junior University was never what it seemed. Stanford was "inward"—a common expression of the late nineteenth century used to describe things that were not as they appeared on the surface. Stanford appeared to be simply another of the new research universities funded by rich people during the Gilded Age: the University of Chicago, Rice University, Vanderbilt University, and Carnegie Mellon University. But Stanford University became much stranger and much darker.

It was more fitting than I originally knew to begin my tour at the mausoleum because it was Jane Stanford's death that saved the university created by the death of Leland Jr. Both, along with Leland Stanford Sr., rest inside. Initially and obtusely, I focused on Leland Stanford Sr., whose fortune derived from the Central Pacific and Southern Pacific railroads. I recognized soon enough that without the dead child—Leland Stanford Jr.—the Stanford campus would be just another patch in the suburbs sweeping south from San Francisco.

But the key figure was Jane Stanford. After the death of her husband and cofounder Leland Stanford in 1893, she wielded power over the university. For a dozen years the dead son and the dead father rested alone in the mausoleum while Jane Stanford kept the university alive during the hard times of the 1890s. She shaped it until her death in 1905. During those years, an empty sarcophagus awaited her inside the family mausoleum. The inscription engraved on its marble surface stopped, incomplete: "Jane L. Stanford. Born in Mortality, August 2, 1828. Passed to Immortality . . ." On March 16, 1905, a workman chiseled in the missing date: February 28, 1905. What Jane Stanford called her earthly life was complete.[1]

Leland Stanford Junior University was not like other universities because Jane Stanford was convinced that not only was she doing God's work, she was also his agent in promoting the education of the soul as well as the mind. In 1900, taking a cure in Bavaria, she imagined the scene at the university, with "carriages rushing up the main drive up to the Arch. . . . I can see the artists at work on the carving bringing out the story of the civilization of the world and prevading [sic] my entire being such a sense of gratitude fills me . . . that I, so unworthy of God's special care, should have been chosen as a humble instrument to do the will of the loved ones gone on to their reward for lives well spent."[2]

Contrary to the selfless image created of her after her death, Jane Stanford always deflected attention back to herself, even as she celebrated her son, her husband, God, and civilization. She commissioned the statue of her family; she built the arch and the church. She dedicated the church to Leland Stanford—"my husband"; she was the instrument of God's and her deceased family's will. The Reverend David Charles Gardner proved a spectacularly poor prophet but correct enough in discerning the church's purpose when he said at its dedication, "This cathedral like church will stand forever a monument to the piety of a woman."[3]

Jane made her Christian devotion, her identity as a mother and wife, and her service to civilization visible, but they also masked what she sought to keep out of public notice: her spiritualism. Spiritualism was both common and controversial in Gilded Age America and, for that matter, in Victorian England. Queen Victoria was a spiritualist; so too were Sir Arthur Conan Doyle, Mary Lincoln, President Ulysses S. Grant, and his wife Louisa. Spiritualism had numerous variations, but essentially it involved communication with the dead.[4] Death was so thin a barrier that spiritualists often refused to use the word, instead resorting to euphemisms like birth into a higher life. In a world full of early deaths, this was comforting.

Jane Stanford did not advertise her spiritualism, but neither did she hide it from those who knew where to look. The nondenominational Memorial Church was Jane Stanford's great solace. She described it as "soul-satisfying," "a work of love." But the church was deeply inward.[5]

The cacophony of creeds and symbols in the ecumenical Memorial Church allowed the voices of spiritualists to babble inconspicuously among the others. Jane Stanford personally gathered the spiritual quotations that covered the lower walls of the east and west sides of the church. She sought to strip Christianity of dogma and make it nonsectarian, but the result spoke mainly to a sect of one: Jane Stanford. The church of Jane rested on two key texts. The first read: "The best form of religion is, trust in God and a firm belief in the immortality of the soul, life everlasting." This she attributed to a letter from her husband. So too the second: "An eternal existence in prospect converts the whole of your present state into a mere vestibule of the grand court of life; a beginning, an introduction to what is to follow; the entrance into that immeasurable extent of being which is the true life of man. The best thoughts, affections and aspirations of a great soul are fixed on the infinitude of eternity. Destined as such a soul is for immortality, it finds all that is not eternal too short, all that is not infinite too small."[6]

I wanted the students on my tour to see the physical signs of these nineteenth- and early twentieth-century beliefs in the edifices built during Stanford's "Stone Age," as David Starr Jordan, the original president of the university, sardonically referred to it. I also wanted them to recognize absences and exiles, to draw meaning from what has vanished and been displaced, and what remains. The bronze statue of the Stanford family originally located just beyond the arch eventually became an embarrassment and was banished to a spot beside the Stanford family mausoleum, a place now rarely visited except by spiritualists who sometimes light candles and leave them on the tomb's steps.

Jane Stanford longed to join her departed husband and son, but things did not end as she expected. She died of strychnine poisoning in Hawaii, in the words of the coroner's jury, "at the hands of person or persons unknown." In 2003 Robert Cutler, a physician at Stanford, published *The Mysterious Death of Jane Stanford*, a book that reexamined the circumstances of her death. Cutler undermined the university's position, which it has held since 1905, that she died a natural death. My initial interest in her death was pedagogical. I used Cutler's book as a source for a class on historical research. I sent undergraduates into the archives to see what they could find out about Jane Stanford's poisoning. They found a lot, but as proud as I was of their work, these were ten-week classes, and they could only scratch the surface.[7]

Historians and detectives both know that the answer is always in the past. Dashiell Hammett might as well be a historian when he opens *The Maltese Falcon* with Sam Spade instructing his client, "Suppose you tell me about it, from the beginning, and then we'll know what needs doing. Better begin as far back as you can."[8]

Sam Spade had living witnesses. Like most historians, I only have the long dead. I can't interrogate them—"sweat them" in the police argot of the early twentieth century. I am left with whatever they left, willingly or unwillingly, behind.

Among the things Jane Stanford left behind was a plaster cast of her face: a death mask made two days after she died. It is in the Stanford University Archives, and the first time I taught the class on her demise, the archivist pulled it from its box and showed it to the students, who reacted with audible gasps as if her corpse had walked in the room. At that moment Jane Stanford leaped across the century and came among us like an apparition at one of her séances. She then disappeared.

So too have many of the sources concerning her life and her death.

Preservation of historical records is always imperfect, but rarely have I encountered more documents that have vanished and more collections and reports that have gone missing than in this research. Jane apparently destroyed most of Leland's records, and many of Jane's have also disappeared. Except for a memoir, most of her secretary Bertha Berner's papers are gone without a trace. These vanished records test my belief that the past cannot be erased, but my faith remains intact. An original letter can go missing, but a response remains. A report can disappear, but accounts of the report survive. Participants in events lie, but it is virtually impossible to find and destroy all the materials that undermine the lie.

I wish I could say that seeing the mask of Jane Stanford's face, only a little more than a day dead, sparked a desire in me to see justice done. It didn't. I saw an aged woman and I initially wondered not who killed her, but why? Why hasten those last few steps to the grave? Someone must have had something at stake.

I was not surprised that in the Gilded Age—a time of breathtaking inequality—the many murders of poor people went unsolved, but why would the investigation of the death of the richest woman in San Francisco be shut down in less than a month? Why would her family, the administrators of the university she cofounded, the police department, the political establishment of San Francisco, and private detectives hired to find the murderer not only give up on finding her killer, but, despite the evidence that she was poisoned, go to all the trouble of denying it and crafting a narrative of a natural death? This was not how I imagined Gilded Age San Francisco worked.

I always intended this book as a history that used Jane Stanford's death to reveal the politics, power struggles, and scandals of Gilded Age San Francisco. And it is. Her life and death were inseparable from Leland Stanford Junior University, Boss Ruef's San Francisco, Chinatown, the urban underworld, nineteenth-century spiritualism, and the people—upstairs and downstairs—of the Stanford mansions.

But the book surprised me in several ways. As a story of Gilded Age privilege, inequality, corruption, politics, and the press, it resonates with the present. In an age of surreal conspiracy theories, it is a reminder that conspiracies can be quite real. In an age of staggering inequality, it is set in another age of staggering inequality. Its main characters are rich people who created monuments to themselves, and whose lives are reminders that the problem with philanthropy is very often philanthropists. We live in a world where murderers walk free, and powerful people go to great lengths to preserve secrets. Such things are not unique to our time.

The second surprise is that while I started out to write a history—which this is—I also ended up writing a detective story that could fit in the true-crime genre. Like a detective, I was sifting through scattered sources to determine not only who killed Jane Stanford but how and why. Finishing the book, confined by the Covid pandemic, I kept going back over the sources, looking for details that I might have ignored. That search produced my final surprise. I had wondered why the police and detectives gave up their pursuit of the suspects. I ended up thinking they did not give up. They found what they were looking for.

POLAND
SPRING
WATER

CHAPTER 1

THE FIRST POISONING

ON SATURDAY EVENING, JANUARY 14, 1905, Jane Stanford prepared to go to sleep in her California Street mansion on San Francisco's Nob Hill—one palace on what Robert Louis Stevenson called a hill of palaces. Someone intended that she never see the next day.

Mrs. Leland Stanford, as she referred to herself, was seventy-six years old, the cofounder of Leland Stanford Junior University, and reputedly the wealthiest woman in San Francisco. Much of the year she either traveled or stayed at her Palo Alto estate, but this winter she had returned to San Francisco to entertain before departing for Europe in the spring.

Her bedroom was one of nineteen in the mansion, whose fifty rooms, spread over four floors, totaled 41,000 square feet of interior space. The architects designed the building for public events and configured it to resemble a seventeenth-century palace. When the doors from the first-floor rooms were opened onto the large central hall, the fountain in the conservatory, the flowers in profusion, and the music from the orchestrion—a machine that imitated an orchestra—combined in a dazzling spectacle.[1]

Yet, with its unoccupied bedrooms and vast spaces, the mansion could seem quite forlorn between the dinners, receptions, and parties. Jane's husband, Leland, had been dead for nearly twelve years; her son, Leland Jr., died nearly twenty-one years before. After all the years, she still missed them terribly, but she was thankful for the friendship of Bertha Berner, her companion and secretary, whose love she regarded as "God-giving."[2]

That winter Bertha Berner had a bedroom on the third story of the mansion, a floor above Jane's room. She was thirty-nine, unmarried, five feet five inches—tall for the time—with gray eyes and abundant brown hair. There are only a few pictures of her. In one she stands in front of the Stanford summer home in Palo Alto, wearing a white dress with the wasp-ish waist of the period. She has full lips and an aquiline nose. She posed with a half-smile. In another she is on a camel in Egypt. Her face is round, her eyes almond shaped, her gaze direct. She was a woman whom men noticed, and Jane Stanford noticed that men noticed. Berner did not usu-ally reside in the mansion. When Jane Stanford was in Palo Alto, Berner shared a home in Menlo Park with her mother and brother.[3]

Jane Stanford might sometimes be lonely, but she was never alone. Servants surrounded her. That winter, besides Berner, there were seven ser-vants: Stanford's personal maid, Elizabeth Richmond; the temporary but-ler William McQuinney; the housemaid Nora Hopkins; Ah Wing, who was the general factotum of the house; Ah Young, who was "the boy cou-rier" and Ah Wing's nephew; Joe Yeng, the cook; and Ah Lee, the assistant cook.[4] But much of the company Mrs. Stanford kept was otherworldly. She told a *San Francisco Examiner* reporter that "I am never alone. Either my husband or son are with me all the time. They never come together, but in turns. Their stay is limited to within two weeks' time, and during that period I enjoy a happiness that the world can neither appreciate or know." She denied she was a spiritualist "according to the popular con-ception," but her dead son and husband were her "two spiritual advisers. In living with these bright visions near me, I am being prepared for the end—the union with my husband and son."[5]

Just before retiring that night, Jane Stanford took a glass of Poland Spring Water—a mineral water produced in Maine. It came in a quart green-glass bottle, and someone had uncorked the bottle and placed it by her bed. The company, seeking to protect its brand, specially marked its cork and offered a $500 reward to anyone who detected that the bottle had been tampered with and the cork replaced. Poland Spring Water promised purity, which gave it the power to cure an array of diseases, among them indigestion and "many of the peculiar diseases of women." It was able "to cleanse the body of 'evil humors,' clear the mind of 'distorted fancies,' and transform the soul."[6] Because she drank Poland Spring Water for her health, it became the vehicle for administering poison. But the poisoner overdid it. The water tasted so bitter that Jane immediately vomited and called for help from Elizabeth Richmond, her personal maid. Richmond was English, and reporters described her as refined and well-mannered: "a quiet little mouse of a woman."[7]

The bottle turned out to contain strychnine.

That someone put strychnine into Jane Stanford's bottle of Poland Spring Water was the only clear thing about what happened that evening. Just three people possessed firsthand knowledge of what occurred: Mrs. Stanford, Elizabeth Richmond, and Bertha Berner.

Their stories—often conveyed in breathless coverage by the city's newspapers—overlapped, changed over time, and were full of contradictions, and that is their virtue. They map attempts to explain, deceive, and justify. None of these accounts is definitive, although it is possible to isolate the events where they agree and the places where they differ. Tracking the differences is a necessary step to understanding what happened.

Mrs. Stanford, Bertha Berner, and Elizabeth Richmond all agreed that at about 8:00 p.m. on Saturday evening, January 14, 1905, Bertha Berner said good night to Jane Stanford in her second-floor bedroom. She went upstairs to her own room, drew a bath, and then retired for the night. Jane Stanford busied herself in her bedroom with Elizabeth Richmond nearby in the adjacent sewing room. About 9:00 p.m. Mrs. Stanford called out to tell her there was something wrong with the Poland Spring Water. She had taken a drink, and it nauseated her. Richmond tasted the water and agreed it was bitter.

At some point, Jane Stanford told Elizabeth Richmond to go upstairs and summon Bertha Berner, which she did. Berner put on a wrapper and came down the stairs to Jane Stanford's bedroom. She found Mrs. Stanford standing in front of her washstand, trembling. She said she had taken a drink of the water "and it was terrible." After the first swallow, the water had "come up in a flash," and she vomited repeatedly afterward. Berner dipped a finger in the glass and put it in her mouth. She said it tasted very bitter. She told Jane Stanford to continue vomiting. Stanford took another drink of warm water, stuck her finger down her throat, and the vomit came up clear.[8]

Jane Stanford told Berner to look at the bottle in a strong light. She and Richmond both saw particles suspended in the water. Berner suggested that the water be examined, and Richmond agreed.[9]

Berner and Richmond's accounts concur on the bitter taste in the water, Mrs. Stanford's vomiting, and the decision to send the bottle out to a chemist to be analyzed. These are important things, but their accounts differ on much else.

Richmond said that before going to summon Berner, she went downstairs to get "an emetic of warm water and salt" for Mrs. Stanford.[10] The *San Francisco Bulletin*'s account corroborated Richmond's claim of administering an emetic, but reported that she was gone so long that Jane Stanford "got nervous," went to the stationary stand, and drew two glasses of hot water, vomiting after swallowing each one. When Richmond finally returned, Mrs. Stanford could hardly drink the water, having already swallowed so much.[11] Defensive about her absence, Richmond claimed that she did not go to get warm water, which was available nearby, but salt. Mrs. Stanford's panic made her think that her maid was gone a long time.[12]

Other differences in the stories are more significant. Richmond remembered having seen the bottle between ten and eleven in the morning with about a glass full of water already poured from it. The detail was important. Since Jane Stanford did not complain of the taste earlier, the water must have been originally pure and harmless. Someone contaminated it between 11:00 a.m. and roughly 6:00 p.m. when Jane Stanford returned to the room.[13]

According to the *Bulletin*, Mrs. Stanford corroborated Richmond's story. She said that she ordered a bottle of Poland Spring Water to be brought to her that Saturday morning, poured a glass, and recorked the bottle. She also drank another glass of Poland Spring Water from a separate bottle downstairs at lunch.[14] Richmond said Ah Young uncorked the original bottle and brought it to Mrs. Stanford's room, but Nora Hopkins, another maid, said it was Richmond.[15]

Berner disputed Richmond's account. She said the bottle was in the same condition as when it came from the case, and that Richmond must have put the thought in Jane Stanford's mind that the bottle was only partially full.[16] If the bottle in the room was full, it contained the poison when it arrived and had been contaminated before reaching the room. This widened the window for the poisoning and the roster of possible suspects.

Berner and Richmond also differed on what happened to the bottle following the poisoning, or rather they originally agreed but Berner changed her story. Richmond said that at Mrs. Stanford's request she immediately carried the corked bottle to Wakelee's pharmacy to be analyzed. Cable cars ran up California Street on Nob Hill, but Richmond walked from the mansion at Powell and California to the drugstore at Bush and Montgomery because she was afraid of having the bottle spill or break on the cable car. The clerk at Wakelee's remembered her coming in. Because of its bitter taste, Richmond told him the water might contain quinine, which was also apparently Jane Stanford's initial suspicion.[17]

Berner originally accepted this account. After Richmond went downstairs, dressed, and departed for Wakelee's pharmacy, Berner stayed with Jane Stanford, who continued drinking warm water and putting her finger down her throat until Richmond returned. Mrs. Stanford said she felt weak but not ill. Richmond brought Jane Stanford a cup of warm milk, and Berner left. When Berner checked on Mrs. Stanford the next morning, "she assured me that she had a better night than she enjoyed for some time, and experienced no ill effects."[18]

Berner told a different story in her memoir. As she recalled thirty years later, "Mrs. Stanford had a very severe cold, with a congested head, and slept little that night"; her lack of sleep was the result of her cold and not the Poland Spring Water. Berner now said that it was not until the next morning that Richmond took the bottle to the drugstore.[19]

It was unclear who besides Ah Young, Richmond, and Berner entered Mrs. Stanford's room that day. Berner did not believe an outsider could gain access to the bedroom, but she admitted that if anyone else had, she would not have noticed them. This raises the question of whether any outsiders were present that Saturday. In the story she told in 1905, Berner did not mention any other visitors in the house that day, but in her memoir she wrote that Jane Stanford met with her lawyer Russell J. Wilson in the morning and held a meeting of university trustees in the afternoon. But there was no trustee meeting that day, and Mrs. Stanford could not have met with Russell Wilson. A stroke had felled him years earlier, and he no longer practiced law.[20]

Bertha Berner could have mixed up Russell with his brother, Mountford, who still represented Jane Stanford. And according to the *Bulletin*'s account, Jane Stanford did meet with "one of the trustees and another person."[21] If accurate, then there were at least two more unnamed people— and thus two more at least peripheral suspects—in the house the Saturday of the Poland Spring Water incident. If Mountford was "the other person," he could have been in the house that day.[22]

After her meeting, Jane Stanford put on her hat and cloak to take the evening train to Palo Alto. She would attend services in the Stanford Memorial Church; Berner would "spend the day with my family, as we had been away so long." A Saturday evening and a full Sunday with her family was something Berner was unlikely to give up easily. In her memoir, Bertha Berner explained that they postponed the trip this Saturday because of Jane Stanford's exhaustion and bad cold. But no one at the time mentioned Jane Stanford's being sick that Saturday night. Elizabeth Richmond mentioned only a sore throat the next morning, which was not surprising in a woman who had repeatedly stuck her finger down her throat to induce vomiting. Berner said that she, rather than Stanford, suggested delaying the trip. They would instead take one of the Sunday morning trains to Palo Alto, which left at 6:10 and 7:00 a.m. After eating dinner, Jane Stanford went to her room and Berner said good night to her there.[23] Intentionally or not, Berner became the proximate cause of the poisoning. If Mrs. Stanford had gone to Palo Alto that evening, she would not have had the opportunity to drink the poisoned water.

THE TRIP TO THE TRAIN STATION the following day brought an additional surprise. Jane Stanford and Bertha Berner encountered David Starr Jordan, the president of Leland Stanford Junior University, and told him of the incident. Jordan was in the city to attend a dinner held in honor of Jacob Riis, the author of *How the Other Half Lives*, at the Palace Hotel on January 14. He probably arrived on the afternoon of the 14th.[24]

Jordan and Jane Stanford agreed that they met coincidentally, but differed on where they met and what they said. Jordan claimed that he met Bertha Berner and Jane Stanford on a streetcar on January 15, and they told him of the Poland Spring Water incident, which Mrs. Stanford "appeared to take . . . lightly." Streetcars were not cable cars, but rather trolleys that ran along the flat parts of the city. Meeting on the streetcar involved a significant element of chance. Stanford, coming from her California Street mansion on the way to the Southern Pacific Depot at Third and Townsend, would need to transfer to a streetcar that passed the Palace Hotel on Market just as Jordan was boarding. Jane Stanford told friends that the meeting took place on the train to Palo Alto, which seems more likely given that there were far fewer trains than streetcars. She said she described her symptoms to Jordan, who declared the water must have contained strychnine, which makes his report that she "appeared to take the matter lightly" odd.[25]

A month later, long after the arrival of the chemist's report that there was strychnine in the water, Jordan denied any poisoning. He either forgot his conversation with Stanford or she did not inform him of the chemist's report. Or he lied.[26]

There was one sign, an admittedly ambiguous one, that Jordan knew something untoward had happened to Jane Stanford. On January 20, before Stanford received the chemist's report on the Poland Spring Water, Jordan wrote to the *Daily Palo Alto*, which had a student correspondent working for the *San Francisco Chronicle*. He demanded that "all matters containing the name of Mrs. Stanford be submitted to the president's office." He was not privy to the investigation of the poisoning, and no one besides the person who placed the strychnine in the bottle, or those to whom the poisoner confided, as yet knew there was poison in the Poland Spring Water. The correspondent, W. K. B. Fowler, replied that the *Chronicle*'s policy prohibited such preapproval.[27] Jordan warned Fowler against letting "statements injurious to the University and especially painful to Mrs. Stanford" appear in the newspapers.[28]

Over the years Jordan continued to revise his story. In a 1921 letter to Ray Lyman Wilbur, then president of Stanford University, he said that Stanford told him of the poisoning soon after it occurred and that she was planning "to go away for a time."[29] Jane Stanford did tell Jordan of her plans for a trip, but it was in early February, weeks after the poisoning, when she was in San Jose.[30]

CHAPTER 2

STRYCHNINE

WAKELEE'S PHARMACY, where Jane Stanford's maid, Elizabeth Richmond, brought the suspicious bottle of Poland Spring Water on Saturday night, January 15, could not perform the analysis requested, so the pharmacist sent the bottle to the Falkenau Assaying Company located nearby on Sacramento Street below Montgomery. Mrs. Stanford and Bertha Berner meanwhile left for Palo Alto, where the newspapers reported that they remained until Wednesday or Thursday, when Jane Stanford returned to host a dinner on Friday, January 20. The results of the analysis had still not arrived.[1]

Old friends from her Sacramento days made up most of the guest list. The theme was gold and the gold rush, and the dining room dripped yellow. Charles Lathrop, who was both Jane's much younger sibling and her employee, sat at the head of table with his wife nearby. He owed his own fortune to his employment first on the railroads and then at the university belonging to Jane and Leland Stanford. Also attending were Jennie Lathrop—Charles's daughter and Jane's niece, who hated her stepmother and was close to Jane—and Bertha Berner. Jane sat at the middle of the table.[2]

Timothy Hopkins, the adopted son of Mark Hopkins, one of Leland Stanford's old railroad associates, sat at the other end of the table. Hopkins and Jane Stanford shared lawyers—the Wilson brothers, Russell and Mountford. Hopkins, disinherited by his widowed mother because he objected to her second marriage to her interior decorator, contested her will. His case seemed lost until the Wilsons recruited Joseph Choate, a New York attorney, to serve as Hopkins's attorney in the case. Hopkins's stepfather surprisingly settled, granting him two or three million dollars but requiring him to acknowledge that he possessed no rights as an adopted son. Hopkins had blackmailed his stepfather, who was an invert, as gay men were called during the Gilded Age. Choate negotiated the settlement.[3]

The guests later reported that Mrs. Stanford had a slight cold but seemed "bright, active, and cheerful." After the dinner, she had a return of "bronchial trouble."[4]

Elizabeth Richmond began telephoning Wakelee's the day after the Poland Spring Water incident to get the test results. On Tuesday, the druggist said the results were ready, but the store did not put them in the mail until the following Saturday, January 21, a week after Richmond brought in the bottle. The report arrived that same Saturday, the day after the dinner party.[5] The Lathrops were still at the mansion.

When the report arrived, Jane Stanford asked Berner to read it. The chemist concluded that a glass of the Poland Spring Water contained three-quarters of a grain of strychnine. Half a grain usually proved fatal. The strychnine was not pure. It was a commercial poison sold to kill rats and squirrels.[6]

Upon hearing that the water contained strychnine, Jane Stanford threw up her hands and uttered what others would take up as the refrain of the next two months: "Oh, God. I did not think any one wished to hurt me. What would it benefit any one?" Then she calmed herself and said that no one was to say anything about this.[7]

Elizabeth Richmond left Berner, Mrs. Stanford, and Mrs. Lathrop alone to talk it over. When Richmond returned, she suggested an investigation. Jane Stanford told her that she had already decided to call the Pinkerton Detective Agency.

Charles Lathrop did not contact the Pinkertons nor did he contact the police; instead he alerted Mountford Wilson, Jane Stanford's attorney, and they engaged the Morse Detective Agency. Given the California dinner, Morse was a serendipitous choice. Harry Morse was, like Leland Stanford, "Old Californ'": an Argonaut—as the 49ers called themselves—and during the Civil War a member of the Oakland Guard, which was the local militia organized to suppress Confederate sympathizers. As sheriff of Alameda County, Morse hunted Narciso Bojorques, Tiburcio Vasquez, and other Californio and Mexican "desperados" whose banditry made some of them folk heroes among the Spanish-speaking population. He killed Juan Soto in a famous gunfight. The people Morse helped convict were not necessarily guilty. When required, he perjured himself and presented dubious evidence. In 1878, unsure of reelection and seeking more lucrative employment, he resigned as sheriff. Soon after, he founded the Harry Morse Detective Agency.[8]

Wilson and Lathrop did not go to the police because they preferred to avoid a scandal and wanted to keep the Poland Spring Water incident out of the newspapers.[9] Morse put Jules Callundan on the case. He hired Callundan in 1881 as a sixteen-year-old office boy, which made Callundan roughly the same age as Bertha Berner. Callundan rose to become a captain in the agency, its general manager, and eventually a partner.[10]

Callundan broke strikes, tracked down embezzlers, and supervised security guards, but he came on to the Stanford case for another talent. He knew how to keep things out of the newspapers. In a revealing incident two years earlier, he had protected his sister-in-law—the daughter of Congressman Eugene Loud—after she was involved in a midnight accident in Golden Gate Park during a night of drinking and gambling with a man who was not her husband. Her companion died, and she abandoned the body while passersby sought help. Callundan averted a scandal and made the incident go away.[11]

The chief concern of private detectives like Callundan was doing what their employers asked, which might or might not involve actually solving a crime. For nearly a month he kept the story of the poisoning out of the papers.[12]

Charles Lathrop also telephoned Dr. William Boericke, Jane Stanford's physician, to come and see his sister about her cold, but he did not mention strychnine. Jane Stanford had not seen Dr. Boericke for nearly two years. She only called doctors when extremely ill. He visited her on Saturday and returned on Sunday. By the time Dr. Boericke saw her, she was very sick. She had the grippe, as influenza was called. She was coughing with a high fever. Despite this, on Monday, January 23, Stanford and Berner left San Francisco and went to the Hotel Vendome in San Jose. She did not tell Dr. Boericke about the strychnine until he made a third visit to check on her progress. She told him she could not imagine who would want to poison her.[13]

CHAPTER 3

WATCHING
THE DETECTIVES

WHEN JULES CALLUNDAN and the other Morse detectives set to work in January of 1905, they knew three things. First, someone had put rat poison in Jane Stanford's bottle of Poland Spring Water. The chemist's report established that. Second, their job was to keep this quiet, which is why no one went to the police. And third, Jane Stanford insisted that no one had any reason to harm her.

The detectives also had three goals. First, find the source of the strychnine in the bottle. Second, try to find those with a motive to kill Mrs. Stanford. Third, narrow those with a motive down to a list of suspects with access to Jane Stanford's Poland Spring Water.

The only accounts of the investigation are Callundan's brief interview with the *San Francisco Call* in December of 1905, and David Starr Jordan's story of a supposed conversation with Callundan years later.[1] There are no surviving records of the Morse Agency in regard to the case. The police became involved later, but their records seem to have perished in the earthquake and fire of 1906. I have had to rely largely on newspapers, which is never a good thing.

The detectives made Elizabeth Richmond, whom Charles Lathrop disliked and mistrusted, their chief suspect. Richmond said Lathrop's animosity arose from Mrs. Stanford's confiding in her and telling her of the troubles she had with relatives, presumably including the Lathrops. Other stories circulated that Mrs. Stanford thought Richmond "cold and distant." Richmond admitted she noticed suspicion in Mrs. Stanford's eyes. After the test results arrived, Jane Stanford moved Richmond out of the room she occupied near her bedroom and had another maid, Nora Hopkins, sleep there. Richmond "was rather put out by having others doing my duty toward Mrs. Stanford."[2]

On January 26, one of Lathrop's clerks came to the mansion with Elizabeth Richmond's back wages and terminated her services. By then two weeks had passed since the poisoning and a little under a week since the chemist's report. The clerk told Richmond to pack and go to Palo Alto to retrieve her possessions at the summer house. A detective tracked her. He spied on her when she got a room in a San Francisco boardinghouse. Detectives continued to stalk her for two weeks.[3]

The detectives were not subtle. On Sunday, February 5, an annoyed Richmond went to San Mateo, located between Palo Alto and San Francisco, to visit Albert Beverly and his wife. Like Richmond, Beverly was a British immigrant and was previously Jane Stanford's butler. Richmond intended to stay only a day but remained until Thursday. On Saturday, after she returned to San Francisco and while sick in bed at her rooming house, two men who refused to give their names interviewed her at great length. They said she was no longer under suspicion and asked if she had theories on the case. On Monday the 13th, Mountford Wilson and Jules Callundan came to see her. Callundan asked her a great many questions.[4]

Richmond originally said that she gave Mrs. Stanford notice before the poisoning, but she repeatedly changed the story of her resignation. She admitted to the detectives that she and Jane Stanford quarreled, and that she got her back up when unjustly accused, but she denied stories that she was prone to rages. She said Stanford must have been out of her mind if she accused her of blind rages. She was not the first or the last to question Mrs. Stanford's sanity.[5]

They quarreled, Richmond said, on the Tuesday following the poisoning—which would have been January 17—when a hook for eyeglasses broke off of Jane Stanford's dress and Richmond mislaid it and failed to sew it back on as quickly as Mrs. Stanford wanted. Jane Stanford snapped at her and told her to telephone for May Hunt, the woman who would replace her. Richmond went downstairs to do so, but Bertha Berner ordered her back upstairs because Mrs. Stanford now wanted her again. Richmond replied she could not be in two places at once. Berner tried to soothe her, telling her it was okay and she should just go upstairs. But Richmond was angry. She told Jane Stanford she wished to leave her service as of the 1st of February. At the time, the report revealing the presence of strychnine in the Poland Spring Water had not yet arrived. Richmond said that if she knew of the poisoned water, she would not have said a word.[6]

The chronology of Richmond's story did not fit with other accounts. Jane Stanford could not have admonished her on January 17 if she and Berner went to Palo Alto on the 15th and stayed for several days, but Richmond changed her story again. The incident with the hook—whenever it occurred—was not the reason for her quitting. She said that part of her duties involved massaging Mrs. Stanford, and because Richmond was recovering from malaria, she found this difficult and decided to leave. Then she changed this story. She decided to leave on the morning after the poisoning when she went into Jane Stanford's room to massage her neck because of her sore throat. Jane Stanford reacted angrily, "You go away. I don't want you to put your hands on my throat. You go away."[7]

Pressuring Richmond proved a mistake. The ex-butler Albert Beverly was not a man to allow his friends to be pushed around. Indignant at Richmond's treatment, he claimed to have laid the case before the British consul. But Beverly appears to have been bluffing; there is no record in the consul's files in the British archives of a complaint, and there was never any intervention by the consul even though consuls intervened in far less notorious cases in 1905. Instead, Beverly urged Richmond to talk to the press. Once she did, the newspapers erupted in stories, which was precisely what those employing Callundan had sought to avoid.

Callundan and the other Morse Agency detectives responded by lying, but it took a few days to agree on the lie. They told the *San Francisco Call* on February 21 that there had been no poisoning, and they had devoted only a day to the case. They attributed Jane Stanford's nausea to indigestion, and said she called detectives only to make sure the rest of her Poland Spring Water was pure. But this was what the marked corks were supposed to guarantee. Stanford didn't need detectives to look at corks. Callundan then told the *Chronicle* that there had been a two-week investigation, and he was willing to "stake my good right eye against $1 that there was no attempt to poison Mrs. Stanford." Other servants staged the whole episode to discredit Bertha Berner.[8]

The detectives also searched for the source of the strychnine, but if the papers reported it correctly, the hunt was odd from the beginning. The chemist's report clearly identified the strychnine as coming from rat poison, which was readily available for over-the-counter purchase, but Callundan went looking for pure strychnine. He did so because he said Berner and Richmond saw crystals in the bottom of the bottle.[9]

Morse detectives claimed they went to every drugstore in San Francisco and the surrounding cities examining the poison registers to find recent purchasers of strychnine, but reporters for the *Examiner* claimed they contacted pharmacists who were never interviewed by the detectives. Strychnine was, the *San Francisco Chronicle* reported, "a drug rarely purchased in the crystal form." Pure strychnine was apparently usually sold as a powder. Every purchase the detectives discovered was legitimate. They also found no strychnine of any kind in the mansion.[10] There was, unsurprisingly, strychnine to poison rats and ground squirrels on the Stanford estate in Palo Alto.

———

THE SEARCH FOR A MOTIVE proved no more successful than the search for the poison. Those around Jane Stanford insisted that no one in their right mind would wish to harm her. Jane Stanford had no enemies because she was kind, good, and philanthropic. Nor, her relatives asserted, was there anyone who would benefit by her death.[11]

By the end of February Jules Callundan and the Morse Detective Agency seemed to have convinced San Francisco that the Poland Spring Water poisoning was only a jealous quarrel between servants. Mrs. Stanford was never in danger. This story—purposefully or inadvertently—made Bertha Berner's relationship with Jane Stanford, her own liminal relationship as employee and friend, and her relationships with the other servants—past and present—at the California Street mansion the center of the case. Jane Stanford retreated to the margins. The police never even opened an investigation, and the press moved on to other things.

———

NEITHER JANE STANFORD nor Bertha Berner believed Callundan's story. Nor did George Crothers, Jane Stanford's confidant on the Board of Trustees. I don't think for a minute it was what Jules Callundan really thought. The detectives reported what their employers wanted them to report. Why their employers did not want them to report an attempted murder is, in a nutshell, my problem.

CHAPTER 4

AH WING AND WONG TOY WONG

JANE STANFORD EMPLOYED both white and Chinese servants. Her Nob Hill mansion sat at the very top of California Street; Chinatown began near the bottom. In one of his *noir* stories, Dashiell Hammett describes Chinatown as jumping "out of the shopping district at California Street and [running] north to the Latin Quarter—a strip two blocks wide by six long. Before the fire nearly twenty-five thousand Chinese lived in those dozen blocks."[1] Nob Hill and Chinatown might seem worlds apart, but physically they were nearly adjacent.

When Wong Toy Wong sought to talk to Jane Stanford, he had to walk uphill, but he did not have far to walk. According to Morse Agency detectives, Wong Toy Wong wrote Mrs. Stanford a letter claiming to have been defrauded out of $30,000 from his account at the Stanford University Trust Bank. Someone had impersonated him and withdrawn the money. Wong Toy Wong lurked about the California Street mansion seeking an interview with Mrs. Stanford and the return of his funds. All this occurred before the poisoning of the Poland Spring Water bottle.[2]

The story was puzzling. There was no Stanford University Trust Bank, and Jane Stanford neither met nor talked to Wong, but some of her Chinese servants may have. These servants lived in the mansion when Mrs. Stanford was in residence, but most presumably lived in Chinatown when she was absent. After the January 14th poisoning, Wong Toy Wong passed from annoying to ominous, and a watchman roughed him up. Wong had angrily told the guard he would kill Mrs. Stanford. On the testimony of Morse detectives John Cleary and Callundan, Wong Toy Wong was brought before a judge, and on February 11 he was put in the state asylum at Mendocino.[3]

The doctors who admitted Wong described him as homicidal and destructive, but they recorded a different story than the one told by the Morse detectives. Wong Toy Wong said he was a wealthy man. Although a servant, he was about to marry his white employer's daughter. Because of this, Chinese merchants put a price of $5,000 on his head. A man claiming to have had his money stolen from a bank that did not exist was certainly delusional. A Chinese man claiming to be involved with a white woman and with a price on his head was less so, but Wong Toy Wong ridiculously overestimated the cost of killing him. A few hundred dollars would have bought his death.

Wong Toy Wong would remain in the asylum until June 21, 1914. The notation of his release said "Unimproved (Deported)."[4]

IN GILDED AGE SAN FRANCISCO with its deeply entrenched Sinophobia, Jane Stanford's Chinese servants were bound to come under suspicion. Wong Toy Wong triggered that suspicion, but the detectives did not consider him a real danger. He had no access to the mansion. Mrs. Stanford worried about another possibility: Wong Toy Wong might have convinced one of her servants to become his accomplice.[5]

Whites in San Francisco often knew just enough about Chinese to confuse themselves. A white employee of Mrs. Stanford claimed that all the Chinese servants were members of a single family—the Wong family, which is why Wong Toy Wong came to the mansion. But to think all Wongs were related was like thinking all Smiths or all Cohens were members of a single family. Wong was the most common surname among the immigrants from Guangdong province. The vast majority of Chinese emigrants to California came from four counties on the western side of the Pearl River delta. The large majority of this majority came from a single county, Xinning.[6]

When the employee said the Chinese all belonged to a single family, he may have meant the servants were members of the same *huigan*, which were native place associations. *Huigans* translated as meeting halls; whites referred to them as companies. The *huigans* functioned as mutual aid associations for those from the same region of China; they worked like similar associations established by other immigrants. They mediated disputes among members, protected them from abuse by whites, and when necessary protected their interests from other *huigans*. The Six Companies, an association of *huigans*, formed a shadow government for Chinatown.[7]

If any Chinese servant talked to Wong Toy Wong, it brought pressure to bear on Ah Wing. Ah Wing was from "the Old Wang Kwong (Crooked Stream) Village in the District of Sun Ning, Province of Kwong Tung [Guangdong]," near Hong Kong. His place of birth indicates that he would belong to the See Yup (Si Yup) *huigan*. He started working for the Stanfords in 1881—"the tenth year of the Reign of Emperor Kwong Hau [Guangzu]"—when Leland Jr. was still alive. It is unclear when he came to the United States. As the senior Chinese servant, he would be asked about the activities of the others as well as his own.[8]

If Ah Wing as a senior trusted servant recruited relatives like his nephew Ah Young and others for work in the mansion, then they too were probably See Yups, San Francisco's largest *huigan*. They may also have shared membership in a *tongxianghui*, or clan, another association that blended kinship, place of origin, and dialect. And some of them might have belonged to tongs, secret societies or brotherhoods that created fictive kinship among unrelated men and provided solidarity, resources, protection, and access to sex for single men who lacked family and money. In both China and the United States, the tongs could shade into criminal activities. Protection of their members could become aggression against outsiders. The resources they provided could come from prostitution, gambling, blackmail, opium, and theft. The sporadic tong wars that erupted in California usually involved turf disputes in the vice trades. If Wong Toy Wong was a member of the same *huigan*, clan, or tong as some of Jane Stanford's servants, they may very well have talked to him.[9]

JULES CALLUNDAN WAS QUITE FAMILIAR with the See Yups. In the 1890s the See Yups arranged for the assassination of Fong Ching (Fong Jing Tong) or "Little Pete" as the newspapers called him, one of the best-known Chinese in San Francisco. Little Pete employed Callundan's brother, Ferdinand, along with other white detectives and Chinese fighting men, to protect him.[10]

Little Pete belonged to the Sam Yups, a *huigan* whose concentration of cosmopolitan merchants from Canton and its environs gave it disproportionate influence. He ran a shoe factory, but he also engaged in "questionable enterprises" that included smuggling opium and trafficking in women. Little Pete was convicted of bribery in 1887 and sent to Folsom prison, but the Supreme Court of California overturned the conviction in 1889. This did not lead Little Pete to cultivate a low profile. He was famous as the only Chinese bicyclist in Golden Gate Park, exuberantly careening past white riders, smoking a cigarette with his queue flowing in the wind. He was also passionate about Chinese theater, and not just because he used it as a front to smuggle in women sold into prostitution in China. He wrote plays. He also fixed races by bribing trainers and jockeys.[11]

Horse racing involved Little Pete with the Callundans. The Bay District Track banned Little Pete before it closed for good in the spring of 1896, which also kept him from owning horses or betting at the new Ingleside Racetrack. The group that ran the new track, the Pacific Coast Jockey Club, hired the Morse Agency for security, and Morse put Jules Callundan in charge of a squad of twenty men.[12] It was Jules Callundan's job to make sure Little Pete got nowhere near the Ingleside track, which was probably one reason Little Pete hired Callundan's brother, Ferdinand.[13]

Little Pete adjusted. He operated through a trainer, James Rainier, buying horses but racing them under the names of prior owners. He corrupted jockeys, and patiently set out to fix races. James Rainer contended they were on the verge of a big score before the assassination.[14]

Little Pete also cultivated the police. His reputation as a police asset probably came from his willingness to turn in others to advance his own operations. The See Yups accused Little Pete of being a police informer. Little Pete probably was.[15]

Ah Wing was not involved in any of this, but he would have known of the Callundans just as the Callundans knew of the See Yups. Little Pete paid Ferdinand Callundan to lead a squad of men who, while posing as regular police, smashed the See Yup headquarters with axes. Such attacks were a regular police tactic earlier in the decade, justified as a weapon against the tong fighting men, the so-called highbinders. Callundan and his associates were arrested but let off with a warning. It was the kind of thing that left memories.[16]

The See Yups took their revenge on Little Pete in January 1897. He was in a barber's chair, having sent his bodyguard down the street for a paper because he wanted to check the horses running the next day. The assassins were waiting. Knowing he was rumored to wear chain mail under his shirt, they shot him twice, once in the forehead, once in the eye.[17]

———

CALLUNDAN CERTAINLY ASKED Ah Wing about Wong Toy Wong, and about the other servants. And since the See Yups were involved in a war over gambling that was roiling San Francisco politics in 1904–1905, he probably asked Ah Wing about his relation to Chinatown and its fighting men. And Callundan would have asked him about his relationships with Bertha Berner and Jane Stanford. These, it turned out, were complicated.

CHAPTER 5

THE WAY TO SAN JOSE

FOR A WOMAN WHO HAD NO ENEMIES, Jane Stanford was obsessed with vengeance during the winter of 1905. Well before the Poland Spring Water incident, she had launched a crusade to reform Leland Stanford Junior University, which she and her husband had founded following the death of their son in 1884. Mrs. Stanford intended to force David Starr Jordan out as president of the university. The Poland Spring Water poisoning did not divert her.

David Starr Jordan had become as synonymous with Leland Stanford Junior University as Jane Stanford. It provided the platform from which he preached pacifism, anti-imperialism, conservation, and eugenics. He thought all were tools of progress. Jordan defined his own life in terms of his work: "a naturalist, teacher, and minor prophet of democracy."[1]

When on January 23 Jane Stanford went to the Hotel Vendome in San Jose to rest and recover, she enjoyed a pleasant time with old friends who happened to be staying there.[2] But she also had business to transact at the upcoming meetings of the Stanford board of trustees. Her relations with Jordan had been deteriorating and were no longer pleasant.

In the draft of his annual report on the university in 1905, Jordan made matters public that Jane Stanford wanted kept private. He also requested more money for faculty members whom Jane Stanford regarded as his pets. Most irritating of all, he made it seem that the only one "connected with the management of the University . . . was the president." The university did not revolve around Jordan; it revolved around Jane Stanford.[3]

The two had substantial disagreements. Jane Stanford no longer supported coeducation, which was one of the defining innovations of her university. She declared that public opinion was coalescing against it. It would soon be "tabooed" and Jordan, who supported it, must gracefully submit to public opinion. As long as women students remained, their actions, dress, deportment, and social lives needed to be closely monitored.[4]

Jane Stanford's goal was not a large research university—that was the destiny of the University of California at Berkeley—but a small college whose graduates would be "men of the highest moral character whose influence will always be for the good and the glory of God." She intended to limit enrollment, with less wealthy students given preference. Both sororities and fraternities tended toward aristocracy and should be tightly regulated. The church and school needed to be integrated, with unpaid students assisting the minister.[5]

Mrs. Stanford denied opposing everything that Jordan did, but she "had a woman's sense of right and wrong," and was forced to swallow much about the university that "caused her heart to ache." She wanted to bring things to a head at the winter trustees' meetings. She insisted to trustee Samuel Leib that Jordan's power of appointment be curtailed. All projected hires would have to be approved by the board.[6]

The poisoning derailed the meetings. The January meeting failed to achieve a quorum, and it was rescheduled for February 1. Her recuperation in San Jose meant she could not attend, but she set forth an agenda for the meeting that consisted of a series of rebukes of the president. This meeting, too, was postponed.[7]

Even as she maneuvered to restrain and eventually remove Jordan, Jane Stanford remained outwardly cordial. On February 5, when she had been in San Jose for nearly two weeks, she sent Jordan a "Dear Friend" letter, thanking him for his solicitude about her health. The rain kept her indoors, but she walked for an hour the day before. She began walking for her health five years earlier and often covered from five to seven miles a day. She was not a fragile woman. She planned to return to San Francisco that week, but she still did not feel well enough to resume her duties and was planning a trip.[8]

The letter was a velvet glove over her iron fist. Although the trustees had still not met, Jane Stanford believed that they were ready to do her will. She had Samuel Leib inform Jordan that he would have to pare his salary raises back to $15,000. When Jordan tried to finesse this, Leib replied testily, saying that he thought he stated the matter clearly and was astonished that Jordan failed to understand. Jordan was to make no other appointments unless approved by the board, which would decide how much to appropriate for them.[9]

Jane Stanford's animus took its toll on David Starr Jordan. He was falling apart. He pulled out of a series of lectures that he had promised to deliver, saying he was too distracted and could not devote to them the attention they deserved "until the pressure of many things grows less." He consulted Dr. Ray Lyman Wilbur, a future president of Stanford, who refused to charge him for personal care rendered a fellow "medical man." Wilbur prescribed some capsules for Jordan to use when suffering circulatory defects or an undue susceptibility to colds. What he really needed, Wilbur told him in early February, was a "long vacation and rest."[10]

It was Jane Stanford who took a vacation. Dr. Boericke urged a change of scene from the damp and cold of that northern California winter, suggesting a trip to the southern part of the state. But that winter the weather in southern California was no better than the Bay Area, and she decided not to go. She was concerned about more than the weather. She told Boericke that leaving the country made her feel safer.[11]

On February 15 she announced that she was about "to take a short sea voyage for the benefit of my health." She would go to Japan by way of Hawaii. She also left directions for the disposal of her jewels and the use of her Palo Alto home after her death. The house should be used for educational purposes. She said that it was too expensive to maintain as a residence for the president.[12]

———

ON FEBRUARY 6 JANE STANFORD left San Jose and took the train to Palo Alto. She and Bertha Berner went to the Stanford Pharmacy on University Avenue, where W. E. Jackson, the "chief prescription clerk," waited on them. Among other things, he sold them three ounces of bicarbonate of soda.[13]

Following the purchase, Bertha Berner went to the home that she shared with her mother Maria and her brother August, while Jane Stanford stayed at her Palo Alto estate. It was her second visit in a month. Berner remained with her family for two days before rejoining Jane Stanford for the trip back to San Francisco.[14]

Berner's family was acting strangely. I don't know what Bertha Berner said to her mother and brother during these visits, but I know that at some point she gave her mother information about the poisoning that upset her a great deal. Maria Berner believed that Bertha knew who placed the poison in the water. August Berner kept his silence, but his efforts to make sure that his mother stayed quiet attracted attention. He worked in real estate, and in January and February of 1905 he ceased going to work. He did not dare leave his mother alone. She was upset, nearly distraught.[15]

August Berner later claimed he had been protecting his mother from reporters since the middle of January, but in January there were no reporters trying to contact her. The story of the poisonings did not break until mid-February.[16] In January the only people looking for information about the poisoning were the Morse detectives. They had already talked to Bertha Berner, and talking to her brother and mother would presumably only get them secondhand what Bertha had given them firsthand—unless Bertha lied to the detectives and told her mother and brother more than she told them. August did not want whatever his sister had said to leave the house. He declared that his mother was "a sickly woman and did not know what she was talking about."[17]

He eventually began answering the door with a shotgun in hand.

ON HER RETURN TO SAN FRANCISCO, Jane Stanford, at the suggestion of Samuel Leib, checked into the St. Francis Hotel "to get the peace I cannot get at home" while she prepared for the trip to Japan. She took rooms on the fifth floor, but she did not register. She and Bertha Berner ate at a private table. Jane Stanford refused bottled water. Bertha Berner became her taster, reassuring her by carefully examining the ice water brought to the table. She also supervised the packing of the trunks at the mansion.[18]

Jane Stanford apparently spent much of her days on Nob Hill selecting the items for her trip to Japan. She reengaged May Hunt, whose mother she knew and who worked for her previously, to replace Elizabeth Richmond, and between February 9 and 15, May Hunt assisted in the packing of Mrs. Stanford's wardrobe. She also placed needed items in Mrs. Stanford's medicine basket. Mrs. Stanford selected the medicines. May Hunt thought a bottle of bicarbonate of soda sat on a table for the entire six days of the packing. Hunt, Berner, and Jane Stanford

often left the room; when they did, other servants also could pass unob-
served in and out of the room, which remained open during the day
but locked at night. The medicine basket was placed inside a new telescope basket. An express company took all the luggage, including the
telescope basket, to the steamer. The telescope basket was taken to the
stateroom occupied by Mrs. Stanford.[19]

ON FEBRUARY 13, THE SUNDAY EVENING before her departure, Jane Stanford summoned George Crothers to the St. Francis Hotel. They talked
for four hours. Crothers had been an undergraduate at Stanford before
serving Mrs. Stanford as a legal adviser and university trustee. That night
she told him for the first time of his resemblance to her dead son, Leland
Jr., and how—though the term is an anachronism—she had stalked him
when he was an undergraduate, driving around campus in her carriage
to find him. She told him that on her return she would fire Jordan and
remove Hopkins and other trustees who opposed her.[20]

IN 1937 A LETTER that Jane Stanford wrote to Crothers before her departure resurfaced. He lost the original in the 1906 earthquake and fire, but
he said that he always remembered it. His memory of the letter was hardly
exact. He recalled that she wrote it on a Tuesday, the day before she sailed
for Honolulu, but the letter was dated Wednesday, February 15, the day
she sailed. He thought she had written "that if anyone wanted to kill her it
would not be hard to do." That phrase was not in the letter, but she might
have told him this during their conversation or it may have been in a second letter that he said she wrote.[21]

She wrote Crothers because it "would be doing my heart injustice, were
I to go away from my home, my sacred interests, the University—without
giving expression to all I feel in regard to your helpfullness [sic] to me for
the past few years." He had soothed her and comforted her in the midst
of doubt about the university's future: "Is God and my loved ones in sympathy sustaining me, is it pride, self glorification that is actuating me? Or
what can it be that keeps me here, no taste for the allurements of life, no

longing to stay away from the country where my loved ones are dwelling."
He had reassured her about the university's future and how much good
Stanford had done. She said, "I placed my son in your place and was glad
that I knew you." He was a "gleam of sunshine."[22]

She told him that he knew the "peculiar circumstances" that prompted
her voyage.

"I am not quite so sure of health and life as heretofore—death in a
natural way would not be a calamity for I have much and dearly loved
ones waiting for my advent there, but I am startled even horrified that
any human being feels that they have been injured to such an extent as
to desire to revenge themselves in a way so heroic as has happened." She
hoped God would spare him from sickness, sorrow, and death for many
years, and that he would "take the same deep interest in the University
you now feel—even though I 'fall asleep' I shall awake in the Fair Land
beyond." She would pray that once there, she could continue to work for
the university and its students.[23]

Crothers regarded it as a farewell letter. He showed it to only two other
trustees, Whitelaw Reid and Samuel Leib. He said he forgot that he also
gave a copy to his friend Walter Rose. This was the copy that resurfaced
in 1937.[24]

Jane Stanford wrote a second, similar letter to May Hopkins, thanking her for her "sweet sympathy" and regretting that she could not bring
her "friend" to allow Hopkins to visit her during her illness. She had, she
wrote Hopkins, "more than sickness, a troubled heart." She could not tell
her why, but Hopkins would know when a few more weeks passed. She
regretted having to cancel the "at house" for her niece, Jennie Lathrop,
but the doctor would not allow it. She was departing that day on doctor's
orders for Honolulu and Japan. She went unwillingly since she wanted to
be in Palo Alto for the beautiful spring and then go to Europe with Jennie. She thanked both May Hopkins and her husband "Tim" for their aid.
She could not go away without letting her know what was in her heart.
What was odd, or duplicitous, about the letter was that, no matter how
genuine her feeling for May Hopkins, she thought Timothy Hopkins was
working against her and was determined to dismiss him from the Board
of Trustees.[25]

She conducted a final piece of business. She signed a statement drawn
up by Crothers "concerning her acceptance of the trust." This was designed
to prevent any legal challenge to the money she left the university. Croth-

ers intentionally wrote the document in the past tense because the trust in question was now nearly two years old. It was a sign of Crothers's lingering doubts about the legality of the Stanford bequests to the university. The document does not appear to have survived. Her signing it signaled the possibility of her not returning.[26]

FOUNDING A UNIVERSITY

CHAPTER 6

BERTHA BERNER
WRITES A LIFE

WHEN JANE STANFORD SAILED to Hawaii in 1905, Bertha Berner accompanied her. That trip ended Mrs. Stanford's life, and it formed the last chapter of *Mrs. Leland Stanford: An Intimate Account*, the book Berner wrote thirty years later. The book has become the chief source on Jane Stanford's life. Berner said she wrote it because so many people had forgotten so much about Mrs. Stanford and knew so little about her personal life. She also wrote the book because Mrs. Stanford expected Berner to "write about me when I am gone."[1]

Now Bertha Berner, Jane Stanford's companion, has become my companion. When I go backward from Jane Stanford's death, I have no choice but to rely on Bertha Berner. She is the only one who attempts to tell a coherent story for the period from Leland Jr.'s death to Jane Stanford's demise. George Crothers, the Stanford trustee and Jane Stanford's confidant, is valuable but only for the last few years of her life. Other sources have vanished. Jane's niece Jennie was working on a book of her own when she died in 1934. She said that she had sent her research materials to Stanford University, but they seem to have disappeared as thoroughly as the materials from which Berner compiled her own book.[2]

George Crothers warned Orrin Leslie Elliott, who wrote a history of Leland Stanford Junior University and consulted Berner, that she was "far from accurate in her memory and statements." Crothers also warned

Elliott not to trust Crothers's own memory. It was a wise warning. Crothers compounded Berner's misstatements with mistakes of his own.[3]

Like all memoirists, Berner claimed to tell the truth, and like all memoirists she is an unreliable narrator. Memoirs convey the meaning of lives and the events that made them, but not necessarily what actually happened. Memoirs may seem to be built on the accumulation of actions, relationships, thoughts, and words over the course of a life, but they are really built from the elimination of everything that would complicate, or falsify, the morals and meanings the author wishes to impart.

I mention this because Berner's memoir is critical to what follows. Bertha Berner lies in her book, but historians, like detectives, not only expect people to lie, they depend on it. If people did not lie, historians and detectives would not have work, at least not interesting work. They don't assume that everyone lies all the time, just that some people lie some of the time. Lies are as revealing as the truth—they just disclose different things.

Berner's memoir fooled me into thinking that my task was simply to catch the lies. I was as easily distracted as a dog chasing a stick. Crothers warned Elliott of mistakes in Berner's account of the Poland Spring Water incident, and the lie that first struck me was her account of what happened when the chemist's report of strychnine in the bottle of Poland Spring Water finally reached the California Street mansion. Berner recalls that "consternation ruled," and she writes that "the belief entertained was the Poland Spring Water bottle had been used to hold some cleaning solution and taken to Mrs. Stanford's room by mistake."[4]

The statement was nonsensical. On that day in 1905 Jane Stanford read a report that clearly said the strychnine came from rat poison. Cleaning solutions do not contain strychnine.[5] Berner's lie—ridiculous on its face and easily disproven by anyone who investigated—puzzled me.

I found it easy to catalog Berner's lies about what happened during the time between the Poland Spring Water incident and Jane Stanford's departure for Hawaii and Japan. She gave an implausible—indeed impossible—account of her return to San Francisco from San Jose. She wrote that she and Mrs. Stanford took the train to San Francisco only to be met at the depot by Charles Lathrop, Mountford Wilson, and Samuel Leib, who told Jane Stanford it was too dangerous for her to return home. Leib lived in San Jose and was in communication with Mrs. Stanford while she was at the Hotel Vendome, and she had just seen her brother in Palo Alto. Why would either travel ahead of her to San Francisco to give her a message? Why not tell her in Palo Alto?[6]

Berner also lied when she said Jane Stanford did not originally plan to go to Hawaii and Japan, but was prompted to go by the strain of staying at the St. Francis for "two weeks" and "the circumstances [that] existed which prevented her from entering the home she loved [which] was almost more than she could bear." They left San Francisco for Hawaii, according to Berner, on February 10, 1905.[7]

For Berner's account of a two-week stay at the St. Francis to be correct, they would need to have left San Jose for San Francisco on January 27, but on February 5 Stanford was still in San Jose writing Jordan of her plans to return to the city, and on February 6 she was in Palo Alto. Her ship would not depart for Hawaii until February 15.

Berner's account was wrong in virtually every detail of this period. The decision to stay at the hotel came after the decision to take the Pacific voyage. Jane Stanford wrote May Hopkins, Timothy Hopkins's wife, that Leib suggested she would be more comfortable at the St. Francis Hotel while preparing for her trip than in her mansion. She stayed there for over a week "to get the peace I cannot get at home."[8]

The lies Bertha Berner told about the Poland Spring Water incident and its aftermath created a narrative of careless housekeeping and ulti-mately needless worrying about Jane Stanford's safety. There was nothing more to the "poisoning" than that.

As easy as they were to catch, Berner's lies worked. They diverted me, at least temporarily, from a more revealing search for what she did not talk about at all. In concentrating on the lie about the meeting with Lathrop, Wilson, and Leib in San Francisco, I neglected her failure to mention the stop she and Jane Stanford made in Palo Alto, a stop that is critical to the mystery.

Berner's lies and omissions did not spring from forgetfulness. She clearly kept journals, and she wrote and received letters, because she pro-vided abundant, sometimes excruciating, detail about her years with Jane Stanford. Without written records she was unlikely to remember that Mrs. Stanford took apartments at the Hotel Meurice in the Rue de Rivoli and spent three weeks there in 1899. She would not remember the stand in the Bois de Boulogne where Mrs. Stanford ate waffles and drank tea.

The location of a glove shop, and when and how the women who owned it shopped, were not the kinds of things she would recall. Nothing remarkable happened on that trip to Paris to fix such details in her mind.[9]

Bertha Berner's *Mrs. Leland Stanford: An Intimate Account* is essential to understanding why Jane Stanford died. There is no uncovering the mystery of Jane Stanford's death without going into Jane Stanford's life, a life to which Berner had the greatest access. Berner was there when Leland Stanford Junior University was just an ambition of grieving parents and did not yet have a physical form. She was there as the institution grew. Berner watched Jane Stanford nurture it, and eventually she watched Jane Stanford die.

Memories are not chronological; their dates of origin vary, but they mix together in the mind like pennies in a jar. But a life is chronological—it moves through time, one year following another. Think of a life as a mansion with each room a year. Berner's book is full of empty rooms. All the furniture has been removed. I am drawn to the empty rooms and to what is missing from the still-furnished rooms. These are the places, I think, where the answers lie.

Bertha Berner and I are both authors seeking to turn lives into books. We both track the same terrain. She did so to memorialize Jane Stanford's life for never fully disclosed purposes that it took my writing this book to fathom. I am a simpler person. I am just trying to understand Jane Stanford's death. That Bertha Berner lied and dissimulated makes her all the more interesting and revealing. Her book demands careful reading; it is not all one thing or the other.

Her memoir begins in 1884. That is where I will go, too.

❖

CHAPTER 7

LELAND STANFORD JR.

THE DEATH OF LELAND STANFORD JR. marked the beginning of Jane Stanford's public life. Conceived during his parents' middle age, their only child died in Florence, Italy, in March of 1884. Typhoid fever killed him just short of his sixteenth birthday. Leland Stanford Jr. died, but he never departed.

His bedroom in the California Street mansion was across the hall from his mother's. Jane Stanford turned the adjacent tutor's room into a study where she worked with Bertha Berner, but she kept the bedroom as it was when Leland died. She would go "into dear Leland's room and kneel down and tell all my sorrows to the blessed Jesus. I feel my darling boy and my dear husband are pleading with me." In 1893, nearly a decade after the boy's death, curators from the university museum took exact measurements of every furnishing and its position in the room, and transported his possessions into the university museum. They told Jane they arranged the room "just as it was in your city home."[1]

Herbert Nash, Leland Jr.'s tutor, wrote a biographical sketch of the boy that portrayed Jane as the sun around which her son revolved: "young ladies' company and the conventionalities of society had no attractions for him," but "toward his mother he would display the most attentive gallantry." Nash's account of Leland Jr. became gospel, not to be questioned. In appreciation, Jane made him the university librarian.[2]

The Stanfords raised their son to be their companion, including him in their conversations and taking him on their long European tours. Leland Jr. had an audience with the Pope. He spoke fluent French, met celebrated painters—Meissonier, Bonnat, and Carolus-Duran—and watched them work. He did not hesitate to criticize them. While in Europe, he sent home instructions about the care of his dogs, horses, boat, and machinery. He was the kind of child who could write that his dog had "developed vagabond propensities." His precociousness and privilege could be annoying. He treated his uncle, Jane's brother Ariel, who then managed the Stanford estate, like a servant, detailing the tasks he wanted performed in his absence.[3]

IN DEATH, the child only increased his influence over his parents, whose grief was deep and affecting. He became a household deity, who could not be offended or replaced, and this fractured the extended family. When Ariel made a slighting reference to the dead boy, questioning his genius, Jane banished him. He lost his job and returned to New York. This was when Charles, a younger brother, took his place.[4]

Charles and his family lived in the shadow of the dead Leland Jr. Charles's first wife died when their daughter Jennie, who was born the year after Leland Jr.'s death, was only four months old. She asked Jane to "take care of her little daughter if she did not recover." Jane agreed, but Leland Stanford was "most decided in his objections" to Jane's taking responsibility. Among his objections was that some might think that they were adopting the child. This could never be since there was no room in their hearts for anyone but their dead son. Jane acceded to his wishes and persuaded her sister Anna to come and live with Charles and take care of Jennie. Anna became more than a devoted aunt. She raised the girl, until being called to a "higher and better life." She died when Jennie was seven. On her death bed Anna asked Jane to do what she could for "her dear little girl." Again, Leland and Jane talked and agreed that they must be careful so that both Jennie and the world understood that they had not adopted her. Anna made Jennie her heir, leaving her $50,000, and asked that she be sent to convent school until she was eighteen. Jane paid for her education.[5]

After Anna's death, when Jennie was not at school, she often lived with Jane and Leland. Leland changed his will to give the girl an additional $100,000. Jane expected Jennie to stay with her "as long as I live." She believed she had done all she could for her niece, who she thought loved her dearly. She impressed upon both Jennie and Charles, who remarried and whose second wife Jennie came to despise, that she would not adopt Jennie, but, as it turned out, she still expected Jennie to follow her wishes and commands.[6]

Leland Jr.'s presence extended beyond memory and spiritual visitations. Leland Jr. lived on in his things. At thirteen, he began collecting arms, armor, art, antiquities, and bric-a-brac, intending to present them to San Francisco for a public museum. Gathering objects for the museum became an obsession. It occupied him for much of his final, fatal, European trip.[7]

The Stanfords converted some of the bedrooms in the Nob Hill mansion into storage rooms to hold their son's collections. Jane Stanford created the university museum in large part to fulfill the boy's dream and to house his stuff. The museum formed a shrine to the dead child within a much larger shrine: the university itself. He inspired his father to found it.

The stories of Leland Jr.'s message to his father differ in detail—and many of the details are clearly wrong—but they are of a kind. "Ghost Builder of University" and "Spirit of Son Made Request" were representative headlines. In some stories the grieving parents engaged a psychic to talk to "the son who had gone over the border, and Leland Jr. advised them to use their estate to found the university."[8] In others Leland Stanford sank into his chair in a stupor after his son died, and Leland Jr. appeared to him, saying, "Father I want you to build a university for the benefit of poor young men, so they can have the same advantages the rich have."[9] In still others, Stanford, watching over his sick son and thinking there was nothing to live for if his son died, fell asleep and dreamed of Leland Jr., who told him to live for humanity. When he awoke, his son was dead.[10]

The last story appears to have been true. Jane Stanford destroyed most documents concerning her husband, but before disposing of her own journals, she copied out two entries. In 1892, two years before Leland Sr.'s death, Jane and her husband spent an evening in Bern, Switzerland. They were on their way to "Battenburg on Lake Thurr." Leland was sick, afflicted with gout, overweight, going deaf, hardly able to walk at times, and much discouraged. He lay down on the sofa, and Jane played the piano for him. They had a "quite unusual" conversation that caused her to make a note of it. They talked about their dead son, the school they founded to commemorate him, and education. Leland Stanford was not an educated man, nor did he know much about education. He thought in terms of vague clichés: he wanted "his scholars to be taught that they can know the finite, can never reach the infinite, but can approach it." He wanted "to better humanity," and he taught Leland Jr. to appreciate virtues that his father did not noticeably embody: "to always be sure and to so conduct himself to respect himself, and then he would be pretty sure to be happy . . . he was a truthful boy, too, and did not care to read books that were not true."

Leland Sr. recollected his dream the night "Leland went away." He did not remember all of it, but he knew "it was a great help to me, it made all the difference in the world, something to live for and make that University a place to send boys out to do missionary work."[11] This recollection and even the phrasing of it became something of a trope for the elder Leland. In the second conversation Jane Stanford copied from her journal, he remembered the dream again in September in France saying, "I know from that moment I resolved to build the University, and we both from that night resolved on this."[12]

For Jane the critical part of both conversations and Leland's remembrance of the dream was the Stanfords' joint partnership. As Leland said in Switzerland, "And you too are just as much interested as I am and have done all you could and if you live can go on with it."[13] There is a startling line in Bertha Berner's memoir that is easy to glide past. "For about twenty years before the University was founded," Berner wrote, "Mrs. Stanford had had literally nothing to do." Jane Stanford played billiards; she doted on her son; and she also grew large, fleshy, and prone to headaches. She became imprisoned in her body, unable to walk more than short distances; she traveled to European spas for her health. To Bertha Berner, a woman who worked since she was a teenager to support herself, her mother, and, for a while, her brother, it was extraordinary that Jane Stanford spent her time doing little beyond being rich. Then her son died, and the loss of the one she loved above all others freed her. She disciplined herself and regained her health. The university gave her a purpose.[14] Going on with it would be the story of the rest of her life.

These are the elements from which the Stanford docents, backing across campus, construct their story.

⬙

CHAPTER 8

GHOSTS AND MONEY

THE UNIVERSITY MRS. STANFORD COFOUNDED, her enduring love for her dead child, her philanthropy and ardent religiosity, all seemed prima facie evidence that only a mad person could wish to kill her. The newspapers insisted she had endeared herself to the citizens of the state.[1]

There was truth, if not the entire truth, in the portrait of the dedicated and grieving mother. But there were people who could have told a different story. Some of these people employed the detectives; others lied to them; and still others stayed silent.

Bertha Berner knew Jane Stanford's past better than anyone else except perhaps Jane's brother Charles. She slipped into Mrs. Stanford's life in the sliver of time between Leland Jr.'s death and when Leland Stanford Junior University became his mother's life's work.

Leland Stanford Jr.'s memorial service on December 1, 1884, brought the two women together. As she told the story—and she was the only one who told it—Bertha Berner first encountered Jane Stanford at the Episcopal Grace Cathedral in San Francisco at California Street and Stockton Street. She was part of the crowd attracted to Leland Stanford Jr.'s memorial service.[2]

Berner was nineteen and had only recently arrived in San Francisco. She said that she, her brother, who was thirteen, and her mother had moved to California to find relief for Maria's asthma. She did not mention her father.

Maria had a husband, also named August, and they had seven children, but only Bertha and August lived to adulthood. After the family emigrated from Germany, August senior became a merchant in Wisconsin, and then moved to Caldwell, Kansas, where the census listed him as a tinsmith. Bertha went to work as a bookkeeper. Kansas friends said she was self-conscious about being German. She wanted to be called Ruby, a name she thought more fitting for the American girl she aspired to be. Then, sometime between 1880 and 1884, the remainder of the Berner family exploded. When the Berners left Caldwell for the coast, they did not go as a unit. Maria and the children appeared in San Francisco, but according to the 1885 Minnesota state census, August lived in Minneapolis. Then he disappeared. Having lost all but two of her seven children, Maria Berner would understandably be obsessed with dead children. Bertha Berner, the support of her sick mother and brother, would just as understandably be protective of her.[3] By the time they arrived in San Francisco the Berners were Episcopalians—unusual for German immigrants. The memorial service for Leland Jr. at Grace Cathedral was "of our denomination."

On November 27, days before the memorial service, Leland Jr.'s parents conducted a simple funeral at their Palo Alto estate. They interred their son in a temporary, brick mausoleum with the spiritualist inscription "born in mortality . . . passed to immortality." It contained both a sarcophagus and a richly decorated anteroom where Mrs. Stanford could sit, read, pray, and commune with the dead child. Jane Stanford kept the only key in her possession.[4]

The memorial service was as spectacular as the funeral was simple. Publicity for the service claimed that it would feature the greatest floral displays ever seen on the West Coast—supposedly costing $20,000—but the chief attraction was the Reverend John Newman. In an age of celebrity preachers, Reverend Newman was as much an actor as a minister. Handsome and eloquent, he drew "the young ladies." He attracted more people than could fit in the church.[5]

Unable to gain entry, the Berners were about to leave when, so Berner claimed, "a curate came over to my mother and said that Mrs. Stanford had seen us and had asked if we would like to enter, since there were a few vacant seats left." The story of a distraught mother filling up the seats with strangers seems unlikely, but Bertha said he seated them behind the Stanfords.[6]

Reverend Newman eulogized a boy who had died nearly eight months earlier. In between his death in Florence on March 13, 1884, and his interment, Leland Stanford Jr. had been traveling. His parents could not bear to let him go. Leland Jr.'s journey toward California created the backdraft that drew Reverend Newman west, which in turn attracted Bertha Berner and thousands of others to Grace Cathedral that Monday.

Too distraught to leave Florence when their child died, the Stanfords had lingered before traveling to Paris with the body. Leland Jr. rested in the mortuary of the American Church in Paris as his father continued to regain his health and composure, but as her husband improved, Jane Stanford broke down. When she was well enough to travel, they went to New York, where the Sunday school room in Grace Church on Broadway served as a mortuary chamber for Leland Jr. In New York they often met with ex-President Grant and his wife Julia. Grant was dying of cancer and struggling to complete his great memoir.[7]

The Grants introduced the Stanfords to the Reverend Doctor John P. and Julia Newman. All three couples shared an interest in spiritualism. They all attended a séance in New York after the Stanfords' return from Europe.[8]

A Methodist minister, Newman was previously chaplain of the United States Senate and pastor at the fashionable Metropolitan Memorial Methodist Episcopal Church in Washington, DC. His congregations included the rich and famous. Dollar signs festooned newspaper stories about him: the amount of money he raised, his salary, how much he was paid for a talk. The Metropolitan Memorial Church opened the same year that Grant assumed the presidency and was described as the "Westminster Abbey of American Methodism." The Grants were Methodists and occupied the presidential pew, but, like the Stanfords and Newman himself, they moved easily between Protestant denominations. Newman relocated to New York, as did the Grants at the end of his presidency, and between 1882 and 1884, Newman was pastor of the Madison Avenue Congregational Church, also a resort of the wealthy and famous. The Grants were again his congregants.[9]

In 1884, having left his pastorate in New York City, Dr. Newman was between positions. The Stanfords persuaded him to return to California with them and preach at Leland Jr.'s memorial service. They reportedly promised to pay him $10,000, an extraordinary sum at the time, equal to his quite formidable annual salary.[10] When the Stanfords finally departed for California in November, Newman went with them. Leland Jr. traveled in a special funeral car, draped in black with a bier in the center and floral tributes alongside it.[11]

The mourners who flocked to the memorial service in San Francisco were not disappointed. Newman's eulogy soared; his delivery was affecting. But if it were not for the deep grief of the parents, Newman's hyperbolic praise of a rich dead boy he had never known would have been risible. His sermon provoked accusations of blasphemy for its comparison of the young Leland with Christ, and it sparked a dispute over whether a non-Episcopalian clergyman should have been allowed to participate in an Episcopalian ceremony.[12]

What followed the memorial service was as plausible as Bertha Berner's account of being seated at the service was unlikely. The death of five of Maria Berner's seven children gave her reason to empathize with Jane Stanford's grief. Maria Berner said it looked like Jane Stanford's eyes had been wept blind, and she surely could not use them to read or write. Over objections from her mother, Bertha Berner wrote to Jane Stanford, asking for work in helping her handle her correspondence. Such work would be in the Stanfords' home and not bring the disrepute that many women working and living outside the home faced. The Stanfords interviewed her, and then Jane Stanford asked to meet her mother. Bertha Berner began work at the mansion in December of 1884.[13]

That December the Newmans stayed with the Stanfords on Nob Hill before going on to the Palace Hotel. The trip west and the memorial service cemented Jane's relationship with Reverend Newman. She credited her belief in spirit communication and soul development after death to Newman's residence in San Francisco. Although the university tried to pretend otherwise, Newman's influence never diminished. Months before her own death, Jane Stanford remembered how "the great Bishop Newman . . . gave us such spiritual enlightenment as no other minister of the gospel had ever given to me, and my husband, who has passed and is now enjoying the light which he brought to our darkened souls."[14]

According to Berner—or at least Berner in her memoir—Reverend Newman cultivated the Stanfords because he wanted money to support a church; according to the Newmans, it was the Stanfords, particularly Jane, who offered money to keep Dr. Newman on the West Coast. Reports in the newspapers in early 1885 indicated that the Stanfords were buying Newman a church to get him to remain in San Francisco. The church would be nonsectarian, just as the Stanford Memorial Church eventually would be.[15]

Newman denied that his new church would adhere to any extreme version of spiritualism, but his preaching, like his letters, was full of visitations of angels and saints. And he numbered Leland Jr. among those angels, saints, and ministering spirits. He promised the Stanfords that their dead son "shall . . . come to you with messages of love, and wisdom and protection."[16]

Berner reported that the Newmans told the Stanfords that the ministering spirits were about their altars morning and evening, and they conducted séances in the Stanford mansion seeking to contact Leland Jr. In describing them, Berner's language was significant: ". . . no great or even perceptible results were expected right away because we were all new mediums of approach, which caused a difficulty." We? It seems Berner not only participated but considered herself a medium. Friends and relatives of the Stanfords later claimed she acted as a medium. Berner said Leland Stanford did not participate but indulged Jane, hoping it would rouse her from her depression.[17]

Mrs. Newman acted as the chief medium of approach. She was not inexperienced. She published *Golden Links in the Chain That Connects Mother, Home, and Heaven* in 1890, which contained her book of a similar title published in 1872. She received her first glimpse of heaven when her own mother died, and "the golden light shone down on earth, which has ever since gilded my life's pathway." During a séance at the Stanford mansion, she claimed to see "luminous clouds forming," and tried to persuade Berner that she saw them, too. Jane was "almost dying of the longing" to see Leland Jr. again, but her son did not appear. Instead, Ensign did. Ensign was the spirit of a child whom the Newmans had intended to educate, but he had died. He informed Mrs. Newman that her husband was called "St. John the Divine" in heaven. Ensign also said that heaven rejoiced in Mr. Stanford's decision to "dedicate his fortune to the glory of God and the church." There had apparently been a failure of communication between the spirits and Leland Stanford Sr., since this news surprised Mr. Stanford. "From now on not much more was spoken regarding spiritualism," Berner wrote, "and before long the Newmans returned to the East."[18]

But this was not exactly what happened. The Newmans did return to the East, but so did the Stanfords. Newman departed to minister to ex-President Grant in his last illness. He would preach Grant's funeral sermon and then resume his lucrative ministry in the nation's capital. Leland and Jane Stanford, too, would go east. Stanford had bought his way into the United States Senate.[19]

In her memoir Berner insinuated that the Ensign episode ended the Stanfords' connection with the Newmans, but this was also not true. In 1894, the Newmans wrote to Jane Stanford of their visiting the hotel room where Leland Jr. had died in Florence—"your Gethsemane"—which was both creepy and predictable. Until her own death in the early twentieth century, Julia Grant regularly sent news of the Newmans, and Jane Stanford not only continued to express her admiration and gratitude toward them but also corresponded with them.[20]

Leland Jr. failed to communicate with the Newmans, but he did speak to his uncle, Leland Stanford's brother Thomas Welton Stanford, who had departed California for Australia in December of 1859. After acquiring the exclusive Australian franchise for Singer sewing machines, he had made a fortune. He married Wilhelmina Watt in 1869, but she died within a year. Heartbroken, he gravitated to spiritualism hoping to contact her. In 1870 he founded the Victorian Association of Progressive Spiritualists, and gradually, except for the circle of spiritualists in Melbourne, grew more reclusive and more interested in the dead than the living.[21]

Slate writing became a staple of Thomas Welton Stanford's communication with the dead. Henry Slade, an American medium, was credited with creating slate writing, and, over time, several different variations developed. Some mediums had two blank slates examined and then tied together. They placed them on or under a table in a dark room with a piece of chalk nearby. The medium would either have his or her hands tied or would sit holding hands with those attending the séance. Another method was to have the medium and a member of the séance hold the slate against the underside of the table, again with the chalk nearby. These were "test conditions" to make sure that the medium could not surreptitiously write on the slates. The medium then channeled a spirit that would write its message directly on the slate. Although the spirits often brought apports—relics, sometimes from the ancient past—to séances, they could not be depended upon to bring their own chalk.

Thomas Welton Stanford eventually donated transcriptions of his séances, apports, and some of the slates to Stanford University. He carefully noted the circumstances of their creation. "This slate," he wrote about one, "was secured by a padlock key which was in the pocket of Mr. Stanford whose hands held the edges having staples . . . whilst the medium Bailey held the hinged edge."[22] Another paired set of slates in the

Stanford Special Collections are fastened together with screws. The slates with the name of the medium inscribed on the labels were "produced under test conditions."

Test conditions were a sham. The trick took place before the séance and involved recording the messages on the slates and then disguising the writing with a cover that could be quickly taken away when the medium unbound the slates.[23]

The messages that spirits sent to Thomas Welton Stanford fill volumes that are now in the Stanford archives. A few slates came directly from Leland Stanford Jr. The first that Stanford attributed to the dead boy is dated 1884, which means Leland Jr. had wasted little time contacting an uncle he never met in his earth life. He described how his body had been placed in an aboveground tomb in the garden of the summer house. His mother, he said, sat for hours alongside the tomb, and sometimes he spoke to her clairvoyantly when she asked for him. It had taken Leland Jr. a while to master turning himself into an actual apparition, but when he did, so he told Thomas Stanford, he had appeared to his father to reassure him that he lived.[24]

If the slate writings were any indication, the spirits' major goal was to cultivate spiritual understanding in those attending the séances and to promote confidence in the mediums. Leland Jr. cautioned his uncle not to be too eager to persuade others about spirit communication. They would be convinced in time. The immediate aim was to deepen Thomas Welton Stanford's spiritual understanding.[25]

Mediums were the immediate apertures to the spirit world and critical for cultivating the insight necessary for people like Thomas Stanford to gain direct access on their own. The slates were small, without much room for messages—sort of tweets from the dead—but the spirits devoted an inordinate portion of their writing to advertising the virtues of the mediums. Leland Jr.'s slates seemed a billboard for Fred Evans, the medium who recorded them, proclaiming his virtues and setting out his rules.[26]

Leland Jr. didn't reveal much that his uncle could not have learned from Jane and Leland Stanford, although he promised to give his uncle a history of his life in the spirit world at a future date.[27] But it really did not matter what Leland Jr. did or did not reveal; what mattered was that both Thomas Welton Stanford and Jane Stanford thought they could commune with the dead. It shaped what they did, and as significantly it shaped what others thought of them. It raised the possibility, among those who did not think the dead communicated with the living, that not only the poisoner but also Mrs. Stanford might be deranged.

If Mrs. Stanford had listened to ghosts in drawing up her grants and wills to fund Leland Stanford Junior University, then there was a problem. Ghosts, so to speak, lacked legal standing. Documents whose contents reflected advice from the afterworld not only raised eyebrows, they might also be open to legal challenge.

CHAPTER 9

LELAND STANFORD
JUNIOR UNIVERSITY

COLLIS P. HUNTINGTON HAD KNOWN Leland Stanford Sr. since the 1860s when they were both merchants in Sacramento. They became two of the Associates who controlled the Central Pacific and then the Southern Pacific Railroad. One of the great disadvantages of living a public life and destroying your papers is that it delivers your posterity into the hands of your enemies. Leland Stanford left virtually no papers; Collis P. Huntington left abundant papers. Many of them reference Stanford, whom Huntington came to hate. He probably understood Stanford better than any other man alive.

Leland Stanford became the monster to Collis P. Huntington's Dr. Frankenstein. Huntington gave Stanford economic and political life, and then Huntington tried to destroy him. Because of the peculiar financial structure created by the Associates of the Central Pacific and Southern Pacific railroads, which combined their assets into a common pool, the men who controlled the Central Pacific—Leland Stanford, Collis P. Huntington, Mark Hopkins, and Charles Crocker—could never be rid of one another. Huntington wrote that Stanford "has never made any money but he has had a good deal made for him and knows no more of its value when he gets it than he does of the way in which it was obtained."[1]

Until he fell in with Huntington, Leland Stanford's life was a series of false starts. Born, like his wife Jane, in upstate New York, he had failed as a lawyer, and then, thanks to his brothers who had preceded him to California, righted himself and gained some stability when he joined them in the grocery business. He branched out, ran his own saloon while serving as a justice of the peace, and, after three years apart, his wife Jane joined him. When his brothers departed to start new ventures, he took over the store. He seemed destined for the modest success of a Sacramento merchant and small-time politician.[2]

Stanford and Huntington both attached themselves to the new Republican Party, but Stanford's first political efforts were not auspicious. He lost a race for alderman in Sacramento, getting only 87 votes out of 3,068 cast, and then lost as a candidate for state treasurer in 1857. He was unlikely material for a gubernatorial run, but Huntington helped him gain the nomination in 1859. He lost again, but the Republicans were on the rise in California. They were the party, according to Stanford, of "free labor, of justice, and of equal rights." They were also the party of "free white citizens," and Stanford wanted "the country settled by free white men." In 1861 he ran for governor and won, as the majority Democrats split their vote between two candidates.[3]

Once in office, Stanford aided the free white men in their genocidal (and I use the word advisedly) campaign to "exterminate" the Native population of California. (It began with the gold rush and proceeded over a quarter century in which the Native population plummeted from 150,000 to 30,000.) In his inaugural address Stanford also warned of the danger presented by the Chinese: "a degraded and distinct people must exercise a deleterious influence upon the superior race, and, to a certain extent, repel immigration." This was before he realized how useful the Chinese were in building railroads and staffing his mansion.[4]

Huntington and the Chinese helped make Stanford rich. The building and operation of first the Central Pacific Railroad and then the Southern Pacific involved bribery, subsidies, fraud, and an inordinate amount of lying, cheating, self-dealing, and backstabbing by all of the Associates. The railroads lost money, but those who controlled them could still funnel vast sums into their own pockets. Their business plan was to drain assets into their own accounts and leave others—stockholders, bondholders, and the government—saddled with the debts.

The Associates were not equally able. Huntington and Mark Hopkins were men of more talent than scruples; Stanford and Crocker lacked both. But their interests had become so intertwined and their money so comingled that they would necessarily rise and fall together. Thanks to Huntington, they rose, although their finances were often precarious.[5]

As far as I can discern, the Associates agreed on a single moral line that they would not cross: no matter what they did to others, they agreed not to betray or cheat each other. Leland Stanford could not stay on the right side of that line. Huntington had recognized his partner's ineptitude in business early on, but only when Stanford began to withdraw money and bonds from the common funds without his partners' consent, and bribe legislators without Huntington's knowledge, did the rift become open.[6]

For all his limits as a politician and railroad man, Stanford had succeeded at two things: he financed a stable that raised some of the best trotting horses in the nation, and he was a good and adoring father. Huntington recognized where Stanford's interests and talents lay. "I am disposed to think," he wrote Charles Crocker in 1871, "Stanford will go to work for the railroad company as soon as the horse races are over. Of course, I do not expect anything until then."[7] Huntington did not envy him his horses, but he did envy him his son.

The death of Leland Jr. brought a momentary sympathy between the two men, but it did not last. When a grieving Stanford betrayed the railroad's candidate for senator and took his place, Huntington erupted, forcing him from the presidency of the Southern Pacific in 1890, which Huntington then took over. They never reconciled.[8]

In the aftermath of their break, Stanford joined the U.S. Senate and opened his university. This infuriated Huntington, who thought California had a perfectly good university in Berkeley. The funds Stanford would devote to the school instead of the railroad would be wasted, since Leland Stanford would botch the university as he had botched virtually everything he touched since Huntington first knew him. Jane Stanford would inherit the quarrels with Huntington.

The university made the Stanfords as much as the Stanfords made the university. Without the university, the Stanfords would be barely remembered, and Leland Jr. would not be remembered at all. The couple began planning for it in the immediate aftermath of their son's death. In 1884 they visited Cornell, Harvard, MIT, and Yale during the long journey to bring their boy's body home.

The Stanfords were not intellectuals. Bertha Berner remembered that Leland was "not a great book man." He had a library, which during his senatorial years he used for naps.[9] But in its early years the university treated them as if they were: quoting and preserving the Stanfords' views on education, praising their wisdom and insight. George Crothers, the shrewdest and most calculating member of the Board of Trustees, thought publicly if not privately that the Stanfords' theories of education compared well with the "highest authorities on education, both ancient and modern." They were "in advance of all existing institutions."[10]

Like her husband, Jane Stanford regarded a classical education as useless and cruel. Graduates of Harvard and Yale, she claimed, were of benefit to no one, including themselves. Her husband employed "six of them as car-conductors on the Market Street Line now." Their university would train students for "usefulness in life." It would be open to both men and women, the poor as well as the rich, and would encompass the liberal arts, the sciences, and the practical arts, including agriculture. They would make the university a center of research and invention.[11]

The Stanfords laid the cornerstone for Leland Stanford Junior University on what would have been their son's nineteenth birthday: May 14, 1887. Frederick Law Olmsted, whom they hired as the university's landscape architect, wanted to place the buildings in the foothills, but the Stanfords did not care about vistas. They wanted the buildings on flat land. Olmsted suggested and Charles A. Coolidge designed the low neo-Mission campus buildings that formed what is now the inner quadrangle below the hills. These, Encina Hall, and some small engineering buildings comprised the campus that sat at the end of the long drive Stanford planted with Mexican fan palms and Canary date palms. Palm Drive ran to the campus from the small railroad station in what would become Palo Alto. The university opened for its first class on October 1, 1891.

For Andrew Carnegie, the leading advocate of philanthropy at a time of growing inequality, Leland Stanford the man and Stanford the university stood as exemplars: rich men and institutions that could use their wealth to place "within . . . reach the ladders upon which the aspiring can rise." Stanford epitomized "the man of wealth" using his "superior wisdom, experience and ability" to administer his fortune to benefit his "poorer brethren . . . doing for them better than they would or could do for themselves."[12]

Others took a dimmer view of Carnegie, Stanford, and philanthropy. Doing great harm seemed to be the prerequisite for gestures of amelioration. They regarded Carnegie and Stanford as the kinds of men who, having cut off your leg, offered you a crutch. Ambrose Bierce, the San Francisco newspaperman, had Carnegie and Stanford in mind when he sardonically defined *restitution* in *The Devil's Dictionary* as "the founding or endowing of universities and public libraries by gift or bequest."[13] To its critics, Leland Stanford Junior University was a giant exercise in money laundering.

It wasn't just Bierce or radicals who viewed the origins of the university with cynicism. President Charles W. Eliot of Harvard insinuated that the Stanfords had "tried to raise a personal monument by the good use of ill-gotten money." David Starr Jordan objected that no one was a penny poorer because of Stanford's fortune, but much of California rightfully believed that the Stanford fortune came at their expense. The strangling of the possibilities of others was precisely what earned the Southern Pacific the nickname of the Octopus.[14]

Most eastern university officials thought the Stanfords well-intentioned but naive. The couple shared the common conviction of the rich that, as Nicholas Murray Butler, who turned down the Stanford presidency, later wrote, "money could buy anything and could do anything and [Stanford] was both surprised and chagrined when he found sometimes it could not."[15]

Gilded Age philanthropy produced resentments where its donors expected gratitude and admiration. In universities the faculties chafed at the control of the rich and powerful who held the power of the purse. Horace Davis, one of the university's original trustees and one of its few discerning ones, described Leland Stanford Junior University between its founding and Jane Stanford's death as a system of absolutism, a place rotten with imperiousness, mismanagement, ineptitude, and fear. Jane Stanford, a woman supposedly without enemies, cultivated enmity and harvested a bountiful crop.[16]

The founding documents of the university made the conditions Davis described nearly inevitable. Stanford himself supposedly drafted an Enabling Act, passed by the state legislature in March of 1885, for the establishment of Stanford University. On November 11, 1885, less than a year after Leland Jr.'s interment, he issued a Grant of Endowment— the so-called Founding Grant—that established Leland Stanford Junior University, provided for its funding, and named its trustees. Three days afterward the trustees convened, and Leland Stanford issued them a deed of trust to the university.

The Enabling Act and the Founding Grant created a legal nightmare.

The Enabling Act failed to create a legal entity necessary for Stanford's purposes in founding the university; it did not even provide for a legally constituted board of trustees. The California constitution limited the life of any corporation to fifty years—after that the state could dissolve or modify it—but Leland Stanford incorporated the university to exist in perpetuity. The Founding Grant, which funded it, created perpetual trusts illegal under existing California laws on trusts, and the governing structure of the university did not conform to constitutional requirements for the administration of the trusts.[17]

The university was less than met the eye. The Stanfords' initial gift was small. They retained control of the vast bulk of their fortune. The Board of Trustees was merely decorative. It could not receive or administer additional gifts to the university. Leland and Jane Stanford, as the grantors, reserved to themselves the power to change the grant; they also assumed the powers of the trustees during their lifetimes. Leland Stanford Junior University was for all practical purposes whatever the Stanfords wished it to be at any moment. But Leland Stanford managed to muck this up, too. Because the Founding Grant did not conform to the terms of the Enabling Act, it rendered his subsequent delegation of powers to Jane Stanford as the surviving original trustee open to challenge. Jane Stanford compounded this by exceeding even the broad powers granted her in the founding document.[18]

CHAPTER 10

DAVID STARR JORDAN

IT ALWAYS EMBARRASSED David Starr Jordan—the first president of Leland Stanford Junior University—that he owed his job to a message from a dead child. He hated spiritualism. When he wrote his autobiography, he recounted his own experience with it. In 1875 while in California to collect and catalog fish, he had for entertainment in San Francisco "attended seances of some of the many professional mediums operating in the city." He thought "all their manifestations were frauds." Jordan spent his career at Stanford trying to distance himself and the university from the Stanfords' spiritualism, but Jane Stanford did not prove to be easy to escape.[1]

Jordan had not been the Stanfords' first choice for the presidency, nor their second nor third. The Stanfords assumed that getting a president for the university simply involved paying the necessary price. Even though Leland Stanford started high and then doubled the offer, he failed to hire Nicholas Murray Butler, who would later become president of Columbia University and subsequently the Republican vice-presidential candidate in 1912. They had already failed to hire Francis Walker, the president of MIT and one of the leading intellectuals in the United States.[2]

Andrew White, the president of Cornell, also refused the position, but in 1891 he suggested a Cornell graduate: David Starr Jordan. Jordan was forty and the youngest college president in the country. In 1885 he had received the "undesired and unexpected" offer of the presidency of Indiana University when student "Peeping Toms" saw the previous president—the Baptist minister and professor of theology Lemuel Moss—engaged in "immoral acts" with "a pretty blonde teacher connected with the institution." Moss threw all the blame on the blonde teacher, but it did him no good.[3]

Jordan's rise was less rapid than it seemed. Born, like the Stanfords, in upstate New York, he obtained his education at Cornell, then studied briefly at a summer research institute with Louis Agassiz —the most famous naturalist in the United States, an opponent of Darwin, and an ardent racist who advocated polygenesis to explain racial difference. Jordan became a Darwinist, but he continued to idolize Agassiz. He attended medical school, where he received, in his own words, a "scarcely earned" degree as a doctor of medicine, while also teaching high school in Indianapolis. He never intended to practice; he thought the degree would help him teach physiology better.[4]

Jordan taught at Butler University and made his name as an ichthyologist cataloging the fish of the South, but he aspired to positions at larger research institutions. They repeatedly rejected him. In 1879, he accepted an offer at Indiana University, which contained a preparatory school and was then as much a high school as a university. He continued to do his work, and his research led him all over the country and the world. A trip to California left him enamored of the state, but it appeared his future would be in the Midwest.[5]

Doggedness and an optimism that would seem to border on delusion if it had not so often succeeded became Jordan's leading traits. Progress— individual, professional, national, and evolutionary—formed the great theme of his life. He studied fish for a larger purpose. His goal was to create a taxonomy that would reveal not just the order in the world but an order that bespoke future improvement. The classification of living things also provided the markers by which science could detect decline and degeneration. Every setback could be, would be, overcome, but only by weeding out the immoral and the unfit. Jordan made a name for himself as a moralist as well as a scientist, and for him the two were connected. Education was not for everyone. "For the fool, the dude, and the shirk," he said, "the college can do nothing."[6]

Personal loss accompanied his professional success. His wife Susan, who had resented his travels, died in 1885, and the next year his infant daughter followed. Jordan became a trustee of Cornell, his alma mater. And although university trustees do not normally court undergraduates, in 1887 he married Jessie Knight, a twenty-year-old student "with whom I had become acquainted in connection with my attendance at a trust-

ees' meeting" at Cornell. Jessie had him send his surviving children off
to boarding school. His daughter Edith, ten at the time, hated her for it.
"I knew then that I would never call her mother," she later wrote. Jessie
traveled with Jordan. He coupled their honeymoon in the Adirondacks
with reading the page proofs and doing the index of his *Manual of the
Vertebrate Animals*.[7]

When in 1891 Leland and Jane Stanford came to Bloomington and
offered him the presidency of Leland Stanford Junior University for
$10,000 a year, Jordan accepted and began in the fall of that year. The sal-
ary was half what they had offered Butler, but far more than Jordan made
at Indiana. More critically, the Stanfords informed Jordan that the ultimate endowment of the university would be about $30 million, which at a
5 percent return would yield $1,500,000 a year. With a great deal of effort,
Jordan had increased the budget at Indiana to $50,000. At Stanford, Jor-
dan would not have to deal with either state politicians or a board of
trustees, which would be "without function during the lifetime of either
founder." This more than made up for having to please aging benefactors.
What could go wrong?[8]

While he was at Stanford, Jordan also continued and expanded his own
work. He sympathized with the Stanfords' vision of a practical university.
He had since his days with Agassiz adopted the slogan "study nature not
books," and he persuaded himself that this desire to learn directly from
the world created an affinity with Leland Stanford's idea of training students for "usefulness in life."[9]

Businessmen like Leland Stanford were naive about education, but
educators like Jordan were equally naive about businessmen. Stanford
promised Jordan an eventual $30 million, but the actual endowment he
gave the university before his death consisted of three ranches containing 85,000 acres. The largest, Vina, had never turned a profit, and all
of its grapevines soon died of phylloxera. The Gridley Ranch produced
grain, but its production was in steep decline. The Palo Alto Ranch, which
housed the university, also was famous for its trotting horses, but the stables usually lost $7,000 a year. George Crothers complained that the
ranches brought "nothing but taxes." This was also not exactly true, but
they did cost more in taxes than they brought in revenue. The university's
founding documents prohibited their sale.[10]

To construct the first buildings and finance the university, Stanford
had borrowed $1.5 million from the Pacific Improvement Company, nick-

named the Private Interest Company because it was essentially the slush fund for the Associates. The PIC drained corporate railroad assets and turned them into private assets. The PIC made distributions when times were good; at other times the Associates could borrow from it. The PIC itself borrowed heavily during the depression of the 1890s, and it owed $28 million, of which Stanford and his estate were liable for 25 percent.[11]

WHEN THE UNIVERSITY OPENED in 1891, it was just an island in the Stanfords' Palo Alto estate whose stables and tenant farms continued to function around it. It had fifteen faculty, virtually all of them hired because of Cornell or Indiana connections, and five hundred and fifty-nine students, mainly from California, which made it the largest college in the far west. The faculty members, mostly young and little known, owed their positions to David Starr Jordan, to whom Leland Stanford delegated the power to hire and fire.[12]

Within two years it was all in danger of collapsing. Leland Stanford died in 1893 and left the university $2.5 million in cash, far less than the $7 million he gave largely to his—not his wife's—relatives. The bulk of his wealth, the actual worth of which remained uncertain, went to Jane, upon whose largesse the university depended. The Panic of 1893 had just taken hold, and the depression that followed, the deepest in American history to that point, lasted into 1897. The Southern Pacific Railroad, which was the basis of the Stanford fortune, faced bankruptcy. Its stocks did not pay dividends. It could not pay full interest on its bonds.[13]

When it seemed things could not get worse, the federal government in 1894 sued the Stanford estate for $15 million, freezing its assets, including the bequest to the university. The government sought to recover loans it had made to the Central Pacific Railroad. The Central Pacific had been incorporated under California law, and the law made stockholders liable for debts the corporation did not pay. Leland Stanford and his Associates had drained money from the railroad into their own pockets, sold the derelict Central Pacific to British investors, and then had the Southern Pacific, which they still controlled, lease it back. Because the British feared the California law making stockholders liable, the Associates kept the stock in their name. In 1894 it seemed time to pay the piper; the government came after the Stanford estate to recover Stanford's share of what was owed. "People think," Jane Stanford said, "that Governor Stanford left me a very rich woman. I thought so myself, but it now seems that I was left a legacy of debt, trouble and worry." Jane Stanford kept the university open through the household allowance allowed her by the court, an insurance policy, and the sale of personal belongings. She cut salaries by 10 percent.[14]

This was not what David Starr Jordan had anticipated. His faculty would have gladly deserted if they had any other place to go in the midst of a depression. Jordan had no choice but to defend the Stanfords and the institution. He tried to rally support for "the cause of Higher Education in America." He argued that the suit was without basis and that prolonged litigation could kill the university.[15]

To save the university and the Stanford fortune, Russell Wilson, Jane Stanford's lawyer, turned to Joseph Choate, the luminary of the New York City bar who had aided Timothy Hopkins, to argue the case before the U.S. Supreme Court. Choate was valuable for his political connections. He would in 1899 succeed John Hay as ambassador to Great Britain. In 1896 the court ruled that there was no individual liability for the railroad stockholders, even if California law at the time of the incorporation of the railroad had imposed it. The government would have to recover its funds from the Central Pacific.[16]

In official accounts of the university, the victory solved the money problems of Jane Stanford and Leland Stanford Junior University. It did not—it only complicated them. In 1896, just before the court handed down its decision, Choate at Wilson's urging wrote to Jane Stanford with advice. He told her that her victory in the Supreme Court would provide her with more money than she anticipated—perhaps $40 million. This was a considerable exaggeration, but he urged her immediately to rewrite her will "with the aid of the very best counsel." The new will should bestow on her executors "the most full and complete powers" to "manage and control" that portion of the estate that was under the joint control of her and the Associates. This was the vast bulk of her estate. Nothing, he wrote, would be more disastrous than to leave the management of these securities to "the caprice and bad judgment of the [university] trustees," who were no match for Collis P. Huntington. Choate was not done. He and Wilson agreed that the amount of her estate was much larger than the university should be allowed to hold. A bequest of that size would only make it a target of "plunder and attack." He advised fixing a maximum amount that would go to the university. Choate's advice was contrary to Jane Stanford's public pledges about what she would do with the funds if she won her case.[17]

Unsurprisingly, the "very best counsel" turned out to be Russell Wilson and his brother Mountford Wilson. She drew up a new will in 1896, but no copy of it seems to have survived. The Wilsons advised her not to transfer the securities that Leland Stanford had left the university in his will, since this would make the university liable for taxes that it could not pay. This was true, but it was also true that Jane Stanford would be equally liable for the taxes. This the Wilsons did not tell her.[18]

CHAPTER 11

INDEPENDENCE

AS BERTHA BERNER WITNESSED the transformation of Jane Stanford into a woman of purpose in the late 1880s, she underwent her own transformations. As a young woman seeking work when she first met the Stanfords in 1884, she was in an unenviable position. If she left her family and found employment, she became a "woman adrift"—regarded as a danger to herself and society. If she worked and remained in her mother's home, she could retain respectability but at the price of independence. With enough education, she could have become a teacher, a nurse, or a doctor, but such professions usually foreclosed marriage and family. If she did not marry, she would become, in the vernacular of the time, an old maid.[1]

Bertha Berner was part of a demographic. Of American women born between 1865 and 1874, eleven percent never married; others were widowed, divorced, or deserted. Her generation produced some remarkable women. Charlotte Perkins Gilman, five years older than Berner, would suffer from postpartum depression, endure a "rest cure" popular at the time, and leave her husband. Her 1890 short story, "The Yellow Wallpaper," became the Gilded Age's classic account of the price women—and their children—paid for their lack of autonomy. Jane Addams, also five years Berner's senior, would forge a life as a social reformer, but she began it with an acute sense of the limits American society imposed on women, particularly educated women. Lizzie Borden, also born in 1860, felt the same constraints on her possibilities, but she did not internalize them. She murdered her father and stepmother—inspiring the famous children's rhyme, "Lizzie Borden took an ax"—and she got away with it. The jury did not think a middle-class woman was capable of an ax murder. They acquitted her.[2]

Women gained no liberation by moving west. San Francisco society, of which Jane Stanford was a pillar, monitored middle-class women closely, watching their associations and behavior. Charlotte Perkins Gilman, who lived in Oakland and San Francisco during these years, "knew well the ordinary risks of a woman in my position among San Francisco–minded people, and took extreme precautions to give no least hand for criticism in behavior. . . . I made it a point to be seen nowhere with a man, to receive no slightest 'attention.'"[3]

Gilman, Addams, and Borden were all Gilded Age possibilities.

When, in 1885, after Leland Stanford's election as senator, Jane Stanford offered to take the young Bertha Berner with her to Washington, DC, she seemed to open a route out of the constraints ambitious American women faced. Bertha would be in Washington part of the year and return to California, where her mother and brother lived, when the Stanfords returned to San Francisco or to their Palo Alto estate. The *Curran Directory*—the standard directory for San Francisco—listed Bertha as Jane Stanford's secretary, but she also became a confidante.[4]

Berner in her own memoirs wrote as if her life with Jane Stanford was largely uninterrupted until Mrs. Stanford's death. This was not true. She did not mention the quarrels and fissures. Many of them involved Berner's duties to her own family. Others involved men.

Acquaintances of Mrs. Stanford spoke about these tensions. In 1889 Bertha Berner left the Stanfords' employ after Jane Stanford denied her permission to go to California to see her mother, saying she "didn't think it was right to leave at the time." According to Grace Gilmore, a daughter of one of Jane's friends, when "Bertha said she was going anyway," Jane Stanford told her, "if you go now, you will go for good." Berner left, and Gilmore came to stay with Jane Stanford for about three months, "and then Bertha came back." She did not stay long. While living with the Stanfords, Berner became quite close with a male secretary of Leland Stanford's. They spent a great deal of time in each other's company, and, as Grace Gilmore put it, Jane Stanford, being "rather old-fashioned," again sent Bertha Berner away "for a time."[5]

Stanford had a private secretary, Herbert Nash, Leland Jr.'s old tutor, and another secretary for his work as a senator. The newspapers reported that the secretary involved with Bertha Berner was "Ashe," which would indicate Herbert Nash, but the newspapers were not always reliable. That Berner never referred to Nash in her memoir, even though Nash would work for the Stanfords or the university until his death in 1902, is not surprising. She did not mention any of the men she was rumored to be involved with by name.

The other possibility is that the male secretary involved with Berner was J. B. McCarthy, who was far more worldly and aggressive than Nash. In a 1929 interview, Berner surprisingly—given later accusations about her—spoke about McCarthy and the kickbacks he had taken on household expenses. The opportunities were large. Stanford delegated to him the design and building of the stables he constructed in Washington, DC, which given Stanford's devotion to his horses was no small thing. Berner had mixed feelings about McCarthy. She described him as a "bright and capable man, but inclined to glorify himself and not too trustworthy. . . ." She apparently was in a position to know.[6]

Jane Stanford may have sent Bertha Berner away again in the spring or summer of 1890 when the Stanfords and Nash departed for Europe seeking to recover both health and spirits following Stanford's resignation from the presidency of the Southern Pacific. Bertha said she remained at home because of the ill health of her mother, which may also have been true. Jane Stanford sent her weekly letters, and she came back to the Stanfords when they returned.[7]

But again Berner seems to have stayed with the Stanfords only a short time. She was with them in the spring of 1891 when they traveled to Bloomington, Indiana, to recruit David Starr Jordan to be president of their new university, but there seems to have been another departure soon after. Both McCarthy and Nash were still around. Jane Stanford over the years became obsessed with the sexuality of young women. She was apparently determined that there be no romance under her roof or at her university. This may again have produced Berner's departure. Berner later admitted that she left for two and half years, only returning to Stanford's employ in 1893, the year Leland Stanford died. Berner does not appear to have attended the senator's funeral, although she later said she was very fond of him.[8]

She did not immediately resume the role of Jane Stanford's secretary. Herbert Nash was Jane Stanford's assistant until he became the head librarian at the university in 1896.[9] Whatever was going on in the Stanford household indicates that Jane Stanford did not regard Bertha

Berner's private life or what she did with her body to be Bertha Berner's personal affair.

Charlotte Perkins Gilman complained about but conformed to the mores of women like Jane Stanford, but increasingly young women like Bertha Berner did not. Jules Callundan, the Morse detective who later took charge of the Poland Spring Water investigation, also investigated a pair of San Francisco murders that revealed ugly sexual tensions.

Theo Durrant was a church librarian, an assistant superintendent of the Sunday school at Emmanuel Baptist Church, a student at Cooper Medical College—which would eventually become part of Leland Stanford Junior University—and a member of the California National Guard. In 1895 he murdered two young women and left their bodies in his church.[10]

The murders, which gripped Gilded Age San Francisco, were very different—the first nearly ritualistic, followed soon by the second, which was impulsive, brutal, and bloody. The case evoked the same kind of panic over the social consequences of women's sexual freedom to which Jane Stanford proved so vulnerable. If the victims had been prostitutes, the story would probably have faded more quickly, but they were church-going women who also asserted the independence of traveling alone and choosing their own companions. According to Gilded Age norms, such women courted danger and tempted men, but it seemed unimaginable that Theo Durrant—devout, devoted to his mother and sister, handsome, living at home, and studying to be a doctor—could be a killer. This became the core of his defense: a respectable person like Durrant could not be a murderer.[11]

A San Francisco police detective, Edward Gibson, who would also be involved in the Stanford case, discovered the second body, and worked to convict Durrant. Harry Morse and Jules Callundan joined his defense. They attempted to clear Durrant by creating suspects among the classes presumed more likely to kill. Morse contended he was never paid but undertook the work because he believed Durrant innocent. The jurors quickly and unanimously decided that the middle class, professional, religious, and respectable, could kill. They sentenced Durrant to death. He denied the crime until the end. Harry Morse learned that the respectable could sometimes be convicted, and it might be best if they were never brought to trial.[12]

In this world Bertha Berner, a young woman seeking independence, lived a life that came to be balanced between two old women, her mother and Jane Stanford. After Leland Stanford's death, she always traveled with Jane on her lengthy trips to Europe and beyond, but she tried to carve out at least a small realm of independence. She did not live in the California Street mansion. In the 1890s she listed her addresses as houses her mother rented on Hayes and Powell streets. She remained respectable but gained some freedom from the monitoring of her relationships by Jane Stanford.[13]

Her attempts to fulfill her obligations to two older women while retaining at least a modicum of freedom proved a challenge. It was one she would fail.

CHAPTER 12

SURROGATES

JANE STANFORD DOMINATED Leland Stanford Junior University following Leland Stanford's death in 1893. She controlled the endowment, the school's growth, its construction, and its priorities. She relied on men—dead and alive—but she used them for her own purposes. Leland Stanford delegated the power to hire and fire to Jordan, and Jane Stanford told the trustees in 1897 that the president alone would select and remove professors. She reiterated his authority in 1903.[1]

In the early days, the faculty largely regarded Jordan as a benevolent dictator, protective of their interests. Jane Stanford only intervened when a position or issue was important to her. In 1896 she instructed Jordan to hire Herbert C. Nash, Leland Sr.'s former secretary, Leland Jr.'s old tutor, and possibly Bertha Berner's lover, as head of the library. Nash's academic credentials consisted of the short account that he published of the young Leland. After his appointment as librarian, Jane Stanford lamented that Nash failed to receive the respect from the faculty that she thought he deserved.[2]

In 1899 she decided to use her own funds to endow a Professor of Personal Ethics, either a strange or a necessary choice given the financial origins of the university in a fortune accumulated through fraud and dishonesty. Jordan understood that she had the Reverend George Hepworth in mind, and he set out to find out "just what manner of man Mr. Hepworth is." Mr. Hepworth was a spiritualist. As one of Hepworth's characters in his book, *They Met in Heaven*, says, "the departed are nearer to us, very much nearer than we dare think. As God is here, at this moment, so perhaps are they." There were times "when they make themselves known to us." Jordan acknowledged that he had "of course . . . to be guided largely by Mrs. Stanford's wishes in this particular matter."[3]

Faculty who departed from Jane Stanford's wishes endangered their jobs. In 1898, not realizing Jane Stanford was in attendance, H. H. Powers, a Stanford economist, told students at a religious meeting that they should pay more attention to the prosaic side of life than to "youthful ideals." A shocked and angry Jane Stanford went directly to David Starr Jordan's house at 10:00 p.m., got him out of bed, and told him Powers must go. Jordan dismissed him midsemester.[4]

Powers was not an anomaly. While traveling in Europe in 1899, Jane Stanford informed Jordan that she would "take a more active interest in the internal workings of the university." She "resolved to keep the University on the highest level morally and spiritually. The latter is more deeply interesting to me from the fact that it seems to be lost sight of in a sense." The "development of the soul" "was the university's essential task." It was "by far the most essential thing in life, all education should tend toward this one aim, and this is only attained by following the teachings and maxims of that greatest of all teachers our world has ever known—a precious Savior, Jesus Christ and this phase in the education of youth is far more important than professors as a rule realize."[5]

She was right. Professors did not realize this, but now she had told them. In her address to the trustees of February 11, 1897, she directed that entering students "be taught that every one born on earth has a soul germ, and that on its development depends much in life here and everything in the Life Eternal. Cultivating the soul intelligence will endow them with that which is beyond all human science and reveal to them God's very self."[6] This was "in direct violation of Section 11 of the Enabling Act, which specifically prohibited the right of any grantor to demand any form of religious instruction or to try to influence religious belief," but this did not deter her.[7] She used her addresses to the Board of Trustees to amend the Enabling Act at will.

Over the course of her addresses she instituted an alarming array of changes to the university. The amendments she attempted ranged from the illegal to the unconstitutional, to the unworkable, to the unreasonable. She routinely violated the constitutional rights of faculty members and made the trustees mouthpieces for her own decisions.[8]

Jane Stanford considered herself an agent of her deceased husband and son. Ghosts ran the university. Jane Stanford told a newspaper reporter that she could not go on if her husband and son did not continue to visit her. "I never," she said, "transact any business, or in fact do anything worthy of consideration without asking their advice. . . . What would I have done with all my business cares and worries, if I had been deprived of my two spiritual advisors?"[9]

Spirits, admittedly, were not the whole story; Leland and Leland Jr. left surrogates, who tried to limit the influence of the deceased even as they stepped into their shoes. When Jane Stanford claimed to delegate the power over appointments to President David Starr Jordan, it was because he, at least for a while, became a substitute for her deceased husband.

David Starr Jordan could have departed during the university's years of crisis that followed the government's suit in 1895, but he decided to remain. When in 1896 he turned down the directorship of the Smithsonian Museum, Jane Stanford gushed her gratitude. She trusted Jordan to lessen her "cares and anxieties" and to take onto his "broad shoulders" all university duties that might upset her. "You have," she assured him, "been more to me since my dear husband departed from the mortal life to the life immortal, in keeping at its helm guiding and steering through the fog that obscured the sunlight . . . thanks be to God, your power and your strength, and . . . high Christian character . . . commands the love and respect of all of the students and commands my tenderest love and gratitude." She wanted his loyalty and promised him hers.[10]

Jordan and Jane Stanford did not necessarily agree on the direction of the university, but Jordan believed he could steer her, and she gave him reason to believe she was willing. She was even more ardent about her devotion to him in 1899, when the newspapers were highlighting her differences with Jordan over the expansion of the university. She wrote to Jordan's wife, Jessie Knight Jordan, saying that she loved him as a son, although in practice she relied on him more as a husband. She admired his intellect, his generosity, and his purity, even when she disagreed with him. Nothing could come between them.[11]

Jordan recognized that success as Leland Stanford's surrogate involved paying homage to his wisdom and his vision for the university. In 1907 Jordan published a small book, *The Human Harvest*, a product of two lectures, the first delivered in 1899. In it Jordan praised Leland Stanford and turned his most famous horse—Electioneer—into a parable that reflected Jordan's vision of the world. That vision centered on eugenics, his belief in racial rankings, and the necessity to limit the reproduction of inferior humans and encourage the reproduction of superior men and women.[12]

The main theme of Jordan's book was the human waste of war. For Jordan the waste was in the shedding of blood and the racial traits that expired with the bearer if not passed on. His parable portrayed "a man, strong, wealthy and patient, who dreamed of a finer type of horse than had ever yet existed." This man, of course, was Leland Stanford, and Electioneer was one of the horses he bred to a mare—Beautiful Bells—who "excelled all others in retaining all that was good in fine horses and in rejecting all a noble horse should not have." As with horses, for Jordan, so with human beings. When "real men"—those who died on the battlefield—gave way to "mere human beings" in producing children, a nation was doomed. When war culled out the fit—whether in ancient Rome or the current United States—then the unfit would take their place and reproduce. The unfit produce more unfit; the fit produced the fit. "True history" always repeats itself.[13]

In humans as in horses, only blood and descent really mattered:

> . . . a Jew is a Jew in all ages and climes, and his deeds
> everywhere bear the stamp of Jewish individuality. A
> Greek is a Greek; A Chinaman remains a Chinaman. In
> like fashion the race-traits color all history made by
> Tartars, or negroes, or Malays, or Japanese.[14]

David Starr Jordan pandered to Jane Stanford in praising her dead husband's virtues, but he also knew that too close an embrace of Jane Stanford could be dangerous. To create some distance between his own academic reputation and Jane Stanford's spiritualism, he began to publish a set of articles that ridiculed spiritualism. He must have believed that neither Jane Stanford nor those around her read much.

In 1896 Jordan published the "The Moral of the Sympsychograph" in *Popular Science Weekly*. He satirized the belief that photographs could capture mental images. On their outer reaches such beliefs merged with spirit photography. Spiritualists, among them Jane's brother-in-law Thomas Welton Stanford, produced photographs of spirits or astral projections, examples of which still exist in the Stanford archives.[15]

DAVID STARR JORDAN did not anticipate that lurking among the first graduating class of Leland Stanford Junior University was Jane Stanford's surrogate son, George Crothers. Crothers became Stanford's youngest trustee and Jane Stanford's confidant. He did not marry until he was forty-one, well after Mrs. Stanford died. This made him attractive and available to Jane Stanford—not sexually but quite the opposite. His absence of any overt sexuality allowed him to conform to her ideal image of her son. Leland Jr. died, she told Leland Sr., before the temptations and burdens of life could reach him. He was now "safe from all harm, his soul is free from sin, and he is acceptable to our Lord Jesus." She would not have him back if she could; she would join him in heaven.[16]

Crothers's marriage, when it came in 1911, proved brief. His wife died in 1920, and he never remarried. Like Leland Stanford Sr., Crothers was a devoted Mason, but above everything else, he gave his devotion to Leland Stanford Junior University. He lived a long life, dying in 1957, but his only progeny were the campus buildings named after him.

In an archive some things survive by chance, but most documents have been preserved for a purpose. Little in an archive is innocent, and the loudest voices are often the ones to discount. The earthquake and fire of 1906 destroyed much, but not all, of Crothers's early correspondence, but he formed the habit of writing himself memoranda. He drafted these first in longhand—sometimes on legal papers, sometimes on odd scraps of paper—and then had some of them typed up later. He wrote them from the early twentieth century into the 1940s. The later memoranda might be based on earlier notes.[17]

Those memoranda, filed neatly by subject, are the most interesting parts of his papers. Having spent years in the archives, I know historians are not neat. In a heavily researched collection, the papers do not align and are often not in order. When I first went through the Crothers papers they aligned like a new deck of cards. A danger of waiting too long to say what you know is that no one is any longer listening.

Crothers waited so long because he feared that revealing what he knew would endanger the very trusts and endowments he sought to protect. He could not reveal the people trying to subvert the endowment without revealing how easily it could be subverted. So he confined his enemies to the memoranda. The people who run through the memoranda without ever surfacing in the *Outline*, his published account of the founding of the university, are the Wilson brothers. Crothers succeeded in obscuring their efforts to drain away the university's funds.

I never came to trust George Crothers completely, but I came to understand, for good or bad, his motives. Jane Stanford was devoted to him. He was devoted to Stanford University. He formed a one-man Greek chorus, a complicated witness, to Jane Stanford's struggles and demise.

In 1898, when he and a colleague went to see Jane Stanford to discuss a minor matter—the removal of a fraternity house and the transfer of its lease to another location—George Crothers had only begun to make a name for himself as a lawyer. And although he did not know it at the time, he already had an unusual relationship with Jane Stanford. When she first saw him as an undergraduate, she later told him on the eve of her final trip to Hawaii, she was struck by his resemblance to her dead son.[18]

At their meeting in 1898, Mrs. Stanford turned the conversation from the fraternity house to Collis P. Huntington. Desperate to keep the railroad solvent and fearful of Stanford's desire for a distribution of assets, Huntington had bullied her in an attempt to replace a Stanford appointee on the Central Pacific or Southern Pacific with one of his people. She said she told Huntington that "when her Stanford University boys grew up they would settle with him for his treatment of her." He told her she would never see the day when one of them would lift a little finger in her defense. In telling the story, she burst into tears.[19]

Crothers thought both the conversation and the tears tactical. Jane Stanford also mentioned the tax problem that Mountford Wilson had discovered. When the pooled assets of the Southern Pacific were divided, Jane Stanford would gain control of her one-quarter share of the railroad's stock and bonds. But she could not convey her stock or bonds to the university since the taxes on a stock transfer alone would have exceeded the entire income of the university, and the stock itself produced no income.[20] The California state constitution did not grant tax exemptions to colleges or universities.

Crothers concocted a solution: an amendment to the California constitution that would exempt Stanford University from taxes. In 1898 he began drafting an amendment and organizing a campaign to pass it. In doing so, he discovered that he had barely sampled the rich stew of stupidity, ignorance, and arrogance in the university's founding documents.[21]

Like Jordan, Crothers always remained publicly reverential to the founders. He learned early that to influence Jane Stanford, it was necessary to flatter her and protect her. In his published accounts of the campaign to amend the California constitution, Crothers concealed as much as he revealed. He admitted in his memoranda that he wrote "with meticulous care to avoid any disclosure in detail of the medley of apparently trivial to colossal and wholly illegal provisions of the specific amendments or attempted amendments to the university trusts provided for in the so called 'addresses' of Mrs. Stanford. . . ." "[S]ome if not all of Mrs. Stanford's amendments were clearly invalid," as were her grants to the university. Crothers referred to these as the "illegal, impossible, and undesirable" provisions. According to most legal criteria, there was no Stanford University.[22]

Crothers originally conceived of his amendment as a way for the university to escape taxation, but he quickly turned it into a measure to legalize and legitimize the university and protect it from potential Stanford heirs and their attorneys, who wished to carve it up like a goose and feast on its pieces. The first part of Crothers's amendment provided for the ratification of the trusts and estates created by the Founding Grant. The second permitted the trustees to receive property by any form of conveyance to existing trusts, which allowed for new gifts. The third authorized the legislature to grant the trustees corporate powers and privileges.[23]

As Crothers organized his campaign to have the legislature approve his amendment and put it on the ballot for voters to approve, he eliminated the amendment's original content: a blanket exemption of the university from taxation. It would doom the measure. Not only would it deprive one county of one-eighth of its tax base, but because Jane Stanford retained the right to change the purposes of the institution, it also seemed a classic bait and switch. California would give a permanent tax exemption to an organization that could change its purpose whenever Jane Stanford chose. Under the revised amendment, the state government could exempt Stanford from taxation, but it did not have to do so.[24]

Jane Stanford wanted a tax exemption, and she refused to fund a campaign for the amendment without it. The state's voters should bestow it on her out of gratitude. But Crothers's revised amendment went forward, and only grudgingly at the end of the campaign did she pick up some of the costs.[25]

Not everyone in the Stanford inner circle was as devoted to the university as Crothers.

In crafting the amendment, Crothers corrected problems that Leland Stanford had created in founding the university, but he discovered that the Wilson brothers and others were working just as strenuously to undermine his efforts.

QUARRELS

CHAPTER 13

FOLLOW THE MONEY

THE DISPOSITION OF large Gilded Age estates regularly unleashed feeding frenzies among potential heirs. George Crothers and the Wilson brothers came to know each other when they were on opposite sides in the long, tangled, corrupt, and allegedly murderous battle over the estate of James Fair, Crothers's uncle and a man nearly as rich as the Stanfords. The dispute began in 1895 and would continue for a quarter of a century.[1] George Crothers's campaign for the constitutional amendment to protect the Stanford endowment was one consequence of Jane Stanford's 1896 victory in the Supreme Court that secured her husband's fortune, but it was only part of the scramble over the eventual settlement of his estate. Crothers became convinced that he and the Wilson brothers were no more allies in battles over the Stanford estate than they were in the contest over the Fair estate.

When Leland Sr.'s estate finally emerged from the probate court in December of 1898, the university's troubles did not end. Jane Stanford's fortune consisted of land that yielded no net income, $2 million in bonds—half of which paid only 4 percent—and a one-quarter interest of the Associates' pooled holdings in the Southern Pacific Railroad and the Pacific Improvement Company. The railroad holdings represented the bulk of her fortune, but until she sold the stock it remained only paper, since the railroad stock paid no dividends.[2]

In 1898 selling the stock was impossible. Neither the Pacific Improvement Company nor the Southern Pacific stocks and bonds were fully under her control. The property of these companies could not be divided or sold without mutual consent of the original Associates or their heirs. The railroads were teetering on bankruptcy, and they avoided receivership mainly because the large bond holders did not demand the interest payments that were in arrears.[3] Collis P. Huntington needed every dollar to keep the corporations solvent. He was not about to let Jane Stanford start withdrawing large amounts of money from the pool.

As executrix of her husband's will, Jane Stanford found herself besieged by other legatees, particularly the children of Leland's dead brother, Charles Stanford. They demanded their inheritance in cash that she did not have, and seven percent interest until they received it. They refused her offer to compensate them with real estate, which she could not then sell at what she regarded as a reasonable price. Furious, she considered them ungrateful.[4]

She also felt betrayed by her own relatives, the Lathrops. Charles Lathrop supported his sister's efforts to keep the university open when others advised closing it, but he did not like responsibility even if he coveted authority. He mostly desired money. He was rich, but he very much wanted to be richer. His best opportunity lay in receiving a share of the Stanford fortune. Jane Stanford was not totally unsympathetic. She was always torn between a desire to provide for her relatives and fear of their greed.[5]

She felt crossed when, in 1897, Leland Stanford Lathrop, Charles's adult son, sought to renege on an agreement to take property for money promised him in Leland Stanford's will when it cleared probate. Jane Stanford did not forget this. She retaliated by cutting him out of her own will. Jennie Lathrop, Charles's daughter, was a different case. She was a minor and very close to Jane. Mrs. Stanford wanted a guardian appointed for the child, who would then agree to take the real estate. Charles apparently would not consent.[6]

What happened next plumbed the depths of Jane's vindictiveness. She punished Jennie, at once professing her love and taking her revenge. She gave David Starr Jordan a letter to be used, if necessary, after her death. She hoped Jordan would never have to reveal it, "but I have learned by very sad experiences the greed for gain tempts beyond the ability to resist." The letter disinherited Jennie. She added that she was sure her brother Charles would "never deviate from his love and loyalty to me and my memory."[7]

The will Jane Stanford signed in 1896 turned out to be just the beginning of her adventures in will writing. Over the years between 1896 and 1905, her wills and trusts would leave the university and all those around her the playthings of her whims, convictions, resentments, and desires. Nobody could be fully sure what would happen to her fortune until she was dead.

———

IN 1899, WITH THE ECONOMY improving and their stocks finding a market, the remaining Associates and their heirs finally agreed to allow Jane Stanford to remove her shares in the Southern Pacific and Pacific Improvement Company from the common pool. She now held those stocks in her personal control, but there were still dangers. The U.S. Congress had appointed a new commission to pursue repayment of the debt, then amounting to $59 million, of the Central Pacific.[8] Jane Stanford's remaining stock holdings in that railroad were minor in and of themselves, but the repercussions would have spilled over into the Southern Pacific, the main source of her wealth. She had before her the example of the Union Pacific, which was sold at foreclosure in 1897.

In the wake of the new commission, James Speyer, of Speyer & Co., negotiated a settlement between the Central Pacific, the Southern Pacific, and the government. Under the complicated agreement, Speyer & Co., the bankers for the Associates, refinanced the debt owed the government. The Southern Pacific agreed to guarantee the bonds necessary to pay the debt. Congress approved the arrangement on March 3, 1899.[9]

The Speyers were not done. That spring Edgar Speyer, James's younger brother, followed Jane Stanford through Europe from hotel to hotel. She arrived in a new city to find his gifts of flowers and fruit awaiting her. She grew suspicious; he was resolute. He conveyed an offer to buy her stock in the Southern Pacific.

She had reason to sell. She needed income. And the Crockers had already sold their shares, leaving Huntington in control of the company and Mrs. Stanford a minority stockholder without dependable allies. On the other hand, with a recovering economy and consolidation of the railroads into great systems, Southern Pacific stock was nearly certain to appreciate. The Speyers knew this.[10]

Stopping in New York on her return from Europe, she sold the Southern Pacific stock on May 31 for a reported $11 million. Russell J. Wilson advised her when she made the sale, which George Crothers considered one of the great disasters to befall the university. It was, he claimed, $7 million less than the Speyers received when they sold the same stock to E. H. Harriman the next year. Writing in the 1930s, he calculated that the interest on that $7 million would have added up to more than the present endowment of the university, and this did not count the vast profits that much later came to the railroad from the sale of its oil company to Standard Oil.[11]

THE STOCK SALE left Jane Stanford flush with cash, but it was not certain that all the money could or would go to the university. Crothers, who was still working on getting a constitutional amendment before the voters to regularize the university's status, had a more immediate problem on his hands. On May 31, 1899, the same day as her stock sale, Jane Stanford made a mammoth gift to her university, transferring most of her estate through the so-called Great Deed, which Crothers called her "great but defective grant." The deed contained a clause, inserted by Mountford Wilson, that, according to Crothers, "practically destroyed its effect as a grant." That clause gave Mrs. Stanford the authority "to grant, bargain, sell, convey or lease" all the property she gave the university. Jane Stanford retained such extensive control over the money in the grant that it was as if the grant had never been made.[12]

According to Crothers, Mrs. Stanford regarded the deed "so lightly that she withdrew millions from its effect, and at least two millions of the money so withdrawn was bequeathed to her relatives, and many millions so withdrawn" went into a trust for her own benefit. It would go to the university only on her death and only if she did not change her mind before then. Jane Stanford often changed her mind.[13]

The money that Jane Stanford took back into her own hands after she withdrew it from the Great Deed could not flow easily back to the university even if she so desired. California law allowed only one-third of an estate to go to "eleemosynary institutions." Unless her lawyers found a way to circumvent the law, two-thirds of the money that remained with Jane Stanford when she died would go to other legatees and not the university.[14]

George Crothers began to suspect that the Wilsons were behind all these defects not because they were bad lawyers but because they were corrupt lawyers. Their opposition to his efforts to pass the constitutional amendment and their role in drafting the Great Deed were all calculated. Jane Stanford paid them extravagantly–they received $50,000 in 1899, presumably for drawing up the Great Deed—but they may have anticipated a greater payday from the heirs to the part of the fortune that did not go to the university.[15]

Crothers claimed that probate records verified that Russell Wilson and Timothy Hopkins, a university trustee and friend of Jane Stanford, were borrowing heavily from Charles Lathrop and other potential Stanford heirs, a claim that Charles's daughter, Jennie Lathrop, seconded. In 1897 Jane Stanford wrote to Jordan that Russell Wilson did his very best "to persuade me to give my personal property to the legatees" and not the university. Crothers believed that the Wilsons' amendments to the Great Deed were designed to invalidate the whole gift. He also thought that they allowed the "preposterous" method of Jane Stanford amending the trusts through "long rambling 'addresses,' mainly of her own composition," in order to open the trusts up to challenge. More money would thus go to Lathrop, to whom Wilson and Hopkins were in debt.[16]

The Great Deed was sloppy and dangerous, but things could always get worse at Stanford. In 1899 Jane Stanford did not understand what was in Crothers's amendment, but she worried that if the constitutional campaign failed, her Great Deed to the university would fail with it. She took an extraordinary step. She deeded the entire university endowment of $25 million, without any reservations or trust provisions, to another lawyer and trustee, Samuel Leib. The rationale was that if Stanford's gifts were to be ruled illegal, Leib could then reconvey the property to the university.[17] She had signed over the entire endowment to a single trustee.

Crothers later reflected on this "strange procedure," wondering how a future historian would explain Jane Stanford's actions, since had Leib died or acted on the deed, the university might not have been able to recover the money. But in 1899 Crothers seems to have endorsed it as a way to counter the Great Deed. He told Jordan that since under the Great Deed Jane Stanford "reserves the right to convert the securities to her own or any other use without accountability of any kind, in the event of her death, what evidence of her not having so converted them can be given, other than their possession by the trustees or their agents? We have made this suggestion and several others to Mr. Leib." Leib, for his part, assured Jane Stanford that if he survived her, her wishes would be carried out. She apparently did not believe him, for she later denounced him for accepting her gift. Leib destroyed the conveyance.[18]

Universities were not supposed to work like this.

CHAPTER 14

COMINGS AND GOINGS

IN HER MEMOIR BERTHA BERNER largely skips the period between February 1897 and the spring of 1899. May Hunt, who first went to work for Jane Stanford in 1898, said Bertha Berner was gone at that time. Leaving Jane Stanford and then returning became the pattern of Berner's employment. In the spring of 1899 she was back, accompanying Mrs. Stanford, who planned a visit to Europe "for a rest, intending to travel leisurely as fancy dictated." There was a day that spring that encapsulated what Berner gained, her frustration at the price she paid for it, and why she longed to leave. Jane Stanford and Bertha Berner were in England, taking rooms at the White Hart Inn located across from the main gate to Windsor Castle. They took drives every afternoon.[1]

Queen Victoria—"the little old lady" as Berner called her—was in residence, and from her window Jane Stanford enjoyed watching the garden parties and the coaches that arrived from London. When Mrs. Stanford received an invitation to one of the garden parties, she accepted.

The day was bright and sunny, and the military bands with their shining instruments "made the scene very gay." Members of the royal family moved through the garden chatting with friends. Guests promenaded on the marble walk.

Officers opened the side gate by which Jane Stanford entered. Among them was Lord Kitchener, famous for defeating the Dervishes at Khartoum in Sudan and soon to depart for battle against the Boers in South Africa. He offered Mrs. Stanford his arm. "As in duty bound," Bertha

Berner wrote, "I started to follow, but he smilingly asked me to be seated." Jane Stanford said something about Bertha being her shadow.

The other officers offered Bertha a chair and began to question her about the United States. They were, Bertha thought, "fine earnest men," and she was earnest in turn. She said that the United States had more opportunity than any other place she had seen in the world and good land that could be owned by those who worked it rather than a landlord. Wages were normally good, but the country was still recovering from the depression of 1893.

When Lord Kitchener returned, he took Bertha Berner on his arm and walked her around the garden. She flirted, saying that she treasured the story that she would tell her friends on returning home about walking around the Queen's garden on the arm of Lord Kitchener. He laughed and said titles were just words. She said she did not mean his title of Lord but rather that of "K. of K."—Kitchener of Khartoum—"which means very much to Americans." She leaned into him to examine his decorations, and he, a tall man, stooped toward her so that she might see them. What she remembered was the "earnest look in his bluish gray eagle eyes." Kitchener was hardly known for his charm, but Bertha Berner seems to have charmed him. It was a skill she had obviously mastered and used previously, but it did not here prove as useful as she may have hoped. Kitchener was reputed to be an "invert."[2]

Kitchener escorted her back to Mrs. Stanford, who was talking with the Princess of Wales. Children played around them, including the future Edward VIII, who was then a little child "in a white dress and blue bows."[3]

At the garden party Bertha Berner was briefly the center of attention. Bold, flirtatious, charming, quick, and calculating, she was much more than Jane Stanford's shadow. But when the party ended, she again became the traveling companion of an old and demanding woman.

IN FEBRUARY OF 1900 Jane Stanford inscribed a book of Bible stories to Bertha Berner, her "faithful friend and secretary for eighteen years," thanking her for her "constancy and attentions through years of sorrow and tears." She asked that Berner remember her when she read it. The inscription had the feeling of a farewell.[4] Jane Stanford's correspondence is incomplete, but she was meticulous about keeping letters from those she regarded as famous, particularly when they praised her. A letter from Julia Grant to Stanford survives from May of 1900.

"In your last letter," Grant wrote, "you mentioned wanting to secure a maid and companion that spoke German and French. If Bertha is not with you any longer, as I infer, I would like to recommend to you in Bertha's place Miss Annie Held . . . a German woman," who was a "strong, healthy, capable person." She spoke both French and German. She previously had served the family of Julia Grant's son as a governess and another friend as a maid. Julia Grant wished Jane Stanford a pleasant trip abroad.[5]

———

STANFORD REPLACED BERTHA but not with Annie Held. In June of 1900 a census taker enumerated the occupants of the California Street mansion: Jane Stanford, a butler, a German maid, a Chinese cook, a Chinese housekeeper, and a private secretary, Lula Rice.[6] Lula Rice may have been only a temporary secretary. Five years later Mrs. E. D. Benson said she had succeeded Berner as secretary, serving for about a year after Berner's departure and traveling with Mrs. Stanford to New York. When she left, Bertha Berner returned. Rice may have been the brief bridge between them.[7]

That same day in 1900 another census enumerator went to 732 Powell Street, just downhill from the Stanford mansion on Nob Hill, where Bertha Berner was living with her sixty-four-year-old mother, Maria, in a rented home. Maria was listed as the head of household. Bertha was thirty-four years old and listed herself as a private secretary. In the parlance of the time, she was a spinster.[8]

Bertha Berner made no mention in her memoir of the 1899–1900 rupture with Jane Stanford. But in 1912 she wrote to David Starr Jordan about her attempts to create some distance between herself and Mrs. Stanford. She told Jordan that twice she and Mrs. Stanford agreed that Berner would have a month off "to do as I pleased and both times after the second day she came to my home and said she would like to spend the vacation with me. Poor lonely dear." Berner claimed that the memory was now precious to her, but it does not appear to have been so at the time.[9]

The rupture may have been over Jane Stanford's plans for yet another foreign trip in 1900. With Maria Berner aging, the long trips seem to have grown worrisome and onerous for her daughter. But then in early June something changed. Bertha Berner applied for a passport to travel with Mrs. Stanford, a servant, and her niece.[10]

There is an odd element to this reconciliation. Bertha Berner took care of the details of Jane Stanford's travels. She arranged purchases from the European dealers who sold Mrs. Stanford art and antiquities. She had a life and friends in San Francisco. So why was Mountford Wilson the witness for her passport? She did not need his help.

Mountford Wilson wrote Jane Stanford's 1899 will, which contained a $10,000 bequest for Bertha Berner. Berner may not have known of the bequest, or she might have known of it and feared that Stanford, to whom changing wills became something of a hobby, might alter it. Wilson also may have conveyed Jane Stanford's willingness to pay for Berner's return. But he may also have been acting as an agent of Charles Lathrop, who was rumored to have personally supplemented Berner's salary more than once to secure her return as Mrs. Stanford became more exacting, and caring for her more demanding. Berner was earning $2,400 a year in 1905, a substantial amount, more than most professors at Stanford, but her actual income was much greater.[11]

Most likely, money brought Berner back. In her memoir Berner compared Stanford to Queen Victoria, whom Stanford admired. "Mrs. Stanford," she wrote, "came to rule people through her wealth, and no crown or title could have made her rule more absolute nor the realization of her power more clear in her mind."[12]

Bertha Berner learned that Jane Stanford was not inclined to be generous with those who quarreled with her or opposed her. On one of the New York trips, she witnessed an encounter between Jane and yet another brother of Leland Stanford, Asa Philips Stanford. Asa Stanford died in 1903, contending that Jane had cheated him out of his fair share of the Central Pacific railroad proceeds. According to his widow, Annie Stanford, his last encounter with Jane occurred just before his death. He was aged, sick, and poor. Annie Stanford wrote and visited Jane asking for aid, and when she failed she made a last desperate attempt by placing Asa in Jane's hotel in a place where she could not fail to notice him. Bertha Berner spotted Asa first, and watched as Jane Stanford coldly denied aid to her dead husband's brother, saying, "When your brother died, our relations were severed. I don't know you." Berner knew the price Jane Stanford would charge for her own return. She would become Mrs. Stanford's subject. Wilson appears to have negotiated the reconciliation between them.[13]

AH WING SERVED the Stanfords for years. He was literate in Chinese and would leave an account of the earthquake of 1906 that destroyed the Stanford mansion. He was observant—quick to catch meaningful details—but white people paid him little notice. When they did, they often demeaned him.[14]

Ah Wing worked largely at the Nob Hill mansion, where he lived when the Stanfords were in residence and when they traveled. After Harry Lathrop, another of Jane's brothers, stopped working in 1891, he moved in with Jane. Like the rest of the Stanfords and Lathrops, Harry fed from the Southern Pacific trough. He was dying of cirrhosis of the liver. Ah Wing helped care for him before his death from dropsy, or congestive heart failure, in 1899, and Harry supposedly promised to leave Ah Wing money in his will. Instead, he left all the money to Jane and his two surviving brothers. Ah Wing was furious at the betrayal.[15]

The expectation of the money may have been what prompted Ah Wing to schedule his return to China, where he had a wife and child. He reportedly invested $5,000 from his savings there. Jane Stanford, afraid of losing an old servant, conciliated him by giving him $1,000. In return, she exacted a promise from him to stay with her as long as she lived. She pledged that he would not be the poorer for it. According to Bertha Berner, Mrs. Stanford said she would leave him more money in her will.[16]

Ah Wing went to China anyway, apparently over Jane Stanford's objections. It was a dangerous move. The United States had severely restricted Chinese immigration in 1882, and in 1888 the Scott Act limited the right of return for those who had previously immigrated to the United States and then left the country. When the census taker arrived at the Stanford mansion in June of 1900, Ah Wing was not present.[17]

On May 1, 1902, Charles Lathrop wrote his sister about Ah Wing's return. "It was," Charles reported, "a whole week before he could make a landing and they had to wire to Washington to get permission for him to come ashore." Lathrop told Ah Wing that if he ever "went back to China he would have to remain there as it would be impossible for him to get back in America again."[18]

Jane Stanford was traveling in Hawaii and Japan when Ah Wing landed. She took the ocean voyage in part to recover from an operation on her scalp in the winter of 1901–1902 by Dr. William T. Bull, a noted surgeon. He removed multiple wens—benign cysts—from her head. Lath-rop wrote his sister that he "told [Ah Wing] to go to the City house and remain there until you returned as these were your instructions should he arrive during your absence." Stanford would then decide whether to retain him. Jane Stanford rehired Ah Wing, and he expressed his gratitude and devotion.[19] But he made a cruel bargain. He had to remain with Jane Stanford as long as she lived. If he returned to his family, he was unlikely to receive his promised bequest.

CHAPTER 15

EDWARD ROSS

THE BALANCE BETWEEN JANE STANFORD, with her absolute financial control of the university, and David Starr Jordan, to whom she delegated administrative control, proved too precarious to last. Edward Ross tipped the balance. In 1893, the year Leland Stanford died, Jordan appointed the twenty-six-year-old Ross to a chair in Economic Theory and Finance. Six foot five, handsome, a popular teacher, a sought-after speaker, a graduate of Johns Hopkins, and a rising scholar who had already held positions at Indiana and Cornell, Ross became one of the most famous and influential intellectuals of the early twentieth century. Like Jordan and many other Progressives, he was from Protestant, rural, old-stock America, which matched a confidence in its ability to shape the world with a fear of national degeneration from immigrants unlike them. In the 1890s Ross was, like Jordan, a eugenicist who argued that the United States would collapse beneath the burden of racially inferior immigrants.

Ross went to Stanford against the advice of friends and colleagues, who doubted that it offered much of an academic career, but he was not sorry. He loved California, a place of "halcyon days and gentle nights," which was "everything I dreamed—and more." The faculty of "a multi-millionaire's university" were, he claimed, plainer, more down to earth and "homespun" than those at the relatively nearby campus of the University of California at Berkeley. He threw himself into his work and the natural world that surrounded the Stanford campus.[1]

Ross maintained that he and his fellow newly minted PhDs from Johns Hopkins were fearless in those days, not caring "how their utterances will strike powerful outsiders." People who knew and admired him also thought him brash and perhaps too proud of his ability to turn a striking phrase or epigram. He sprinkled his lectures with current slang.[2]

Jane Stanford heard—from whom is unclear—that Ross told a class that "a railroad deal was a railroad steal" and that all great fortunes were based on theft. She told Samuel Leib that Ross called Leland Stanford a thief in his classroom.[3] Ross claimed he had never criticized Leland Stanford personally, although his surviving class notes show that he did criticize his policies.[4] Ross was convinced from his own research on the Southern Pacific Railroad that "everything has not been right in that management," which was something of an understatement.[5]

True or not, the stories could only outrage a woman who went to great lengths to protect her husband's reputation. Her past dominated her present. She retained every memento of her dead child, but she relentlessly destroyed every bit of evidence that could challenge her memories. She destroyed Leland Stanford's papers, which indicates that she knew—or at least suspected—that there were aspects of his career best left unexamined. Every railroad deal might not be a railroad steal, but plenty were.

Jane Stanford took a dislike to Edward Ross. Henry B. Lathrop, a faculty member who knew Mrs. Stanford but was not related to her, later told Ross that she "was moved not by general ideas, but personal feelings." This was condescending and sexist, but when Lathrop said that she regarded the university as "the memorial of a dead son, and of a dead husband," he was only stating the obvious. She took criticism of her husband—implicit or explicit, deserved or not, true or false—personally.[6]

In the fall of 1896 Ross recognized that he was in trouble with Jane Stanford. He taught that summer at the new University of Chicago, giving two lectures a day, including Saturdays. Among his lectures was one that promoted bimetallism—using silver as well as gold as the basis of American currency. This was his answer to the "money question" at the heart of the presidential campaign that year. William Jennings Bryan, a Democrat also backed by the Populist Party, embraced bimetallism. The Republican candidate, William McKinley, stood for the gold standard. Ross turned the lectures into several articles for the *Chicago Record*, and then published the articles as a pamphlet, "Honest Dollars."[7] Although Ross was a Republican, he supported Bryan, and the Democrats distributed the pamphlet widely, supposedly putting 40,000 copies in circulation.[8]

Ross returned to California and the university on the morning of September 14, the first day of classes, to find that he had attained notoriety as one of only two economists who "have come out unreservedly for the free coinage of silver." He spoke at public meetings in California, including Democratic Party meetings. He recognized that Mrs. Stanford and most of the faculty were for gold. He did not know if there would be "any strong pressure to have them put me out of the University."[9]

There was.

In the fall of 1896 Jane Stanford made it clear to David Starr Jordan that Edward Ross was a cause of anxiety, and she wanted him gone. But Jordan chose not to regard her wish as his command, and Ross remained. Her desire to rid herself of Ross led to what became known as the Ross Affair.

In October of 1896, Jordan, who had been in the Pribilof Islands investigating the overhunting of fur seals, sent Ross a letter informing him that the university was "an institution pledged to non-partisanship." Its founder "will never interfere in any way with the religion, the politics or the love affairs of any member of the University." These were supposedly Jane Stanford's own words. But the institution did have "the right to expect its members not to compromise its dignity." Faculty members should not "expose the institution to unwelcome surprises," and Jordan was surprised and humiliated. He did not think it necessary to be more specific.[10]

Jordan made it seem that this was the first mention of his concerns to Ross. But three days earlier, Ross wrote his mother that "I have told the president that I will shun all political writings and speeches, but I will not decline to lecture on money in a dignified way when people invite me to do so." In all probability, Jordan's letter with its praise of Jane Stanford's liberalism and restraint was a record meant less for Ross than Jane Stanford.[11]

Jordan reprimanded Ross and removed him from his chair in economics, but he gave him another chair in sociology, at that time a new discipline. He defended Ross to Jane Stanford. Ross spoke on the issues, but he did not actively campaign for Bryan and thus was not a partisan.[12]

Jordan's actions did not satisfy Jane Stanford. Her animosity simmered and in January of 1897 it boiled over again. Ross, who was not a socialist, gave a speech before socialists. Jane Stanford despised socialists and for that matter unions and politicians who depended on working-class votes. That Ross would speak before socialists "was sufficient to warrant me to say all I did to you in regard to his being retained by the university." She put renewed pressure on Jordan to dismiss him.[13]

Jordan sought to balance his protection of Ross with a general defense of Jane Stanford's right to fire professors for violations of a Stanford University policy that prohibited partisan speech. There were multiple problems with this position; the most immediate was that there was no policy about partisan speech in the Founding Grant. The university's Grant of Endowment did prohibit sectarian instruction, but it said nothing about the faculty being nonpartisan.[14] In compiling material for his autobiography, Jordan claimed that "Mr. Stanford had laid down certain propositions" that became governing statutes. One was that the university "'must forever [be] maintained upon a strictly non partisan and nonsectarian basis'" and that "'it must never become an instrument in the hands of any political party or religious sect or organization.'" The quotes were from a speech that Leland Stanford gave to the Board of Trustees concerning the Memorial Church and its nondenominational status. It proclaimed the university's position and not that of individual faculty members. In saying the university was nonsectarian, Leland Stanford did not mean to say that faculty members could not be active Methodists, Baptists, Catholics, or Jews. So, similarly, in a nonpartisan university, they could be active Democrats, Republicans, or Socialists who spoke on issues of public interest and concern, as Jordan himself did. Stanford, after all, was a Republican senator.[15]

Jane Stanford later claimed that she instituted a strict nonpartisan policy in her address to the trustees on June 1, 1897, but there is no record of this. What she did was put all public responsibility for troublesome professors such as Ross on Jordan.[16]

David Starr Jordan read Jane Stanford's writing on the wall. She wanted Ross gone, but she did not want her hands dirty. Still, Jordan hesitated. He lived in and cared about a much wider academic world agitated by issues of academic freedom. Firing Ross could cause a scandal that would endanger the university's national reputation.

To steer the university away from a wreck on the shoals of academic freedom, Jordan in 1899 undertook an educational campaign for Mrs. Stanford. It proved to be the greatest pedagogical challenge of his career. He failed miserably.

Jordan sent Jane Stanford an article on an earlier dispute at the University of Chicago, in which Professor Hermann Eduard Von Holst condemned President Grover Cleveland's threat to intervene in the Venezuela boundary crisis. President Harper of the university and other faculty, who supported Cleveland, condemned Von Holst and made it clear he spoke only for himself. Jordan's apparent goal was to show that in other universities similar disputes over faculty statements about public issues could be conducted without silencing or dismissing faculty members. Professors like Von Holst—and Ross—could be rebuked by the university president and loyal faculty. There was no need to fire them.[17]

Jane Stanford was traveling in Europe when she replied. She seemed to absorb the intended lesson. She proclaimed her devotion to "freedom of thought, freedom of action, freedom of speech."[18]

But she ascribed her own moral to the story, a lesson that applied to university presidents as well as university professors. A university president, she wrote, should never pursue any object that did not advance the welfare of the university. "When a man assumes to be a leader and campaigner of [a] vital political issue, he really in my humble and womanly opinion, oversteps the boundary line of what is expected from a president of an University." She was not just referring to the president of the University of Chicago, and Jordan knew it. She was referring to him.[19]

Jordan's reply to Stanford survives as an undated draft in a miscellaneous folder separate from the Ross files. He began by referring to her "very kind letter," but then he crossed out "very kind." He was "sure that you do not mean to charge that I have used my position to favor any political party or to further any ambitions of my own," but that was exactly what she implied. The issue in this case was the Philippines. Jane Stanford was, in her words, an "expansionist," who supported their annexation. She was referencing a speech Jordan gave three or four times: "Lest We Forget," opposing American imperialism in the Philippines. He regarded his speaking out as a "vital duty." He had "spoken what seems the plain truth because the country is suffering from error. I could not do otherwise in justice to myself." The newspaper reports of his talk were not entirely accurate, but he had spoken on "behalf of my country because it seemed my plain duty to do so." He had not solicited chances to speak and declined the majority of invitations, and he did "not intend to speak on the subject again." He had "not in any way abused the duties of my position for party, personal, or any other ends." If she regarded him as having done so, then "Stanford University is not a University at all and cannot stand for the free investigation and free proclamation of truth." He did not mean to cause her distress or embarrassment. He would try not to add to her burdens. He, in effect, perfectly replicated Ross's position and justification.[20]

He closed the letter "Your loyal servant" but crossed out "loyal servant."[21]

Having let Jordan know he was in her crosshairs, Jane Stanford shifted her aim back to Ross. "Professor Ross, as you know, overstepped the bounds and entered into a political campaign which was as distasteful to you as to me, and both you and I felt Professor Ross had been an injury to the University."[22] Jordan could escape her censure only by ridding her of Ross. During her European travels in 1899, she thought Jordan had made arrangements for Ross's departure. When Ross remained on the faculty, she blamed Jordan for ignoring her wishes over the course of three years. The president, as George Crothers remembered, "seemed not to have the courage to carry out the policy she thought had been agreed upon."[23]

CHAPTER 16

THE ROSS AFFAIR

IN 1899, WHILE TRAVELING across Europe, Jane Stanford decided to force the removal of Edward Ross. Ross, who was also in Europe with his wife on a sabbatical leave, returned to the Santa Clara Valley that fall. He thought of California as his home, and he was glad to be home. Having performed extraordinary service during the long financial crisis of the 1890s, he believed that with the division of the pooled assets of the Southern Pacific Railroad, the university was entering a period of "good times." Teaching assistants allowed him to escape the "drudgery" of the classroom. He could devote time to planning his classes and his lectures, and he was making progress on his book. "Altogether," he wrote his mother, "the outlook is bright." In early May, Jordan renewed his appointment.[1]

Ross did not realize the extent or persistence of Jane Stanford's animosity toward him. He should have. She personally disliked him for his manner. She did not like what he said and how he said it. She did not like him sitting on a desk when he addressed his class. On May 8, 1900, Jane Stanford read a newspaper account of a speech by Ross to the United Labor Organizations of San Francisco. David Starr Jordan described it as incendiary. Jordan told President Charles Eliot of Harvard that Ross gave the speech at a meeting "in the hands of men against whom Mr. Stanford . . . had struggled in defense of the Chinese." Ross's association with such men "hurt Mrs. Stanford deeply."[2]

What Jordan omitted was that, after declining the invitation himself, he suggested to Ross that he speak. Jordan and Ross shared the same mixture of racism, nativism, and Progressive politics. Jordan thought the French "dissolute and slovenly," he despised southern Italians, and he thought Mexicans "ignorant, superstitious, ill-nurtured, with little self-control, and conception of industry or thrift." They lacked "most of our Anglo-Saxon virtues." The United States was a "Nordic" nation, he believed, and its future depended on remaining "Nordic." Where Ross and Jordan differed was on the Japanese. Jordan carved out a racial exception for the Japanese, whom he considered honorary white people. Ross disagreed. He described Japanese as unassimilable. They were the products of an inferior civilization who would degrade American workers. It would be better, he said, if the United States turned its guns on every ship carrying Japanese rather than letting them land. If he said it, he apparently ad-libbed the gun part. The language was not in his written copy of the speech.[3]

There was more. It was brought to Jane Stanford's attention—by whom was a matter of dispute—that Ross criticized privately owned street railways, which were part of Jane Stanford's stock portfolio through the Pacific Improvement Company. He did not think they should come under public ownership, although he thought they would eventually become publicly regulated private utilities. This infuriated Jane Stanford.[4]

Mrs. Stanford was "weary of Prof. Ross." Jordan should not have to be on the watch for what "your professors may say . . . Prof. Ross cannot be trusted and he should go. . . . He is a dangerous man." Jordan said this was the first time that Jane Stanford demanded a professor's dismissal, but this, as H. H. Powers, Ross's ex-colleague, could attest, was not true.[5]

It was hard to say how Jane Stanford could have been clearer about the reasons for Ross's dismissal. She insisted that his opinions and his speech would not allow him to remain at the university. He held "rabid ideas" that he could not help inculcating into the minds of his students. His talks spurred a "feeling of indignation throughout the community," that the university was "lending itself to partisanience and even to dangerous socialism." She bristled at an attack on "coolie labor"—men who built her husband's railroads and servants who protected her house against the sandlot mobs, who had attacked the Chinese and threatened the rich in the 1870s.[6]

Ross, Jordan admitted, had his faults, but they were "neither dangerous nor incurable." He was rash, but this sprang from an "honest boldness." He pointed out that Ross's opinions were well within the bounds of normal academic and public discussion. They were "neither extreme nor revolutionary." Jordan did not defend socialists; he just denied that Ross was a socialist. He told Stanford that other prominent academics were much more politically active than Ross. He stressed Ross's service to the university. "This matter involves the whole future career of a wise, learned, and noble man, one of the most loyal and devoted of all the band we have brought together."[7]

Jordan's motives went beyond affection for Ross. He wrote Jane Stanford that "[t]he honor of the University is dearer to me than life. It is my life. And this honor forces upon me the need of justice. No deeper charge can be made against a university than that it denies its professors freedom of speech. Of all men in the country, their opinions on public questions are most important." Jordan told Stanford that "while your wish is sacred to me . . . the honor of the University is also sacred," and that he would have to decide what "is wise and right."[8]

Jordan's phrasing—freedom of speech rather than academic freedom— was significant. The Gilded Age battle over academic freedom in American universities had raged since the 1870s and originally centered on Darwin and the teaching of evolution. That battle did not so much array religion against science, since many religious people accommodated evolution, as it pitted scientists against those ministers, college officials, and college trustees who sought to dictate the legitimacy of scientific research. Jordan championed science. As universities professionalized and followed the models of German universities, academic freedom expanded to become the right of university professors to research and report their findings without restraint. In Germany academic freedom did not extend to a participation in politics. This is why Jordan also appealed to a more specifically American right that extended to all members of the public— freedom of speech.[9]

By the early twentieth century the social sciences formed the most active front in the war over academic freedom. The conflicts often pitted conservative boards of trustees—usually businessmen—against more progressive academics—such as Ross. Conservative critics demanded that academics be neutral and take no part in partisan debates. Liberal academics replied that their obligation was not to the universities or the people who controlled them, but to the public and to their profession. They possessed a right to address public questions as long as they did so judiciously and within the bounds of their findings; their status as American citizens allowed them to speak when and where they wanted. They shared the same rights as other citizens.

In the spring of 1900 Jordan informed Ross that Jane Stanford wanted him gone, but he still thought she might change her mind, and he encouraged Ross to write her. Ross did, stating in his letter his reverence for her as the "mother of the University," and insisting that she was being deceived by rumors and gossip. He asked to be judged on his academic writings and his service to the university. He denied he was either a socialist or a "dangerous man." Ross had devoted himself to his teaching and the university at great cost to his publishing. At one point, he had 335 students in his classes, a third of the university. He devoted his "whole soul and strength to the glory of Stanford, trusting Stanford would look out for me."[10]

Jane Stanford played the dowager queen. She softened slightly with Ross's letter, pleased with his recognition that his position depended on her. She thought that he may not have realized that his opinions on silver were objectionable; if he had, he might have been more tactful. But there were the new offenses, and she insisted on his dismissal. She considered it her due. It was her university. As H. B. Lathrop, who sympathized with Ross, wrote, she lived among plutocrats, and "[o]f course she had been spoiled by riches" and become "arbitrary."[11] She put it differently. Her decision to fire Ross was the result of "disappointment, reflection, and prayer."[12]

Jordan started out trying to do what was wise and right, and when he learned that these were mutually exclusive, he selected the wise. A principled stand against Jane Stanford would be useless. With her back up, she would accept his resignation as well as Ross's. Jordan possessed enough vanity to think Stanford could not become a major university without him, and he was not the only one who thought so. Professor Lathrop said if Jordan defied or blamed Mrs. Stanford, Jordan would not retain his position, and this might "destroy Stanford University." As Jane became friendlier with Catholic prelates, there were rumors she would turn the university over to the Jesuits.[13]

Jordan decided it would be best if Ross left quietly, accepting a position elsewhere without fuss or discussion as to why he was leaving. On June 15, Jordan wrote Ross of his fate. He told Ross, falsely, that Mrs. Stanford liked and respected him. She "had no desire to limit freedom of speech, but she feels that the reputation of the University for serious conservatism is impaired by the hasty acceptance of political and social fads or of ideas not approved by conservative thinkers, and administrative schemes not acceptable to serious businessmen." Jordan, in effect, argued that Stanford University endorsed freedom of speech as long as the speech was conservative and supportive of the status quo. The letter put the onus for Ross's dismissal on Jane Stanford. The cause was his expression of unacceptable opinions.[14]

Jordan told Ross that he could show the letter to others, but he must not quote or paraphrase it. He gave Ross a powerful weapon.[15]

Ross thanked Jordan for his support and agreed to resign at the end of the 1900–1901 academic year, not wanting to be "a cause of worry to Mrs. Stanford or of embarrassment to you." In September he wrote his mother in confidence, telling her that he was leaving because railroad people induced Mrs. Stanford, who was "old and crotchety," to dismiss him. Jordan had tried to protect him but failed. Ross was not planning to announce his departure for "a couple of months." The news would "wake a sensation on the Pacific Slope."[16]

Over the summer, Jordan sought to camouflage Ross's departure. Jordan warned Jane Stanford that he thought Ross would remain silent but that with his resignation "the word will go out that he was dismissed for political reasons. Such a statement would do us great injury in the higher circles which make University reputation." Jordan suggested a way to avoid scandal. He would treat Stanford University as if it were a baseball team. He would accept Ross's resignation, but hold it while he tried to exchange Ross with Cornell, Wisconsin, or the University of Chicago for a comparable professor. Jane Stanford agreed. Jordan wrote letters praising Ross as a scholar and a man. He attributed his leaving solely to Jane Stanford's dislike of him.[17] These letters too were capable of doing him damage.

It was no great surprise, except perhaps to Jordan, that this did not work. No economist or sociologist of any reputation wanted to be traded to Stanford, and rumors of Ross's departure created suspicions. Albion Small of the University of Chicago told Jordan that Ross was already one of the most eminent men on Stanford's faculty, and the university's prestige would suffer if he departed. President Charles Eliot of Harvard, who received a letter from Jordan effusively praising Ross, hoped that Jordan could convince Jane Stanford of "the fundamental importance of complete academic liberty for professors, and particularly for professors whose subjects touch on public policies and affairs." He told Jordan "it would be a great calamity for the Leland Stanford University if it should come to be known that a professor had been obliged to leave it because Mrs. Stanford expressed a wish to that effect." No men of "strong character and good abilities" would come to the university in the future.[18]

CHAPTER 17

ROSS STRIKES BACK

WHEN JORDAN'S EFFORTS to trade Ross stalled in the summer of 1900, Jane Stanford grew impatient. She demanded that Ross be gone by the next March. Jordan lost the will to resist. On his return from a trip to Japan, he learned of the death of his youngest child two days earlier on September 12, 1900. She had contracted scarlet fever in the summer, seemed to recover, then succumbed. The loss of Barbara was too much. Twenty years later, when he wrote his autobiography, he said, "the wound seems as deep as yesterday." It was a sentence Jane Stanford could have written. Jordan felt he had done all he could for Ross.[1]

Mrs. Stanford seems to have imagined that Barbara's death would bring a transformation in the Jordans similar to the transformation Leland Jr.'s death produced in her and her husband. She sent Jordan's wife a copy of Ernest Shurtleff's *The Shadow of the Angel*, a sermon in verse that brought her comfort. Shurtleff intended his book to have the same effect "as the humble flight of a butterfly over a little child's grave, leading some grieving mother to look up." Jane Stanford inscribed the book: "I now(?) dare send my secret long cherished loving words that led me to love God as I never loved him before. He called my dear ones from earth life to Heaven." Deaths should be born "patiently and cheerfully" for they were a mark of God's love. That "God bless and keep you from further sorrow is ever my prayer."[2]

The invitation to take comfort in spiritualism could only infuriate Jordan. Before Barbara's death, he had submitted articles to *Science* and *Popular Science Monthly*, which came out in the fall of 1900. In them he satirized invented cults—neminism and sociosophy—which bore a famil-ial resemblance to spiritualism. In one article, photographs of "elderly ladies with serene and smiling faces" covered the walls of the president of the University of Mentiphysics. "Each one had been made whole and happy through Neministic Science." In a particularly cruel touch, nemi-nistic science promised the ability to regrow lost teeth. Jane Stanford had lost virtually all her teeth.[3]

On November 11, 1900, Jordan accepted the resignation letter Ross wrote in June. He had delayed the action in the hope that circumstances would change and lead to a reconsideration. He accepted the resignation with "great reluctance." He expressed his high esteem for Ross's work as a teacher and "his character as a man."[4]

The timing of Jordan's acceptance was notable. The week before Jor-dan's decision, Crothers's constitutional amendment to regularize the legal status of Stanford University came before California voters. Mount-ford Wilson had tried to undermine it. He initially convinced Jordan that the founding documents were sound. When Jordan testified to this point before the California Senate Judiciary Committee, it refused to endorse the amendment, deeming it unnecessary. Crothers and his allies neverthe-less convinced the Senate as a whole that Jordan and Wilson were wrong.

Crothers still had to convince the voters. A high-ranking Mason him-self, Crothers mobilized a network of Masons, Stanford alumni, and local newspapers to persuade voters to approve the amendment. On Novem-ber 6 they did: in its final form it regularized the university's status and allowed the legislature to create a special tax exemption for Stanford's lands and the funds put in trust, as long as they were devoted to educa-tional purposes. In return, students who were citizens of California were not to be charged tuition unless such fees were authorized by an act of the legislature. As Ross and others pointed out, if the news of his dismissal were known before the election—or if Ross had gone to the press—the amendment might have gone down to defeat.[5]

In November of 1900 Edward Ross was finished at Stanford, but he wasn't finished with Stanford. Ross called in reporters for the San Fran-cisco newspapers. He gave them a statement that attributed his dismissal to Jane Stanford's disapproval of his political opinions. The reporters immediately interviewed Jordan, who had not yet read Ross's statement; he praised Ross profusely. That praise would appear alongside Ross's letter in the San Francisco newspapers on November 14. The *Chronicle*'s headline blared, "Dr. Edward Ross Forced Out of Stanford University." Ross attributed his dismissal to his talks on "coolie" labor and on municipal ownership. The story blamed Mrs. Stanford and, in Ross's words, "certain powerful people and interests in San Francisco" for Ross's firing. Jordan tried to save him, and Ross thanked his "great chief" David Starr Jordan. It was a Judas kiss. In praising Jordan, he put the onus for the whole affair on Jane Stanford. Jordan's letters to Ross made it hard for the president to assert either that he—rather than Jane Stanford—made the decision to fire Ross or that Ross was fired for anything but proclaiming his opinions. Jane Stanford was not pleased.[6]

Ross was very pleased. Even papers whose editorial positions differed from his on Asian labor and municipal ownership backed him. He said he had 800 press clippings, 95 percent of which were supportive. The reform journalist W. T. Stead's *Review of Reviews* said his dismissal had caused a "prodigious sensation." The initial academic reaction was scathing. Edwin Seligman, a Columbia economist, hoped Ross could gain a position where he would "not be exposed to the petty malignity of people whose mental horizon is bounded only by the limits of their purse. Leland Stanford has received a blow from which it will never recover during the lifetime of its present dictatress. Its reputation as a University has vanished." At the American Economic Association meetings that winter, Seligman was among a group who organized to investigate and write a report on the Ross Affair.[7]

David Starr Jordan felt betrayed. He had tried to protect Ross from Jane Stanford and to obtain another faculty position for him. In return, he expected Ross to go quietly. Instead he had a public scandal on his hands. He sacrificed Ross to save his own relationship with Jane Stanford, which he thought critical to Stanford's being a reputable academic institution, but Ross sabotaged his efforts.

Once Ross went to the papers, Jordan had no good choices. The key problem was simple: Ross was telling the truth, and he possessed evidence to prove it. If Jordan attacked him publicly, Ross could publish the letters in which Jordan blamed Jane Stanford for Ross's dismissal and praised Ross. But if Jordan let the newspaper accounts go unrefuted, then the loss of Stanford University's academic standing among its peers and its own faculty could cripple the university for years to come.

Jordan tried to disarm Ross. He reminded him that his letters were confidential and not meant for publication. But he also wrote Ross telling him that his association with Stanford University ceased with the publication of his statement. On November 18, he asked Ross to return the copies of letters Jordan wrote on his behalf. He also sent him a cryptic note asking if he had forgotten the meaning involved in *"noblesse oblige."*[8]

Ross offered to return the letters but only on the condition that Jordan write a public letter of "clearance" for Ross addressed to Jane Stanford, repeating his praise of Ross's work and ability. This Jordan could not do without destroying his own standing with Mrs. Stanford.[9]

Jordan sought to stifle further dissent at Stanford by securing the loyalty of key faculty members. The most significant was a historian, George Howard. On November 14, the night Ross's letter appeared, Jordan went to visit Howard; he told him that the faculty should "keep still." Howard informed him that he had already made a statement to the newspapers condemning the university's action. He said he could not "murder" his intellectual freedom. He then offered his resignation. Jordan refused it.

Howard asked Jordan why he had not thrown down the gauntlet to defend academic freedom and allowed the faculty to support him. Jordan replied that such action would have "killed Mrs. Stanford." He acknowledged that her actions were "exceedingly foolish," just the "whim of an old woman."[10]

Jordan told Howard that if the action had come from a real and reputable board of trustees, he would have resigned on principle. But at Stanford the trustees were irrelevant. They possessed no power. Often trustees meetings dissolved for the lack of a quorum. Jane Stanford was the Board of Trustees. Getting rid of Ross was necessary to "save the university." He was, he told Howard, dealing "with the mysteries of a woman's heart." If Jordan resisted further, she would starve Stanford of funds.[11]

Jordan told Howard that three men connected with the Market Street Railway in which Jane Stanford held stock prejudiced her against Ross. The next day Howard denounced Ross's dismissal in front of his class on the French Revolution. He used the information Jordan relayed to him. Jordan repudiated his statements to Howard. He said he had been mistaken about the street railway men influencing Mrs. Stanford. Jordan made it clear to Howard that in the future as president he would follow the demands of Jane Stanford.[12]

Jordan weighed a full public defense. In early December, he drafted a statement about Ross claiming that "the main cause of his dismissal was the loss of faith in his discretion and in the seriousness of the foundation of his economic views and of their application to questions of administration." The trouble sprang from not what he said but rather how he said it. Virtually every factual claim Jordan made in the draft was false and Jordan knew them to be false. He never issued the statement, but it formed a template for what followed.[13]

THE PUBLIC REACTION to the firing of Professor Ross upset, puzzled, and angered Jane Stanford, but she did not retreat. She always regarded the particulars of the Ross Affair as "trivial." Academic freedom did not resonate with a woman who for all practical purposes owned a university. She demanded that political neutering and a respect for conservative opinions be the price of academic life. The university had a right to censure and censor speech she judged to be partisan. She was "within her rights" to dismiss faculty, and when challenged she was always imperious. She did not forgive or forget.[14]

As soon as the storm over Ross broke, Jordan began repairing his standing with Mrs. Stanford. He privately told her that she had been right about Ross all along while he was wrong. Ross was "a consummate fool," and "at bottom just a dime novel villain." An angry Stanford was not satisfied with Jordan's private reversal of position. She wanted him to say this publicly, both to vindicate her and to protect "the character and the well-being of the University." Jordan knew that would be professional suicide.[15]

Upset by the turmoil, Jane Stanford fled to Europe at the end of 1900. Jordan hoped that distance would stop her from interfering further; it did not. Jordan refused Howard's resignation, but from the Grand Hotel in Rome a furious Jane Stanford demanded that Jordan dismiss Howard. In January of 1901 Jordan asked Howard to step down on account of his unjust accusations and discourtesy to "the University management." He said he "waited a reasonable time in the hope that reflection would enable you to see some explanation and apology were desirable." He marked Howard's fault as a "breach of courtesy." The charges of discourtesy outraged Howard. He had no apology to make. He resigned in January of 1901.[16]

Howard was not the first to depart, but his leaving was the most consequential. Morton Aldrich, an economics professor, quit in November 1900 over "unjustifiable interference with the independence of a university teacher within the proper limits of his freedom." A parade of professors from mathematics, history, and English followed Howard. Some Jordan forced out; others resigned in protest. Howard accused Jordan of trying to "befog the real issues by falsehood and evasion," and then launching a "reign of terror." Howard so soured on the president that he thought it best if Jordan could be forced out of education entirely.[17]

Jane Stanford demanded an even larger bloodletting in the wake of the resignations, but Jordan dissuaded her. At the end of January 1901, about to depart up the Nile, she was still filled with anxiety about the fallout from the Ross Affair. Back in Cairo in March, she obsessed about rebel faculty.[18] The resignations continued in February. Horace Davis, who would become president of the Board of Trustees after Jane Stanford's death, referred to the exodus of faculty as the "great secession of 1900–01."[19]

Many of the faculty members who remained wavered. Most were simply terrified. As Julius Goebel, who taught German, wrote Jordan, "a feeling of uncertainty and instability" overtook faculty members who realized they could be removed for their opinions. He urged Jordan to eliminate Stanford's policy of making only annual appointments.[20]

Jordan's defenders proclaimed the loyalty of the bulk of the faculty, but in private Jordan recognized the wreckage around him. In mid-January of 1901 he planned to replace departing professors with instructors. The university, he asserted, "will be all the stronger when its spurious prestige is gone, and it starts up sound from the bottom."[21]

The alumni also threatened to rebel, but George Crothers quelled it. An initial protest meeting was full of Ross sympathizers, but Crothers and his allies captured the committee designated to write a report on the Ross Affair. Two of the committee's leading members—a lawyer, Walter Rose, and Anthony Suzzallo, later president of the University of Washington— consulted Jordan on its content and drafting. Crothers regarded the Ross Affair as a disaster, but his immediate goal was to convince Jane Stanford of the loyalty of the alumni. If the report failed to do so, he thought she would abandon the university.[22]

The alumni committee's investigation was cursory. Although it did hear testimony from Professor Ross, he held back the documents in his possession, and Jordan disclosed only selected files that he asked to be kept secret. The main value of the report issued at the end of January 1901 was that Jane Stanford thought she had the support of her boys— she rarely mentioned the women who graduated from Stanford except when she feared they were seducing boys. The report kept the evidence—

or lack of evidence—secret. The committee blamed Ross's dismissal on his partisanship in the 1896 campaign, an event that had taken place more than four years earlier and a charge that Jordan had denied in writing. Nor did the committee explain why the professors who came out publicly with statements in the newspapers in support of the gold standard and the Republican ticket—among them J. M. Stillman, professor of chemistry, who was then acting president of the university while Jordan was in the Pribilof Islands, and H. C. Nash, Leland Jr.'s tutor and university librarian—were not also dismissed. It did not mention Jordan's own public campaign against the annexation of the Philippines. The other reasons given for dismissal were either vague—Ross's "general conduct" and his "lack of good taste and discretion"—or trivial—his use of slang in the classroom.[23]

Closer to the mark was the committee's charge that Ross made derogatory statements about Leland Stanford. The committee found no evidence that Mrs. Stanford ever objected to his teachings or opinions, which meant that they did not look. It also denied that Ross's opinions on "coolie" immigration or municipal ownership had anything to do with his dismissal. The committee argued that by trying to retain his position, Ross admitted that Stanford did not restrict free speech, since an advocate of academic freedom would not try to remain.[24]

When the report was not false, it was tendentious, and when it was not tendentious, it was nonsensical. The documents in the case disproved every one of the report's major contentions, but since the committee did not see them, they could not know this. The report's vindication of Ross's dismissal had a fatal flaw. It attributed his departure to Jane Stanford, not Jordan, undercutting her denials of any interference in university affairs.[25]

Some of Ross's supporters feared readers would look only at the alumni report's conclusion and not question its reasoning, evidence, or logic. They grew restless and wanted Ross to counter it. Some urged him to release the documents in his possession, but Ross remained publicly silent, although he corresponded with leading journalists. In late December at the meetings of the American Economic Association, an ad hoc committee was formed to investigate the Ross Affair. Ross rested his fate with them. He showed the documents from Jordan to the AEA committee. The letters remained his trump cards.[26]

WHILE AWAITING THE AEA REPORT, Jordan twisted himself into an aca-demic pretzel trying to explain why the university's treatment of Ross was not an abridgement of academic freedom. A December letter to "Garrison Phillips" (apparently William Phillips Garrison, the editor of *The Nation*) asking for patience and denouncing Ross's statement as "essentially unjust and untrue" was something of a template. He rejected claims that Ross was dismissed for his "opinions or teachings," but he refused to provide evidence for the real cause of the dismissal because he said he had no desire to attack Ross's character. He informed correspondents that he had long ago come to believe that Ross was not fit for his position, but, out of kindness, he protected him from Mrs. Stanford until he could do so no longer. He withheld the facts of the case only because he did not wish to do further harm to Ross and prevent his obtaining another position. Listeners noticed the logical flaws of an explanation that tried to reconcile Ross's dismissal as unfit after having retained him for years, with public praise and attempts to get him another, similar position. Confidential let-ters making accusations against Ross gushed out of Jordan in early 1901. The gist of the accusations was that Ross was a liar, long in trouble over issues of character. The dismissal was on the grounds of incivility.[27]

Some of these letters got back to Ross, who watched as Jordan "craw-fished." He thought Jordan would never attack him in print because "I hold letters from him explaining Mrs. Stanford's objections to me." The material Ross gave to the AEA committee was so damaging that when Felix Adler, an admirer and supporter of Jordan, read them and the com-mittee's draft report, he told Edwin Seligman, the head of the committee, that he struck his colors. He abandoned his defense of Jordan and left Seligman's office a "sadder and wiser man."[28]

As its authors admitted, the Report of the Committee of Economists depended on incomplete evidence since Jordan refused to submit doc-uments. The committee concluded that Mrs. Stanford dismissed Ross for his position on free silver, immigration, and municipal ownership. It cited evidence submitted by Ross. For Jordan the committee's report was a catastrophe. It not only made academic freedom and freedom of speech the central issues, but it also placed the blame on Jane Stanford, whom Jordan sought to protect in order to protect himself and the university.[29]

In his formal response Jordan resorted to a combination of lies and evasions. He attacked the authority and competence of the committee. He said it would be necessary for the public and the committee "to assume my

knowledge of all the facts" and accept his "assurances" and "plain statements" of the "important facts." These assurances and plain statements
were that Ross was dismissed because university authorities thought "he
was not the proper man for the place he held," and for reasons of his private character.[30] All important surviving documents validated Ross's version of the affair, not Jordan's.

Jordan lost the public debate, but he hoped to salvage Stanford's academic reputation among his own faculty and those in other institutions.
Jordan had John C. Branner, who served as acting president during Jordan's frequent absences, take up the cudgel. Branner's trip to Chicago in
February of 1901 was not a success. At a dinner at the University Club,
the hosts put him down to deliver a toast to "Free Speech"; he was not
amused. In a later talk he delivered a labored defense of the university
entitled "Freedom of Speech in University Circles." When he claimed that
Stanford protected academic freedom, the audience laughed.[31]

Jordan's future rested on the good will of Jane Stanford, and publicly
he defended everything about her. Writing from the Moana Hotel in June
of 1901, he told Charles Eliot that she was a "most worthy and intelligent
woman . . . unflinchingly loyal to the interests of higher education and
to a wise conception of academic freedom and academic dignity. . . ." He
lamented the "ignorant" attacks upon her.[32]

CHAPTER 18

"HE TOLD IT NICE"

DASHIELL HAMMETT WAS CYNICAL but not completely wrong when he had Sam Spade claim in *The Maltese Falcon* that "[m]ost things in San Francisco can be bought, or taken."[1] The Ross Affair was not the only scandal that roiled San Francisco in 1900. Earlier in the year an attempt to take over the police department provided a dress rehearsal for the investigation of Jane Stanford's poisoning. It had nothing to do with Jane Stanford, but it had a lot to do with the people who would investigate her poisoning. Jules Callundan, the private detective who would head the Poland Spring Water investigation, was at the scandal's center. So too was Fremont Older, the editor of the *San Francisco Bulletin*, whose paper covered Jane Stanford's murder.

The Octopus—as Frank Norris called the Southern Pacific Railroad machine in his 1901 novel—had strongly influenced but never totally controlled San Francisco governance. Norris made the Southern Pacific's machine more competent than it was—Leland Stanford, after all, ran it; but the railroad corporation certainly corrupted politics, bought the press, and repressed labor. It helped shape the San Francisco where Jane Stanford lived and died. A reaction against the corruption of the Southern Pacific and the San Francisco street railways, as well as the Spring Valley Water Company—a private utility that overcharged and underserved the city for years—fueled the good government reform movement spearheaded by James Phelan.

Phelan was a second-generation Irish American born to money. As a rich man with intellectual ambitions, he inevitably had contact with

Leland Stanford Junior University. He and David Starr Jordan exchanged volumes of poetry. He opposed the Market Street Railway, in which Jane Stanford held stock, as corrupt and exploitative. He shared speaking platforms with Edward Ross, whom he supported in his conflict with Jane Stanford. Later, as a U.S. senator Phelan would pledge to "Keep California White."[2]

In 1897, Fremont Older of the *San Francisco Bulletin* persuaded Phelan, a Democrat, to run for mayor. Older was a nominal Republican who moved toward reform partially from disgust at corporate control of politics and the press, but mostly because he thought that being instrumental in electing a reform mayor in San Francisco would be good for business. It would boost the *Bulletin*'s circulation and thus its advertising and income. Older convinced the paper's publisher, R. A. Crothers—his brother-in-law and no relation to George—that the *Bulletin* could remain Republican in everything but city politics. Like the Republicans, the Phelan campaign had to pay for the *Bulletin*'s support, but not much, and Older claimed Phelan never knew. The *Bulletin*, like other city newspapers, took money from everyone willing to pay. None of the city's half dozen major newspapers could be trusted, but their bitter competition also meant that none of the stories they floated went unchallenged.[3]

The Phelan administration (1897–1903) was "conventionally honest." It combatted graft, opposed the Southern Pacific's influence in the city, paved streets and sidewalks, and monitored city contracts. It supported a new city charter, which established commissions that would prove hard for the railroad to control. When R. A. Crothers was tempted to make more money by selling the *Bulletin*'s influence to the Southern Pacific, Older struck a compromise. The paper supported the Republican candidate for governor but backed Phelan and his new city charter.[4]

The Harry Morse Detective Agency had its own complicated relations with the city government, particularly the police department. On January 8, 1900, Ed Byram, a San Francisco police detective, wrote in his journal that Jules Callundan had resigned as superintendent of Harry Morse's patrol system and taken a job as an ordinary patrolman with the San Francisco Police Department. Callundan was then thirty-five years old, ancient for a patrolman. He was not physically imposing. He was short, squat, the kind of man for whom a derby seemed simply an extension of his physiognomy. As a patrolman, he would make less than half the amount he did at the Morse Agency. When Byram ran into Callundan at the Bank of California, Callundan gave him "a yarn about better pay and a chance of promotion with the other men. He told it nice."[5]

What Callundan told nice, he often did not tell true. Callundan's odd career move was part of a byzantine scheme that took shape when San Francisco voters in 1899 passed a new modernizing city charter giving the mayor the right to make the appointments to the city's commissions, including the police commission. They then reelected James Phelan as mayor of San Francisco. It was the new charter that led Jules Callundan to decide to become a patrolman.

Phelan chafed at his lack of control over the police department, which Republicans dominated at its highest ranks, and the charter gave him the chance to change that. His ambition led him to make a deal with a devil.

The devil was "Long Green," as Alfred B. Lawrence was known. Lawrence was editor of the *San Francisco Examiner*. He rose in life by staying close to the Hearst family—first George Hearst, the mining millionaire, who said at least one true thing: "If you are ever inclined to think there is no such thing as luck, just think of me." There was no explaining his career without luck, and bribery. Like Leland Stanford, George Hearst used his money to become a senator from California. Hearst picked Lawrence, then an *Examiner* reporter, as a candidate for the state legislature, where he was accused of soliciting a bribe.[6]

When Alfred Lawrence returned to newspaper work under George Hearst's son, William Randolph Hearst, he mixed journalism and blackmail. In 1896 he retained Wyatt Earp, the Western gunfighter and gambler who straddled the border between law enforcement and crime, as a bodyguard. He listed him on the *Examiner*'s payroll as a library attaché.[7]

In any other city but San Francisco, editors with bodyguards might have seemed excessive. Charles de Young, the original publisher of the *San Francisco Chronicle*, was shot and killed at his desk in 1880 by the son of Isaac S. Kalloch, who was then mayor. To be fair, de Young had previously shot the mayor. Michael de Young, who succeeded his brother as publisher of the *Chronicle*, was shot by the son of Claus Spreckels, the sugar baron, in the same office where de Young's brother was killed. Michael de Young accused Spreckels of abusing his workers and swindling his stockholders. Spreckels eventually acquired the *San Francisco Call*. Fremont Older, who as editor of the *San Francisco Bulletin* helped make Phelan mayor, would be assaulted on the streets, kidnapped, and have a contract placed on his life. Long Green was only being prudent when he kept Wyatt Earp around.[8]

Jules Callundan was very much part of this world. Having headed the Morse patrol at the Ingleside racetrack, he would have known Earp. In 1896 Earp had been down on his luck. He would testify that he had "only the clothes on his back." Among his debts was a bill of $200 at the race-track restaurant. He had come to the racetrack with a string of horses, but he lost them all and became trainer for others. Earp was in need of money, and Long Green gave him an opportunity to earn some by recommending him as referee for the Bob Fitzsimmons/Tom Sharkey prizefight. Fitzsimmons was the favorite, but Long Green bet heavily on Sharkey. Sharkey's managers agreed to pay Earp $2,500 of the $10,000 purse if he would call a foul on Fitzsimmons and disqualify him. Suspicious, Fitzsimmons punished Sharkey for eight rounds, careful not to throw a body blow. When Fitzsimmons eventually threw one, Earp ruled that he hit below the belt, declared Sharkey the victor, and quickly left the ring.[9]

Phelan had no illusions about Long Green, but he had reasons to cultivate him. The *Examiner* was the city's leading newspaper, and it did not have Republican baggage.[10] Phelan's deal with Alfred Lawrence was simple. The *Examiner* would support Phelan for reelection, and Phelan would have his new police commissioners fire the Republican chief of police, Isaiah W. Lees, and allow Lawrence to name his successor. Harry Morse, who hated Chief Lees and was his longtime rival, came in on the scheme in exchange for the promise that Jules Callundan would be made chief of detectives. The goal of both Lawrence and Morse was mercenary. Since crime and scandal sold newspapers, Lawrence wanted the police department to act as bureau for the *Examiner*, giving them privileged access to stories. Morse, for his part, was facing increasing competition in the detective business. Having his right-hand man as chief of detectives would solidify his position. As Detective Byram put it, "Harry Morse would control the force."[11]

The flaw in the plan was that while it was not hard to fix a newspaper, it was impossible to fix all of them. Their rivalries drove them to opposing positions.[12] The *Call* and the *Bulletin* flushed out the plot. The headlines of Claus Spreckel's *Call* blared: "Conspiracy to Betray City to Criminals."[13] Fremont Older did not abandon his support for Phelan, but this was business. He was not going to allow Long Green to control the police department.[14]

The *Call* and the *Bulletin* dredged up old scandals. Callundan's first wife had sued for divorce on the grounds of desertion in 1890. The desertion involved his sudden departure for Australia after failing to make alimony payments. He was also accused of embezzling funds from, among others, his employer, Harry Morse. Morse denied this, and Callundan had returned. He soon accrued enough cash to settle with his ex-wife for a lump-sum payment, and made his advantageous second marriage to the daughter of Congressman Eugene Loud in 1893.[15] The *Bulletin*, the *Chronicle*, and the *Call* also focused on Fred Esola, the candidate for police chief, a close associate of Lawrence and a man with a checkered past. Esola did not get the appointment. Callundan decided to return to the Harry Morse Agency.

The story revealed how intertwined the press, the police, and politics were in Gilded Age San Francisco. Things had not changed five years later when someone put poison in Jane Stanford's Poland Spring Water.

Leland Stanford sowed the wind; his wife reaped the whirlwind.

A SYSTEM

OF

ABSOLUTISM

CHAPTER 19

THE DESPOT

DAVID STARR JORDAN EMERGED from the Ross Affair a diminished, vulnerable, and vindictive man. Some of those at Stanford who disagreed with his actions regarding Ross sought to excuse him. They thought his devotion to the university, his loyalty to Mrs. Stanford, and the death of his daughter had marred his judgment. Many feared, with good reason, that if he fell, she would turn the university over to the Catholic Church.[1]

Even Professor Edwin Seligman, who produced the devastating American Economic Association report, tried to be charitable. He thought Jordan "meant to do what is right, but there is no doubt that he has acted foolishly, and in such matters folly is very close to crime."[2]

Jordan believed that he had saved the university, but he also did real damage. The only silver lining in the Ross Affair was that many college administrators and public officials already regarded Leland Stanford Junior University as so peculiar that what happened there could have no lasting influence on universities as a whole. Charles Eliot of Harvard thought the Ross Affair could set no precedent. No other university had all power in the hands of "one aged woman."[3]

Eliot, who did not understand the actual financial situation at Stanford, gave Mrs. Stanford credit for endowing the university, saving it during the crisis of the 1890s, and making it financially stable. But he also regarded Ross as a substantial scholar and "Honest Money" as "a vigorous presentation of the silver side of the controversy." Eliot noted that Jordan's reversal of his opinion of Ross was something that "so often happens when two men who have been working together are suddenly thrown into adverse relations." He hoped that Jordan would take over the real direction of the university and feared that if Jane Stanford's "mind weakened before her body, great harm might be done."[4] He did not realize that Jordan now depended on Jane Stanford much more than she depended on him.

———

JORDAN THOUGHT his only error was treating Ross "with consideration, showing him the confidence due a gentleman." He would not make that mistake again. He grew more ruthless, determined to protect his friends on the faculty and root out and punish his enemies.[5]

In 1901 rumors reached the San Francisco newspapers of a new scandal—this one sexual—involving Professor Charles H. Gilbert. Like Jordan, Gilbert was an ichthyologist. His career demonstrated how incestuous Stanford was: Jordan's student in high school, Gilbert followed him to Butler, then to Indiana, and finally to Stanford. In the middle of the Ross Affair Gilbert wrote Jordan a fawning letter, telling him that he owed Jordan all his opportunities in life. He signed off "reenlisting for the war," and he proved a key supporter during the conflict over Ross. In the aftermath of the Ross Affair, Jordan relied heavily on scientists like Gilbert and professors in the professional schools for support. To force Gilbert to resign in disgrace would, Jordan thought, be a great triumph for supporters of Professor Ross.[6]

Gilbert was less popular with his students than with the administration. They did not like him. The exception was M. E. Haven, an 1893 graduate of Stanford. She apparently liked him very much.[7]

Gilbert was married, and his sister-in-law worked in the library, which made the library a spectacularly poor choice as a place for Professor Gilbert to be unable to keep his hands off a former student. Gilbert had secured a key that allowed him to enter the building through the basement. He visited frequently, passing Miss Haven notes and meeting her behind the stacks. A librarian, Alfred M. Schmidt, heard in February that Professor Gilbert was "guilty of improper relations with a young woman employed in the university library."[8]

All of this was little more than a scandal over a middle-aged professor's suspected adultery, but as happens often in universities then and now, it sucked in people from across the campus. When Gilbert's lover was dismissed for incompetence, Gilbert not only got her reinstated, he also retaliated against those who criticized her. Meanwhile, Florence Hughes, Gilbert's sister-in-law and the head cataloguer at the library, appealed to Alfred Schmidt for help. Schmidt, in turn, went to Professor Julius Goebel. Both were German, and Schmidt had been Goebel's student. The involvement of Goebel in the Gilbert Affair would have lasting consequences.[9]

This was already a complicated cast for trysts in the library, but it grew wider, pulling in others who would become involved in events leading up to Jane Stanford's poisoning. John Nourse, a recent graduate doing a postgraduate year and soon to become a lawyer, reported the affair to Charles Lathrop, who conferred with John Casper Branner, who was acting president while Jordan was in Hawaii on a research trip. Branner conducted an initial investigation with Professor Green, another crony of Jordan's whose teaching left him time enough to run a grocery and act as a detective. Branner concluded that Gilbert "had been thrown with the lady, Miss Haven, too much," but besides gossip there was nothing more to it. Branner sent letters to the San Francisco newspapers and then visited the managing editors to suppress the story. He was successful everywhere but at the *Examiner*, which suspected that the university was trying to cover up another scandal. The *Examiner* said that Gilbert's friends denounced the rumors as malicious, and that, so far, they appeared groundless. There was a picture of Gilbert looking middle-aged and unhappy. Gilbert offered to resign, but Branner advised against it.[10]

Gilbert neither admitted nor denied the affair, at least in writing. In a letter to Jordan he lamented the public scandal and its effect on family and friends. Gilbert told Jordan that "I need not now discuss the personal aspects of the case," and he didn't. He left it to Green and Branner to "write the facts to you [Jordan]." Jordan assured Jane Stanford that the stories about Gilbert were baseless. It was all, he said, an attempt at revenge against Gilbert. Schmidt was a tool.[11]

Jordan and Branner made Schmidt the scapegoat for Gilbert's affair. Only the fear that there would be a newspaper scandal stopped Branner from firing Schmidt immediately. Instead, he started a campaign to pressure Schmidt to resign because of "his mental and moral condition" and "his morbid state of mind." David Starr Jordan denounced him as "sexually perverted." Branner concluded that Schmidt "should not be in any institutions where there are women."[12]

David Starr Jordan endorsed Branner's campaign. From his room at the new Moana Hotel in Hawaii, he complained that it was "hard to go back to work on fish when there are rascals who need the whipping post." One of the rascals, Nourse, the student who reported Gilbert to Lathrop, would later become a prominent judge and a Stanford University trustee.[13]

In September of 1901 Alfred M. Schmidt wrote a stilted, painfully sincere letter to Jane Stanford. He acted, he said, only at the solicitation of Gilbert's sister-in-law, who asked his help in making sure M. E. Haven's appointment was not renewed for the sake of the family.[14]

In the aftermath of the *Examiner* story and Branner's and Green's "investigations," the other witnesses, fearing Gilbert's influence with the president, abandoned Schmidt. Florence Hughes, Gilbert's sister-in-law, signed a statement disavowing Schmidt's account of their conversations. She later reportedly said that she betrayed Schmidt to protect her family. Branner created a special committee to conduct a second investigation and stacked it with Gilbert's friends and Jordan's supporters. They ridiculed Schmidt's stories and demanded proof of a "criminal relationship," which he could not provide. Branner and Green said Miss Haven was only Gilbert's protégé and acted as his private secretary.[15]

Schmidt considered Branner, Gilbert, and Green part of a clique around Jordan. No one could cross them and obtain justice. He contended that his character was being defamed; he did not say how. He asked Jane Stanford for a reinvestigation of the whole affair with sworn testimony because it was impossible to obtain justice from Jordan, who was prejudiced in favor of Gilbert.[16]

Julius Goebel, the head of the German department, not only heard the stories from Schmidt, he also observed Gilbert and M. E. Haven in compromising circumstances. Palo Alto was a small place, and Goebel saw Gilbert and a woman, whom he initially thought a young relative of Gilbert's, walking along the Embarcadero, then an isolated road. He also saw the same woman resting in his arms, her head on Gilbert's shoulder on the train returning from San Francisco. When an embarrassed Gilbert saw Goebel enter the car, he begged him not to tell anyone what he had witnessed. Branner told Goebel that Schmidt had besmirched an innocent man, but Goebel replied that rumors had been rampant for a year, and Gilbert had brought this on himself.[17]

On his return from Hawaii Jordan pressured Schmidt to resign. When Schmidt threatened to sue, Jordan called in Goebel to help get rid of him. Jordan told Goebel that Schmidt was a "sexually perverted character, who read library books such as Krafft-Ebing's work on sexual perversion." Jordan threatened to have Schmidt committed to an asylum if he did not leave Stanford. That a librarian could be condemned for reading a library book said a lot about Stanford. Goebel went to the library and found that it did not even own a copy of Krafft-Ebing. Goebel, shocked at the lie, still took the threat to commit Schmidt to an asylum seriously. He advised Schmidt to go east. If he stayed, he would be ruined for life. Goebel went to the Santa Fe Railroad station to pick up the pass that Jordan had secured. He said he did so to protect an innocent man.[18]

Jordan's allies later described Julius Goebel as a "pathological liar," but Jordan's account of the affair substantiates virtually all of Goebel's particulars. Jordan wrote Jane Stanford in December of 1901 that he had resolved the Schmidt matter. Schmidt would go east and "not try to make any further trouble." Jordan obtained a written statement from Florence Hughes that all she knew of the matter was from Schmidt. He also obtained a "statement of Schmidt's physician that in view of the disease from which Schmidt suffers, he is not surprised that he is troubled with 'freed Ideas' or semi-hallucinations." Schmidt was only partially responsible for his actions. Investigators found no one "who knows anything whatever to the discredit of either of the persons accused by him." Schmidt resigned. Miss Haven, the report noted, "did miscellaneous work."[19]

———

THE GILBERT AFFAIR revealed Jordan's methods, but its central significance was that Jordan's success in protecting friends and punishing enemies emboldened him. The Gilbert Affair yielded to the Pease Affair in 1902, when Jordan dismissed Professor Ernest M. Pease, the head of the Latin department.[20]

Jordan claimed his decision to dismiss Pease came from a long history of dissatisfaction and that he told Pease that he needed to find a position elsewhere. He wrote Charles Lathrop that the real reason for dismissing Pease was that he was "selfish and intriguing, [and] I have never been able to get along with him."[21]

Pease gave a simpler reason for his firing: he had refused to sign a letter written by Jordan's clique condemning Ross. Jordan told one of Pease's colleagues that he was determined to "root out . . . every man who did not stand by us in our troubles of last year." He considered Pease one of those men. Jordan told Timothy Hopkins, a Stanford trustee, that while he could not prove Pease's association with Ross, he thought Pease was responsible for Howard's turning against Jordan. Hopkins wrote Jordan that he thought activity in the Ross matter should be grounds for dismissal if it persisted after the firing of Ross and Howard.[22]

Like Schmidt before him, Pease appealed directly to Jane Stanford.[23] He had been told that his criticism of the Ross Affair caused her pain, but Pease claimed he had only criticized Jordan. Stanford told him she took no offense, assuring him that if he had ever thought ill of her she would have known it "for you know I believe in telepathy."[24]

In 1903 Pease sent Jane Stanford his correspondence with Jordan along with the letters of support he received from leading scholars. He located the heart of the problem in Jordan's unusual power to hire and fire. As one faculty member said, that power "makes cowards of us all." He claimed that Jordan and his clique so discredited the university that it could not recruit top men. "[A]t least five great University Presidents" thought Stanford could not recover its prestige with Jordan at its head.[25]

Pease portrayed Jordan as a liar, a hypocrite, and a coward, and he told Jane Stanford that Jordan put all the blame for the Ross Affair on her. He brought up one last instance reluctantly because of the pain it would cause her. It was "a feeling at the University which not infrequently finds expression in words that the management of University affairs would be greatly simplified when there could be no further interference from its founders." President Jordan was "largely responsible for that feeling. It was reported to me from more than one source that he had taken certain students into his confidence and in speaking of the difficulties of his administration under your control represented himself as temporarily somewhat of a martyr, a condition which he said he must bear patiently for a time."[26]

Pease phrased the matter more directly in a letter to Julius Goebel that fall. Jordan had anticipated not Jane Stanford's resignation but her death. He had "even said in confidence to certain students that things would be better at the University when she had passed away."[27]

The Pease controversy undercut Jordan's standing with Charles Lathrop, who already disliked him. Lathrop used it to discredit Jordan with his sister. Jordan was weak and "away so much looking for public admiration that he neglects . . . his duties at the University and that in consequence the Professors do just as they please."[28]

The recurrence of these "cyclonic disturbances" at Stanford dismayed Horace Davis, a trustee already alarmed by the situation at Stanford.

"Already the prejudices are so strong in the Eastern universities that number one men do not want to come here, and every year will make it worse." Harvard faculty told Davis that "good men" would not come to Stanford because they did not want to be at the mercy of one man.[29] As Davis would later phrase the problem:

> The trouble with us has been that the University ran on for twelve years without any law: Dr. Jordan managing the Academic part, the inside of the College without even an Academic Council for an advisor and Mrs. Stanford managing the property interests. You can imagine the difficulty of reducing this to a system after so many years of absolutism.[30]

Davis along with George Crothers worried about Jane Stanford and David Starr Jordan; they worried about the Roman Catholic hierarchy, reactionary San Franciscans, and society ladies in Jane Stanford's circle who tried to influence her. They worried about her relatives who wanted the university endowment for themselves. They worried about inept, lazy, and crooked trustees.

They did not devote sufficient worry to Julius Goebel.

CHAPTER 20

THE BREACH

THE ROSS AFFAIR DEMORALIZED Jane Stanford. David Starr Jordan had failed to protect her, and that as much as administering the university was his job. In her anger and hurt, she grew increasingly erratic. After her return from Europe in 1901, she three times drew up addresses criticizing Jordan's administration of the university. If made public, any one of them would have forced him to resign. In 1902 she wrote a pamphlet compiling her correspondence regarding Ross and justifying her actions. She blamed Jordan for the disaster. She had five hundred copies printed. George Crothers convinced her that she should burn them. He persuaded her that "however able she might be, the world of educators could not believe that a woman could possibly know how to run a university," and she would not be able to hire the kind of man she needed to take Jordan's place.[1]

She continued to intervene in the administration of the university. This ran from important matters to small but revealing ones. The more trivial the issue the more humiliating her intervention. There was, for instance, the matter of doorstops in the chemistry building.

Charles Lathrop—insecure and dependent his whole adult life on the good will of his brother-in-law and his sister—missed few opportunities to feed his sister's discontent with Jordan. Irritated by what he regarded as Jordan's intrusions on his own domain, he complained that the president was vain, officious, and incompetent, with a proclivity "to interfere or break into business that does not concern him." In the spring of 1902 Jordan was, Lathrop reported, "in Los Angeles attending some Women's Convention and most of his time is devoted to traveling around the Coun-

try and delivering lectures and making himself prominent with politicians, railroad people and any old thing. I do not think he ever says no
to an invitation that is extended to him to dine or where he may have an
opportunity to talk."[2]

In June of 1903, Jordan received a formal letter from Mrs. Stanford.
The letter was typed, presumably by Bertha Berner. It began, "Dear Sir."
It was about doorstops in the new chemistry building. The doorstops
cost $3.00 each and were not ordered through the business office, run by
Charles Lathrop. "Do you think this disobeying all business rules as laid
down should be tolerated?" the letter asked. Jane Stanford did not. She
ordered Lathrop not to pay for "such an extravagance and useless expen-
diture of money."[3]

No wonder Jordan grasped every speaking invitation offered him. It
is easy to imagine him, reading the letter, pinching his eyes, putting his
head on the desk, and muttering: "Doorstops? Doorstops? I am president
of this university, and she is writing me about doorstops?" Jordan learned
to swallow such things.

The small humiliations pointed to a larger problem. Jordan's lack of
control over university finances constrained his own plans for the institution. The university's salaries might have been high for 1891, but they had
not risen in ten years. Jordan faced difficulties retaining good faculty and
could not replace them at existing salaries. When he paid a few faculty
more, he created inequities in the ranks.[4]

Jordan pleaded with Jane Stanford for higher salaries, but in May of
1903 she reminded him that they were a minor issue compared to the
money she was expending on new buildings. With university income far
below the demands of the institution, building would take precedence.
Her efforts yielded the university's "Stone Age"—the church, the museum,
and the Memorial Arch—all of which memorialized the Stanford family.[5]

THE CHURCH IN PARTICULAR dominated Mrs. Stanford's attention.
David Starr Jordan imagined Stanford as a research university equal to
Harvard, Yale, Columbia, Johns Hopkins, and the University of Chicago.
Jane Stanford imagined a very different place. The center of the campus
would be her new Memorial Church dedicated to Jesus Christ and her
husband. The university would be devoted to the development of the soul.

She believed that the "filling of the pulpit is of vastly more importance than the filling of any other position in the University."[6]

Her choice for the first pastor of the new church seemed perfect. R. Heber Newton was respectable—the longtime pastor at New York's All Souls Protestant Episcopal Church—and he had spiritualist and nonsectarian sympathies and convictions. Jane Stanford had admired Newton since hearing him preach in 1884 following Leland Jr.'s death. He gave a sermon that "comforted her heart to such a degree that its effect had never left" her. Newton was sympathetic to the coming of a new Christianity that would grow out of the old Church by shedding its dead or dying trappings while clinging to the essentials of the Nicene Creed: belief in God, the immortality of the soul, and Jesus Christ. This fit well with Jane Stanford's desire for "no theological doctrines, nor creedisms of any kind, only the simple beautiful truths taught us by our master teacher Jesus Christ."[7]

Newton indexed his readings for reference, and spiritualism has twenty-eight separate entries. He segregated these entries from the other note cards, tying them in a green ribbon. In a folder labeled "Misc. Notes," there is a handwritten notation on the back of one sheet of paper that seems compatible with soul germ theory—the idea, one embraced by Jane Stanford, that the soul continued to grow and develop after death.[8]

Newton thought that knowledge of immortality was evolving. His wife, too, was a spiritualist, and a month before Jane Stanford's death Newton himself would declare "his firm belief in the genuineness of spirit communication with the material world, that mental telepathy and clairvoyance are scientific facts, and that men may wear invisible halos around their heads be they good men or bad." The *San Francisco Examiner* regarded this as "startling" when Newton said it, but it was not. His openness to spiritualism had attracted Jane Stanford to him.[9]

Newton refused the appointment at Stanford twice because of conditions Jane Stanford had imposed—teaching duties and his resignation from the Episcopal Church. He was happy at All Souls with a congregation that "loved him and with whom he had never quarreled." Although "no dissensions have ever disturbed their harmonious relations," he finally left, in part, for his health, something that lured many people to California.[10]

When he agreed to come to Stanford in the fall of 1902, he did so— at least in his own mind—only on the condition of "a free hand in the administration of worship and work of the church along the general lines laid down by you and accepted by me." Newton was still recovering from a grave illness that laid him low that spring, and his wife broke down under the strain of caring for him. She could not undertake housekeeping, and, in any case, the house Jane Stanford was building for him on campus was not yet ready. Newton would spend two months as a guest in Jane Stanford's home. He told her that all he wanted was to please her, but he learned that this meant doing exactly what she desired. She promised him full authority over the church but repeatedly undermined him and countermanded his orders.[11]

Jane Stanford wanted to be loved and admired, but she needed to be obeyed. Obedience was the condition of working for her, and virtually everyone around her, except George Crothers, worked for her in one sense or another. The distinctions between her servants, her faculty, David Starr Jordan, her companion Bertha Berner, and her California relatives were ones of degree not of kind. Even her brother was also her employee.

Obedience extended to the Church, and R. Heber Newton became a prime example of how Jane Stanford sought to reduce everyone to her will.

Newton was fanatical about church music. He lectured about it and later wrote a book entitled *The Mysticism of Music* based on his lectures. Music provided a gateway to the invisible, the "inner sphere of life," and the unseen universe, which was the "only real world." Music revealed "the inner life and soul [that] can never die." The moral message of music, particularly church music, was harmony. Music was the "sign of love," and love was "the central reality of life." Newton thought that he would be in charge of church music at Stanford.[12]

R. Heber Newton and Jane Stanford quarreled over music, which was also a quarrel over money, though a trivial amount. But most of all they quarreled over authority. In R. Heber Newton's telling, Jane Stanford came to the Newtons' house for tea in the spring of 1903, and the conversation turned to music. He suggested a paid choir since the music provided by the student choir was ragged and, without regular rehearsal, it would not improve. Jane Stanford disliked paid choirs. She replied that "as long as she lived" she would never consent to such a thing. Newton thought he could persuade her. She took this as a challenge to her authority. He attempted to reconcile. She refused. She went behind his back, giving direct instructions to the organist as to what was to be played during services. All this was an affront to his self-respect that he could not accept.[13]

George Crothers offered a slightly different version. Reverend Newton was upset because attendance at the Memorial Church did not match his expectations, and he thought a paid choir would attract congregants. Meanwhile, he printed out 500 leaflets every Sunday, even though attendance was never higher than 350. Charles Lathrop cut the print run down to 350. An outraged Newton demanded to have full control over his church. Crothers said it was Newton's criticism of Lathrop that was the cause of the rupture. Newton's story has more evidence to back it than Crothers's.[14]

In both versions Newton wrote an angry resignation letter to Jane Stanford, and then regretted his resignation and tried to withdraw it. Jane Stanford thought the letter "petulant and ill-tempered." She asked him to imagine the "horror and agony of heart" that he caused her. He had promised to please her. He had not.[15]

She accepted the resignation even though Jordan, Crothers, and the faculty members she consulted urged her not to do so. She had brought Newton to California when, after thirty years in his pulpit, he was on the verge of a pension. He came in part for reasons of health. It was unconscionable to dismiss him.

Jane Stanford was not a person to see two sides of an issue. She dismissed Newton's complaints as trifles, but she could not "afford to declare myself unequal to the present situation." She had up until now "met all questions of management alone" and brought them, in her view, "to a fairly successful issue." The "ill-temper and petulance" of the pastor of the church would not change her now. It boiled down to a case in which "the servant thinks himself greater than the Master!" She wanted a choir "singing praises to God without money and without price . . . a voluntary effort on the part of those dear boys and girls."[16]

For Jane Stanford the quarrel with Newton opened the old wounds of the Ross Affair. This time she would demonstrate her control over the university.

She decided to call the trustees together to explain her dismissal of Newton, and she wanted also to have the "Ross matter reviewed and set right." She owed this to herself, and "instead of being adversely criticized, it will meet the approval of all right-minded people," who would appreciate her "fearless pursuance of doing what I know to be right." Newton "failed in understanding me personally, and equally failed in understanding the purposes of the Church." The sooner he left, the better. God loved her, and the students, she thought, loved her, and she hoped for the "help-ful strengthening sympathy of the right-minded public" as she sought to do God's will.[17]

She decided Newton's fate, but, here again, she did not wish to do the dirty work herself. She wrote him an effusive note praising his Easter sermon and telling him "God and the loved ones who have passed on will bless you," but she also gave her brother Charles orders to cut him loose.[18]

R. Heber Newton failed to recognize how unerringly God's will and Jane Stanford's will converged. Once Newton grasped his doom, he wrote her a long letter of Christian cruelty as refined as her own. The Ross Affair should have warned him, but he said he learned only after he arrived "of the methods of administration here, the outgrowth of years of absolutely autocratic power," which created "little prospect of happy work in the future." He portrayed her version of the church and university as delu-sional. He found that he was ministering to a constituency "uninterested in church attendance" and indifferent to the church and its services. Those who were interested attended other local churches. The Stanford church was cold in the winter and its acoustics were terrible. He saw music as a way to attract people to the church, and he gradually built up numbers. These congregants were, he claimed, his adherents and would have pressed to retain him but "for the felt powerlessness alike among the faculty and the student body to accomplish anything." The actual desires of the con-gregation, he wrote, were of no more concern to Jane Stanford than if they "were residents of some other world." The church was "really a proprietary chapel, with the inevitable limitation of freedom of administration and lacking of room for initiative and withholding of authority and power necessary for the work, characteristic of such a situation." She had been, he wrote, devious, unjust, and cruel in her treatment of him. The "reports given to the public" about his departure were correct in minor details but false on his reasons for leaving. They were intended only to remove responsibility from Jane Stanford. In writing about the church, he could have been writing of the university as a whole.[19]

Crothers and Jordan ultimately convinced Jane Stanford and R. Heber Newton not to make the conflict public. Jordan defended Stanford. He admitted that the church was proprietary, but Newton should have known that. There was a brief mention of the controversy in the *London Daily News*, with the author rightly enough describing Newton as "preacher and pastor" and Jane Stanford as "pope," and resurrecting the lack of academic freedom at Stanford. The story went nowhere because Newton kept silent. Jordan gave material to Whitelaw Reid of the *New York Tribune* and a Stanford trustee to use against Newton if necessary. It did not prove necessary.[20]

———

JANE STANFORD'S QUARREL with Newton resurrected her memories of her controversy with Ross, which she blamed on Jordan. She did not, it turned out, burn all the pamphlets she wrote denouncing Jordan. In 1903 she sent a copy to Samuel Leib for his opinion, and she read the Ross correspondence as well as her later correspondence with R. Heber Newton to the trustees. She wanted to publish them. Crothers again persuaded her not to do so, and also not to dismiss Jordan immediately but rather bide her time. She continued to harass and humiliate the president, but she disguised her ultimate intention. In May of 1903 she gave Jordan a 20 percent salary increase to $12,000. Jordan, in turn, went out of his way to praise her.[21]

Crothers protected Jordan not because he admired him or feared him but because he thought Jordan's enemies posed a greater danger. This collection of reactionaries, Catholics (who were also often reactionaries), Stanford relatives, and society friends wanted Jordan gone. They thought the university was irreligious, lacked a coherent curriculum, and allowed its students—particularly its female students—undue license. They agitated Mrs. Stanford about all these things and added to her discontent.[22]

CHAPTER 21

THE SURROGATE SON

AS IF THEY WERE PAIRED on a seesaw, David Starr Jordan sank in Jane Stanford's estimation when George Crothers rose. Jane Stanford spent the years after her son's and husband's deaths seeking substitutes for those whom she could not replace. Jordan became her dead husband; Crothers was her dead son. After the Ross Affair, the surrogate son overshadowed the surrogate husband.

Crothers evaluated people according to their relation to the university. He appreciated Jane Stanford as a founder, but he also recognized the damage she was capable of doing to the institution. He distrusted David Starr Jordan, but he knew the harm that would ensue to the university's reputation if Jane Stanford drove him out. He did not trust Bertha Berner.[1] Although he was younger than all of them, he sometimes seemed their caretaker. He tried to prevent them from harming themselves because of the harm that would do to the university.

Crothers paid attention to detail, the kind of detail that glazes eyes and numbs minds. The best way to cheat people is to bore them, to lure them into inattention so that they don't recognize contradictions, omissions, and lies. Lawyers excel at this. Crothers saw that the university was a financial house of sand that could dissolve under the first wave of challenges. His self-appointed task was to correct all this. He was never fully confident that he had succeeded.

Crothers worked for Jane Stanford without pay because he realized if he was compensated, Jane Stanford would treat him with the same arbitrary authority she treated all employees. He became a trustee in 1902, which surprised those who thought another Stanford alumnus, Herbert Hoover, would be chosen. Crothers promised Mrs. Stanford that should she ever increase the power of the trustees, he would "always consider myself bound by your judgements and wishes."[2]

Crothers spent much of his time between 1899 and 1905 crawling down legal rabbit holes in the hope of giving Leland Stanford Junior University at least the semblance of a normal American university. He feared that Jane Stanford would—in anger and despair—either abandon or transform it. Archbishop Patrick Riordan of San Francisco gained considerable influence over her. In 1899 the archbishop unsuccessfully tried to persuade her not to sign the Great Deed, the ineffectual instrument that reconveyed the endowment to the university. The condolences of the sacraments and rituals of the Church attracted her. She contemplated turning Stanford into a boys' school, delivering the university over to the Catholic Church, giving the endowment to Columbia University—a particularly cruel dig at David Starr Jordan since Leland Stanford had first offered the presidency to Columbia's president, Nicholas Murray Butler. She considered simply distributing her fortune among her heirs.[3]

By 1902 Jane Stanford was a catechist taking instruction in preparation for conversion to Roman Catholicism. She had long talks with Crothers, who claimed he was careful not to be critical of either the Church or the Jesuits. He said that he convinced her that joining a hierarchical, authoritarian church, which grew rich over its control of the sacraments, would violate all her liberal Protestant beliefs in a higher and purer religion purged of extraneous doctrines. How this was not a criticism of Catholicism he did not make clear.[4]

Her decision not to become a Catholic turned out to be a postponement and not a refusal; nor did it weaken her determination to have Stanford emulate Catholic colleges. Critics told her that she could only expect "barnyard morality" in a school where, like Stanford, evolution was taught. She obsessed over reports of young men and women "who promenaded the shady lanes of the campus" and shocked her Victorian sense of propriety. A ritual developed. Jane Stanford would summon Crothers, sometimes in the middle of the night when they were both in San Francisco and she was unable to sleep. She would recount the stories she heard about problems at the university. He would promise to investigate and return to her later with what he discovered, which was inevitably that what she was told were either falsehoods or exaggerations.[5]

Jane Stanford originally argued for coeducation at Stanford, but she came to regard young women as a danger. They tempted her "boys," threatening their celibacy. According to Crothers, so alarming was the persistent gossip about evolution, sex, and lax discipline to Jane Stanford that she began to fear the influence of the Catholic prelates and friends who relayed the stories to her. She requested Crothers's presence at lunches with the Catholics present. She began to doubt her ability to withstand the rumors, and told Crothers that it might be best if she resigned as surviving founder before she made some "foolish change" in the institution.[6]

Crothers worked incrementally to protect the university. He rolled the rock gradually up the hill, watched it slip partway down, and then pushed it farther up again. He needed to do what the Great Deed and the Leib transfer had failed to do: provide secure and permanent funding of the university. He also needed to ensure that with Jane Stanford's death additional funds would pass to the university. And he needed to make university governance more than a series of arbitrary decisions by David Starr Jordan and Jane Stanford.

In December of 1901, following the passage of the constitutional amendment, he drew up papers that delivered the bulk of Jane Stanford's estate to the university without conditions. He purposefully wrote the documents so as to disguise his own role, fearing that a future suit by Lathrop and Stanford relatives to overturn the wills, trusts, and grants would claim undue influence on Crothers's part. Jane Stanford submitted the papers authorizing the grant to the university to another attorney, John T. Doyle, who often worked for the Catholic Church and Archbishop Riordan. He advised her not to sign on the grounds that it would cost her control over both her estate and the university.[7]

Jane Stanford asked Crothers to visit her on a Sunday to consider what to do—what property from the estate would go to the trustees, and what would be withdrawn for her own use. Crothers, in this case as in others, sought to provide a prophylactic against a future legal challenge. He agreed to the meeting but only on the condition that her brother, Charles Lathrop, attend. Crothers feared that any agreement signed with only himself and Jane Stanford present would be challenged, and he thought Lathrop was the most likely person to present the challenge. Lathrop desired the money and could testify to Jane Stanford's close relationship with Crothers. But Crothers also thought Lathrop honest enough not to challenge documents he had witnessed. Crothers admitted that the revision of the trusts finalized in October of 1902 and witnessed by Lathrop were all the work of Crothers's own hand.[8]

Jane Stanford signed over $25 million to the university, including the proceeds from the sale of Southern Pacific Railroad stock. She kept for herself $2 million in bonds, the stock in the Market Street Railroad, and her share of the Pacific Investment Company, which alone was worth about $6 million. She planned to use the money she retained as leverage.[9]

In 1902, because a "kind providence" increased the prosperity of the estate, she also changed her will. She enlarged her donations to family, servants, and charity. She gave $1 million to Charles Lathrop and bequests for other relatives. Bertha Berner—"Secretary and devoted friend through nineteen years of trial and sorrow"—received $15,000. Ah Wing, "servant for twenty years," received $1,000, the same as several other longtime servants. She gave detailed directions for the placement of family mementos in the Stanford museum.[10]

Crothers knew that, under state law, Jane Stanford could leave only one-third of the money she retained in her estate at her death to the university or other charitable purposes. He told her that she could get around this by placing the funds in a revocable trust to go to the university at her death. She refused. She did not want the trustees to know of her plans, and she intended to use a portion of the money for other purposes should the heirs of the Associates sell the stock in the Pacific Improvement Company. She created a different revocable trust, and made Crothers the sole trustee. She counted on him to follow her wishes. He also assumed her sole power of attorney.[11]

Despite Lathrop's acquiescence, Crothers continued to fear a challenge to the disposition of the estate from other heirs. Knowing how odd and irregular many of Jane Stanford's beliefs and actions were, he was afraid of efforts to contest her legal competency. He thought that he detected signs of the groundwork for such a move. Timothy Hopkins, an executor of the 1902 will, openly questioned Jane Stanford's "normalcy" and asserted that she had always been "queer." Crothers thought the best strategy was to hold close those who were a danger to the university.[12]

Crothers worried, too, about Jane Stanford's continuing sense of the university as a proprietary institution no matter what the amendments and trusts said. In 1902, not for the last time, she decided that enrollments should be limited to two or three thousand. Crothers doubted that she possessed the power to amend the Founding Grant in that respect, and he thought that such radical changes would amount to frauds upon the voters who approved the constitutional amendment and now faced a bait and switch. A reduced enrollment could also open the endowment up to attack as "in excess of what is necessary," and the surplus could be distributed to her heirs and those of her husband, which is what Crothers thought Lathrop and Mountford Wilson wanted.[13]

In 1903 Jane Stanford changed her will again. It involved the usual intrigue. The new will dropped Russell Wilson as an executor. A stroke had felled him, and he suffered what Crothers called a "softening of the brain." Crothers continued to mistrust both Wilsons. He believed their main concern was lining their own pockets. But as with Hopkins and Lathrop, Crothers did not want an open break with Mountford Wilson, and he sent him a copy of the new will with a promise that Crothers would not try to displace him as the attorney for the estate—a source of substantial fees. Mountford Wilson went to Jane Stanford and told her that dropping Russell as an executor would break his heart. He promised that his brother would not try to exercise his powers. Jane Stanford did as he asked. She also, at the urging of Timothy Hopkins, made Mountford Wilson the sole attorney for her estate.[14]

Crothers encouraged Jane Stanford's desire to resign her sole trusteeship before she did something she would regret. He convinced her that the most effective way to rid herself of Jordan and reform the university was to resign her powers, thus putting the responsibility for Jordan's dismissal on the trustees. Stanford would appear to operate like a normal university. She could then accomplish what she could not otherwise do herself without courting disaster.[15]

But nothing was easy at Leland Stanford Junior University. Jane Stanford was the surviving trustee for life. There was no provision for her resignation. If she resigned, a court of equity could intervene and appoint its own trustees, and the university could slip from both Stanford's and the existing trustees' control. Crothers urged her to wait until he could draw up an amendment to the Enabling Act and have the legislature pass it.[16]

When Crothers accomplished this in 1903, Jane Stanford composed an address to the Board of Trustees announcing her resignation, which meant she could no longer change the "object, nature, and purposes of the University." Crothers read and approved it with modifications. But she also prepared a second address that she did not show him. It was severely critical of Jordan, and it informed the trustees that if at any time they thought coeducation a failure, they should abolish it.[17]

A shocked Crothers stopped the reading of the second address and asked for a short meeting with Mrs. Stanford. In resigning and disavowing her power to arbitrarily change the purposes and nature of the university, she was instructing the trustees to arbitrarily change the purposes and nature of the university. The Founding Grant proclaimed it "to be a University for both sexes." She could not instruct the trustees to flaunt the laws creating the university without risking the overthrow of the university itself. Crothers persuaded her to settle for a maximum of five hundred women at the university.[18]

This did not fully register. In 1904 she still considered coeducation an unsettled question.[19]

Incidents such as this gave Crothers cause to worry that the bequests to Leland Stanford Junior University were not beyond challenge. He obtained from the legislature a special act authorizing a proceeding to establish the legitimacy of the Stanford grants and trusts. He thought the law "absolutely unique," which it probably was, but that made it no more unusual than virtually everything else about the university. He had his brother, T. C. Crothers, bring a friendly suit challenging the validity of the documents and the competence of the founders.[20]

On June 27, 1903, a Saturday morning when no court calendar was available to alert reporters, Jane Stanford, Bertha Berner, and Crothers entered a courtroom in San Jose for a hearing on T. C. Crothers's challenge to the validity of university trusts and Jane Stanford's competence. The judge ruled the various modified trusts and bequests to be valid and the founders competent. As they left the courthouse, Jane Stanford said, "Now I am judicially dead." Crothers replied, "Yes, that is so in so far as the University is concerned." This was not quite true until the judge signed the final decree of July 3, 1903. And even then it was only temporarily true. Three days later, Jane Stanford rose from the dead. On July 6, 1903, to her "great delight," the Board of Trustees elected her as a trustee and president of the newly empowered board.[21]

With the trusts ruled valid, in October of 1903 Crothers moved to clean them up. He removed the clauses that required the university to maintain the Vina winery and the Palo Alto horse farm and to retain lands outside the main campus. He eliminated provisions that the trustees select faculty and that the university confine itself to the Palo Alto campus.[22]

Years later Crothers would think that without careful study no one would realize the long and intricate work he did to protect the university. Yet on the night before Jane Stanford's departure for Hawaii in February of 1905, Crothers clearly still doubted that he had done enough. This was why he had her sign the document he drew up to certify her acceptance of the trust. He worded the document to make it appear that it had been drafted years before.

SECTION 5

TRAVELS

TOWARD A

POISONING

CHAPTER 22

MY MAN BEVERLY

"BEVERLY, MY MAN SERVANT," as Jane Stanford referred to him, was dark haired, tall—six foot one—and had a scar on his upper lip. Albert Beverly had immigrated to the United States in 1883 when he was about twenty. In photographs he looked very British and somewhat supercilious, but he was an American citizen. He married in 1885. His wife had also immigrated from England.[1]

In the late 1880s Lillie Langtry hired Albert Beverly. To her, too, he was "my man, Beverly," but it is hard to imagine two women more different than Langtry and Stanford. Langtry was beautiful, notorious, sexually adventurous, and extravagant. Among her lovers was the Prince of Wales. She was not sure who fathered her daughter. At the urging of Oscar Wilde, she became an actress to capitalize on her fame as a beauty and the lover of famous men. She possessed, as an early reviewer wrote, "no artistic skill. She is simply a pretty amateur playing a part pleasantly." He thought Americans rushed to see her for the same reason they crowded in to see Barnum's Jumbo the elephant; she was the biggest thing of her kind. She was much better at being famous than acting. She acquired an American lover, and in order to file for a divorce that her husband would not grant her in England, she required an American residence. She bought an American ranch in Lake County, California, about 100 miles north of San Francisco.[2]

In Gilded Age America acquisitions could bridge seemingly unsurmountable differences. Jane Stanford and Lillie Langtry both had private railroad cars, unprofitable ranches, and Albert Beverly. Langtry remembered Beverly fondly and vividly. She made him something of a cowboy butler. He preceded Langtry to her ranch and arranged for two stage-coaches to transport her there from the nearest railroad station. Beverly was, Langtry noticed, more popular with the ranch hands than she was. Beverly was taken with the West, acquiring land near Langtry's, but in 1896 he was back in San Francisco. In 1900 he was living without his wife in Lassen County in the northeast corner of the state. He was the butler for Henry Butters, a financier and railroad man. He was probably the only butler in the county.[3] He was a man who could adapt. He took care of his employers.

Jane Stanford needed such a man for her travels. Beverly, along with Elizabeth Richmond and Bertha Berner, accompanied Stanford in April and May of 1902 when she took a trip to Hawaii and Japan. It was perhaps on this trip that Beverly and Berner grew close; how close was a matter of gossip. Elizabeth Richmond, who was about Berner's age and a friend of Beverly's wife, supposedly told others that Berner and Beverly had, in George Crothers's words, "been unduly familiar."[4]

By the time of the trip to Hawaii and Japan, Bertha Berner's life had changed. Her mother's health was declining. In January of 1902 Jane Stanford, presumably at Bertha's instigation, wrote a letter of introduction for August Berner, Bertha's brother, to the trustee Samuel Leib. She requested he assist August in finding property to buy or lease for Maria Berner, who was "in delicate health." In February Mrs. Stanford permitted Bertha to spend a day with her mother in Phoenix, where she was recuperating from an unnamed illness.[5]

This was not the first time the Stanfords helped August Berner. Leland Stanford had secured him a position as machinist's apprentice for the Southern Pacific in the 1880s. He lived in Sacramento and then in Oakland before going into the fruit business in 1892, but he failed in the depression that followed. He then moved north to build mining dredges on the Yuba River. Now he wanted to reenter the fruit business and provide a home for his mother.[6]

August Berner never bought a farm; instead his mother purchased three acres of land near Jane Stanford's summer house and the Charles Lathrop estate on Mayfield Road (the current Sand Hill Road) leading to the now-vanished town of Searsville. The property had been put up for sale in 1899 as part of a real estate development. When Maria Berner purchased the tract in 1902, it presumably had a house on it, because Charles Lathrop saw August Berner and Maria Berner there frequently that spring while Jane and Bertha were in Hawaii and Japan. There would not be time to build a house between January and May.[7]

When Bertha returned to California from Japan in May of 1902, she moved in with her brother and mother.[8]

⸻

THE 1902 TRIP TURNED OUT to be a dress rehearsal for a much longer round-the-world journey Mrs. Stanford planned for 1903–1904. She would go west to Australia, and then anticipated continuing on to India, Egypt, and Europe. She would enjoy herself abroad while the Board of Trustees began the work of ridding her of David Starr Jordan.

Just as 1903 proved a turning point in Jane Stanford's relationship with David Starr Jordan, so her trip across the Pacific that year proved critical to her relationship with Bertha Berner. Things went very wrong. In Australia something upset Berner. She said she had had "enough in Australia." Mrs. Stanford was threatening to send Beverly and Elizabeth Richmond home. Berner could not deal with Jane Stanford by herself.

Stanford's threat to send Beverly home almost certainly involved his relationship with Bertha Berner. Rumored to be lovers, Berner and Beverly also became business partners. Whether this happened before or after the Pacific trip is unclear. Jane Stanford depended on Beverly to handle household purchases and apparently dispatched him and Berner to acquire antiquities and objets d'art for the Stanford museum when they traveled. Beverly followed the customs of European servants entrusted with such duties. He patronized merchants who would pad their bills and kick back the extra profit to him. Bertha Berner, who was in charge of the household accounts, approved the inflated bills, and Beverly split the profits with her.[9]

Beverly refused to travel without the right to the commission. He told Berner, "You don't think I am traveling for pleasure, do you? It costs me to travel nearly as much as I can earn." Jane Stanford's large purchases for the museum made the Pacific trip lucrative. In Australia, angry at Beverly's monitoring of her transactions to make sure he got his commissions, Stanford threatened to send him home. Berner then refused to travel through Ceylon and India, where cholera was raging, without a man.[10]

Beverly was indispensable. He had planned the trip through India. He slept on a board and gave Jane Stanford his comforter. He gave his pillow to Berner. Berner contended that only after leaving Australia did Beverly offer her half of the commissions, which came to $1,500. She claimed that not only did she tell this to Jane Stanford, but she returned her portion to her. This is unlikely. Richmond said that rake-offs had begun in California. Beverly and Berner not only shared his commissions, the two exchanged small gifts.[11]

Why did Berner take the money? Perhaps because she had the opportunity, perhaps because she fell under Beverly's sway, perhaps, resenting the way Jane Stanford used her wealth to dictate to others, it seemed only just. And, perhaps, because she, like Beverly, regarded it as normal and acceptable. She said that J. B. McCarthy, Leland Stanford's secretary while he was in the Senate, took commissions on the Stanfords' household bills. How had she known this? If McCarthy was the secretary rumored to be having an affair with Berner, and he shared the proceeds with her, Beverly may not have been the first with whom Berner combined business and pleasure.[12]

Even as he managed the trip, Beverly remained in the background, as butlers were supposed to do. There is a photograph taken before the Sphinx with the Great Pyramid in the distance. Jane Stanford sits, with Elizabeth Richmond standing nearby. Egyptian guides are gathered around them. Bertha Berner, too, is in the background, seated on a camel. Beside her, on another camel, is Albert Beverly. He is wearing a suit, a tie, and a derby.[13]

At the beginning of the trip, Bertha Berner allowed herself a rare personal entry into her account of Mrs. Stanford. After their ship docked in Auckland, New Zealand, they spent a day ashore followed by a surprise birthday party for Jane Stanford. The birthday dinner also contained a surprise for Bertha Berner. She found a New Zealand greenstone heart on a gold chain beneath her plate. She said she could not discover the donor.[14]

It is not surprising that she had admirers; her mention of one of them was unusual. The greenstone heart wasn't about Jane Stanford, the rich Americans, the maharishis, and the British imperialists who clogged the memoir. It was about more interesting meetings. She presented it as a mystery, but like other mysteries involving Berner, I suspect she knew more than she told.

CHAPTER 23

THOMAS WELTON
STANFORD

ONE VOYAGE ACROSS the Pacific Ocean during his lifetime proved enough for Thomas Welton Stanford. After emigrating to Australia in 1859, he never returned to the United States. Of all the Stanfords and Lathrops, he was the only one who did not hope to profit from Jane Stanford's fortune. When his older brother Leland left him $300,000 in his will, he offered the entire sum to Jane Stanford to use for the university library. She agreed to accept half of it to fund a library that she named after him. Seeing her brother-in-law was one of the reasons for her trip in 1903.[1]

Jane Stanford's visit that August was the first extended stop on her trans-Pacific tour, and Thomas spared no expense. He rented an entire floor in the largest hotel in Melbourne and hired carpenters and decorators to create a large suite. He leased a special carriage, had a special harness made, and procured a coachman and footman, providing distinctive uniforms for the occasion.[2]

Thomas Welton Stanford undermined David Starr Jordan's claim that spiritualism had no influence on the university. Jane could hide her spiritualism within Christian practice, but Thomas Welton Stanford never attempted to do so.

Jordan claimed that Mrs. Stanford's beliefs were orthodox, amounting to little more than a Christian belief in the immortal soul and angelic visitations, but she went much further. She regarded the boundary between life and death as a babbling brook rather than a yawning chasm. Human souls passed easily over it, and as spirits crossed back again. The dead remained accessible to those with the means to see and hear them. For spiritualists such as Jane, punishment and atonement, and with them hell and purgatory, vanished. Heaven became Summerland or the Other Place inhabited by the departed, who retained their physical form now cleansed of disease, decline, and decay. They continued to grow and evolve. They had much to teach and advise.[3]

Thomas Welton Stanford not only made no attempt to mask his beliefs, but—and this could only outrage Jordan—claimed scientific sanction for them. He claimed that spiritualism was the enemy of materialism, not science. He hoped to make Leland Stanford Junior University—named after a child who had visited him as a spirit—a source of scientific validation. All the scientists who "earnestly investigated spiritualism" concluded that "the claims of its advocates are well founded—life continuous, man immortal and progression endless."[4]

In her memoir, Berner describes Thomas Welton Stanford as "tall, very thin, and extremely nervous." She claims that Jane Stanford was impressed with his friends, who were supposedly skeptical of spiritualism and hopeful that his enthusiasm for it was dwindling. She mentions a séance arranged with "Mr. Bailey" that fizzled. The room was dark and silent, "broken only by an occasional request that we have patience." Then Bailey announced that the conditions were unfavorable and there would be no manifestations. On the way back to the hotel, Bailey stopped the carriage, calling out that he had lost his diamond ring. Mrs. Stanford supposedly ridiculed him, ordering the coachman to drive on, and telling Bailey, "Your spirits will, no doubt help you find your ring again."[5]

Berner says that other séances at Thomas's offices frightened Mrs. Stanford, who talked "very earnest and seriously to Mr. Stanford about this matter that had occupied their thoughts for so long without proving satisfactorily that the departed were able to communicate and also return to their loved ones on earth." She begged him to leave his present surroundings and recuperate. Unhappy and "grieving about Thomas Welton," she left Australia early and, according to Berner, never again attended a séance. She had seen no evidence that "the departed returned to this earth." She wanted her conclusions known at the university and wrote to Jordan that "her faith in a hereafter was based entirely on the teachings in the Bible." Berner wrote that Jane Stanford's "statements of this fact will be found in the archives of the University."[6]

Apart from Berner's memoir, there is no evidence that the visit to Australia changed her opinions about spiritualism or T. W. Stanford. There are no "statements of fact" in the Stanford archives that I have found. There is considerable evidence that Bertha Berner was mistaken at best and lying at worst. As Berner confessed, it was she, not Jane Stanford, who was upset by the Australia visit.

A newspaper account of the séances that Thomas Welton Stanford held for Jane Stanford provides a very different picture of the trip. "An exceedingly clever English woman of strictly orthodox views" reported that a number of immense stones slowly floated down from the ceiling. The largest, "covered with Babylonian inscriptions dating 7,000 years before Christ" took three men to move. Jane Stanford was among the thirty-two people who witnessed this. At another séance brilliant tropical birds "unknown to science" flew through the room at the command of the medium.[7]

Addie Ballou was a spiritualist who claimed to be a friend of both T. W. Stanford and Jane Stanford. She said the séances with Charles Bailey—"the mahatma," who was sponsored not only by Thomas Welton Stanford but also later by Arthur Conan Doyle—were a great success. Several years after Jane Stanford's death, Bailey would be revealed as a fraud, but Jane Stanford convinced herself that both the relics and Bailey were genuine. According to Ballou, she arranged another set of sittings to be attended by those who were not convinced spiritualists. Among them apparently was the "exceedingly clever English woman of strictly orthodox views." When they too were convinced, Mrs. Stanford arranged for the relics to be sent to Stanford.[8]

When Jane Stanford wrote Timothy Hopkins's wife, May, from India, she sounded very much like she always had. She considered herself under God's protection ever since she departed on her long trip. She wrote, "He takes my daily messages to my loved ones gone from earth life. He is like an operator at the telegraph taking dispatches from his children on earth to his children in Heaven." She thought she was in better health away from home.[9]

Thomas Welton Stanford wrote her a long, cordial letter in 1904 that contained no hint of trouble between them. He spoke of the university expanding to "lead and light the intelligence of progressive cycles." Creeds and sects were obsolete. Her new preacher for her church "should be a spiritual pantheist, teaching the Universe is God, that the Universal Law . . .

pervades all space . . . and that our religion should be a heart full of loving aspiration for an ever increasing knowledge of, and closer union with that law, Divinity, God, or Superior Being. . . . It is for us, individualized spirit-force entities to strive to understand the conditions necessary to harmonious relations with the Law of which we are a part. . . ."[10]

If she quarreled with her brother-in-law over spiritualism, Jane Stanford would hardly consult him on a preacher, nor would he write as he did to a person who disavowed spiritualism. They agreed on the study of "psychic psychology and other occult forces of Nature . . . as essential to higher education." This is why it was necessary to endow a position at Stanford "for the investigation of Spiritualist and the occult forces pertaining there to."[11]

In October of 1904, just months before her death, she wrote that she was carrying out "the wishes of those who were dearest earth-life to me. I never think of them as being what the world says, 'dead,' or 'lost.' They are living in a higher, better, condition of life . . . and I sincerely believe they are instrumental in guiding and helping me in my work, and acting the part of guardian angels such as the New Testament has promised us."[12]

On her return to the United States, she encouraged her brother-in-law to fund a chair at Stanford in a subject "as close to your heart as psychic psychology."[13] Thomas Welton Stanford funded a fellowship in Psychic Research that was held by John Edgar Coover. He also donated his art collection as well as many of his apports—the objects from the past delivered to him by the spirits—to the university, where they remain today.[14]

CHAPTER 24

HOMECOMING

EVEN AS JANE STANFORD traveled the world in 1903 and 1904, her thoughts were never far from Leland Stanford Junior University. Those thoughts were rarely pleasant. She wrote David Starr Jordan a cordial letter from Egypt in January of 1904, but the letter she sent George Crothers from Cairo that same month complained how "slack and irregular the internal affairs of the university have been run." She told Crothers that in the university as in her household, "willful [*sic*] waste brings woeful want." She was pleased that the trustees were intervening to bring order and discipline.[1]

Despite Jane Stanford's hopes for a quick dismissal of Jordan, Crothers and Horace Davis—the two trustees met every other day—concentrated their initial efforts on curtailing Jordan's powers and reforming Stanford University's governance. When in December of 1903 Jordan departed on another of his long trips, the board informed him on his return that hereafter "he should not leave the University without the consent of the Board."[2]

Horace Davis was a gold rush merchant who recognized that wheat, not gold, would dominate California's post–Civil War economy. He turned to producing flour. A leading Republican, he served two terms in Congress before becoming president of the University of California at Berkeley and then accepting an invitation to be a Stanford trustee. He fancied himself a scholar, and he certainly was more widely read than the rest of the Stanford board. He undertook a systematic survey of other research universities—including Harvard, Yale, the University of Michigan, Columbia, Cornell—to find suitable models for a reputable institution of higher education.³ He also solicited Jordan's advice, and on the surface Jordan seemed accommodating. He agreed that "the university will cease to be one man and take on the form of organization prevailing in other institutions." Jordan could see that the tide was running against him. Nicholas Murray Butler of Columbia understood Davis's effort to be a preparation for governing the university after Jordan's departure.⁴

Jordan did not intend to depart, even though Jane Stanford was using the board to try to curtail his power. At the beginning of 1904, as president of the board, she announced her intention to limit enrollment to 1,600 until all the buildings were finished and paid for. She did not trust Jordan to control expenses; that authority should rest solely with her brother as the university's business manager and treasurer.⁵

She was "determined on radical change both in the University and the Board of Trustees." She wanted to move quickly and decisively because she "anticipated another long absence from home"; she planned a trip to Europe in August. In July of 1904 she read Davis's analysis of the condition of the university "with surprise and interest." She was "startled to learn that we are 'bound hand and foot' because of the great mistakes made in the Ross Affair." The university was "virtually a branch of Cornell and Indiana University." She prepared a letter that embodied her reforms for the next meeting of the trustees, but she showed only part of it to Crothers, knowing he would advise caution. She gave Davis the entire document and asked for his opinion.⁶

The letter was, to use a word coined about the same time, a humdinger. She would be satisfied to see every department in the university become subordinate to church work. She quoted Ralph Waldo Emerson (or rather someone quoting what they remembered Ralph Waldo Emerson as saying) that religious worship was the single most important function in the life of the nation. She needed a strong minister, a man in the mold of the now deceased Reverend Newman, who had preached Leland Jr.'s memorial sermon so long before. Second only to the church would be the museum, which she enlarged so it could contain all the stuff she intended to transfer from her California Street mansion. When she got around to talking about the faculty, things got worse. She wanted the new chair in "psychic psychology" that her brother-in-law Thomas Welton Stanford was to donate to seek a scientific validation of spiritualism.⁷

Broader academic concerns rested at the very bottom of her list, ranking below her determination that the university keep its vineyards at the Vina ranch out of the California Wine Association. Mrs. Stanford intended to intervene even more actively in academic affairs, bolstering some departments and culling those deemed weak. Professors in those departments should be given notice to seek other positions.[8]

Horace Davis and George Crothers had labored for a year to craft proposals to give Stanford University the semblance of the emerging American research university, only to discover on reading her letter that Jane Stanford wanted to turn the university into a cult. Timothy and May Hopkins were already gossiping about how "queer" many of Mrs. Stanford's beliefs and actions seemed to be. And even George Crothers regarded many of her ideas as "impossible." But mixed in among them were departmental reforms that sprang from a detailed knowledge of how the university actually worked—and didn't work—that Jane Stanford did not herself possess. These reforms partially echoed Davis's support for strengthening the humanities and curtailing the power of the sciences, but they did not come from Davis.

The Gilbert Affair turned out to cast a long shadow. The name of that shadow was Julius Goebel, the head of the German department who had defended Schmidt, befriended Pease (who said Jordan would welcome Jane Stanford's demise), and became, despite Pease's warning of the potential cost, Jordan's leading enemy on the faculty. Goebel provided the specific departmental proposals that Jane Stanford adopted.

Jane Stanford consulted Goebel in 1904 because she wanted information that she said she was unable to acquire from the administration. Mrs. Stanford noticed that the amount being spent in several small departments, largely in the sciences, exceeded that being spent in the larger departments that did most of the teaching. She asked Goebel for his honest opinion on enrollments as well as other aspects of the university. He told her that he would prefer that she get the information from the administration. She assured him that she was seeking information from all sides and that he had a duty to help her. She wanted his answers in writing since she desired to put them into a report to the trustees. She promised to keep his role confidential. Goebel reported on the decline of the humanities at Stanford and the dominance of the sciences. He wrote about the practices of German universities—their enrollments, requirements, and basic language instruction. He excoriated the Jordan clique's domination of the university. He made the Gilbert Affair a central example.[9]

On July 6 Mrs. Stanford wrote a long memorandum, almost certainly based on information from Goebel, that named the strong and weak departments and professors. It attacked by name Professors Gilbert and Green—Jordan loyalists at the center of the Gilbert Affair and the firing of Schmidt.[10] Only three people—Jane Stanford, Julius Goebel, and Mrs. Stanford's "private secretary," Bertha Berner—knew of Goebel's report to Jane Stanford, which informed the memorandum.

Jordan began in July to seek some of the reforms suggested in the report to impress Jane Stanford, while using his faculty advisory board to block them. Goebel suspected that Jordan had obtained a copy of the report. If so, he also knew of Jane Stanford's renewed interest in the Gilbert Affair. Since she—at the urging of Davis and Crothers—did not give her letters to the trustees to Jordan, it seems unlikely that she would have given him Goebel's report. That leaves Bertha Berner.[11]

CROTHERS AND DAVIS were understandably alarmed at Jane Stanford's July 6 memorandum, but Crothers was diplomatic. Crothers stressed his support of the larger goal of raising the standards of the university rather than the particular proposals.

Jane Stanford sent an official address to each trustee on July 23, and she then read an address at their meeting of August 1. There are two different documents labeled "Address to the Board of Trustees" in the Stanford archives. In both of them Jane Stanford targeted the administration of her university, attacked the university's current condition, and proposed the reforms contained in her memorandum. She demanded professors sympathetic to a university that provides "food for the mind, but also the richer food which our Lord and Savior gave us for our soul's comfort." Let us not, she says, "be poor copies of other universities. Let us be Progressive."[12]

The second version of the address stated her determination "to revolutionize existing conditions" in order to create an ideal American university in five or ten years. The address disparaged the current version of Leland Stanford Junior University as "only being a college of the Mid-Western type." It criticized the quality of the students and their suitability for college work. It urged more original research and postgraduate education.[13]

The minutes of the Board of Trustees simply noted that Mrs. Stanford addressed the board on "the necessity of raising the standards of the university," and proposed making the departments "equal to any in the world." This was "followed by many favorable comments."[14]

Having become adept at controlling the damage from Jane Stanford's opinions, George Crothers recognized that if either version of her address became public it would be read as an attack on the administration and on at least a part of the faculty, which it was. He told Samuel Leib that "in view of the prospective unpopularity of the proposed measures among University professors throughout the country, and of the fact that our ability to get the right class of professors depends upon our reinstatement in the confidence of Eastern and European professors," it was best to keep it secret that these suggestions originated with Mrs. Stanford. He thought the trustees should take full responsibility for any changes to protect Jane Stanford "from attacks from our numerous and powerful enemies in the East." Crothers remained loyal to her, but his defense doubled as a devastating critique. He was the lawyer who listed all the crimes his client either planned or executed, and then took credit for preventing some of them and avoiding punishment for the others. Crothers took "meticulous care to avoid any disclosure in detail of . . . the wholly illegal provisions" of Mrs. Stanford's amendments—and attempted amendments—of the university trusts in her "so called 'addresses.'" There provisions, he said, ranged from the "apparently trivial to the Colossal."[15]

CHAPTER 25

DOWNSTAIRS

ON MAY 2, 1904, when she returned to San Francisco on a Pacific Mail Steamship from Japan, Jane Stanford did not go to Nob Hill. She took up residence in Palo Alto.[1]

Her return and resettling produced tensions and readjustments among her staff. Albert Beverly left her service almost immediately. When he told Mrs. Stanford that he was leaving to spend more time with his family, she said she was sorry but asked him to stay until she could get resettled. He spent two days in San Francisco clearing her goods through customs and then brought them to Palo Alto. Since he continued to live in a house near the stock farm on the Palo Alto estate for the next several months, the parting seemed amicable. Beverly bicycled daily into town, frequently seeing and talking to Elizabeth Richmond and, so he said, Bertha Berner.[2]

After a few months, when she needed the house for another employee, Mrs. Stanford wrote him a note, and he vacated. They supposedly stayed friendly, and just before Christmas she asked him to return to help with the receptions she was planning for the new year in San Francisco. Only then, Beverly said, was there a sign of trouble. He heard nothing more. "I suppose in the meantime some people got their hammers out and fixed me."[3]

Grace Gilmore, a daughter of a friend who visited Jane Stanford that summer in Palo Alto, gave a different story. She said Mrs. Stanford let Beverly go because of the commissions he took on the purchases he made in India. This surprised Gilmore because Mrs. Stanford always liked and relied on him. She replaced him with Max Magner, who became another of the many people who displeased Jane Stanford.[4]

Bertha Berner's return home did not go smoothly. Jane Stanford still considered Berner's friendship "one that cannot be bought, it is God-giving [sic]," but Berner's personal life made it difficult for her to give Jane Stanford the attention that she demanded. Beverly went back to his wife, and sometime that summer Berner's mother became so ill that Jane reported Bertha "had to go to her . . . and probably will never be able to leave her." This made Jane Stanford's heart go out to Jane Stanford: "you can picture what it is to be without her." Only Stanford's decision to postpone her trip to Europe prevented an immediate rupture.[5]

When Jane Stanford took a short trip to New York that summer, Bertha Berner apparently did not accompany her, but in the fall when she first visited the Louisiana Purchase Exposition in St. Louis and went east to seek a minister for the church, Berner came along. There was a trip to Harvard and Yale to hear ministers preach at each college, and a side trip to Norwich, Connecticut, to meet Stanford's distant cousins. Bertha seemed cheerful. In Connecticut, the cousins showed Jane Stanford their treasures. Bertha Berner dressed in one of them: "a very beautiful light blue costume that had a flowered brocade overskirt and a pointed waist trimmed with rich lace, of the time of Martha Washington." She put plumes in her hair, applied a beauty patch of black court plaster, and "then with a fan . . . made a curtsy in the drawing room."[6] She did this for an audience of old women.

In early December 1904, Jane Stanford was back in New York City, staying at the Waldorf Astoria. She planned a trip to Cambridge to meet with Charles Eliot, the president of Harvard, whom she missed on the earlier visit to Cambridge, but a snowstorm made her decide not to go. She chose to escape the winter and return to California. She wrote Eliot that "Providence permitting," she would meet him before her planned departure for Europe in June.[7]

On December 15, Jane Stanford stopped in Omaha on her way home when the *Omaha News* interviewed her. She was in good health and good spirits. She walked four miles a day: two miles before noon and two miles after. She favored Japan in the Russo-Japanese War and said the "Chadwick case is all the talk in the east," meaning it was what the rich people she talked to were gossiping about. Cassie Chadwick was a confidence woman who claimed to be the out-of-wedlock daughter of Andrew Carnegie in order to obtain loans from banks and rich men across the eastern United States. In November of 1904 the scheme collapsed.[8]

On that train trip across the continent, Jane Stanford, a rich woman never particularly sensitive to the feelings of those outside her immediate family, told Bertha Berner of her plans for the upcoming year. She described an old rich woman's idyll to a woman who was neither rich nor old, but who was approaching middle age with a mother who needed her care. Jane Stanford intended "to give myself a treat this coming summer." She would invite her two elderly Norwich cousins, women who were, she said, "my kind," to accompany her to England. She would secure a nice residence on the Thames from which they would make side trips. She would "take no servants from America but have all engaged in England." In describing her plans, Mrs. Stanford used "we" in her usual imperial sense. It seemed to include Berner, but the ambiguity itself contained a chilling message. If Berner accompanied Mrs. Stanford, she would have to leave her own mother to cater to the pleasure of her employer, and she would not even have the aid and solace of Beverly. If it did not include Berner, she would be without income.[9]

On the return to California that December, Berner found herself for apparently the first time in a long while living in the Nob Hill mansion. Her room was on the floor above Jane Stanford's, which made her relationship with Mrs. Stanford even more stifling.[10]

Berner's presence created tensions and jealousies. Her influence over Jane Stanford was significant, but George Crothers thought that she was "not fully trusted." She did not attend the luncheons and meetings that Mrs. Stanford had with Crothers. Still, her influence was far greater than that of other employees. Albert Beverly later claimed that Lathrop disliked Berner because Jane Stanford placed confidence in her.[11]

For more than a year, with Stanford away first on her world tour and then in Palo Alto and the east, the Nob Hill mansion had been Ah Wing's domain. There was time for whatever lingering resentment he felt over his betrayal by the Lathrops and Stanfords to dissipate. In the hierarchy of the mansion, he remained subordinate to the butler, but Max Magner, who replaced Beverly, did not represent much of a threat. Beverly scorned American butlers as mere "window cleaners," and Jane Stanford never liked Magner, dismissing him after her return from the east in December. Ah Wing's authority expanded to fill the vacuum. Berner and Ah Wing had previously gotten along, but Berner's residence in the mansion changed their relationship. She had developed the habit of taking coffee at about 4:00 every afternoon either alone or in the company of the rest of the staff. Jane Stanford found out. She did not like it and demanded it stop. Berner believed that Ah Wing had told her. He denied it, and the two quarreled.[12]

Some of the other servants seemed gratified by the quarrel between Ah Wing and Berner; they resented the authority Berner assumed over them. Elizabeth Richmond, who knew of Berner's arrangements with Beverly, later claimed that she had denounced Berner for cheating her employer, and the papers reported that Richmond and Berner had quarreled for years. But Richmond, who told many stories, also told the papers that Berner was kind and considerate.[13]

WHEN IN JANUARY OF 1905 Callundan came to investigate who had placed strychnine in Jane Stanford's Poland Spring Water, he was correct in saying that there were quarrels and jealousies among the servants, and that Bertha Berner was central to them.

CHAPTER 26

THE WALLS CLOSE IN

BY THE SUMMER OF 1904, David Starr Jordan's greatest protection from Jane Stanford's determination to remove him was the endless disarray of the aging, dim, and often distant Board of Trustees. Mrs. Stanford had a hard time even getting the board to meet. There were resignations and absences—including her own—following the August 1 meeting where she presented her attack on Jordan and conditions at the university, and these meant poor attendance during the summer and fall.[1] The trustees formed less a wall against reform than a swamp that was hard to traverse. But Crothers and Davis found that with sufficient trudging and a tolerance for slime, it was not impossible.

George Crothers insisted that he liked Jordan personally, but he regarded him as a disastrous administrator—a man without judgment, tact, or principle. His decision about firing or retaining Jordan depended on whether it forwarded reform of the university as a whole. As Jane Stanford grew more impatient and insistent on dismissing Jordan, Crothers sought to avoid the crisis and scandal that a frontal attack on the president would precipitate. He would have the trustees ease Jordan out and give him an honorary research position.[2]

Horace Davis, too, was willing to work incrementally. He thought the president's power to dismiss faculty unilaterally created dependence and demoralization, fed the university's reputation for restricting academic freedom, and made recruitment of outstanding scholars difficult if not impossible. When Davis departed on a voyage to Europe for his wife's health in August 1904, he wrote Jane Stanford regretting that he would not be present to help implement his proposed reforms, but he reiterated the need for change. Stanford was not among the "first class, all around" universities, and would not be until these problems were remedied.[3]

Jordan nominally agreed to reform, but in practice he resisted. He pointed to Stanford's salaries, which were below those of comparable institutions and well below those at Harvard, Yale, Chicago, Columbia, and Pennsylvania. Costs of living at Stanford were also higher. His solution for the university's problems was not reform but greater spending. This had the unintended consequence of fortifying Jane Stanford's conviction that her university was inferior to those other universities. Jordan also erected an administrative framework that seemed to institute the kind of faculty governance that Crothers and Davis wanted, but he crafted an executive faculty council dominated by his allies that could serve as a bastion against Jane Stanford's and the trustees' demands for change. Reform came to the faculty council to die.[4]

Jordan told Crothers that being answerable to the Board of Trustees and the faculty was well and good, but "there arise extreme cases where the President has to act instantly without time to consult anyone." He used as an example his dismissal of a professor of education for sexual misconduct. Pandering to Jane Stanford's panic over sex on campus might have seemed shrewd, but it rather awkwardly ignored the Gilbert Affair. It was also not the best example for a university president who had courted his second wife while she was a college undergraduate and he was a university trustee.[5]

Fearing that his enemies would release additional stories of the turmoil at Stanford and his troubles to the press, Jordan sought to preempt them. He sent out letters to the major papers complaining of the inaccuracies of their stories about the university and demanding that offending journalists be disciplined and reprimanded. As the puzzled editors pointed out, it was hard to make corrections let alone discipline reporters when he gave no examples.[6]

Above all, Jordan sought to regain the good graces of Mrs. Stanford. He tried to aid her search for a new minister, and opened negotiations with "his friend," William James, whom Jane Stanford very much wished to recruit because of his interest in spiritualism.[7] None of this worked. In August, Jane Stanford lectured Jordan about overstepping in his negotiations with Professor James. This was something to be left to her and the trustees.[8] In September she criticized him for scheduling a ceremony to lay the cornerstone of the library without her permission, and for his mocking references to Stanford's "Stone Age," which "has hurt my feelings in that it has given me the impression that you have not all this time been in sympathy and accord with my putting up such extensive and expensive buildings, which I myself considered my duty, and it has afforded me great pleasure."[9]

At their August meeting, the trustees asked Jordan for a report "on the needs and deficiencies of the University." He responded in November of 1904, reporting that the "University has been doing creditable work" and was improving. Teaching had been "satisfactory," but students lacked necessary books and scientific apparatus. Salaries were too low to secure the best instructors or to permit those it hired the time or resources to improve. He agreed to limit the number of students and put a cap on women students. He acknowledged that the humanities needed to be strengthened.[10]

He ignored some of Mrs. Stanford's most troubling demands and tried to turn others to his advantage. He said nothing about the university's spiritual mission. He thought Mrs. Stanford gave him an opening with her endorsement of postgraduate education, and he seized it. He advocated putting no limit on the number of graduate students. He desired to make Stanford a "center of advanced research."[11]

Jordan fought hardest over coeducation and salaries. Women students, he insisted, posed far less of a disciplinary problem than men. And the university needed higher pay, guaranteed sabbaticals, and pensions. His argument for higher salaries shaded into a denigration of the faculty. A professor could afford to teach at Stanford only if they were "rich men or celibates. The man of family without income has no place in them." Rich men did not do much work, and those willing to take faculty positions at existing salaries tended to be "poor men of inactive temperament who could not succeed in other professions." The academy in general was filled with men "of feeble health, narrow experience, and limited force of character."[12]

The report, with its praise of the founders, disparagement of the faculty, and nominal acquiescence to some of Jane Stanford's demands, demonstrated Jordan's tendency toward sycophancy. It also showed he wasn't very good at it. When he took Jane Stanford's advocacy for postgraduate education as an opportunity, he failed to realize that she did not understand what a postgraduate education meant. When he sought to appease her, he only irritated her. He insinuated that the inadequacies of the university came from Mrs. Stanford's failure to fund it sufficiently. He reinforced her sense that the university was a failure, her efforts unappreciated, and her money wasted.

Where Jordan resisted, Jane Stanford refocused her attacks. In their push for reform, Davis and Crothers used the word *discipline* to refer to the academic subjects of study and the reform of faculty governance, admission standards, course requirements, and electives. When Jane Stanford spoke of discipline, she meant financial discipline and moral discipline, particularly for women students.

In 1904 Jane Stanford said she thought coeducation an "unsolved question." She was willing to give it a "fair and impartial trial" until God revealed to the "wise rulers of earth" the answer to this "troublesome and delicate question." She was until then relying on the advice of her trustees.[13]

It was all too clear what advice she wanted. She had named the university after her son, but she did not send her niece there. Jennie Lathrop went to a convent school, where she converted to Catholicism. Nor did Jennie enroll at Stanford when she graduated. Jane Stanford sometimes thought the university corrupted women and sometimes thought women corrupted the university. Sometimes she thought both. In November 1904 Crothers reported that she "made a vigorous protest to me against laxity of student discipline, especially as to the girls, and expressed herself very radically as to the whole system of co-education." Crothers told Jordan that something must be done to pacify her.[14]

Jordan refused to administer the university to satisfy the gossip Jane Stanford heard and the anonymous letters she received. "In spite of the idle talk of gossips of all degrees, it is rare that any young woman on the Campus puts herself in a position where one would not like to see his daughter." His own daughter was at Stanford. He said the "spooning" that supposedly took place on campus came from couples in neighboring towns.[15]

Crothers, who supported coeducation, was dismayed at Jordan's response.[16] Crothers thought the university's "moral conditions on the whole are exceptionally good, but we have neglected to require the girls to be governed by the conventional laws applicable to their sex." He regarded the extreme freedom and informality on the campus as "almost as evil as the extreme rigidity of discipline of the convent."[17]

After meeting with Jordan and Leib, Crothers suggested draconian changes as a way to stop Jane Stanford from rejecting coeducation altogether. The university would apply stricter rules to women and monitor them closely. There would be moral policing to banish any sign of sexual attraction between students on campus. The board would increase the age of admission of women students from sixteen to eighteen and "as soon as possible thereafter from 18 to 20 years. This will practically limit the female students to the advanced and graduate course. The age of the women will greatly exceed that of men." A system of matrons would be put in place "with full authority to enforce discipline" over the female students. Watchmen and mounted guards would report any infractions of discipline "and turn over the culprit to the University authorities for punishment." Warnings would be issued to "those who are conspicuous in their attention to the opposite sex."[18]

In December 1904 Jane Stanford wrote Jordan from New York demanding an end to the "free and familiar intercourse" between men and women. The girls in the sororities were "lawless and free in their social relations with young men." Jordan had the power to restrict this, and he should.[19]

Bertha Berner must have known of this uproar; she must have listened to Jane's rage at the "free and familiar intercourse" between men and women. She must have thought of her own position and Jane's interventions. Beverly went back to his wife, but there was gossip that Berner was being "friendly" with other men. She was an adult, but Jane did not relax her surveillance of her body and friendships.

Crothers was playing a complicated game. He warned Jordan that a large majority of the current trustees did not believe in coeducation, making it all the more important to have a system of student discipline that would protect it from attack.[20] He worked to prevent Jane Stanford from precipitously eliminating Jordan, a move that would trigger a public scandal equal to the Ross Affair, while at the same time seeking to limit Jordan's power, which he regarded as the Achilles' heel of the university. He inserted language in a general revision of the university trusts to transfer the power of appointing faculty to the trustees.

In October Crothers admitted things were moving slowly, but he thought that when Jane Stanford selected new trustees for the board to replace those who had died or were asked to resign because they could not attend the meetings, the board would be ready to act in January. Then he hoped a great deal would be done.[21] The most immediate issue involved limiting Jordan's power over hiring and firing.[22]

CROTHERS FOCUSED ON ORGANIZING a reform majority on the Stanford board. He thought that in addition to himself, Davis, and Jane Stanford, four trustees would support reform. Samuel Leib might join them. Timothy Hopkins and Charles Lathrop, both close to Jane Stanford, were notably absent from the list of reformers. Hopkins never abandoned the old railroad habits of graft and insider dealing. Crothers said that Hopkins routinely examined bids for university work and then put in lower bids of his own for contracts he wanted.[23] Reform was the last thing he desired.

Crothers admitted that many trustees had reasons to dislike him. Usually more informed, always harder working, and inevitably better prepared than his adversaries, he insisted on having his way. Always careful, he made sure that he could not be credibly accused of stacking the board in his favor. In 1904 Crothers suggested Charles P. Eells and William Babcock as new trustees. He did so knowing Eells was likely to oppose him because of his animosity toward Crothers's brother. He intended Eells's opposition to work in his favor since he anticipated a challenge to the will and trusts on the basis of his undue influence over Jane Stanford. Appointing Eells rather than one of his friends would serve as a prophylactic. As Crothers anticipated, Eells became part of a group that sought to "break up the Davis-Crothers combination."[24]

Hopkins fell out of favor with Jane Stanford because he committed a far greater sin than dishonesty. He ridiculed Jane Stanford's museum, which contained, among other things, the re-creation of Leland Jr.'s bedroom in the San Francisco mansion at the time of his death.[25] It was sacrosanct.

Jennie Lathrop acted as a guide for visitors to the museum, and later reported to Crothers that both Timothy and May Hopkins had always "sneered" at Mrs. Stanford's exhibits. They remarked to guests they were escorting around the museum that "Mrs. Stanford was always queer." This, of course, was repeated to Mrs. Stanford. Jane Stanford linked Hopkins with Jordan as "the weak sisters." Both would have to go.[26]

CHAPTER 27

RESURRECTIONS AND SUICIDES

AT THE END OF 1904, David Starr Jordan's enemies could smell blood. One day in either late November or early December, Charles Lathrop stopped John Nourse on the street in San Francisco. Their previous relations were not friendly. Lathrop believed that when Nourse was a postgraduate assistant at Stanford he had participated in a student plot to harass Professor Charles Gilbert for his rumored affair with his ex-student who worked in the Stanford library. Now Nourse was a lawyer in the city, and Lathrop told him that there was going to be a new investigation of the so-called Gilbert Affair, which had seemingly been resolved more than three years earlier. Nourse wrote a friend afterward that "they" were after Jordan, Gilbert, and some others. The friend, T. L. McFadden, who had been Julius Goebel's student at Stanford, told Goebel, the German professor who became Jane Stanford's ally against Jordan, "that if you can give Nourse some data, it will be used to a good purpose." He assured Goebel that his name would not be mentioned, which was the same assurance Goebel earlier received from Jane Stanford. McFadden told Nourse that whatever information he received needed to be held closely. Stanford faculty feared Jordan.[1]

Goebel believed that Jane Stanford now regarded Schmidt, the librarian, as an innocent victim of Jordan's attempts to protect Gilbert. With the creation of a reform majority on the Board of Trustees, a new investigation of the Gilbert Affair combined with Jane Stanford's lingering animosity over the Ross Affair could bring Jordan down. Goebel thought that Jordan knew that "this investigation would result in the exposure of Gilbert as well as of himself [Jordan] and of his entire coterie and he made up his mind *that it had to be prevented at any price.*"[2]

ON DECEMBER 1, 1904, while Jane Stanford was still in the east, Martha J. Soule, the wife of one her husband's old employees—a man Jane Stanford looked out for—took her own life. She was old, tired, and sick. She took a small dose of rat poison; the strychnine killed her. The suicide got publicity in the local papers and made an impact at the university. Jordan sent her husband a condolence letter on behalf of the faculty. The newspapers treated Martha Soule's suicide as prima facie evidence that she was demented.[3]

Martha Soule's death by strychnine stood out because it struck so close to Jane Stanford and her university, but anyone reading the *San Francisco Examiner*—Hearst's paper and the leading daily in the city—in 1904 encountered a parade of suicides, murders, and accidents all linked by strychnine. Most of the strychnine stories came from across the region and the nation—few came from San Francisco itself. In a city with 28 murders and 239 suicides in 1903–1904, only four of the suicides were by strychnine. But since strychnine deaths tended to be both horrible and dramatic, they made good copy.[4]

Strychnine was catholic in its victims. Men depressed by the inability to find work swallowed it. Heartbroken lovers used it to end their lives. Unhappy husbands and wives employed it. Unfaithful spouses used it to rid themselves of unwanted partners. Sometimes the police initially missed, and doctors obfuscated, the cause of death. The old and sick—like Martha Soule—swallowed it, and so did young girls. Some took rat poison, but others, because strychnine was an ingredient in so many medicines, used purer forms. The purer forms were part of a scientific apothecary used at the time to prolong life. The *Examiner* was often more specific about the container holding the poison—usually a vial—than the form of strychnine it contained.[5]

Anyone around Jane Stanford who read the newspapers and contemplated her prospective murder would know about strychnine. Martha Soule's death gave the poison an added attraction for a murderer. By raising the possibility of suicide, strychnine deflected attention away from the killer. But suspicion of suicide also threatened whatever bequests the victim left behind. Suicides were by definition deranged, incapable of judging their best interests. They did not possess the sound mind necessary to execute legal documents.

DEATH COMES FOR MRS. STANFORD

CHAPTER 28

MOANA HOTEL

ON FEBRUARY 15, 1905, roughly a month after the Poland Spring Water incident, Bertha Berner and a maid, May Hunt, accompanied Jane Stanford on the steamship *Korea* departing San Francisco for Hawaii and Japan. There were large crowds and military bands on the dock to salute General Arthur MacArthur, the commander of the Department of the Pacific, who was on board. The passenger list misspelled Bertha Berner's name as Benner and listed their destination as Yokohama.[1]

Bertha Berner did not want to leave San Francisco. With a sick mother, she was not eager to be dragged off to Asia in the company of an imperious and rich woman. Jane Stanford also asked her niece Jennie Lathrop to accompany her, but, according to newspapers stories, Lathrop refused to come if Berner went. The newspapers did not say why. Jane Stanford chose Berner.[2]

Berner supposedly pleaded with Jane Stanford to reenlist Albert Beverly, her butler during her last trip overseas, but Stanford refused. She would not, she said, "take any man along with me."[3]

The S.S. *Korea* was not palatial like the luxury steamers plying the Atlantic, but it was grand enough. It was "handsomely fitted up with all modern improvements." It had electricity, commodious and tastefully furnished saloons, and first-class cuisine. There was a smoking room with a bar attached and a library. The captain was Japanese. The Chinese waiters were neat and attentive, but one traveler described the Chinese crew as a "half-starved, dirty looking crowd." Crew members ran a gambling operation in steerage.[4]

Berner spent the voyage to Honolulu trying to persuade Jane Stanford to return home after their stay in the islands and not to go on to Japan. Her efforts fell on deaf ears. Stanford was prepared for a long trip. She brought $75,000 worth of jewels (about $2 million today), and a vast wardrobe. Berner reported that Jane Stanford was morose when the voyage began, but her health improved on the ocean and her mood lightened when they reached Hawaii. During the voyage she spoke freely of the Poland Spring Water incident to General MacArthur and his wife, and also to Charles Sidney Dole, a Chicago grain merchant. When the *Korea* docked in Honolulu, Jane Stanford looked "well and hearty." She told reporters that she enjoyed ocean voyages and was never seasick.[5]

The United States had annexed Hawaii in 1898 and made it a territory in 1900, but American sugar planters dominated the islands well before that. They staged the coup against the Hawaiian monarchy in 1893 that set the stage for annexation. The islands were not like most other territories. Hawaii alone had a population that was both heavily non-white and heavily immigrant. In 1910 Chinese, Japanese, and Korean immigrants composed 55 percent of the population, outnumbering 26,000 native Hawaiians who made up 14 percent, while another 12,000 people were of mixed Hawaiian ancestry. Those classified as Caucasians made up 26 percent; half of them were Portuguese and about 5 percent Puerto Rican.[6]

As in other territories, the president appointed the leading officials. The economic, governmental, and professional elite of the islands was overwhelmingly Anglo, and some had attended Stanford or had Stanford connections. In 1903 Theodore Roosevelt appointed George W. Carter as Hawaii's new territorial governor. He did so after consulting, among others, David Starr Jordan, who knew the islands from his trips to study fish. Jordan, in turn, conferred with Judge Carl Smith of the Hawaiian legislature, who recommended Carter despite his being "dictatorial and lacking in diplomacy."[7]

Mrs. Stanford checked into the Moana Hotel on February 21, planning to stay for three weeks. The Moana opened on Waikiki Beach in 1901. Four stories tall, it was the costliest hotel on the island, noted for its broad lawn, its gardens, and a dining room—connected by a bridge with the main structure—that extended out over the ocean. Here she would stay among her own kind—affluent Americans, many with California connections.[8]

The hotel guests and May Hunt described Mrs. Stanford as friendly and seemingly content during her stay at the hotel.[9] She again talked openly about the attempt to poison her in January. Lallah Highton, who had known Jane Stanford for thirty years but exaggerated their intimacy, said that Stanford had told her that there was enough poison to kill twenty persons, and that she had come to Hawaii on "the advice of my friends," not her physician. Mrs. Highton said she was incredulous, that Jane Stanford must be deluded, but Bertha Berner assured her that the event had occurred. Mrs. Highton had the impression that Stanford feared the poisoner would follow her, but she never said this in so many words. Highton also reported that Jane Stanford avowed her belief in spiritualism, and her decision to establish a chair in psychic psychology at Stanford.[10]

In Jane Stanford's absence, the trustees' meetings that took place in February 1905 were largely devoted to necessary housekeeping business. When the Stanford Board of Trustees next convened in a special, ill-attended meeting in March, she would be dead. The board passed resolutions of respect.[11]

CHAPTER 29

WHEN SHE MET DEATH, SHE CALLED IT BY NAME

JANE STANFORD DIED in Honolulu on February 28, 1905, a Tuesday. The most thoroughly documented day of her life, it was distinguished only by its ending.

Mrs. Stanford arose about 8:30 a.m., her usual time, and prepared to take a carriage ride with Bertha Berner and May Hunt to the Pali, which was only five miles north of Honolulu and offered spectacular views of the Koolau cliffs along the Windward Coast. They had the driver go slowly; Mrs. Stanford wanted to prolong the trip as she took delight in the scenery. May Hunt recalled she "chartered [chattered] on" and sang during the trip. At about 1:00 they took lunch in a grove, staying there an hour and a half, but the lunch itself may have lasted only half an hour. Berner told the *Hawaiian Star* that the lunch prepared by the hotel consisted of sandwiches made of graham bread, Swiss cheese, tongue and lettuce, as well as hardboiled eggs, gingerbread, oranges, chocolate candy, and cold coffee. Stanford ate heartily of everything but the eggs. They stopped briefly at the royal mausoleum and again at Saks in Honolulu, where Jane Stanford gave instructions regarding a skirt she ordered.[1]

They arrived back at the hotel by 4:00, and Jane Stanford returned to her room and rested. She was in Room 120, while Berner and May Hunt shared nearby Room 122. At 6:30 she came to Bertha Berner's room, and the two women went down for dinner. They stopped on the verandah and spoke to a Mrs. Grinbaum, whom Jane Stanford told of the pleasant day.

Because of their generous lunch, dinner consisted only of a bowl of soup and took only ten minutes. Mrs. Stanford returned to the verandah and sat there until 8:00 or 8:15 p.m. She went to her room with Bertha Berner, asking her on the way to prepare her medicine, particularly the bicarbonate of soda.[2]

In Stanford's room Bertha Berner put a cascara capsule on the bed stand and, taking the small medicine basket from the larger telescope basket, removed a small bottle of bicarbonate. The bottle was two to two and a half inches tall and had a wide mouth big enough for a teaspoon. Berner asked May Hunt for a spoon, took out the half teaspoon of soda Jane Stanford requested, and left it beside the capsule. Jane Stanford said she wished to drink some water and "give it time to get out of my stomach" before taking the medicine.[3]

The cascara capsules were *cascara sagrada*, a laxative and a popular over-the-counter remedy at the turn of the century. The capsules commonly contained small amounts of strychnine mixed with cascara in the belief that they hastened the action of the laxative. The capsules had been prescribed for Berner, who took them for years and who swallowed one later that night with no ill effects. Jane Stanford apparently also took them. She urged Berner to take some of the bicarbonate also, but Berner demurred.[4]

Hunt and Berner left the room at about nine, but Jane Stanford called May Hunt back because she was having trouble locking the door. Hunt demonstrated how to use the lock and then went to bed. She woke to the sound of vomiting. It came from a man in the room next to hers, and she went back to sleep. Berner thought Stanford fell asleep without taking the medicine but awoke later and swallowed it. It's unclear why Berner thought this, unless she connected Stanford's death with the bicarbonate.[5]

Berner eventually went to sleep, only to be roused by Mrs. Stanford calling for her and May Hunt. Both women rushed to Jane Stanford's room and found her clutching the casing of the doorway. She was in distress, but conscious and articulate. "I am so sick," she said, and ordered them to get a doctor. She said she was awakened by a spasm and thrown from bed.[6]

They were apparently not the first ones to reach the room. The coroner's jury did not summon Adam Heunisch, who was in a room across the hall from Mrs. Stanford, but he did talk to a *Hawaiian Star* reporter. Mrs. Stanford's loud groaning awakened him, and on opening his door he found her standing in her doorway. She threw up her arms as if in great pain, proclaiming, "Oh I am so ill. Get me a doctor." Heunisch ran to the elevator to get Dr. Humphris, who lived at the hotel.[7]

While Berner, too, sought a doctor, May Hunt tried to get Jane Stanford back to her bed; Mrs. Stanford refused, continuing to cling to the door casing. Berner told the elevator boy to summon Dr. Humphris immediately, saying it was urgent and the doctor should not even bother to dress. Berner also mentioned a man, presumably Heunisch, rushing up the stairs to get Dr. Humphris. Humphris had retired at about 10:45 and was not yet asleep when he heard someone calling for a doctor. This was followed by a knock on his door. He could not remember the man who summoned him.[8]

Berner returned to the room and saw Jane Stanford coming toward her. Mrs. Stanford put her arm around Berner's shoulder, saying again, "I am so sick." She, too, tried to get Jane Stanford to go to bed, but when Mrs. Stanford again refused, they urged her to sit in a chair. She said she had no control over her body and that she had been poisoned again. Berner drew some warm water from the washstand and sought to get Stanford to drink it in order to induce vomiting, but Jane Stanford could not swallow. Her jaws were set. Berner rubbed her face with warm water and, when the spasm ended, got her to drink a glass of water. She and May Hunt were rubbing Mrs. Stanford's limbs when Dr. Humphris arrived.[9]

On seeing the doctor, Jane Stanford told him that she had been poisoned and wanted a stomach pump. When he asked how she knew, she said she was poisoned before and turned to Berner for verification. Berner told him of the poisoned Poland Spring Water, saying there was arsenic in it, then corrected herself and said strychnine.

Jane Stanford told him of being thrown from the bed by a spasm, but she said she was presently in no pain. He asked if she had taken any medicine. She said yes, and Berner told him about the cascara and the bicarbonate. Jane Stanford said that she took them after Berner and May Hunt left. Humphris asked for the bottles. He tasted the bicarbonate and was struck by its bitterness, which he associated with nux vomica or strychnia. Mrs. Stanford was by now drinking hot water very quickly, and Humphris, oddly for a doctor who said he detected the taste of strychnine, thought there was nothing wrong with her except for her "nervousness." He kept the bottles and left the room to get mustard and water to precipitate vomiting. He returned and while she drank the mixture, he went downstairs to telephone Dr. Day, another local physician, to bring a stomach pump.

Her attempts to vomit produced little result. There was a man standing in the doorway—presumably Adam Heunisch—whom Humphris asked to go to his room and bring his medicine bag, emergency bag, and chloroform or anesthetic bag. Mrs. Stanford continued to say she had been poisoned and was afraid she was dying.

May Hunt put Mrs. Stanford's feet in a basin of hot water and rubbed her legs. Dr. Humphris mixed new remedies hoping they would make her vomit. He was about to give her a mixture of chloral and bromine when she said her jaws were stiff. When Dr. Humphris felt them, the muscles were tight. He took the glass from her hand. As Bertha Berner watched the last powerful spasm overcome her, Jane Stanford said, "Oh God, forgive me my sins," followed by "Is my soul prepared to meet my dear ones?" Then she said, "This a horrible death to die." Her first words were predictable. Her last words were surprising. Jane Stanford rarely if ever used the word *death*. Confronted with death, she spoke its name.[10]

As the final spasm took hold, her body went rigid. The soles of her feet were turned inward toward each other, with the insteps arched extremely and the toes pointing forward. Her knees were widely separated. Her eyeballs protruded, her pupils dilated, her jaws were fixed, her fingers contracted, and the thumbs dug into the palms of her hands. Her respiration stopped. She never breathed again. From the time the doctor entered the room until the last spasm, ten minutes had passed.

This was not the end she expected. Jane Stanford imagined gliding into the afterlife as easily as her body would slide into the sarcophagus. The Reverend Ernest Warburton Shurtleff, the author of *The Shadow of an Angel*, one of her favorite books, wrote that the boundary between this life and the next was no more than a "bourn"—a brook easily passed over. "We hasten towards that bourn our loved to greet, / And death is but the kiss with which we meet." Rather than a kiss, her death proved a pummeling, and Jane Stanford struggled against it.[11]

Humphris had also sent for Dr. Murray, one of Honolulu's most respected physicians. He entered Jane Stanford's room as she expired. Dr. Humphris wordlessly motioned to the arched feet, the clinched hands, and the fixed jaws. These were the classic signs of strychnine poisoning. They each felt for a pulse. There was a slight flicker, and then nothing.

Humphris asked Murray if there was any reason for them to disguise the truth from themselves or others in the room. He said, "I don't think so." Humphris went downstairs to meet Dr. Day, who arrived, too late, with a stomach pump. Day and Murray examined the body. Murray's description of the body was the same as Dr. Humphris's. The evidence of the last spasm remained, and the rigidity and the arching of the feet struck Dr. Day, who had never seen them before. Humphris took possession of the vessel that contained a small amount of vomit, and the tumbler and spoon "with which the medicine had been mixed." He ordered a carriage so he could go and notify the authorities. Dr. Murray and Dr. Day took charge of the medicine containers.[12]

Through undersea cables that connected San Francisco and Hawaii after 1902, Dr. Humphris, presumably using information obtained from Bertha Berner, sent the news of Mrs. Stanford's death to her brother, Charles Lathrop. When the cable reached San Francisco, the operator placed a long-distance call to Palo Alto. Lathrop learned of his sister's death at 4:00 a.m. on March 1.[13]

Acting San Francisco Chief of Police John Spillane got word of the death that same day. He cabled the district attorney in Honolulu "suggesting that the stomach and body of Mrs. Stanford be chemically analyzed for poison before embalming take every precaution to detect evidence of crime." He clearly suspected she had been murdered.[14]

Leland Stanford, Jane Stanford, and Leland Stanford Jr. in 1878. *Stanford Family Photographs, Stanford University Special Collections & University Archives*

TOP LEFT: Jane Stanford with photographic brooch of Leland Stanford Jr., c. 1880s. *Stanford University Special Collections & University Archives*

TOP RIGHT: Thomas Welton Stanford, Jane Stanford's brother-in-law, university donor, and a leading spiritualist in Australia. *Stanford Family Photographs, Stanford University Special Collections & University Archives*

BOTTOM: The site of the first poisoning attempt: Jane Stanford's bedroom in the Stanford mansion, Nob Hill, c. 1880. *Eadweard Muybridge Photographs. Stanford Special Collections & University Archives*

Bertha Berner in front of Jane Stanford's summer house on the Palo Alto stock farm, c. 1900. Berner was in her thirties at the time. *Stanford University Special Collections & University Archives*

In Egypt, 1904: Jane Stanford (seated center), Elizabeth Richmond, her maid (at left), with her secretary, Bertha Berner, and her butler, Albert Beverly, on camels. *Stanford Family Photographs, Stanford University Special Collections & University Archives*

The "Stone Age" at Stanford before the earthquake of 1906: the Memorial Arch, the statue of the Stanford family, and the Memorial Church, all funded by Jane Stanford to commemorate her family. *Stanford University Special Collections & University Archives*

Some of the undergraduate women whose presence so alarmed Jane Stanford during the last years of her life. *Stanford University Special Collections & University Archives*

TOP LEFT: David Starr Jordan, the first president of Stanford University, who served from 1891 to 1913. *Biographical Photographs, Stanford University Special Collections & University Archives*

TOP RIGHT: Edward Alsworth Ross, professor of sociology, whose dismissal provoked a crisis at Stanford in 1900. *Biographical Photographs, Stanford University Special Collections & University Archives*

BOTTOM LEFT: George Crothers, the shrewd lawyer and trustee of Leland Stanford Junior University, whose resemblance to Leland Jr. attracted Jane Stanford. Crothers knew where all the bodies were buried. *Biographical Photographs, Stanford University Special Collections & University Archives*

BOTTOM RIGHT: Charles Lathrop, Stanford official and Jane Stanford's younger brother. *Stanford Family Photographs, Stanford University Special Collections & University Archives*

TOP: Market Street, San Francisco, 1905, showing the *San Francisco Chronicle* building (background right with clock tower) and the *San Francisco Call* building (background left with dome). *William M. McCarthy Photograph Collection, California State Archives, Sacramento*

BOTTOM LEFT: Fremont Older, the crusading editor of the *San Francisco Bulletin* from 1895 to 1918, whose war against Boss Abe Ruef of San Francisco involved him in Chinatown and the investigation of the poisoning of Jane Stanford. *San Francisco Historical Photograph Collection, San Francisco History Center, San Francisco Public Library*

BOTTOM RIGHT: Jeremiah Dinan as chief of police. He was earlier a detective investigating the poisoning of Jane Stanford. *San Francisco Historical Photograph Collection, San Francisco History Center, San Francisco Public Library*

Officers of the Chinese Six Companies. The Six Companies operated as an unofficial government of Chinatown. *Bancroft Library, University of California, Berkeley*

Chinatown Police Raiding Squad, 1890s. The raiding squad was notorious for its extralegal assaults on Chinese organizations, both criminal and legitimate, in Chinatown. *Bancroft Library, University of California, Berkeley*

Jane Stanford's death mask. *Iris & B. Gerald Cantor Center for Visual Arts at Stanford University; courtesy of Department of Special Collections, Stanford Libraries*

View of Memorial Church through the Memorial Arch following the earthquake of 1906: Leland Stanford Junior University in ruins. *General Photographs, Stanford Special Collections & University Archives*

CHAPTER 30

GEORGE CROTHERS
COMES HOME

WHEN HE RECEIVED NEWS of Jane Stanford's death, George Crothers was standing on a railroad platform in Tucson, Arizona. He and his brother had invested in a Mexican mine—the San Juan Grande—and he was traveling to Chihuahua to conclude its sale. Twenty minutes later, he was on his way back to San Francisco.[1]

Crothers returned to California with as much fear as sorrow. He held Jane Stanford's power of attorney, and he expected her family and heirs to contest her will and attack the Pacific Improvement Company Trust, of which he was the sole trustee. To do so, they would attack him by accusing him of undue influence, which was why he had long sought to mask his very real influence over Jane Stanford.

That was only one danger and not the chief one. For some reason, Crothers had carried a copy of Jane Stanford's farewell letter with him to Arizona; he left it with his friend and ally in the Ross Affair, Walter Rose. Crothers did not mention the letter to the police or the Morse detectives, "lest its contents be misjudged and its importance exaggerated in consequence of its possible misinterpretation." As he said later, "one reason I did not disclose the Stanford letter to more than one . . . [was that] the public would have said that she must have committed suicide." Suicide could indicate a lack of mental capacity and create an opening for challenges to her wills and trusts. Her letter could provide a thread that if pulled could unravel everything, including the very survival of the university. He was determined to transfer her assets that he controlled to Stanford University before his authority and the legitimacy of Jane Stanford's gifts and grants to the university could be questioned.[2]

On his return to San Francisco, Crothers immediately tendered the Pacific Improvement stock to the Stanford Board of Trustees. It represented several million dollars that the university could not receive under California law and the terms of Stanford's will. He asked the trustees for a waiver of liability for any claims made against him by Jane Stanford's heirs, but the board members refused, afraid they would be deemed financially liable. Fearing that the board's delay would invite a challenge that would prevent the transfer, Crothers delivered the stock anyway. He and his brother waived their trustee and attorney's fees. He, with Charles Lathrop's help, moved quickly to settle the estate and avoid challenges.[3]

CROTHERS NEVER SUSPECTED that Mrs. Stanford would die as she did when he persuaded her not to dismiss the Wilson brothers as her attorneys, and to retain Timothy Hopkins, Mountford Wilson, and her brother Charles Lathrop as executors for her estate. Crothers thought it "expedient" to hold them in line as "friends." He feared all could credibly accuse him of undue influence.[4] Protecting the university's endowment meant that three men Jane Stanford distrusted and wanted dismissed—Mountford Wilson, David Starr Jordan, and Timothy Hopkins—would play crucial roles in the investigation of her death.

Protecting the university took precedence over solving the murder for Crothers. No one else who knew so much said so little, at least in 1905. Only years later did Crothers reveal the existence of the two letters Jane Stanford had sent him. He said Berner's shorthand notes for the second letter should be in the university archives. Like all other Berner materials, they have disappeared.[5]

Even as he withheld evidence, Crothers, virtually alone among the Stanford inner circle, publicly insisted that she had been poisoned. "Facts," he said, "are stubborn things," and he believed the same person was responsible for both poisonings. He said, "I know that Mrs. Stanford desired the apprehension of the culprit and I believe that every effort will be made to carry out her wish."[6] But he knew that the second half of the sentence was not true.

THE INVESTIGATION BEGINS

CHAPTER 31

THE HIGH SHERIFF

BEFORE MIDNIGHT ON FEBRUARY 28, Dr. Humphris left Jane Stanford's body in her hotel room and took a carriage to report her death. Given that his patient died claiming to be poisoned, that a witness verified a previous attempt to poison her, that the body showed the classic signs of strychnine poisoning, and that the bicarbonate of soda the victim ingested tasted of strychnine, reporting the death to the authorities seemed the prudent thing to do. High Sheriff William Henry dispatched Deputy High Sheriff William T. Rawlins to the Moana Hotel. He arrived a little after midnight, inspected the room, and took possession of the bottle of bicarbonate of soda from Dr. Humphris. He was told "by people at the hotel" that there was strychnine mixed with the soda. He tried to talk to Bertha Berner and May Hunt but could not get a coherent account from either one. They were "completely prostrated by the shock." As required to assess suspicious deaths, he enlisted a coroner's jury. It was made up of employees and others associated with the hotel.[1] The Hawaiian investigation had begun.

High Sheriff Henry, in office only since October, was a prominent Republican whose previous police experience was as a prison warden. His ascent was messy and secretive. Territorial Governor George W. Carter had hired a private detective to investigate Henry's predecessor, Arthur Brown, to whom Carter was related by marriage. The detective discovered that Brown "had not only debauched the office, but that his private life was immoral." The corruption was the usual stuff—"gambling and vice," blackmail, and bribery "carried on with the Orientals"—and difficult to prove. Carter removed Brown from office, but did not give the cause "for it would be such a cruel blow to his wife."[2] He kept the investigation quiet.

Deputy High Sheriff Rawlins possessed even less police experience than Henry. He was born in Hawaii and received a law degree from Yale. He became deputy high sheriff in 1904, having previously served as a magistrate and a referee in bankruptcy cases.[3]

Henry and Rawlins could not compensate for their own inexperience by tapping a deep pool of experienced homicide investigators. In 1904 there were only eighteen arrests for murder in the territory, and these resulted in five convictions, an unimpressive record for the police. High Sheriff Henry regarded serious crime as the domain of the darker races—Japanese and Puerto Ricans; this was also his opinion of lesser crimes. Hawaiians, Japanese, and Chinese filled the local jails and prisons for gambling, liquor offenses, and disorderly conduct. Judges sentenced few women of any race to prison.[4]

The poisoning of an immensely wealthy white woman traveling with white servants in which no one was drunk, no robbery seems to have occurred, and sex does not seem to have crossed anyone's mind left the high sheriff and his deputy adrift on uncharted seas. It also put them under a national spotlight. Governor Carter made it clear from the beginning that he was watching the investigation closely. Carter met with Henry and his attorney general on March 1, the same day that Acting Chief of Police Spillane in San Francisco cabled, urging an autopsy and a criminal investigation. Carter delegated authority over the investigation to the high sheriff. Henry guarded it jealously, seeking to avoid any interference from the attorney general's office, but the two men continued to confer.[5]

On the morning of March 1, between 9:00 a.m. and noon, Dr. Clifford B. Wood conducted an autopsy on Jane Stanford's body in the morgue of Queen's Hospital. Dr. Humphris, Dr. Murray, Dr. Day, and Professor Duncan, who was a chemist, were all present. Other physicians also observed the autopsy, as did the undertaker. There was no solid food in the stomach. Wood examined the organs and found nothing notable. There was no evidence of "blood clots in the heart." She had not suffered a heart attack.[6]

Dr. Wood, told of the suspicion of strychnine, was looking for it. Since the only other cause of death that produced symptoms similar to strychnine was tetanus, he examined the body carefully for wounds. He found none. He then looked for the telltale signs of rigidity indicative of strych-

nine poisoning. He found it in the jaws, legs, and feet, but he was surprised not to find it in the upper arm and neck. The undertaker explained
that rigidity was present when he received the body, and he was forced
to break it up to put a gown on the corpse. The forearms were still rigid.
Wood particularly noted the feet: they "were turned in; that is, the soles of
the feet were turned inward towards the center of the body more than they
naturally would. The instep was arched, the bottom of the foot drawn up
and the toes were strongly extended," that is "turned backward and not
turned down." He concluded that the "post mortem appearances found in
cases of strichnia poisoning . . . correspond with the post mortem appearances . . . found at this autopsy." His examination of the body failed to
detect any other "sufficient cause of death." The symptoms "were indicative of death due to strichnia."[7]

Dr. Wood turned the heart over to Dr. Day for preservation. Professor
Duncan had already received the bicarbonate of soda and cascara capsules,
and the small amount of vomit collected in the hotel room. According to
the autopsy report, he now received urine extracted from the bladder. He
also received the stomach and its contents, the intestine and its contents,
the kidneys, and the liver.[8]

There was a discrepancy between what the autopsy report said Professor Duncan was given and what he later testified he received. He said he
received "a bottle containing urine, the contents of the stomach, the contents of the intestinal tract below the stomach, contents of intestines, the
two kidneys, the liver, I think that is all."[9] His omission of the stomach
and the intestines themselves is puzzling. Duncan and Dr. Shorey would
conduct the chemical analysis. They, too, were looking for evidence of
strychnine.

Only after the autopsy did Jane Stanford's body go to the undertaker
for embalming. The next day, on March 2, Joseph Rosenstein made a
death mask, which today is in the Stanford Special Collections.[10] Stanford's skin is wrinkled particularly on her neck, with crow's feet near her
eyes. Her hair seems matted and wet, as if it had merged with the wax or
plaster cast. Her eyes are shut, her lips thin, her mouth pursed. She looks
stern and, unsurprisingly, dead.

High Sheriff Henry decided not to release the results of the autopsy
until he received the chemist's report. The failure to make an official statement contributed to leaks and rumors. On March 1, both the *Hawaiian
Star* and the *Pacific Commercial Advertiser* reported that Mrs. Stanford

died of strychnine poisoning. They also reported that there was strychnine
in the bottle of bicarbonate of soda, which bore the name of a druggist in
Adelaide, Australia. The papers claimed that "[h]alf a dozen people recognized the bitter sign of the deadly crystal."[11]

By March 2 there were reports that the autopsy indicated "tetanus of
the respiratory organs," rendering it "almost a certainty that death was
due to strychnine and that the bicarbonate of soda contained strychnine."
High Sheriff Henry reportedly sent a cable to San Francisco's Acting Chief
of Police Spillane stating that there were 662 grains of strychnine in the
bicarbonate. This was enough to kill a regiment. He then denied having
sent the cable, and the San Francisco police could not find the original.
It is possible that Henry confused the amount of bicarbonate and the
amount of strychnine and tried to cover up his mistake. The controversy
over the cablegram persisted for a month. On March 3, Dr. Murray stated
that strychnine definitely caused the death of Jane Stanford.[12]

BERTHA BERNER AND MAY HUNT remained secluded immediately following Mrs. Stanford's death. The first newspaper stories described Berner as
a middle-aged woman, but in succeeding stories the papers printed photographs in which she appeared young and attractive.

Berner soon seemed to have a compulsion to talk.

On March 1, the same day as the autopsy, High Sheriff Henry interrogated both Bertha Berner and May Hunt at the Moana Hotel. Berner
also gave a statement to a *Hawaiian Star* reporter that morning detailing
the events of the previous day and affirming the attempt to poison Jane
Stanford in San Francisco. She provided specific details. She described the
bottle thought to contain the poisoned bicarbonate "as an ordinary small
bottle with a top that screwed on." That afternoon Deputy High Sheriff
Rawlins interviewed her again.[13]

From the beginning, High Sheriff Henry's investigation bumped up
against influential men with Stanford connections. Dr. Humphris asked
ex-judge W. L. Stanley, who was staying in the Moana Hotel, to represent temporarily the interests of the Stanford estate. Humphris wired
Jordan, who approved Stanley, even though Jordan had no authority to
act for the estate.[14] On March 2, Mrs. Stanford's official representatives—
presumably Charles Lathrop and Mountford Wilson—took charge and

appointed J. F. Hackfeld to represent the estate. Hackfeld was not a lawyer but was one of the richest and most powerful men in Hawaii.[15] Stanley also continued on as counsel.

Reporters noticed that, although he claimed to do no questioning, Stanley worked closely with the police and was present at examinations of Bertha Berner. He and Hackfeld accompanied Deputy Rawlins in the search of the effects of the dead woman.[16]

On March 3, High Sheriff Henry said May Hunt was not under suspicion. He did not clear Bertha Berner, saying only that she was not under surveillance. The same day the *San Francisco Call* reported rumors circulating in Honolulu that Berner told police that she thought Ah Wing placed the poison in the Poland Spring Water in the earlier incident.[17]

The tension between Berner and Ah Wing could only have increased when Berner learned that Ah Wing had told Callundan during his January investigation in San Francisco that Berner was the only one who ever gave Jane Stanford her Poland Spring Water. If Berner did accuse Ah Wing, she quickly retracted it. She said that neither she nor Jane Stanford ever voiced any suspicion as to the identity of her poisoner.[18]

It appeared the suspects were implicating each other.

CHAPTER 32

THE CASE IN
SAN FRANCISCO

JANE STANFORD'S DEATH slammed like a torpedo into Jules Callundan's narrative of the Poland Spring Water poisoning. His story of a quarrel between servants that never endangered Jane Stanford floated on a living Jane Stanford. Now that she was dead and once again there was strychnine in a bottle, the story listed and threatened to sink. Her demise took over the front pages of San Francisco newspapers and remained there for days.

Lathrop, Wilson, and the detectives did not abandon ship. Charles Lathrop and Mountford Wilson insisted that Jane Stanford died a natural death. Lathrop and Wilson dismissed the reports of a second poisoning as absurd. They offered a grab bag of causes: she was sick with bronchitis, or killed by a heart attack, or apoplexy, or "some similar trouble" killed her. Harry Morse said he could not bring himself "to believe that Mrs. Stanford has been poisoned."[1]

The newspapers floated other options: suicide or murder. Some of her friends—usually anonymous—asserted that she had shown no signs of depression or derangement, but the *Examiner* reported "tales that Mrs. Stanford had brooded some since Christmas and that poison was ever in her mind. It is thought by some that she wished to hasten the end—that she yearned to leave a life of loneliness and join her husband and son in the life beyond—the life of which she thought she had evidence of eye and ear through spiritual revelation." The papers thought the evidence pointed toward murder rather than suicide, but they hedged. They continued to say that no one possessed a motive for murder.[2]

Leaks by the Honolulu doctors, and Bertha Berner's acknowledgment that there was an attempt to poison Jane Stanford in San Francisco, began to erode the wall of denial. Harry Morse shifted to agnosticism: "I do not know what to think about it." If it turned out that she died of strychnine poisoning, he would "certainly be stumped." David Starr Jordan scoffed at the idea of suicide or an accidental poisoning. But Jordan also said that with the news from Honolulu "he was almost compelled to believe that Mrs. Stanford was foully murdered."[3]

―――――

JANE STANFORD'S DEATH brought San Francisco's police department into the investigation of the first poisoning, which inevitably bled into the poisoning in Honolulu. The department was in deep disarray. John Spillane served as acting chief because the Board of Police Commissioners had suspended Chief George Wittman while it investigated a Chinatown gambling scandal.[4] Spillane regarded Jane Stanford's death as suspicious, but information from the authorities in Hawaii was slow in coming. The department took its cues from Mountford Wilson and Charles Lathrop. The Morse Agency detectives worked alongside the police.

The so-called yellow press put its collective nose to the ground at any hint of scandal. Reporters swarmed the case, filling the newspapers with contradictory interviews, conjectures, gossip, and stories. They wanted scoops to sell newspapers. Even as the newspapers reported on the investigation of her death, they investigated on their own, sometimes more thoroughly if no more reliably than the police department. For all its energy, the press had a short attention span; it would not stay with Jane Stanford's death unless it produced a constant stream of sensational discoveries.

―――――

ACTING CHIEF SPILLANE put Chief of Detectives Joseph Burnett in charge of the investigation of the Poland Spring Water incident. The stakes were high. Murders focused attention on motive, and motives led to money, and money involved trusts and wills. Jane Stanford's wills and trusts were already open to questions regarding her testamentary capacity, but the publicity of a murder trial would amplify the danger to perilous proportions. A murder trial could reveal the controversies within the university, resurrect old scandals, and reveal new ones. All this would embarrass and threaten important people and institutions.

Anyone who cared to glance at the San Francisco legal newspaper, *The Recorder*, could grasp the grounds for challenging wills and trusts in assertions of testatrix insanity. Civil procedure admitted the testimony of intimate acquaintances. Crothers had long feared that Timothy Hopkins and others could repeat their comments about how "queer" Jane Stanford was, and no one wanted testimony on her reliance on spirits. Wills could be challenged because they went against "natural instincts of justice," and here Jane Stanford's treatment of Jennie Lathrop and Asa Stanford presented embarrassing dangers. Undue influence on the person signing the wills and trusts was, as George Crothers recognized, a landmine that threatened to blow up everything he had drafted for Stanford. He did his best to disguise his work, but the evidence remained that without his intervention far more Stanford money would have gone to the family and probably to the Catholic Church. The legal bar for overturning wills and trusts was high, but even failed attempts would reveal information that would batter Leland Stanford Junior University's already shaky reputation.[5]

Suicide would be even worse. Many would regard it as prima facie evidence of insanity, which if it tipped over her will could send that document careening backward to take down the trusts established for the university.

The Stanford estate and the university feared both murder and suicide, but the investigation also depended on what Mayor Schmitz and Abe Ruef wanted. Abe Ruef headed the Union Labor Party machine that ran San Francisco and elected Eugene Schmitz as mayor to succeed Phelan. If Acting Chief Spillane wanted to please Schmitz and Ruef, then the detectives assigned to the case needed to please Spillane. Two of these detectives, Jerry Dinan and Ed Wren, were quite accomplished at pleasing their superiors.[6]

Jerry Dinan practiced the "stool pigeon" school of detective work. He managed the San Francisco underworld by cooperating with it. Joe "Kid" Sullivan, a notorious pickpocket, was head of a ring of other pickpockets, thieves, and bunko artists who divided the city up among them. Sullivan fed information to Dinan about criminals outside his organization. Dinan, in return, protected Sullivan's men, and when Sullivan flagged the arrival of out-of-town thieves, the police made sure they left or were arrested. When Sullivan's cronies robbed connected and influential people, the police made the thieves restore the goods. If out-of-town victims filed complaints that made it to court, Sullivan intervened, made restitution, and ensured that the victim did not show up. This was witness tampering and a felony, but the police did not go looking for the witnesses. Dinan and Sullivan became friends as well as associates.[7]

The police regularly took payments from those whose livelihoods were proscribed or regulated by law: prostitutes, madams, brothel keepers, liquor dealers, saloon owners, and gamblers. These payments came from the Barbary Coast, from Chinatown, and from the city's French restaurants that rented out rooms for prostitution. Only some of the money stayed in the pockets of the patrolmen and detectives who collected it. The police funneled cash upward into the hands of politicians, which by 1905 was the administration of Schmitz and Ruef.[8]

The newspapers make it clear that neither the Morse detectives nor the San Francisco police were the type of sleuths who left no stones unturned. Reporters kept stumbling onto rather obvious leads unexplored by detectives. Nora Hopkins (no relation to Timothy), the maid who cleaned Mrs. Stanford's room in the mansion, for example, would seem high on the list of people to question, but until reporters talked to her, no one else did. She had her own resentments. She quarreled with Mrs. Stanford, who refused to allow a male employee from the stock farm to visit her. She, like so many others, resented Stanford's interference in her private life.[9]

CHAPTER 33

THE MEDICINE BOTTLE

THE STORY OF THE MEDICINE BOTTLE that contained the strychnine-laced bicarbonate that Jane Stanford swallowed was all over the papers in March of 1905. The bottle had a wide mouth to accommodate a teaspoon. It had its place of origin—Adelaide, Australia—written on it. Bertha Berner recognized the danger the distinctive bottle presented to her; in 1905 it became a kind of daemon demanding that she speak its name. High Sheriff Henry regarded it as the key to the entire investigation.

Bertha Berner's story kept changing. On March 1, she told the *Hawaiian Star* that Mrs. Stanford bought the bottle in Adelaide. She insisted that she never refilled the bottle for Mrs. Stanford and possessed no knowledge of how it got refilled. She said Jane Stanford took bicarbonate only occasionally.[1]

Two days later she still maintained that Mrs. Stanford took bicarbonate only when her stomach was upset, but she was evasive, claiming that she was not "clear as to that bottle with the label bicarbonate of soda. The label says Adelaide, Australia, but I do not recall her having purchased a bottle at that place. I did not purchase it nor do I know of anyone who did or when Mrs. Stanford came to buy it. In any event she had that bottle a long time, but I have no distinct recollection of the purchase of it. It was brought here [to Hawaii] from California, but how much medicine there was inside it when we left San Francisco I cannot say. I supposed it contained bicarbonate of soda. I cannot recall ever having had the bottle refilled for her or getting any medicine for her. I presume, however, she kept the bottle for such a purpose and had it refilled either by sending it out or getting someone to buy soda for her."[2]

She contradicted that account the same day. She and Hunt agreed that the bottle had been filled in San Francisco and left untouched for five weeks before Jane Stanford departed for Hawaii. But May Hunt had no way of knowing this. She had not been employed by Jane Stanford five weeks before the departure. She was hired only days before Mrs. Stanford left for Honolulu.[3]

Berner suspected that she had said too much, or more likely, representatives of the Stanford estate realized it. Judge Stanley monitored her, and acting on the advice of the police and her "attorney," she said she would no longer talk to reporters about the poisoning.[4]

Berner's stories about the bottle, meant to dispel suspicion, only intensified it. While detectives were looking for the strychnine, reporters discovered the provenance and history of the bottle. In reality, there was very little mystery about it. Albert Beverly purchased the bottle in Adelaide, Australia, and it originally contained candy. When Jane Stanford admired it, he gave it to her. She used it for her bicarbonate of soda when she traveled. Elizabeth Richmond, who said Jane Stanford used bicarbonate frequently, remembered that Mrs. Stanford filled the bottle in New York, presumably during her trip in November and December 1904.[5] If Jane Stanford did not regularly use bicarbonate of soda, the bottle should not have needed refilling as soon after the new year as Berner remembered.

Detectives and reporters reasoned that if they found an uncontaminated source for the soda in the bottle, then accidental poisoning could be ruled out. The strychnine must have been added after the bottle was filled. Detectives found cans of pure soda in the Stanford mansions in Palo Alto and San Francisco; the Palo Alto can was full, but the San Francisco can was missing a scoopful.[6] Someone could have replenished the bottle from the can in San Francisco, and maybe someone did, but there was no telling when—nor if it was the bicarbonate in the bottle that went to Hawaii.

Locating a purchase of bicarbonate just before the departure for Hawaii seemed the most likely way to identify the source of the soda in the bottle. The closer the time of purchase, the fresher the bicarbonate, and the more likely Jane Stanford bought it for the trip. On March 3, the *Examiner* announced that the bicarbonate that contained the dose of strychnine that killed Jane Stanford was purchased at the Palo Alto Pharmacy in late

December or January. They identified a purchaser: "a person by the name of Schwab who was formerly a drug clerk here."[7]

Schwab worked at the Stanford Pharmacy for a year, and "being discharged" went to work at Weingarten's drugstore. He left Palo Alto for San Francisco in early or mid-February—the same time that Bertha Berner and Jane Stanford returned to the city—but he was accused of embezzlement, arrested, and brought back to Palo Alto. He settled the charges and returned to San Francisco.[8]

Despite his checkered experience in Palo Alto, Schwab was not suspected of being "in any manner connected with the crime, but, owing to his knowledge of drugs and chemicals, is supposed to have been requested to make the purchase as a matter of accommodation for the person under suspicion." The *Examiner* identified the "person under suspicion" as "a discharged ex-employee" of Jane Stanford. The details made it clear that the paper referred to Albert Beverly. "[H]e was in league with some other persons who were in a position to gain access to the Nob Hill mansion." The ex-employee in question had been discharged for taking rake-offs on Mrs. Stanford's purchases and supposedly threatened to get even. The information came from members of the Stanford/Lathrop household—almost certainly Charles Lathrop and a night watchman, Peter Pohl.[9]

As an attempt to smear Beverly, the story was clear enough, but otherwise it made no sense. There was no special knowledge necessary to purchase bicarbonate, and no one needed the cooperation of an ex-druggist to get it.

The next day, March 4, an *Examiner* reporter—maybe the same one, maybe not—interviewed W. E. Jackson, a clerk at the Stanford Pharmacy in Palo Alto. He said that on February 6, Bertha Berner and Jane Stanford visited the store to buy, among other things, bicarbonate of soda. Mrs. Stanford asked if he had a wide-mouthed bottle into which she could put a spoon, but Berner interrupted and asked him to put it into a package because "we have a bottle home that we always use for bicarbonate of soda." He prepared a package of soda and recorded the sale in the pharmacy's account books.[10]

Bertha Berner clearly knew about the bottle, and she was involved in a recent purchase of bicarbonate. Jackson dated the purchase a little over a week before Jane Stanford departed for Hawaii. He contradicted virtually everything Bertha Berner had said about her knowledge of the bottle and the bicarbonate.

Reporters apparently cabled Berner for comment on the *Examiner* stories. She now recalled her visit to the pharmacy. She and Mrs. Stanford drove—presumably in a carriage that met the train—to the drugstore, opposite the depot. Jane Stanford wished to purchase some cologne and "a few other articles." Jackson said that it was Berner who asked for the bicarbonate in a package so they could put it into the bottle themselves, but Bertha, still trying to distance herself from the bottle, said she asked the clerk to put the soda in a bottle, but he could only find a narrow-necked bottle not large enough to admit a teaspoon. Mrs. Stanford then asked that he put the soda in a paper package, which was bundled with their other purchases. Mrs. Stanford retained the soda. In San Francisco, preparing for the trip to Hawaii, the drugs were packed last. In looking at the various bottles and packages on the table, Mrs. Stanford declared that she did not wish to take a whole apothecary's shop and brought out an old bottle of bicarbonate, which could only have been the Adelaide bottle. She packed it, saying she did not want to be "a hypo," "her favorite expression for hypochondria." To the best of Berner's recollections, the new bicarbonate bought in Palo Alto was not placed in the bottle and was left behind.[11]

The *Examiner* published Jackson's interview in a column next to Bertha Berner's revised account, and they added excerpts from Berner's previous statements, which put Bertha Berner's inconsistencies and contradictions into such stark relief that they looked very much like lies. She clearly wanted nothing to do with the Palo Alto bicarbonate. The *Chronicle* asked how Berner could have forgotten the Palo Alto purchase on February 6, while she remembered the exact date—February 9—that May Hunt placed the bicarbonate in the trunk. The paper used the two dates to create a window of three days—seventy-two hours—in which both the new bicarbonate and/or the poison could have been placed in the bottle in San Francisco. Richmond and Beverly could not have been involved. They had left Stanford's service long before those seventy-two hours.[12]

The story of the purchase proved problematic for Berner, but it also served as a red herring distracting readers from other equally significant developments. Without a connection between the bicarbonate and Beverly, reporters largely lost interest in Schwab. They should not have. Buried in a larger *Examiner* story, there was an account that on the evening of March 3, the police "interviewed James Guilfoyle of Eighth and Howard Streets about the disappearance of T. J. Schwab from Palo Alto." "Guilfoyle" was actually Guilfoy. He lived on Capp Street, not on Eighth and Howard, but he and his sons did operate a metal factory at the Eighth Street address. They made cornices.[13]

The detectives were looking for Schwab because "[i]t has been stated that Schwab was on such friendly terms with Miss Berner that he could have given her the poison without making a memorandum of the fact while he was employed in a pharmacy near the university. Guilfoyle could tell nothing, however, of importance, and his statement was passed over as mere conjecture."[14] The *Examiner* did not report how Guilfoy knew Schwab or what he said about him. Although the newspaper published two addresses for Schwab, there was no report that the detectives visited him.

Someone—the paper did not say who—connected Schwab with Bertha Berner. Schwab had access to strychnine, which he could have obtained without making an entry in the poison book all pharmacies were required to keep. Somehow—no one explained how—this was connected with James Guilfoy in San Francisco.

T. J. Schwab was a person of interest who potentially linked Berner and a source of strychnine, but who was T. J. Schwab? The *Examiner* not only got Guilfoy's name wrong, it also got Schwab's. He was actually P. J. Schwab.

Well over a century later, I can find Paul J. Schwab in the city directory for Palo Alto in 1904. He lives in the University Hotel and lists his occupation as an insurance salesman. Other records show he lived previously in the nearby communities of Santa Clara, San Jose, and Mountain View, where he was employed as a clerk and a druggist. He was married and well enough established in Mountain View to have become the clerk of the new town. He ran his own drugstore there, but it seems to have ended badly with a sheriff's sale in 1903.[15]

So why was he living in a hotel in Palo Alto in 1904? That summer his wife, Katie, whom he married in 1900, filed for divorce on the grounds of "cruelty and desertion." By 1904 the Schwabs' marriage had collapsed, and he left his wife and moved to Palo Alto where, gossip had it, he was friendly with Bertha Berner. Schwab was in his mid-thirties. He was a German immigrant, and she spoke German. The detectives talked to Guilfoy and dropped the matter.[16]

Their lack of curiosity is stunning.

THE

INVESTIGATION

CHAPTER 34

SUSPECTS

IN HAWAII AND SAN FRANCISCO the official investigation of Jane Stanford's death held fire until the coroner's jury assigned an official cause of death. But this did not stop the San Francisco papers from becoming a kaleidoscope of suspects and suspicions. In their reporting, the Poland Spring Water poisoning merged with the Hawaii poisoning. Two poisonings of the same person within six weeks were more likely connected than coincidental. Reporters and editors promised startling revelations, suspects in high places, and detectives with tightly held secrets.[1]

The *San Francisco Post* claimed that the Hawaii high sheriff had placed Bertha Berner under virtual arrest in Honolulu, and that she would return to San Francisco in the custody of Detective Sergeant Harry Reynolds of the San Francisco Police Department. There were rumors of an "arch-instigator," who fashioned the entire plot. Charles Lathrop and those connected with him suggested that Albert Beverly masterminded Jane Stanford's death. George Crothers later said that rumors circulated that Beverly put Elizabeth Richmond up to it.[2]

The newspapers agreed that Bertha Berner, Ah Wing, Elizabeth Richmond, and Albert Beverly were the leading suspects in the Poland Spring Water poisoning and, by extension, in the Hawaii poisoning. They sometimes included Ah Young because he was the only Chinese servant besides Ah Wing with access to Mrs. Stanford's room.[3]

Bertha Berner became the human homonym at the center of the case: on hearing her name people took away different meanings. She provoked both suspicion and sympathy. The Morse detectives, the Stanford family, the Stanford estate, and David Starr Jordan proclaimed her innocence. The San Francisco Police Department initially thought her a potential suspect, as did the high sheriff in Honolulu. Reporters recognized that her stories did not add up.[4]

Jules Callundan, still heading the Morse investigation, resisted any theory of either case that implicated Berner. He had already made her the real victim of the Poland Spring Water poisoning by arguing that the rat poison was added to the bottle so that the blame would fall on her; to suspect her of the murder was to say he had bungled that investigation and cost Jane Stanford her life.[5]

San Francisco reporters had to rely on Hawaiians to interview Bertha Berner, but they could talk to her brother and mother. Or rather, they could try. They demanded to know what August Berner, who was still guarding his mother with a shotgun, was trying to hide. When they discovered that Bertha and her mother exchanged letters in German, reporters concluded that they must be trying to hide something. On March 2, Maria Berner reportedly "intimated" that her daughter had told her that both Bertha and Jane Stanford suspected Ah Wing, but the reporters may have jumped to that conclusion. Maria Berner said only that it was "a man and some others connected with him." This could have been Ah Wing, but it also could have been Albert Beverly and Elizabeth Richmond. It could also have been David Starr Jordan. After a visit from Morse detectives, Maria Berner refused to repeat or explain the accusation.[6]

———

THE BERNERS KNEW SOMETHING. The newspaper stories of March 4 about Bertha Berner's purchase of bicarbonate, her friendship with Schwab, and renewed attention from reporters panicked an already alarmed August Berner. David Starr Jordan and Timothy Hopkins were to depart for Hawaii on March 4 to escort Jane Stanford's body home. A frantic August Berner rushed more than thirty miles to San Francisco to talk to them. He arrived too late.[7]

Although there was no way he could have directly introduced the poison into the bottle, Albert Beverly emerged as the central suspect in the Poland Spring Water poisoning in the week following Jane Stanford's death. He supposedly instigated the crime, and someone else acted as his agent.[8] And if he could be linked to the San Francisco poisoning, then investigators might be able to connect him to Jane Stanford's death in Hawaii.

Reporters needed a motive, and they repackaged the Morse Detective Agency theory of quarrels among the servants. The details, often contradictory, varied between papers. There was a falling out between Richmond and Berner over Beverly. Or, perhaps, Beverly and Berner quarreled, with Beverly blaming Berner for his departure. A bitter Beverly with the aid of Richmond sought revenge on both Jane Stanford and on Bertha Berner. Richmond, too, supposedly disliked Berner.[9]

The newspapers painted Beverly as an angry man who had lost his job and his home, and who anticipated a legacy in Stanford's will and feared losing it. After either Jane Stanford or Charles Lathrop asked Beverly to leave the house near the stock farm, it flooded, causing significant damage. The cause was variously given as broken pipes, water left running, and purposefully detached pipes. The *Oakland Herald* dismissed Beverly's claim that he resigned because he was tired of traveling; Jane Stanford herself did not plan to travel, according to the *Herald*. But this was not true. She originally planned to go to Europe in the summer of 1904 for "another long absence from home."[10]

This stew of jealousy, greed, and vengeance supposedly produced the poisoning of the Poland Spring Water. But the exact rationale remained murky. To get the supposed legacy, Beverly would have had to kill Stanford, but in the dominant narrative Beverly and Richmond only sought to harm Berner, who was supposedly the sole person who ever served Mrs. Stanford her bottled water.[11]

The accusations in the papers angered Beverly. The *Examiner* interviewed him at his home in San Mateo, south of San Francisco, on March 3. Both his wife and Elizabeth Richmond were present. His class resentment spilled over. "Rich people are all right to work for as long as you give them all your time. Just as soon as you want a half a day to yourself so you can see your family, they get the idea that you aren't doing your duty. Anyway, I had all the travel I wanted. I wanted to settle down." Like Berner, he resented Jane Stanford's assumption that she owned him and his time. He refused to incriminate anyone. He avowed his friendship with Berner. "Miss Berner never gave any trouble to anybody." When asked about the Chinese servants, he said that "the China boys minded their own business. They thought a lot of Mrs. Stanford."[12]

The butler denied any complicity by either himself or Richmond in the poisonings; he said the detectives were allowing the real murderer to escape by concentrating on them. He insisted his relationship with Jane Stanford had remained friendly. She considered inviting him back to supervise her winter entertainments. Stanford never recalled him because of Charles Lathrop.[13]

Beverly blamed Lathrop for the accusations circling around himself and Richmond. Although unwilling to say his sister was murdered, Lathrop was more than willing to insinuate that Elizabeth Richmond and Albert Beverly put poison in her water in San Francisco.[14]

When a reporter pointed out that strychnine to poison rats and squirrels was available on the Stanford stock farm where he had lived, Beverly admitted that it was, but he claimed he never used the poison. He silenced his wife when she began to give an account of their loss of that house, insisting on doing so himself. When after a few months Mrs. Stanford needed the house for another employee, she wrote him a note, and he vacated. He blamed the story of an acrimonious departure on Lathrop. Phil Atkinson, a Stanford watchman and Lathrop's man Friday, accused Beverly of cutting pipes. Beverly admitted disconnecting the pipes to the boiler, but denied cutting the water pipes, which were twenty-five years old and broke constantly.[15]

Throwing off, as the *Examiner* put it, "the habit of servitude," Beverly lashed out at Lathrop. He was "a knocker" who carried "a hammer for everybody." He scoffed at Lathrop's devotion to his sister, insinuating he cared only about her money. Jane Stanford once said that Lathrop "was very good to her, because he took her to church one day. . . . That was a wonderful thing to do wasn't it? Who wouldn't go to church with a woman with millions."[16]

The *San Francisco Chronicle* floated a different story that hinted at a midlife romance between Beverly and Berner. Although newspaper illustrations of Berner often pictured her as youthful, even beautiful, both Beverly and Berner were "well advanced in years." The two had traveled together extensively, with Beverly responsible for both Berner's and Jane Stanford's comfort, and "it would not be unnatural if under such circumstances and after a companionship of years, the man and the woman . . . should conceive a strong friendship for each other." But Beverly was married and "not free to follow his inclinations." Beverly, for his part, admitted he was friendly with Bertha Berner "for whom I have always felt a high regard and still do. If there is anything criminal in that, make the most of it." The rest he dismissed as gossip. For romance to lead to poisoning, Elizabeth Richmond needed to become the instigator rather than an accomplice. Jealous of Berner, she put poison in the water so that Berner would be blamed.[17]

Richmond denied any jealousy of Berner, and she, too, blamed Lathrop for the stories. After Lathrop put Morse detectives on her trail, she asked him to his face why she was being "shadowed like a pickpocket." Lathrop claimed he knew nothing about it even though he employed the detectives.[18]

On March 4, the *Chronicle* predicted that Beverly would be arrested, but there were no arrests. The police and the Morse detectives said they were satisfied with his explanations. On March 4, the police told Beverly and Richmond that they could move about as they wished; they were not under surveillance.[19]

When on March 5, the newspapers published the terms of Jane Stanford's will, suspicion turned toward Bertha Berner and Ah Wing. Berner received $15,000 from Mrs. Stanford's will. Ah Wing received $1,000. The will did not mention Beverly. A special messenger went to Menlo Park to give August Berner the news of his sister's good fortune. He shouted down from the window that he knew nothing about it and did not wish to talk. Bertha Berner told reporters that the money she inherited meant nothing to her.[20]

The revelation that Berner would profit from Jane Stanford's death— and thus possessed a motive to speed it along—demonstrated how many defenders she possessed. Judge Leib vouched for her. "I have known Bertha all these years, and she has been loyal and devoted and good and true. I do not believe that a good man or good woman can become suddenly bad. I know that Bertha Berner has been . . . faithful to Mrs. Stanford." Dr. Charles A. Wayland, who saw Jane Stanford and Berner in San Jose, described Berner as "a good girl and too much of a lady" to poison Jane Stanford. "Besides what could she possibly gain by Mrs. Stanford's death?" She was getting a good salary—$200 a month—more than the interest on $15,000 would bring. Why, in effect, would she kill the goose that laid the golden egg? He posed this as an answer, not a question. By March 11, Berner was no longer listed among the *Call*'s suspects.[21] The *Examiner* reported that Berner was shocked to find that San Francisco newspapers considered her a suspect. This was disingenuous.[22]

Beverly's and Richmond's respite from police surveillance proved brief. The police pulled both back in for sweating on March 7. Beverly held to his denial of the rumors that he took kickbacks on the purchases he made for Jane Stanford. They were, he said, lies. But, contrary to what he had said earlier, he abandoned his claim of continuing friendly relations with Berner. He admitted that he had not seen her since he left Mrs. Stanford's employ.[23]

CHAPTER 35

JORDAN AND HOPKINS CROSS THE PACIFIC

THE S.S. *ALAMEDA* DEPARTED San Francisco on March 4, with David Starr Jordan and Timothy Hopkins on board to retrieve Jane Stanford's corpse and escort it home. It had been Stanford's intention to fire both of them on her return. Hopkins, who rarely did anything that did not directly benefit Timothy Hopkins, was not eager to go, but he wrote his wife that it was the "right thing—hard as it is." To Hopkins's relief, David Starr Jordan decided to join him as the representative of the university.[1]

The night before the *Alameda* departed, there was a further change of plans. Mountford Wilson, Charles Lathrop, and San Francisco's Acting Chief of Police Spillane added two more passengers to the party: Jules Callundan of the Morse Agency and Detective Sergeant Harry Reynolds of the San Francisco police. Reynolds was a veteran detective who specialized in escorting suspects who posed little danger back to San Francisco. He would bring back Bertha Berner and May Hunt. Callundan came along to do the bidding of the estate in shaping the investigation of Jane Stanford's death. The Stanford estate paid all their fares.[2]

Wilson and Jordan conferred on the dock before the *Alameda*'s departure to discuss plans "for conducting investigations at Honolulu." They were less interested in discovering whether a crime had been committed—that was a matter for the police and detectives—than in making sure that the stories about Stanford's death would not support challenges to her will that might hurt the university. Jordan wanted to avoid murder or suicide as a cause of death. His secretary, George Clark, wrote "Mrs. C.T. Mills," the president of Mills College, that Jordan, having apparently changed his mind again, had no doubt that Mrs. Stanford had been poisoned, although he was inclined to think it was "gross carelessness rather than a willful crime."[3]

Mountford Wilson wanted a sane Jane Stanford to have died a natural death, but that story faced considerable headwinds. There were newspaper reports two days before the *Alameda*'s departure that Jane Stanford thought she had a summons from the spirit world to join her husband and son.[4] The morning the ship departed, the *Examiner* featured a long interview with Mrs. J. J. Whitney, who had also lost her only son and claimed to be Jane Stanford's medium. Mrs. Whitney testified to Mrs. Stanford's spiritualism, her frequent communication with her dead relatives, and a terrifying dream she related in which a veiled woman forced Mrs. Stanford to drink poison.[5] On March 5, the *San Francisco Call* ran a story headlined "Secretary Said to Be a Medium" next to a column questioning Jane Stanford's sanity. It quoted Jane's brother Ariel Lathrop, and his wife affirming her enduring belief in spiritualism. They attended séances with her in New York and named Berner, a Mabel Lor, a Miss Stryker, and a Miss Carroll as mediums.[6]

Jordan appeared wan and haggard on the dock in San Francisco. A man in love with the sound of his own voice, he uncharacteristically refused to talk to newspapermen. The only exception was significant: he launched into a vehement denial that Jane Stanford was a spiritualist.[7]

The suicide narrative gained traction as the *Alameda* made its way to Hawaii. The *Los Angeles Examiner* published a story, riddled with errors, arguing that her death was a suicide and that she had been deranged for months. When Attorney General Andrews of Hawaii pursued a line of questioning before the coroner's jury that the *San Francisco Call* thought was designed to broach the possibility of suicide, there were more alarm bells.[8]

The newspapers published far more dubious stories. A tourist reported a deranged Jane Stanford having visions in front of the Sphinx and being terrified of the "natives" in Egypt in 1904. She was sure they wished to murder her. Richmond and Beverly, the tourist said, were desperate to leave her service.[9] Jordan and Wilson did not want such stories gaining currency.

THE *ALAMEDA* WAS A LESS lavish ship than the S.S. *Korea* and was not equipped to receive news while at sea. Its six-day passage was unusually cold and choppy. Jordan was often seasick during the voyage, but Hopkins wrote that the president stayed "sympathetic & congenial & even in his illness . . . he has remained unruffled & as full of information as an egg is of meat."[10]

Most early twentieth-century steamships offered passengers a combination of intimacy and isolation. Hopkins was a man who, unsurprisingly for a servant's son adopted into wealth, had a fine eye for the class gradations of Gilded Age America and sought to avoid those beneath him. The passenger list initially disappointed him as lacking in "possibilities," but he eventually found a few "pleasant traveling companions."[11]

Quarters were tight enough that he could observe even those he avoided, which gave his letters a voyeuristic quality. He wrote of a young woman his daughter's age whose "beauty is as well marked as her slang." He stayed clear of a "San Francisco girl going out she says to get married. Of all the vulgar common products of our great and wonderful state, this young lady is entitled to a special prize in a special class by herself." She was "knitting a baby's jacket in full view of an admiring audience—& she not to be married until Sunday next." There was a "half-Hawaiian" who played the piano and sang ragtime. The ship's second butcher, who danced the hula, ran "needles through his cheeks in a very realistic manner" and finished his performance by standing on his head and drinking beer from a glass on a rolling deck without spilling a drop.[12]

Such distractions did not relieve the "great anxiety" Jordan and Hopkins felt over their ignorance of what was taking place in Honolulu and San Francisco. The last news Jordan and Hopkins received from the newspapers on the day of their departure was that Bertha Berner had changed her story about the bicarbonate of soda; the investigation was stalled, and there was no definitive report on the presence of strychnine in Jane Stanford's body.

Before landing, Jordan and Hopkins agreed to arrange a large church service in Honolulu for Mrs. Stanford, ideally on the day of their departure and including both Presbyterian and Episcopalian ministers. Hopkins wanted Jane Stanford's favorite hymns sung, but even though he had known her since he was a child, he had no idea what these were. He would ask Bertha Berner. He said that since there was no telling what might happen on the voyage home, he wanted the service "complete in the essentials."

The *Alameda* rounded Diamond Head and landed on March 10, the same day that the newspapers published the verdict of the coroner's jury.[13]

CHAPTER 36

THE CORONER'S JURY

ON THE AFTERNOON OF MARCH 6, while San Francisco newspapers speculated about the identity of the murderer and Hopkins and Jordan were still sailing across the Pacific, Deputy High Sheriff Rawlins finally convened the coroner's jury at the Moana Hotel to determine the cause of Jane Stanford's death. The attorney general of Hawaii took part in the questioning. Judge William F. Stanley, representing the Stanford estate, sat next to Rawlins and whispered questions in his ear. On the first afternoon and evening, the coroner's jury heard from Bertha Berner, May Hunt, and two doctors, Dr. H. V. Murray and Dr. Francis Root Day, both of whom had arrived in Jane Stanford's room just after she died and told what they witnessed.[1]

The newspapers reported that Berner verged on "utter collapse." Her reaction may have been grief, but it may also have been a response to the troubling news reports in San Francisco papers, triggered in part by her own changing stories about Ah Wing and the bottle of bicarbonate of soda. The day before she testified, it became public that she had inherited $15,000 from Mrs. Stanford, which established a motive for murder. And there was Ariel Lathrop's assertion that she was a medium.[2]

Although two stenographers were present, there was no transcript of Bertha Berner's testimony. It survives as a long statement, which, if read carefully, exhibits the outlines of the questions Berner was answering. The Hawaiian newspapers also preserve some of the questions that Deputy High Sheriff Rawlins and Attorney General Andrews asked.[3] The answers do not indicate that she was overwhelmed.

Reporters for the *Pacific Commercial Advertiser* and the *Hawaiian Star* provide the fullest account of what she said and how she acted. They described her "as a well groomed woman getting on in middle life." Her hair was flecked with gray, swept back into a pompadour; her "long white hands . . . flashed a dozen rich rings." She was "under intense strain but was marvelously well controlled." Her answers were frank—"perhaps too engagingly frank," as if rehearsed—but the reporter conceded that with the danger of her testimony being twisted, it was best that her words be measured and careful. Only when she described the death did she grow emotional. It appeared that she had already talked with Deputy High Sheriff Rawlins so much that she could anticipate his next questions, but she hesitated at some of Attorney General Andrews's questions, and her pauses were laden with meaning.[4]

What, Andrews wanted to know, prompted Mrs. Stanford to seek the advice that brought her to Hawaii?

"How will I begin?" Berner replied.

"Was it merely a pleasure trip? Do you understand the question?"

"Oh yes, I understand," Berner said, and went on to describe the first poisoning.[5]

In these moments, it is possible to glimpse her—self-possessed, thoughtful, and, most likely, calculating. She had learned that everything she said mattered by already saying too much.

If her testimony was rehearsed, then its ambiguities and misstatements may have been intentional. Bertha Berner testified that since 1884 she was continuously in the service of Mrs. Stanford, but this was not true. It eliminated the ruptures, long absences, quarrels, and disagreements. She indicated that Hawaii was their destination. She did not mention Japan, the much longer trip that Jane Stanford had planned, which would tear Berner away from her sick mother.[6] She culled out everything that might give her a motive or an opportunity for killing Mrs. Stanford.

She no longer disavowed knowledge of the bottle of bicarbonate; instead she provided a detailed account of its whereabouts at various times. To the best of her knowledge, the last time Mrs. Stanford took bicarbonate from the wide-mouthed bottle was the first week of January. Berner used it at the same time without incident. When they fled to San Jose, they took the bottle with them. It returned with them to San Francisco, but Jane Stanford did not take it to the St. Francis Hotel. Instead it sat on a table in the bedroom of her mansion for a week. The bottle—packed in a medicine bag that was placed inside a telescope bag—was in Mrs. Stanford's state-room during the trip to Hawaii. It then went to her room at the Moana Hotel, where it remained untouched until she took the fatal dose.[7]

Berner testified that Mrs. Stanford usually took bicarbonate once a week and never went more than three weeks without it. Only Berner herself, Richmond, and another maid, Nora Hopkins, were aware of her regular use of bicarbonate. Attorney General Andrews recognized the inconsistency between Mrs. Stanford's regular use of bicarbonate, never going three weeks without it, and Berner's saying that she did not touch the bottle for eight weeks. Berner explained that Mrs. Stanford never took bicarbonate while under a doctor's care, which she was after contracting the flu in January of 1905. At the St. Francis they ate only two light meals a day, and so she was not troubled with acidity. This still left unexplained Mrs. Stanford's purchase of bicarbonate at Palo Alto.[8]

Berner did not deny that someone put strychnine in the bicarbonate. She did attempt to extend the window during which someone might have inserted it. At its widest, it stretched from early January, when Jane Stanford took some bicarbonate, to the last day of February. This was what made the Palo Alto purchase critical. If the fresh soda purchased in Palo Alto was put in the bottle, then the window narrowed considerably and along with it the possible suspects. It would eliminate, among others, Elizabeth Richmond, who by the time of the purchase had already left Mrs. Stanford's employ.

Berner described how she measured out the bicarbonate on that last evening. "I put in the spoon, tilting the bottle a little, and dipped out the soda. I think I did not let the soda pile up on one side when I tipped the bottle . . . I dipped the soda right out, probably from the top, but I am not sure on this point." She thought, in other words, she had taken the bicarbonate from the top, which meant that if the strychnine was concentrated at the top, Jane Stanford got a heavier dose than was present in the rest of the bottle. Because the strychnine grains were larger than those of the soda, they would have remained on the surface even if the bottle had been shaken or moved. Later, Mr. Stanley asked the doctors whether Mrs. Stanford's taking a smaller amount of bicarbonate—a half teaspoonful—and thus less strychnine would alter their opinions. Dr. Day emphatically answered no.[9]

When questioned about the possibility of suicide, Berner said Mrs. Stanford found suicide repugnant and incomprehensible. Attorney General Andrews found her answer unsatisfying. Over the objections of Deputy High Sheriff Rawlins, he pursued a series of questions designed to explore a suicide theory. This did not appear in the report of the coroner's jury.[10]

Berner did not deny Jane Stanford's spiritualism, but she merged it into conventional Christian belief. She said Jane Stanford frequently spoke of her husband and son and hoped to meet them sometime.[11]

On the morning of March 7, High Sheriff Henry preempted the testimony of the chemists by announcing to the press that tests had produced evidence of strychnine in Mrs. Stanford's stomach and in the bicarbonate of soda. The presence of strychnine in the bicarbonate had already been leaked to the newspapers, but the combination of strychnine in both Mrs. Stanford's body and the bicarbonate seemed conclusive. She had been poisoned.[12]

The chemists themselves testified on the afternoon of March 7, and although they were quite precise, their testimony understandably confused reporters. R. A. Duncan testified that he and Dr. Edward Shorey of the U.S. Agricultural Station had conducted three separate analyses of different ten-gram batches of the bicarbonate of soda. They found .07, .13, and .14 grains of strychnia in the batches. They extrapolated this to only half a grain of strychnia in the entire 43-gram bottle.

According to Thomas Price, a chemist who wrote for the *Examiner*, "about half a grain" was the minimum lethal dose for an adult. A dose as small as 1/16th of a grain had killed a two-year-old child, and Dr. Murray thought those of advanced age—like Mrs. Stanford—were equally susceptible to a low dose. He guessed she swallowed 1/12th of a grain, plus the 1/30th grain of strychnine in the cascara capsule. Since there was no way of knowing how concentrated the strychnine was at the top of the bottle, it was impossible to gauge the actual dose Mrs. Stanford received.[13]

In other experiments, the chemists first analyzed separately the vomit, urine, part of the stomach contents, intestinal contents, and the stomach, intestines, and one kidney. Only the contents of the intestines showed the color reaction diagnostic of strychnine. They then blended all the organs in their possession—including the liver—and their contents and performed the "fading purple test," which to Duncan's and Shorey's knowledge was the most reliable test for the presence of strychnine. "The color reaction we obtained is not produced except by strychnia."

Duncan did not find strychnia in the body because, he testified, "the amount was too small and distributed in the body of matter." What he found were the clear signs of the presence of strychnine in the chemical tests. Dr. Shorey made the same point. They did not find strychnine, but their tests "produced the color reaction which strychnine causes." It was, the *Bulletin* reported, "not known to be produced by another substance than strychnine."[14]

The cascara capsule that Mrs. Stanford swallowed complicated the conclusion. It contained nux vomica, which had among its ingredients 1/30th grain of strychnine. This fell within the normal medicinal dose of from 1/160th to 1/20th grains. A standard work at the time said that the fading purple test would identify strychnine down to the level of .0025 milligrams if it was pure and uncontaminated with organic materials. The strychnine in the nux vomica alone would have registered on the fading purple test, but it was contaminated with organic materials. The same manual noted that brucine—another component of nux vomica—interfered with the reaction. So the nux vomica alone would probably not produce the fading purple reaction unless there was additional strychnine present.[15] Other contemporary experts cautioned that tests of diluted samples taken from the body would not necessarily produce the same results as pure samples taken from outside the body.[16]

To muddle the analysis even more, contemporary authorities said that in order to detect the small amount of strychnine required to kill, it was best to dice up as much as 12 percent of the body mass, including not only the stomach, intestines, liver, and kidneys, but also the blood, brains, spinal cord, and a quantity of muscle. The Hawaiian chemists used a much smaller sample, but still found it produced positive results in the fading purple test.

The newspapers cherry-picked this testimony. The *Chronicle* headline read: "Little Strychnine Found in Body or Bottle," and ran an interview with Dr. C. L. Morgan, a toxicologist, who said that he did not believe she had died of strychnine poisoning. The *Examiner* was more equivocal. Under the headline "Only a Trace of Poison in Mrs. Stanford's Entire Body," its story said the amount of strychnine found was insufficient to kill, but the "autopsy shows poison symptoms." The *Call* reported that she had been poisoned.[17]

The Honolulu papers regarded the sum of the evidence as definitive: Jane Stanford died of strychnine poisoning. There was strychnine in the organs and strychnine in the bicarbonate. The brucine and strychnine in the cascara capsules could have left a trace of strychnine in the body, but the evidence provided by the physicians made the "fact of death by poison conclusive."[18]

The coroner's jury inquest made it clear that the fatal poisoning was radically different from the Poland Spring Water episode, even though the police attributed both poisonings to the same person. Instead of a massive dose of rat poison, the killer had used a precise amount of pure strychnine, distributing it so that only a small residue would remain. Either the killer had done research or had gotten more expert advice.

Attorney General Andrews and High Sheriff Henry conferred on March 7. The next day Henry and Deputy High Sheriff Rawlins declared that it was not the responsibility of Hawaiian authorities to investigate the murder. They were sure the murderer was in San Francisco. They denied, without providing evidence, that the poison could have been placed in the bottle in Honolulu, although the bottle had rested for long periods in the unoccupied Moana hotel room. They wanted to save Honolulu the expense of a trial.[19]

Although scheduled testimony ended on March 8, High Sheriff Henry postponed the conclusion of the proceedings. He said another day was necessary to allow the stenographers to prepare copies of the testimony for the witnesses to sign. In Hawaii and California, everyone—the police, Berner, Richmond, Beverly, and Mountford Wilson—awaited the jury's verdict. Beverly went fishing.[20]

In Hawaii, rumors circulated that "those interested in the estate of Mrs. Jane L. Stanford are having great influence in the management of the local inquiry on account of a possible will contest raising a question of sanity." As a headline succinctly put it: "Insanity May Void Mrs. Stanford's Will." Bertha Berner resumed talking to the newspapers, who reported her as "excitable and nervous" since she was "under extreme strain." Like her defenders in California, she claimed she had nothing to gain and everything to lose from Mrs. Stanford's death, citing her salary of "nearly $200" per month and the "many gifts of clothing and money" she had received from Jane Stanford. She had saved, she said, nearly all of it. She seemed interested in refuting the suicide theories. Like other legatees, Berner would lose her inheritance if challenges voided the will.[21]

The *San Francisco News*—while floating the theory of a mysterious new suspect—reported that the detectives regarded Mrs. Stanford's death as murder, but the influence of the estate allowed Wilson to seal the lips of the police and chemists in San Francisco and Honolulu. This was not the first time that a rich estate "had so abhorred a scandal that it had sealed up the police department." The *News* interviewed Dr. W. C. Bailey, a chemist and toxicologist at the California Medical College. He knew and respected Dr. Humphris, and he agreed with the physicians in Hawaii that despite the small amount of strychnine recovered, everything pointed to strychnine poisoning.[22]

THE CORONER'S JURY finally delivered its verdict on the evening of March 9. They first heard an additional witness who had seen Bertha Berner deposit something in May Hunt's folded umbrella on the day of the poisoning. The something turned out to be a pair of gloves. Dr. Shorey was recalled and asked what kind of strychnine had been used. He said it was alkaloid, the purest and strongest form. The jury's deliberations took only a few minutes, and newspapers carried the verdict the next day, March 10.

> Jane Lathrop Stanford came to her death at Honolulu, Island of Oahu, Territory of Hawaii, on the twenty-eighth day of February, A.D. 1905 from Strychnine poisoning, said strychnine having been introduced into a bottle of bicarbonate of soda with felonious intent by some person or persons to this Jury unknown and of the contents of which bottle Jane Lathrop Stanford had partaken.[23]

In reporting the verdict, the *New York World* said the soda containing the strychnine had been purchased by Bertha Berner in Palo Alto. Although Sheriff Henry had said that he believed the murderer was in San Francisco, both the *World* and the *San Francisco Examiner* reported that Attorney General Andrews would not allow either Bertha Berner or May Hunt to leave until the detectives arrived from California. This in no way implied their guilt.[24]

Not everyone accepted the verdict. The *Pacific Commercial Advertiser* ran a story that wondered if Callundan would agree, although as it turned out they did not really know who Callundan was. They thought he was a San Francisco police detective "who could not have reached the rank he

212 WHO KILLED JANE STANFORD?

had attained" without becoming an expert at his job. The paper stressed the small amount of strychnine found in the bicarbonate, and thought the fading purple test unreliable.[25]

Jules Callundan arrived in Hawaii with David Starr Jordan and Timothy Hopkins on the day the verdict was published. The hopes of Jordan and Hopkins that the jury would rule out both murder and suicide were blasted. They assured reporters that they did not come to investigate the death. They were only there out of respect to escort the body home. Jordan was subdued until a reporter raised the question of spiritualism. Then, as in San Francisco, he vehemently denied that Jane Stanford or Bertha Berner were spiritualists. He defended Berner, repeating the refrain that she had no motive for killing Jane Stanford since her present position was worth more to her than the bequest.[26]

THE

COVER-UP

CHAPTER 37

PAST IS PROLOGUE

WHAT GEORGE CROTHERS SAID PUBLICLY often was not what he thought privately. He was not so much a hypocrite as a lawyer. He appreciated honesty, but he used it instrumentally. In giving his account of the origins of the university, he wrote, perhaps sardonically, that David Starr Jordan was a great scientist "but above all he was a great national preacher of clean living and high thinking." Privately he had a very different opinion. Which one he shared depended on which one best served Stanford University.[1]

It is unclear when George Crothers wrote his memoranda on David Starr Jordan. It could have been before Jane Stanford's death, or perhaps afterward. It doesn't much matter. By 1905 Crothers thought David Starr Jordan's faults and virtues were as set in stone as the campus buildings that Jordan derided as the "Stone Age."

The two handwritten memoranda address the same question: Was David Starr Jordan's presidency successful?[2]

Crothers's answer included a list of Jordan's faults. He offered no evidence for his claims, but anyone familiar with Stanford during the decade before 1905 could have provided it. There were his personal qualities: dishonesty, vindictiveness, vanity, egotism, arbitrariness, and arrogance. There were the repeated "affairs": Ross, Gilbert, and Pease. There was his insistence on maintaining personal control over hiring and firing, dismissing faculty when they crossed him, favoring his pets, and yielding only when necessary to the even more arbitrary Jane Stanford. There was a curriculum without rhyme or reason. There was his resistance to the reforms—common at other American research universities—that George Crothers and Horace Davis urged upon the school.

George Crothers did not bother to recount the evidence he knew so well, he just provided headings under which to organize it. He then listed the headings as answers to his question.

As a person, Jordan was unable to stand the strain of any difficult situation without "being self-centered." He "made promises which he has afterwards repudiated without explanation."

Jordan tortured the truth. He manifested an "inability to adhere strictly to the truth when it conflict[ed] with his personal interest, however harmful and unjust a deviation it may be to another." He was unable "to engage in a personal controversy with a professor without making unfounded verbal accusations against him and written statements of an ambiguous nature affecting his character."

He showed no judgment in "the choice of men," and selected faculty on the basis of personal connections rather than merit. "He has not retained the best men, but those who were willing to submit to him without question."

He was a tyrant with "no conception or respect for the most elementary rights of persons, especially of those charged with wrongdoing." He possessed no respect "for rules or code" and "objected to setting out clear academic or disciplinary policies." "Guided by no rules or principles," he made "secret rulings on individual cases [that] lack consistency and freedom from partiality." "He has intimidated the men under him."

Jordan never showed "a grasp of the place or function of the University," nor did he give "utterance to any clear or original idea of the purposes of the university." He demonstrated "a complete lack of administrative ability and failed to track and judge accurately the work of the departments." He could not see defects nor remedy them. He followed the "line of least resistance without any abiding conviction upon fundamental principles."

He was not an educator, but instead wanted to convert the university into "a bureau of research."

This was Crothers's evaluation of the man who sailed to Hawaii to take control of the investigation of Jane Stanford's demise. From San Francisco Crothers wrote his memoranda, which seem to have gone unread, and watched events unfold.

CHAPTER 38

EVERYONE WAS LYING

BY THE TIME DAVID STARR JORDAN and Timothy Hopkins reached Honolulu, it was apparent that all the suspects were lying.[1]

On Saturday, March 4, Elizabeth Richmond supposedly told Albert Beverly that she wanted to come clean.[2] Richmond didn't come clean, at least not immediately, but under grilling from the police, Beverly, knowing Richmond's resistance had waned, did. On March 6, he reversed his previous denials and admitted to taking rake-offs on the purchases he made for Jane Stanford.[3] Beverly justified the rake-offs as a commission, a customary part of an English servant's due.[4] He said that he took "perquisites" only when Mrs. Stanford traveled in Europe, although Beverly did not travel with Mrs. Stanford in Europe, only in Australia, Africa, and Asia. In the United States he only received his $75 per month. He implicated Berner, but tried to mitigate her role. He said she did not take commissions directly, but he split his with her.[5]

Richmond confessed to the police that she knew of the rake-offs and said that Berner and Beverly shared them, but she said they also occurred in California. She described Berner as strong-minded and self-assertive, exerting an undue influence over Jane Stanford. The money involved was substantial. The total rake-off during the Pacific trip alone was about $2,100, split between Beverly and Berner. Beverly's share would have been more than a year's salary. Berner gained about five months' salary.[6]

Richmond also accused Berner of lying. She once confronted Berner over the rake-offs after an outdoor "fete" in Palo Alto. This would seem to date it either to 1902 or to the spring or summer of 1903. After the

1903–1904 trip across the Pacific to Egypt, Beverly almost immediately left Jane Stanford's service, and it was unlikely that the rake-offs continued without him.[7]

Berner, too, admitted that she had lied. Beverly did give her half the commissions, but she insisted that the rake-offs occurred only during the Pacific trip of 1903–1904, and she claimed to have returned everything that Beverly gave her to Mrs. Stanford. She estimated that her share was $1,500.[8]

As the detectives continued to sweat Richmond, she changed her stories of why she resigned. Stanford's friends claimed Elizabeth Richmond was often subject to "spells," and on March 12 Richmond fainted—or feigned fainting—under continued sweating by the detectives. Each change in her story revealed more tension between her and Mrs. Stanford. As Mrs. Stanford's unidentified friends weighed in with their own accounts, the dates and details of Richmond's stories seemed more and more unstable.[9]

Richmond acknowledged that her proximity to the first poisoning and her shifting stories made her a suspect. She said she understood why, but she proclaimed her innocence.[10]

BEVERLY'S, BERNER'S, and Richmond's ever-changing accounts all involved the Poland Spring Water poisoning. The presumption remained that solving one poisoning would be to solve them both.

Like the bottle of bicarbonate in Hawaii, the bottle of Poland Spring Water in Jane Stanford's bedroom became the key piece of evidence in San Francisco. But while the bottle in Hawaii was singular and distinctive, the bottles of Poland Spring Water were multiple and identical. The detectives needed to determine which bottle contained the poison and when it arrived on Mrs. Stanford's night table. By March 11, interviews with the house servants led them to conclude that the staff never brought a fresh bottle of Poland Spring Water upstairs until the previous one was emptied. The bottle containing the poison was, therefore, not the one Richmond saw the morning of the poisoning—what happened to that one was not explained. The bottle in question was opened immediately before the evening meal. Mrs. Stanford took a glassful with dinner, and then someone brought the bottle upstairs. The poison must have been inserted between 6:00 and 9:00 p.m., since Mrs. Stanford drank from it at her meal without ill effect.[11]

If this was true, the poisoning was either a crime of opportunity or, if planned, the work of Bertha Berner. Only Berner knew that Jane Stanford would sleep in the mansion that night. Before dinner Mrs. Stanford was ready to leave for Palo Alto until Berner suggested they wait until morning. Everyone else on the staff presumed she would be leaving. And if Berner planned to put strychnine in Jane Stanford's nightly water, it was best to do it in San Francisco. Berner stayed with her own family in Palo Alto, and she would not have the same opportunity to tamper with the evening water in the summer house. None of this means that Berner did poison her. Other servants might have inserted the poison, but they could have done so only on the spur of the moment.[12]

The police did not pursue this lead. The press had lost interest in Berner, who was still in Honolulu; instead they focused on the fluctuating accounts Richmond gave as to who uncorked the Poland Spring Water on the night of the poisoning.

The police reverted to the original Callundan theory. There had been no poisoning. Richmond placed strychnine in the water *after* rather than before Mrs. Stanford tasted it. She did not intend to poison Mrs. Stanford but only to discredit Bertha Berner, whose place she wished to take. There was no poison in the Poland Spring Water bottle when Jane Stanford first swallowed it. The theory was no more coherent than when Callundan formulated it. Why did Jane Stanford taste the bitterness of strychnine? Why did Richmond and Berner both see flakes floating in the bottle? And why would Jane Stanford suspect Richmond of poisoning her? All went as unexplained as before. If Richmond wanted to have Berner fired, why didn't she just reveal the rake-offs and accuse her of an affair with Beverly?[13]

When Richmond admitted that she took strychnine tablets for her heart, reporters made this new information seem a significant disclosure, even though they admitted that the strychnine was of a different type than that found in the bottle. Richmond's pills contained only infinitesimal amounts, and she had stopped taking them before entering Mrs. Stanford's employ.[14]

AH WING ALSO LIED. Chief of Detectives Burnett, Detective Sergeant Edward Gibson, and Detective Cleary joined Harry Morse, Mountford Wilson, and Charles Lathrop in interrogating him. The presence of Morse, Wilson, and Lathrop revealed how fully the estate remained involved in the investigation. Under constant pressure, Ah Wing supposedly lost twenty-five pounds. He altered his story. Although he claimed complete access to the entire mansion and that he often entered Mrs. Stanford's bedroom, he said that he did not enter the room on the Saturday of the poisoning. He was in the kitchen all day polishing silverware after a dinner the evening before. But there was no dinner party the evening before, and Richmond, Nora Hopkins, and Ah Young all denied that Ah Wing spent all day in the kitchen.[15]

CHAPTER 39

JULES CALLUNDAN AND HARRY REYNOLDS

DAVID STARR JORDAN INSISTED that he was neither a detective nor interested in investigating Jane Stanford's death. But Jordan knew the conclusion that he wanted the detectives who accompanied him to reach: Jane Stanford died a natural death. At some point during the ocean voyage, he decided that Jane Stanford's symptoms were not typical of strychnine poisoning. He assisted "the detectives to the extent of suggesting questions, as a physician, during their inquiries regarding her symptoms and the results of the autopsy."[1] David Starr Jordan was no more a physician than a detective. In his autobiography he would describe his medical degree as "scarcely earned," and he never practiced.[2] Jules Callundan did not question Jordan's credentials. He came to Honolulu to find what his employers hired him to find.

The presence of Detective Sergeant Harry Reynolds with instructions to bring back Bertha Berner suggested that the San Francisco police still considered her a suspect. Reynolds, a veteran of the Civil War, had joined the force in 1882, but until 1902 he worked on "horseradish cases"— investigating complaints of thefts from the fields of truck gardeners— and other small-time burglaries. Then, through the influence of unnamed "friends outside the department," he gained the favor of Chief Wittman and later Chief of Detectives Burnett, and he began to get plum assignments that involved travel to attractive places after others had done the actual work. He went to New York City and to the St. Louis World's Fair.

He specialized in transporting suspects who presented little danger—like Bertha Berner—to San Francisco. Such work demanded neither investigative talent nor much judgment, a good fit for Reynolds. Later, in 1905, he went to Europe to retrieve an embezzler. Reynolds left a loaded gun in his stateroom on the ocean liner bringing them home, and then left the prisoner alone in the room. The man, to the embarrassment of the department, committed suicide.[3]

Reynolds came to bring Berner home, but as a man with friends outside the department, he might also have come for other purposes. The Stanford estate picked up the costs of the trip. If the executors did not own him, they were at least renting him. If the estate was not interested in finding the murderer, then Harry Reynolds was their man. Once in Hawaii, he stopped communicating with Captain Burnett.[4]

Detectives Callundan and Reynolds re-tilled the ground already plowed by the Hawaiian police. They interviewed Bertha Berner and May Hunt. They talked to High Sheriff Henry and the attorney general. They questioned Dr. Humphris and Dr. William Taylor, who attended part of the autopsy as a guest. They examined the physical evidence and reviewed the testimony presented to the coroner's jury. They hired stenographers to copy depositions. The most palpable result of their presence was that it allowed High Sheriff Henry to wash his hands of the case and turn it over to them.[5]

They did look in some places that the Honolulu police had neglected, although it is not clear why. They went into Honolulu's Chinatown. They did not say who or what they were looking for. The *Honolulu Evening Bulletin* connected the visit with Ah Wing, but only because Ah Wing was Chinese.[6]

There were new discoveries, but Callundan and Reynolds did not make them and did not pursue them. On March 11, the *San Francisco Chronicle* revealed that the paper package of bicarbonate of soda purchased by Jane Stanford and Bertha Berner in Palo Alto had surfaced in Hawaii and "from its contents was removed sufficient of the soda to have filled Mrs. Stanford's bottle." The paper credited Callundan and Reynolds with the discovery, but the Hawaiian police found the package before the arrival of the detectives. They notified both the San Francisco police and Mountford Wilson, who in turn told Callundan and Reynolds. This was the same paper package that Bertha Berner said was never opened and was left in California.[7]

Jane Stanford's maid, Nora Hopkins, remembered placing the packet in a steamer trunk. Why she would separate it from the other medicines, she did not explain. She did not say if the packet was opened before she packed it, nor did she say if it was used to refill the Australian bottle. Whether the package was opened in San Francisco would seem to be important for determining when the strychnine was added to the bottle, but if reporters or detectives asked Hopkins, there is no record of their questioning. May Hunt had already testified that she packed the bottle in the medicine case at Mrs. Stanford's orders after it sat on a table for days.[8]

Any connection between the packet of bicarbonate and the soda in the bottle that killed Jane Stanford would add to the circumstantial evidence linking Bertha Berner to the murder. She was the only person present at both poisonings. She had access to both the Poland Spring Water and the bottle with the bicarbonate. She repeatedly lied or dissembled about the bicarbonate. There still remained the possibility that the bicarbonate was tainted with strychnine before Berner and Stanford purchased it. The police went to the Palo Alto pharmacy and seized the bicarbonate of soda from which Mrs. Stanford's order was filled. They tested it. It was pure.[9]

HIGH SHERIFF HENRY WATCHED the San Francisco detectives and decided they were not very interested in finding the killer. They wanted to eliminate the murder, not the murderer. The transcripts of the detectives' interviews have disappeared, but it is very hard to destroy documents without a trace. Documents produce responses and references in other documents. They throw shadows that reveal their shape and form.

When the San Francisco papers later reprinted a section of the transcript of Callundan's interview with Dr. Humphris, reporters for the *Chronicle* quickly recognized that Callundan and Reynolds were trying to get Humphris to repudiate his conclusions of strychnine poisoning and agree that Jane Stanford died of a heart attack. They failed. Humphris had seen other cases of strychnine poisoning. He regarded the physical manifestations in Mrs. Stanford as irrefutable. He gave details. Her hands were clenched so hard that the fingers cracked when later pulled apart; the jaws were locked and he could not separate them; he could not give her chloroform to relax her during her last spasm because she had ceased breathing. Asphyxiation was the ultimate cause of death from strychnine.[10]

They had more luck with Dr. William E. Taylor, who was finishing a distinguished medical career. He possessed impeccable credentials, having served as coroner in San Francisco and been a member of the faculty at the University of California at Berkeley. He did not question the results of the autopsy, nor was he present at Jane Stanford's death; instead he focused on the testimony that Jane Stanford had managed to swallow glasses of water after the onset of spasms. He told Callundan and Reynolds that he "had never heard of a person suffering from strychnine poisoning who was able to take a glass of water."[11]

Taylor was correct that in the midst of a strychnine spasm it becomes impossible for the victim to swallow, but the medical literature contained accounts of physicians successfully administering liquid antidotes in between spasms. Jane Stanford said she could not swallow—"my jaws are set"—but before and after this spasm she did swallow several glasses of water.[12] Taylor's statement was too narrow to be useful.

The detectives interviewed Bertha Berner at least twice. Given her own shifting stories, and the changing accounts given by the servants in San Francisco, Berner needed to answer a lot of questions. The questions Callundan and Reynolds asked her are missing, but their traces remain in Berner's answers.[13]

From the structure of Berner's denials, the detectives seem to have peppered her with short staccato questions, making her wonder what other witnesses—Richmond, Beverly, or Ah Wing—had said. She told them, referring to the Poland Spring Water incident, that "Wing did not at that time say, 'Bertha, I think you did this.' He did not say, 'Bertha, I didn't see you do it, but I think you did, and you know if you did or not.' No conversation of that kind occurred. Mrs. Stanford never told me that Wing openly accused me to her. I know that if Wing ever made an accusation, Mrs. Stanford would have told me. Mrs. Stanford never told me that she thought Wing had done the thing. She never made the statement that Richmond did it. She never said to me, 'Bertha do you think Richmond did it.'"[14]

The detectives seemed to focus on her relations with Ah Wing. She claimed that Ah Wing never accused her of the Poland Spring Water poisoning, nor did she accuse him. She said that the poisoner must be someone in the house, and she went through the servants, either clearing them or saying she did not know them.

The only exception was Ah Wing. Having said she never accused him, she then asserted that he was the only one in the house with a motive to kill Mrs. Stanford. With Mrs. Stanford's death, he would get his promised inheritance and could return to China. Left unsaid was that the same motive—an inheritance—would apply to her.

Berner added a story damaging to Ah Wing. While she and Mrs. Stanford were staying at the St. Francis Hotel and coming daily to the mansion to pack, Jane Stanford, after a meeting with her brother and trustee Leon Sloss, returned to the mansion and encountered Ah Wing downstairs. Ah Wing was agitated, more excited than she had ever seen him, and he frightened her. "He thinks," Mrs. Stanford told Berner, "that you are not his friend." Stanford asked Berner to see him and "find out what it means."

Berner saw him in her room at the mansion the next day—the day before she and Jane Stanford left on the *Korea*. Ah Wing told her that he was "very cross about coffee," referring to her accusation that he informed on the staff's drinking coffee. Berner told him to think no more about it, and Ah Wing replied, "You and I friends long time. You no friend now." Berner replied that she was still his friend, and he should not frighten Mrs. Stanford.[15]

By the time she sat down with Callundan and Reynolds, Bertha Berner knew that Beverly and Richmond had told the story of the kickbacks. She admitted she received the money from Beverly, but insisted it had only happened on the Pacific trip and that she returned her share to Mrs. Stanford. A desire to disguise her graft from Mrs. Stanford for fear of losing her job and inheritance could be a motive for murder, but not if Jane Stanford already knew.

Berner did not attack either Richmond or Beverly. Instead she briefly, and perhaps inadvertently, revealed the burden of traveling with Jane Stanford: "if Mrs. Stanford were sick or annoyed all the others were sent away, and I was beside Mrs. Stanford to help her over it again. I had enough in Australia. I could bear no more." She said that she could not, would not, proceed without Beverly.[16]

She told the detectives that after their return Beverly sent her "an all-around bad letter . . . in which he criticized me severely." She said it was in her Palo Alto home. Berner later gave the letter to Callundan, who retained it. He released only one line of it. "I never overlook or forget an act of treachery." The papers said this referred to Berner's having revealed the kickbacks to Jane Stanford. Perhaps it did, but the timing of the denunciation was odd. If Berner's revelation was the treachery that caused Beverly's dismissal, why did he continue to live on the estate?[17]

The treachery may have involved something else, something personal, that was the subject of gossip. Crothers heard the gossip. Richmond, he said, knew of the undue familiarity between Berner and Beverly. If so, Berner must have feared that Richmond would reveal the affair to Jane Stanford. In the past, Bertha Berner's romances and flirtations had led to Jane Stanford's sending her away.[18] The detectives chose to keep the letter but did not reveal its contents.

WITH BERNER ACUTELY AWARE of her precarious position, David Starr Jordan and Jules Callundan underlined the danger she faced not to convict her but to make her an ally. They asked her to talk to a doctor that Jordan had recruited to review the materials on Mrs. Stanford's death. They wanted her to rethink what she had witnessed. This would serve her well.

On March 14, Jordan once more expressed his confidence in Berner's innocence. She had served Mrs. Stanford faithfully for twenty years. She loved Jane Stanford and, most of all, she had nothing to gain and a comfortable life to lose by Mrs. Stanford's death. Berner's actual history with Jane Stanford did not interest Jordan, Callundan, or Wilson. What concerned them was what Bertha Berner might say if she were accused and tried. There was no earthly way that Berner's testimony on what she knew about the relationships of Wilson, Hopkins, and Jordan with Jane Stanford would aid them or the university.[19]

The *Pacific Commercial Advertiser* reported that the California detectives "uncovered many things the local authorities did not uncover," but what they uncovered did not amount to new evidence. They cast doubt on existing evidence. Although neither one was a chemist or a physician, they concluded that the evidence provided by the chemist did not prove poisoning. They rightfully criticized the coroner's jury—composed of employees at the Moana Hotel—as being made up of men who should properly have been witnesses, but this did not discredit the evidence the jury heard. The detectives experimented variously with poison, having in this "the aid of a scientist of no less note than Dr. David Starr Jordan." It is unclear what experiments they conducted, why an ichthyologist was the best person to advise them, or what the experiments revealed.[20]

Jules Callundan was not an honest man, but neither was he a stupid man. Even as he and Reynolds followed Jordan's and Wilson's bidding, they insisted that they were keeping their options open. They told report-ers that they had found nothing new. Callundan said there were four different theories of Stanford's death, and he was not going to bend the evidence to fit the theories. Once back in San Francisco, he would come to a conclusion about the solution of the mystery. Both Mountford Wilson and Captain Burnett said they were waiting for the return of the detec-tives. Callundan finally concluded that there was no proof of murder, but Reynolds went off script, declaring that he saw no reason to question the conclusions of the coroner's jury or the high sheriff.[21]

Reporters detected a clear message. On March 14, the *San Francisco Examiner* reported that "the detectives have evidently abandoned the mur-der and suicide theories in the Stanford case and are now working to prove Mrs. Stanford's death was due to natural causes." The next day the *Pacific Commercial Advertiser* reported that "it is believed" they concluded that Jane Stanford had not been poisoned. The *Hawaiian Star* said that Jane Stanford mistook a case of indigestion for poisoning, and this prompted hysteria that duplicated exactly the symptoms of strychnine poisoning. She supposedly died of fright.[22]

Callundan and Reynolds claimed they would write reports of their investigations, but if they did, the reports have not survived.

CHAPTER 40

REFRAMING THE INVESTIGATION

A WEEK INTO THE INVESTIGATION of Jane Stanford's death, the San Francisco newspapers grew suspicious. "There is much strange about the entire investigation," the *San Francisco Call* reported on March 7. "Various people . . . are given to making denials in a manner that is absurd." Fremont Older's *San Francisco Bulletin* blamed Mountford Wilson. His attempt to control the investigation "succeeded in making a pretty thorough mess of it."[1]

Wilson often graced the front pages of San Francisco newspapers in March of 1905. His face looked like an egg with a pince-nez and a carefully drawn mustache. He and his wife were staples of society columns, but his involvement in disputes over the wills of the well-to-do put him on the front pages. His role in the ongoing and endless Fair case—the suit over the wealthy ex-senator's will that entangled him with George Crothers—was not unique. He and his clerks were the last ones to have possession of the will of Mrs. Lizzie Hemphill, which disappeared days before her unexpected death on March 20 from "fatty degeneration of the heart," the same diagnosis he came to favor for Jane Stanford. The Dunsmuir estate case involved the alleged incompetence of Alexander Dunsmuir and multiple suits as family members scrambled for the fortune. By the end of the year, Wilson faced charges of conflict of interest.[2]

Wilson said his abuse in the papers would not affect his actions. He denied that Sheriff Henry's seeming hesitation in releasing the report of the Hawaiian chemists "was due to any instructions emanating from the city or the Stanford interest." All they asked was that the analysis be so thorough that there would be no doubt as to the cause of death.[3] Wilson denied that he told Berner or anyone else of the contents of the will, or that he knew anything more about the identity of the poisoner.[4]

Charles Lathrop gave Wilson cover. The coroner's jury verdict staggered Lathrop, but he stressed the lack of motive for murder, and insisted that "we must find the motive" before assuming a murderer. Privately he knew that his sister's vindictiveness created multiple enemies with reasons to want to see her gone. He had witnessed her will and knew who would benefit from her death. He almost certainly knew that she had planned to dismiss Jordan.[5]

Fremont Older was not about to stop his abuse of Wilson. Older moved easily in San Francisco politics and society and had a deep suspicion of both. He started as a newspaper reporter, became an editor of the *San Francisco Call*, and then built the *San Francisco Bulletin* into the city's largest afternoon paper. Older's involvement with Mayor James Phelan gave him a "social sense." He became what was derisively called a "goo-goo" by machine politicians: a good government proponent.[6]

The ascent of the Ruef machine and the Union Labor Party in 1902 threw Older into more permanent opposition. The *Bulletin* was preoccupied with Mayor Eugene Schmitz and Boss Abraham Ruef, but Older possessed enough bandwidth to distrust the Stanford investigation. He suspected the estate wanted a natural death to avoid scandal and an investigation of the failure to turn the Poland Spring Water poisoning over to the police. Above all, a natural death would lift the specter of suicide and challenges to the will. The *Bulletin* thought the actions of the estate and the involvement of Judge W. L. Stanley in Honolulu were all suspicious and came "dangerously near compounding a felony." Taken together, "the whole thing looks like the development of a careful program, cleverly conceived and promptly executed by agents at various points to shut off suspicion, quiet curiosity and establish the desired theory of Mrs. Stanford's death from acute indigestion."[7]

Other papers followed the *Bulletin*'s lead. In the great tradition of San Francisco will contests, the *Post* suggested on March 10 that a second will had been drawn up in the fall with a much larger bequest to Bertha Berner and religious charities. No one ever produced such a will.[8]

In a gossip column on March 11, the *Call* bundled the denial of murder stories, the spiritualism stories, and the insanity stories into a dangerous package. Mrs. Stanford had been delusional for so long that her friends were loath to believe her accounts of being poisoned in San Francisco, or that her death in Hawaii was murder. If she was long deranged, then nothing she said—or signed—could be trusted.[9]

Wilson had allies in the press. W. H. Mills, an old creature of Leland Stanford and his Associates, paid off a large swath of California newspapers, including the *San Francisco Post*, on behalf of the Southern Pacific, now controlled by E. H. Harriman. The *Post* denounced the stories of murder and praised Jordan and Wilson for refusing to accept them. Wilson and Lathrop had presumably asked for a favor, and Mills granted it. But it was often difficult to distinguish ineptitude from treachery within the Southern Pacific, and, in this case, the *Post* proved less helpful than it appeared. The paper denounced private detectives as "oftener employed in cases where it is necessary to hush up a scandal than in cases where the ends of justice are to be subserved." Since in the Stanford case Wilson and Lathrop were employing the Harry Morse Agency and had sent Callundan to Hawaii, the less said about private detectives, the better.[10]

⸻

THE SUSPICION THAT Mountford Wilson controlled the investigation gained credence because the police were making so little progress. Captain Burnett insisted that the department could not act without more information from Hawaii. He knew nothing about the Hawaiian evidence "except what I have read in the newspapers." In San Francisco his detectives busied themselves interviewing servants and ex-servants.[11]

Even as he denied running the investigation, Mountford Wilson continued to be its voice. The coroner's jury verdict did not sway him. "We are not thoroughly convinced that a murder has been committed; suspicions do not convict, nor do Coroner's juries hang." There were "a number of things about which we are in doubt and which can be solved only by the fullest reports. No arrests are contemplated at present; what may be done after the reports are received from Honolulu will be determined after they are thoroughly considered." The statement with its imperial "we" and passive voice made it seem that Wilson, not the police, was in charge. When the

San Francisco district attorney came to Wilson to consult about the case, he only reinforced the impression that the Stanford estate made the decisions.[12]

The San Francisco police appeared as interested in preventing challenges to the will as in solving the murder. They were reportedly investigating relatives who might have acted from greed or from revenge at being left out of the will.[13] This was certainly a legitimate line of investigation, if not the most promising one, but it was also a warning shot to relatives who might consider going to court.

When Mountford Wilson recruited "six expert physicians" in San Francisco who insisted that the cause of death was angina pectoris, Dr. Wood in Hawaii reacted with outrage. The natural death theory was "simply rot." How, he asked, did the San Franciscans explain the strychnine in the bicarbonate of soda?[14]

THINGS GREW INCREASINGLY INWARD—newspaper stories were not always what they seemed. On March 11, a columnist in the *Oakland Tribune* seemed to attack Jordan, Wilson, and even Jane Stanford. He alleged that the investigation with its focus on the servants was biased against the poor. If "a poor aged and fleshy unknown old woman" died, no one paid attention, but Mrs. Stanford was different. The investigation ignored the vagaries and delusions of a wealthy old woman to persecute and accuse the poor. The only virtue of the investigation was that it kept the police busy and cut down on graft. The poison theory besmirched "the reputations of a lot of people who probably are as honest as the day—but they are poor and 'the poor always ye have with you.'" It was necessary to remember "that the honor of a poor servitor is just as sacred as that of a rich benefactress."

The column ridiculed the no-motive argument. "Who under all heaven would want to kill Mrs. Stanford? . . . an aged woman, afflicted with some narrow ideas." Mrs. Stanford "was a clog on the great university at Palo Alto, as everybody from David Starr Jordan up or down accurately knows. But nobody would venture to put her out of the way just to free the university from the influence that crowded out Ross and lost Howard and left Jordan still genuflecting before his golden goddess; still worshipping his bread and butter."

The writer repeated the accusations that Wilson, Lathrop, and Jordan most feared: Jane Stanford was "a woman of delusions." She was a victim of "senile dementia with [its] ghosts and phantasms" who believed that people were poisoning her. The columnist vilified her dead husband, who "did more to corrupt the politics of California than any other five men the State had known." He repeated the false accusation that Leland Stanford founded the university out of spite at being denied a place on the Board of Regents at Berkeley.

Having vilified the rich, defended the poor, and raised issues feared by the estate and the university, the writer turned around and reached the same conclusion as Wilson and Jordan. There was no murder. "The bold fact is Mrs. Stanford died of senile pneumonia, resulting in angina pectoris." She "gave most of her millions in a spirit of love for humanity and desire to help the poor youth of California." "[S]he didn't die of poison." The author accepted her natural death "because I have been moved to it in consideration of the living poor."[15]

The publisher of the *Oakland Tribune* was William Dargie, a leading Republican politician accused of being a tool of the Southern Pacific under both Collis P. Huntington and Harriman. He hated the *Bulletin* and the *Call*, and their editors despised him in return. They waged a newspaper war that would go on after Jane Stanford's death.[16]

Two days later Older's *Bulletin* summoned the memory of President McKinley's assassination four years before to ridicule the natural death theory. "Had President McKinley been shot at San Francisco instead of Buffalo, the local police detectives, if the murderer had not been seen and arrested, would have asserted, no doubt, that angina pectoris was the cause of death, and that the report of a pistol at the moment he fell and the presence of a bullet in his body were mere coincidences not sufficient to offset the presumption that no person would endeavor to kill so good and noble a man." Anything that demanded "brains, persistence and hard work" was beyond the ability of the police department, and "fearing to add another to the long list of their failures, they are quick to deny that a crime has been done."[17]

The *San Francisco News* described the "aimless daily wanderings" of detectives Ed Gibson and John Cleary. "It is plain to be seen that the idea of a murder having been committed is repugnant not only to the attorney for Mrs. Stanford as well as her brother and other relatives but to the police, both private and civic, who have been called into the case, despite the facts to the contrary." The *News* concluded that "the disposition of Attorney Mountford Wilson and the Stanford heirs is to deprecate the theory of murder and to erase the entire matter from the public mind as rapidly as possible."[18]

The *Bulletin* did not stop with Wilson. It taunted Jordan as a syco-phant who was willing to bend his own principles as required. He was glad to be rid of Jane Stanford and her spiritualism, and was concerned only with his and the university's reputation.[19]

CHAPTER 41

JORDAN AND WATERHOUSE

WHEN HE ARRIVED IN HONOLULU on March 10, David Starr Jordan needed a doctor willing to question the verdict of the coroner's jury. He consulted Judge Carl Smith, the Stanford alumnus who had advised Jordan on his recommendation for the governorship of Hawaii. Smith admired Jordan, but Jordan offered other incentives. He dangled an appointment at Stanford Law School. Smith suggested Dr. Ernest C. Waterhouse, whom he described as "the best-informed physician in Honolulu." Jordan later described him "as the ablest physician we found available," which may have translated as the ablest physician willing to do what Jordan asked. Dr. Waterhouse would die decades later living as a transient in San Francisco's Tenderloin.[1]

By 1905 David Starr Jordan did not aspire to be a servant of the truth; he was its employer. His approach to truth was instrumental, fitting crudely into William James's theory of pragmatism. "Any idea upon which we can ride, so to speak; any idea that will carry us prosperously from any one part of our experience to any other part, linking things satisfactorily, working securely, simplifying, saving labor; is true for just so much, true in so far forth, true *instrumentally.*" When Jordan mounted an idea with "cash value," it could run roughshod over what other observers regarded as established fact. Jordan epitomized pragmatism run amuck. His experience at Stanford taught him that truth should serve his interests, and that other people sometimes needed incentives and persuasion to understand this. Jordan's interests required Jane Stanford to have died a natural death. Since the Hawaiian authorities failed to reach his desired conclusion, Jordan needed to discredit them and replace them with other authorities.[2]

Waterhouse labeled the report he submitted to Jordan "Testimony of Dr. Waterhouse," but it was not legal testimony. He did not attend the autopsy, nor did he witness Jane Stanford's death. Waterhouse was not under oath nor was he cross-examined. Nor did Jordan make his "testimony" public.

Waterhouse answered three questions posed by Jordan. First, did the evidence convince him that Mrs. Stanford died of strychnine poisoning; Waterhouse answered, "decidedly not." He claimed that witnesses saw only a single spasm, one that did not have the severity typical of strychnine poisoning. In addition, he said that when Berner and Hunt rubbed and massaged her, and put her hands and feet in warm water, this should have sent her into violent convulsions but did not. The case lacked "the exaggerated reflexes and muscular excitability" typical of strychnine poisoning. "If this had been a typical strychnine poisoning convulsion she would have known she was poisoned—nothing is more frightful." He used her exclamation, "I think I am poisoned," to argue that she was not in fact poisoned because if she was, she would have known and not just thought it. He omitted any mention of her saying, "This is a horrible death to die." He attributed her symptoms and statements to hysteria—the classic contemporary diagnosis of unexplained illness in women.[3]

Jordan next asked whether there was any sign that the death could be due to angina pectoris or any other cause. Waterhouse said yes. Mrs. Stanford overate at lunch, and although the autopsy found her stomach to be empty, she must have had considerable gas, which would have created pressure on her heart. This would have prompted hysteria, while either the gas or too much water triggered a heart attack. She presumably could have been saved by a fart. The autopsy found no evidence of a heart attack, but he characterized the autopsy report as meager.[4]

The final question concerned whether finding traces of strychnine in the intestine would have changed Waterhouse's opinion. He answered no.[5]

Waterhouse said he based his report largely on an afternoon of interviews—with Jordan present—of May Hunt and Bertha Berner. He supposedly took no notes (nor did Jordan), which was remarkable for a physician preparing any kind of a report, let alone one for a suspected murder. Nor did he interview the attending physicians.[6]

Waterhouse may have taken no notes because he had access to the transcript of Callundan's separate examinations of Bertha Berner. The *San Francisco Call* reported that Callundan and Reynolds also called on Dr. Waterhouse. An account in the *San Francisco Chronicle* published when Callundan arrived in San Francisco gives details of Jane Stanford's death and other aspects of the case that clearly quotes from and depends on an at least partial transcript of the detective's examination of Berner. The "Testimony of Dr. Waterhouse," in turn, bears a remarkable resemblance to the *Chronicle* story. Both seem to have derived from the same source.[7]

The *Chronicle* reporter noted that in her interview with the detectives, Bertha Berner reversed critical portions of her sworn testimony before the coroner's jury and what she told the *Hawaiian Star* the day after Mrs. Stanford's death. She told the *Star* that Mrs. Stanford suffered "great agony and her legs and arms became rigid," and that later her jaws became rigid. She testified under oath that Mrs. Stanford said she lost control of her body and that "another spasm" was coming on. But when she talked to Callundan she seemed to be describing a different death. There was no twitching or jerking of the head or limbs. She had told both the coroner's jury and the *Star* that Mrs. Stanford's jaws were set. She told Callundan the opposite. She testified that Stanford's last words were "God forgive me my sins . . ." and "This is a horrible death to die." She told Callundan that the only sounds Stanford made at the end were "Oh!" She testified that the end came amid a "violent spasm." She told Callundan that Mrs. Stanford passed away peacefully. She said that far from being rigid, Mrs. Stanford's head and neck slumped and needed to be supported. Her face did not darken but grew pallid. When they laid her on the bed she looked "as natural and as sweet as ever."[8]

Small details predictably vary when witnesses are reexamined, but Berner removed every detail that pointed to strychnine as if she were reading from a script. How much Callundan and, later, Jordan led her to do so can't be fully ascertained. Since the newspapers were full of the details on the effects of strychnine, Berner could deduce what she should not say.

Berner's interest in finding that Jane Stanford died a natural death coincided with the interests of Callundan and Jordan. If Jane Stanford was not murdered, there could be no murderer, and no further investigation or trial would be necessary. Why question an account that freed her from suspicion?

So thoroughly did Berner scrub away the details of strychnine poisoning that Jordan seems to have worried that she went too far. It appeared that she was purposefully eliminating evidence. Jordan went out of his way to assure Mountford Wilson that during the interview "Miss Berner had no other conception than that Mrs. Stanford had died of strychnine poisoning."[9]

Nearly a century later Robert Cutler, who taught at the Stanford Medical School, obtained access to both Waterhouse's report and the testimony before the coroner's jury. He noted Waterhouse's lack of clinical experience, his apparent unfamiliarity with any actual case of strychnine poisoning, and the absence of a medical library at Queens Hospital in Honolulu where Waterhouse practiced.

Cutler's evaluation was scathing. Waterhouse mistook the textbook account of strychnine poisoning—what Cutler termed a gestalt and which included all the possible symptoms—for the more limited range of symptoms present during specific instances of strychnine poisoning. Cutler explained that the gestalt was pedagogically useful but less useful diagnostically since not all symptoms occur all of the time. They vary according to the amount of poison, the age and condition of the victim, and the circumstances surrounding the administration of the poison. There were cases in which 1/16th of a grain produced alarming symptoms, and others in which 8 grains resulted in only an unsteady gait and recovery.[10] A doctor needed to consider such variations in cases.

Waterhouse was wrong in thinking that Jane Stanford's symptoms did not fit quite comfortably within the range of the manifestations of strychnine poisoning. If he had done the research:

> He would have encountered descriptions of Mrs. Stanford's terminal symptoms: the "sense of impending death . . . eyeballs prominent and pupils dilated during convulsion . . . patient quite conscious." He might even have found reports of patients thrown out of bed by a spasm. . . . [He] would have learned that . . . a firm grasp does not trigger a convulsive spasm.[11]

Waterhouse's analysis can be chalked up to his inexperience and lack of knowledge, but I think more was involved. Waterhouse played by Jordan's rules: he ignored the evidence given to the coroner's jury. He relied fully on his and Jordan's interview with Berner and Callundan's and Reynold's separate interview with her.[12]

Waterhouse said there was only one spasm, but there were three: the first one that threw Jane Stanford from bed and caused her to call for help; the second, during which Mrs. Stanford said she could not control her body, and her jaws tightened so she could not swallow; and the final spasm, which killed her. Jane Stanford herself referred to multiple spasms, telling Dr. Humphris, "another spasm is coming on."[13]

Although Waterhouse claimed that none of the classic symptoms of a fatal seizure of strychnine were present, Drs. Humphris and Murray, who were present at the death, described virtually all of them: the protruding eyeballs, the head thrown back—implying a rigid neck—jaws fixed, hands gripped so tight that the thumbs were dug into the palms of her hands, feet arched, purplish red spots over the face and ears. Dr. Day added testimony to the extreme arching of the feet and the ankles turned inward in a way he had never seen before.[14]

Berner gave Waterhouse a set of written responses to follow-up questions that he submitted after the interview. They were not as helpful as Waterhouse hoped. Berner did not deny there were spasms. She only said she doubted the first spasm, despite Jane Stanford's statement that it threw her to the floor, because, like many old people, Jane Stanford had difficulty rising and so Berner thought she could not have gotten up. She said Stanford had trouble getting out of low chairs and porcelain bathtubs, but difficulty in rising was not the inability to rise.[15]

Berner said that if Stanford had fallen and gotten back up, she was sure that she would have told her. But Mrs. Stanford told May Hunt that a fit had thrown her out of bed. She might have said this before Berner arrived or while Berner was seeking a doctor. That she did not repeat the statement to Berner hardly proved that the spasm did not occur.[16]

Waterhouse rearranged the supplementary Berner statement into a claim that Mrs. Stanford had "jumped" from her bed. And ignoring Berner's testimony that Mrs. Stanford enjoyed the day and was neither tired nor worn out, he said Mrs. Stanford was subject to a fatiguing day.[17]

Waterhouse could not provide evidence of indigestion let alone a heart attack, but he insisted the heart attack was "more probable."[18] In part, he relied on Berner's revised account of the picnic. She said that during the picnic on the afternoon of Stanford's death, she and May Hunt had helped her up after Mrs. Stanford sat an hour in a full and chilly wind. Berner had not mentioned this in her earlier accounts. They ate lunch in a grove, presumably out of the wind. And in any case the temperature that day was in the seventies.[19]

On March 13, Waterhouse and Jordan dined together at the University Club in Honolulu and agreed to treat the report as a privileged communication. Why Waterhouse wrote the report is more mysterious than why Jordan commissioned it. Waterhouse admired Jordan and seems to have been flattered to have been consulted. The report was the work of three or four days, and it yielded a hefty fee. Carl Smith said that Jordan paid for the report, but the Stanford estate eventually paid Waterhouse $350.[20]

The money hardly seemed worth the pummeling Waterhouse took from his colleagues in Hawaii once they discovered that he was the doctor Jordan relied upon to discredit the autopsy. But it appears that Waterhouse did not think that his future lay in medicine. He planned to move into rubber cultivation. Jordan, who apparently invested in rubber plantations, could help him. Waterhouse's fee presumably financed a trip he took to Ceylon to examine plantations. He planned to leave Hawaii in April, but he did not depart until May.[21]

Jordan got the report he wanted, but it was useful to him only so long as he never revealed it. He referred to it repeatedly, but he never published it. He couldn't. He had trapped himself. As the *Chronicle* reporter noticed in Callundan's interviews of Berner, she contradicted the sworn testimony she gave to the coroner's jury as well as her previous accounts of Jane Stanford's death. Publishing Waterhouse's report—which repeated the same information Berner gave to Callundan—would highlight those contradictions. Berner either lied to the court or she was lying to Waterhouse. Instead of removing the possibility of murder, the published report would point to an organized attempt to suppress the investigation of the murder. In the Waterhouse report, the fates of Jordan and Berner were joined.

CHAPTER 42

A MELODRAMATIC DETECTIVE STORY

ON MARCH 15, FOUR COAL-BLACK HORSES drew Jane Stanford's coffin to the Central Union Church in Honolulu. Although it was not yet eight in the morning, thousands of people lined the street. Governor George Carter, Judge Carl Smith, David Starr Jordan, and Timothy Hopkins—all in Prince Albert coats and tall silk hats—served as pallbearers. Dressed in an academic gown, the Reverend William Kincaid read the text, "I have fought the Good Fight . . ." from Paul's second epistle to Timothy. Episcopal Bishop Henry Bond Restarick conducted a simple ceremony, and the choir sang "Beneath the Cross of Jesus," "Nearer, My God, to Thee," and "Lead Kindly Light." Hopkins presumably discovered that these were Jane Stanford's favorite hymns by asking Bertha Berner. Berner, heavily veiled and leaning on May Hunt, showed "intense grief." The *Pacific Commercial Advertiser* thought that no one who saw her could doubt the sincerity of her sorrow or hold the "slightest suspicion against her." From the church, a police escort took the casket to the steamer *Alameda*. Berner, Hopkins, Jordan, May Hunt, and the detectives accompanied it back to San Francisco.[1]

The night before the funeral Jordan and Hopkins drew up a statement declaring that Jane Stanford had died of natural causes. Her death, they said, "was the result of conditions and circumstances." The causes were her "advanced age, the unaccustomed exertion, a surfeit of unsuitable food, and the unusual exposure of the picnic party." These were "perhaps" aggravated by the strychnine in the medicinal capsule and the small amount in the bicarbonate. The strychnine in the bicarbonate was, they thought, the result of a pharmacist's error, although no one could find a source of bicarbonate that contained strychnine. Jordan and Hopkins, referring to the "evidence in our possession" but not to the Waterhouse report that contained the "evidence," concluded that she had not died of poisoning, either purposeful or accidental.[2]

The newspapers anticipated Jordan's conclusion. High Sheriff Henry told the press that Jordan, Hopkins, and the detectives did not come to solve the crime but instead to cover it up. Jordan had sown doubt about the coroner's jury, the Hawaiian police, and the doctors ever since his arrival. The Stanford estate wanted Jane Stanford to have died a natural death despite the presence of strychnine in the bicarbonate, all the symptoms of strychnine poisoning, and the results of the autopsy. Deputy High Sheriff Rawlins, who was to have gone to San Francisco to coordinate the Hawaiian and San Francisco investigations, canceled his trip after Jordan's statement, which left nothing to coordinate.[3]

Timothy Hopkins made it clear that desire rather than evidence was the midwife of his and Jordan's statement. When a reporter pressed him for his opinion, he replied, "Well, we all wish it to be a death from natural causes, don't we?"[4] Jordan argued from his authority as a scientist and a physician. As a scientist, Jordan knew about poisons. He used them to collect fish. As a physician, he did not know much. Jordan made pronouncements on medicine, just as he made pronouncements on virtually everything, but his medical opinions were often regrettable. Just before Jane Stanford's death he denounced mandatory vaccinations and reportedly said he considered most physicians ignorant men.[5] When he said "unaccustomed exertion" contributed to her death, he did so in the knowledge that for years she walked miles a day.

Jordan predictably supplemented his official statement with ad hominem attacks. He told an *Evening Bulletin* reporter that "Dr. Humphris . . . knew little or nothing about strychnine poisoning." In regard to the "scientific side of Mrs. Stanford's death . . . Dr. Humphris and his associates don't know what they are talking about."[6]

Jordan had no intention of publicly defending this statement. Fearing the response of skeptical reporters, the Hawaiian police, and outraged Hawaiian physicians, he told Carl Smith to release the report of his conclusions after he was safely on board the *Alameda*. As the *Exam-*

iner pointed out, he would be "beyond the interviewer and beyond the cross-questioner."[7]

Among the many peaks in the mountain range of doubt about his statement, one loomed above the others. Jordan provided no credible explanation for the presence of strychnine in the bicarbonate. Coupled with the strychnine in the Poland Spring Water, even the most credulous must have wondered why strychnine repeatedly appeared in the palliatives of a woman whom Jordan adamantly insisted did not die of strychnine poisoning.[8]

Jordan tried to render the questions irrelevant. He gave Smith an additional statement to cable to Mountford Wilson once Jordan left Honolulu. "Miss Berner took the same doses of bicarbonate and the same capsule as Mrs. Stanford did at the same time, and experienced no discomfort." If Berner took the same medicines without effect, then the cause of death must lie elsewhere. Smith dutifully cabled the news to Wilson.[9]

The story was false, and Jordan was caught in the lie. Unable to keep his mouth shut, before the *Alameda* departed he talked to Robert Beverly Kidd, a former *San Francisco Examiner* reporter who now worked for the *Hawaiian Star* and the Associated Press. Jordan told Kidd that Berner also took the bicarbonate. He seems to have thought Berner would support whatever he said. But Kidd had already talked to Berner, and he replied that this was not what Berner told him. Nor was it what she had told the coroner's jury and the newspapers: "She [Mrs. Stanford] suggested that I take some soda, too. I told her I would not take any soda."[10]

Jordan backtracked, claiming Callundan told him the story, but instead of abandoning his own lie, he cut it in half. He said that he went to Berner's cabin and "learned the fact that she had taken the same capsule but only half the amount of soda. . . ." He sent Kidd a written message telling him to ask Smith to hold the cable since it was "not quite true." Kidd telephoned Smith, and an incredulous Smith demanded Kidd show him the instructions in writing. Kidd did so. It was too late. Smith could not recall the cable.[11]

Jordan was at sea when the story hit the papers, and Smith was left holding the bag. He, too, tried to cover one lie by telling another. He said Berner was not "cross-examined" until the day before departure, so it was only recently discovered that she took the bicarbonate. Jordan told Smith "[i]t makes no difference." An exasperated *Examiner* reporter trying to reconcile the various accounts complained that no "forthright" move or statement seemed possible in the Stanford case. "Everything must be fogged like a melodramatic detective story."[12] This was just David Starr Jordan in action. Edward Ross knew how he worked; so did George Howard, Alfred Schmidt, John Nourse, Julius Goebel, and Ernest Pease. So had Jane Stanford.

Above all, George Crothers knew it. Crothers largely stayed quiet as the investigation unfolded, but on March 14 he told the *Chronicle* that in his opinion "Mrs. Stanford was poisoned . . . and by the same hand that poisoned the bottle of Poland water." We know, he said, that "she went to Honolulu in the hope of escaping a second attempt . . . the only possible link that is missing is the failure of the chemists to find strychnine in appreciable quantities in the organs they examined." It was only, he noted, in recent years that finding traces of strychnine in the organs had even become possible.[13]

Privately, Crothers wrote to Horace Davis on March 10 that he had no doubt Stanford was murdered by a servant, but that he did not suspect Bertha Berner because of the strong attachment between them. In a later letter, he thought the attempt on Jane Stanford's life in San Francisco was made "by either a maid or a Chinaman." He thought the strychnine in the bicarbonate was "a part of the original plan" but there was not enough to kill her.[14]

Crothers wanted to distance himself from Jordan and Wilson, but he did not desire to tell what he knew and open up a challenge to the money bequeathed to the university. His paramount goal remained protecting the university, even if this meant staying quiet about men he despised. He was now on record as disagreeing with Jordan and Wilson, but he went no further.

JANE STANFORD COMES HOME

CHAPTER 43

TAY WANG AND CHIEF OF POLICE WITTMAN

ON MARCH 12, THE *SAN FRANCISCO CALL* reported that the city police had narrowed their Poland Spring Water investigation to Albert Beverly and Elizabeth Richmond, who were presumed to have worked together, and Ah Wing.[1] But if the same person or persons were responsible for both poisonings, it became impossible to explain how either Beverly or Richmond could have put strychnine in the bicarbonate of soda that Jane Stanford took in the Moana Hotel. This left Ah Wing as the main suspect among the servants.

Ah Wing had access to both the Poland Spring Water and the bicarbonate of soda bottle, which had sat for days in Mrs. Stanford's room waiting to be packed. He had the opportunity, and he had a motive—the bequest in Jane Stanford's will and revenge for his betrayal by Harry Lathrop, Jane's brother, who had left him out of his will. Bertha Berner stated, retracted, and then stated again her suspicion of him. She similarly equivocated on Mrs. Stanford's suspicion of him.

The detectives caught him in his contradictions, but his greatest vulnerability remained his race. Since the 1850s, white Californians blamed virtually everything wrong with the state on the Chinese. Philip Atkinson, who worked for Charles Lathrop, told reporters that "a Chink would not hesitate at anything if he saw his way clear to receiving a wad of money" that could buy a return to China.[2]

Ah Wing did not need any more trouble, but in March of 1905 he got it. The trouble came out of Chinatown.

IN FICTIONAL MURDER MYSTERIES a key piece of evidence appears. Although its significance at first goes unrecognized, it eventually opens the door to solving the crime. On March 15, the day David Starr Jordan left Honolulu with Jane Stanford's body, "Tay Wang" wrote a letter to Jordan asking for a meeting. It is the strangest piece of evidence in the strange story of Jane Stanford's death.

Tay Wang complained that "mob men" engaged in forgery, fraud, blackmail, robbery, and bribery had kidnapped his wife. He indicated this was connected with both Jane Stanford's death and an ongoing investigation of Chief George Wittman and police corruption in Chinatown. In places the letter is nearly indecipherable. Tay Wang most likely wrote it in Chinese and then had the characters translated into English by someone who was not a fluent English speaker.[3]

As far as I can tell, the critical section of the letter reads: "The infidel De Lung [or De Sung] with the mob men consider impostur by name deceitful Mrs. Jane. Chas. Lathrop. They dare does action. Secret plot." The jumble of names asserts some connection without making that connection explicit. The letter proposed a meeting between Tay Wang and David Starr Jordan to take place at the Occidental Hotel, the building that housed Wakelee's pharmacy, where Elizabeth Richmond took the Poland Spring Water for testing. Presumably, Tay Wang would then reveal how these events were associated.[4]

When I found the letter, I was not sure what it meant. I am still not sure, but I think the letter was intended as Ah Wing's death warrant.

Tay Wang, who also went by an English name—Charles Eyre—sounds like Wong Toy Wong, but the Wong Toy Wong who threatened Jane Stanford in January of 1905 was locked up in the mental hospital in Mendocino. There are Tay Wangs and Tay Wongs and Tai Wongs in the census. It is impossible to identify any of them with the author of the letter. Tay Wang's use of the word *infidel*, a term not ordinarily used by the Chinese, indicates that he may have been a Christian convert.[5]

The letter never mentions Ah Wing, but without Ah Wing I find it hard to understand its timing, and why Tay Wang had sent it to Detective

Sergeant Gibson to forward to Jordan. Gibson was interrogating Ah Wing at the time. If Tay Wang were simply a crank with no information to offer, Gibson would not have bothered to forward the letter to Jordan. Nor would Jordan have segregated the letter out from his other papers unless he thought it might prove useful. He treated it as he did another letter from 1894 that involved an allegation that Leland Stanford had fathered a son out of wedlock, whom Jane made sure was neither acknowledged nor included in his will.[6] Jordan apparently thought the letter might prove helpful in his struggles with Mrs. Stanford.

Gibson provided a gateway to Jordan, but there was also a gateway to Gibson. In forwarding Tay Wang's letter, Gibson attached both his own card and a second card for Kwong Chun Yuen & Co. on Washington Street. The company paid taxes in 1896, and contributed five dollars to a reception for volunteers returning from the Philippines in 1901. Its storefront was severely damaged in a fire in 1904, only a few months before Tay Wang wrote his letter.[7]

It took me a long time to find plausible connections between Kwong Chun Yuen & Co., Gibson, and Tay Wang. Tay Wang complained about blackmailers in his letter, and two years earlier Gibson was involved in hunting down blackmailers who belonged to the Si On tong. He roughed them up and threatened them. Chief among them was a "Chong Yuen," dubbed the "Black Devil."[8] Chong Yuen could have very well been Kwong Chun Yuen, which would explain the connection with Gibson. Like Little Pete before him, and like his contemporary Kid Sullivan, Chong Yuen could have been a criminal who protected his own interests by feeding information to the police.

Gibson may have attached Kwong Chun Yuen's company card to the letter and forwarded it to Jordan because Tay Wang used Chong Yuen to contact Gibson. Chong Yuen in some way vouched for Tay Wang and his claims about the mob men and the Chinese underworld.

The clearest thing about the letter is that Tay Wang wanted his wife back, and that a De Lung or De Sung had kidnapped her. Unable to find Tay Wang, I looked for De Lung or De Sung. More players appeared.

IN 1903 GIBSON HAD BECOME involved in a tong war between the Suey Yings and Hop Sings. Both tongs belonged to the See Yup *huigan* (as did

Ah Wing), but this did not lessen their animosity. The conflict went badly for the Suey Yings, some of whom asked for police protection. Among them was Sun Lee Lung, who was apparently a member of both the Suey Yings and the Chinese Educational Society, which claimed to be a benevolent society connected with Christian missionaries.[9] Sun Lee Lung may have been the mysterious De Lung or De Sung. Phonetically, "De Lung" is close to "Lee Lung."

This is admittedly a guess, but if true, then the Tay Wang letter begins to make some sense. At the beginning of 1903 a person could be both a See Yup and a member of the Chinese Educational Society, but that would not be possible for long. In the spring of 1903 the See Yups and the Chinese Educational Society went to war. In choosing loyalties, part of the line of demarcation might have been Christianity—thus the reference to infidel.

The press and public exoticized Chinatown for what a writer for *Town Talk*, a San Francisco weekly, called "its foul dark depths, its stifling labyrinths or its ill-smelling alleys, for the tragedy, medieval romance and the repellant Oriental coloring with which that habitat of the heathen abounds." But there was a real Chinese underworld full of what Tay Wang called "mob men." Chinatown's depths and alleys were the haunts of the "highbinders," as Chinese fighting men were called. They engaged in extortion, blackmail, murder, and theft. They offered protection to gamblers for a price. And they trafficked in women. Some of the fighting men belonged to tongs; others were independent. Still others by the turn of the century belonged to the Chinese Educational Society.[10]

The Chinese Educational Society was a creation of American-born Chinese. In the early twentieth century, San Francisco's Chinatown was becoming very American, a product of Chinese immigrants and their children, who, like Little Pete, adjusted to the United States.[11] The Society drew its members largely from native-born Chinese, many of whom spoke some English. They were citizens, and the Society's public face advocated Western education, reform, Christianity, and progress. Its members also acted as labor contractors. Some were connected with the Ruef machine, even though his Union Labor Party ran racist anti-Chinese advertisements to solicit the votes of white workers. And the Society operated as a criminal syndicate, engaged, among other things, in the "importation of women for immoral purposes." They blackmailed or protected gamblers as circumstances dictated.[12]

In 1903 the Chinese Educational Society and the See Yup *huigan* and its tongs went to war over the gambling houses of Chinatown. The gamblers paid the Eight Statesmen, as a syndicate of See Yup tong presidents called themselves, to protect the owners of gambling houses from robbery and extortion by Chinese criminals and the police. The Statesmen used a portion of the payments to bribe the police. Chan Cheung or Big Cheung, one of the Eight Statesmen, acted as paymaster.[13] When the Educational Society tried to muscle in, the See Yups resisted. The Educational Society and the See Yups mustered allies in the newspapers, the courts, the police department, and the Morse Detective Agency.

The war sucked in Chief Wittman and the police commission, the board that oversaw the police department. Grant Carpenter, who was both a reporter for the *Examiner* and the lawyer for the Chinese Educational Society, helped secure indictments of the Eight Statesmen. He also went after Chief Wittman in order to stop the Chinatown patrol from favoring the See Yups. The See Yups recruited powerful allies of their own. Hiram Johnson, who would within a few years become governor of California, served as attorney for Nguen Lun, one of the Eight Statesmen who was indicted. In May of 1904 the judge declared a mistrial after a juror reported an attempt to bribe him to acquit Lun.[14]

Fremont Older of the *Bulletin* became Carpenter's ally, thinking that bringing down Wittman would aid his crusade to destroy the Ruef machine. He thought that the bribes from Chinese gamblers went much higher up the chain than the beat cops and detectives of the Chinatown patrol. He set his sights on Mayor Schmitz, Boss Ruef, Chief Wittman, and two of the police commissioners: Thomas Reagan and John A. Drinkhouse. Older published his accusations on November 30, 1904, with pictures of his targets on the front page. After Older entered the fray, Grant Carpenter told him that Chan Cheung was the keystone. Bring him down, and Ruef would fall.

Older discovered that Detective Sergeant Tom Ellis of the Chinatown patrol was getting $200 a month from Chan Cheung, and under pressure of exposure, Ellis agreed to testify before a grand jury in exchange for being put on the staff of the *Bulletin* at $125 a month. In court Ellis produced $1,400 he received from Chan Cheung, and said that the scheme was ongoing when he was assigned to Chinatown. But he refused to implicate anyone above him. Older wryly noted that Ellis's refusal meant that Older gained nothing except having to pay Ellis for the next two years.[15]

Under the dubious authority granted by a cooperating member of the grand jury, Older had Chan Cheung kidnapped and stashed him in the same Occidental Hotel where Tay Wang wanted to meet Jordan. The hotel was a bridge between Chinese and non-Chinese San Francisco. Traveling dignitaries from both China and Japan stayed there, and a Chinese guest would not have attracted notice.

Since Chan Cheung was an opium addict, Older thought ensuring his cooperation was a simple matter of cutting off his opium supply. The plan was to bring him to the grand jury, parade before him a series of fighting men who would implicate him in Chinatown murders, and then offer him a deal. He could give the names of city and police officials taking bribes and then be allowed to return to China to live out his days, or he could be indicted for murder and hanged.

Older underestimated his man. Cheung recognized the irregularity of his arrest and detention. He had been kidnapped. Although sick and shaking from opium withdrawal, he refused to talk. The grand jury locked him in a county jail, where he received "the worst kind of treatment." He remained silent. As Older later remembered, "And all the while Chief Wittman and Ruef and Schmitz were smiling around the streets of San Francisco. They knew the Oriental. They knew we could boil him in oil and he would not talk." Older admitted that he was beaten. Chan Cheung was released on a writ of habeas corpus. Older abandoned his attack on Chinese gamblers as a way to get at Ruef, Schmitz, and Wittman, and turned his attention to prostitution.[16]

Ellis's appearance before the grand jury bared the corruption in the police department. The grand jury indicated that they thought the corruption extended to the Board of Police Commissioners, but they lacked enough evidence to indict. The members of the police board were as indignant as they were probably guilty. They put the blame solely on Ellis and Wittman. Ellis denied he had confessed to the grand jury and invoked the Fifth Amendment against self-incrimination. On February 15, 1905, the board unanimously voted to remove him from the force. If Ellis was representative, San Francisco cops had a sense of humor. Since the grand jury did not indict him, Ellis asked for the return of the $1,400 Chan Cheung had given him.[17]

In March, Wittman became the Schmitz administration's scapegoat for the scandal in Chinatown.[18] The Board of Police Commissioners did not accuse him of taking bribes, but rather of allowing "open and notorious gambling to flourish" in Chinatown between November 7th and November 29th of 1904.[19] The specificity of the dates told the tale. November 7 was the day an injunction obtained by *huigan* lawyers against interference with Chinatown's gamblers expired. November 29 was the date of a raid by Police Commissioner Hutton on a See Yup gambling house. Older's article appeared on November 30. Chief Wittman was to take the blame for a supposed brief resurgence of gambling.[20] The police commissioners exonerated Ruef, Schmitz, and themselves of any involvement in the Chinatown scheme in what the *Chronicle* called a "whitewash report" written by Grant Carpenter. They left Wittman "unwhitewashed."[21]

This was the moment when Tay Wang intervened. Gibson, an ally of Wittman, certainly knew that the Chinese underworld was behind the assault on Wittman. What Tay Wang offered was evidence that they were also involved in the murder of Jane Stanford. By linking the two, he could vindicate Wittman and hurt the police commission.

The problem is that I am not sure what side Tay Wang was on. His English name, Charles Eyre, indicated that he was possibly a member of the Chinese Educational Society. He wanted revenge on De Lung or Lee Lung, who was both a See Yup and was, or at least had been, a member of the Chinese Educational Society. I do not know where Lee Lung placed his loyalty when forced to choose. Tay Wang could have linked him to either the See Yups or the Educational Society.

My guess is that Tay Wang did not care who won the struggle between the Educational Society and the See Yups, or if Wittman was convicted or not. If attacking the Educational Society and giving information on Jane Stanford's murder would lead Gibson and Jordan to help him get his wife back, he would do so. Maybe he did know something about Jane Stanford's murder. If he did, that information could help decide the fate of Ah Wing, the most available Chinese suspect. Any insinuation that a plot against Stanford originated in Chinatown would cast more suspicion on Ah Wing. Gibson may have already been convinced of Ah Wing's guilt; he and the Morse detectives had been sweating him since the news of Jane Stanford's death turned the servants into suspects.

Gibson needed a murderer, and he presumed Jordan did also. Gibson delivered Tay Wang's letter, which awaited Jordan on his return from Hawaii. He moved to set up the meeting between Jordan and Tay Wang at the Occidental Hotel, where he would also be present. It was hard to see how this could work out well for Ah Wing.

It all came to naught. Jordan no longer needed or wanted a suspect. He and Wilson had decided that Jane Stanford died of natural causes. Ah Wing's life dangled on a slender thread. Jordan's decision may have saved him.

There was no saving Wittman. His enemies on the police commission led by Hutton removed him, and just as Police Commissioner Hutton turned on Wittman, so Boss Ruef turned on Hutton. When Hutton and Ruef quarreled over the system of payments for liquor licenses by San Francisco's French restaurants, which rented rooms to prostitutes and paid legal fees to Ruef, Ruef had Mayor Schmitz remove Hutton from the police commission. The Educational Society lost an important ally.[22]

All of this mattered more to the police than who killed Jane Stanford.

CHAPTER 44

DEATH OF AN INVESTIGATION

ON MARCH 21, 1905, THE *ALAMEDA* arrived in San Francisco with Jane Stanford's body. The state legislature adjourned in her honor and flags flew at half-staff—the first time, so the newspapers reported, that this was done in California for a woman in civil life. Thousands of spectators and an extraordinary police presence that included acting chief of police Spillane, soon-to-be chief Dinan, and more than a hundred officers greeted the *Alameda*. Reporters were banned from the revenue cutter that met the ship in the harbor, but they came aboard at the dock. They did not have access to Bertha Berner and May Hunt, who remained secluded, guarded by a steward and several assistants.[1]

During their days together at sea, Bertha Berner, David Starr Jordan, Timothy Hopkins, Jules Callundan, Harry Reynolds, and May Hunt tried to coordinate their roles in presenting the circumstances of Mrs. Stanford's death to the public. Jordan wanted to shape the press narrative and the San Francisco police investigation. He had his work cut out for him.

News by cable traveled far faster than the *Alameda*, and Jordan's and Hopkins's departing statement brought reactions in Hawaii that bounced to San Francisco and created an atmosphere of incredulity. In Hawaii, High Sheriff Henry said that Jordan and Hopkins "were not led by the evidence" in their conclusions that Mrs. Stanford had died a natural death. Drs. Humphris, Day, and Murray tore into Jordan's statement in a public response on March 17. They summarized the evidence: an unknown quantity of strychnine in the bicarbonate, a rapid death consistent with strychnine poisoning, and all the well-known physical manifestations of strychnine poisoning. They found "astonishing" Jordan's statement that there were no characteristics of strychnine poisoning present. They quoted Berner's and Hunt's statements before the coroner's jury describing exactly those symptoms. They repeated their own testimony describing those symptoms. They quoted the 1904 edition of the *Reference Hand-book of Medical Science* describing precisely Jane Stanford's symptoms as those diagnostic of strychnine poisoning. They quoted Dr. Potter's *Medica Materia* to say that only 1/12th of a grain was enough to produce the symptoms of strychnine poisoning. With a toxic dose, according to Dr. Potter, the spasms could be strong enough to jerk the victim from the bed, which was what Jane Stanford reported.

As for Jordan's theories of acute indigestion, there was no food in the stomach and intestines. All her vital organs—including her heart—were normal. It was "imbecile to think that a woman of Mrs. Stanford's age and mental condition might have died of a hysterical seizure in half an hour." No board of health would ever certify the causes Jordan and Hopkins gave for her death.[2]

In San Francisco, the newspapers sided with the Hawaiian doctors. The *Post*, changing sides once more, dismissed the Jordan/Wilson theory of a natural death as absurd.[3] If anything, the statement by Hopkins and Jordan, which offered no plausible cause of her death, increased suspicion that the university and the estate were trying to whitewash a murder.[4] The *Bulletin* shredded Jordan's statements, and the *Chronicle* dismissed them as being without evidence.[5] Only the *San Francisco Star*, a weekly of little influence, thought the natural death theory correct.[6] At the university, the faculty and students reportedly upheld the theory of a natural death, but this could only have been written by someone with no knowledge of the university and its intrigues.[7]

Jordan's and Hopkins's statement and the press reaction put the San Francisco police on the defensive. Captain Burnett once more denied that Mountford Wilson was trying to subvert the murder investigation. He awaited the return of Reynolds and Callundan. The police insisted that they would not be a party to any attempt to "hush up" the poisoning of Mrs. Stanford, which was what the authorities in Hawaii were accusing Jordan of trying to do.[8]

Mountford Wilson said he was awaiting necessary proof for the natural death theory.[9] The proof was supposedly aboard the *Alameda*. Jane Stanford's brain, heart, and kidneys would be retested; the transcripts of witnesses examined by Reynolds and Callundan in Hawaii would be studied, and Berner and Hunt questioned yet again.[10]

Jordan orchestrated the presentation of the proof. The start was not auspicious. Timothy Hopkins told reporters that Bertha Berner would have nothing to say because she had told everything to the coroner's jury already, and she stood by her testimony. Perhaps Hopkins did not actually read Berner's original testimony, or perhaps he did not read the Waterhouse report, which contradicted Berner's original testimony. Or perhaps Timothy Hopkins was just confused. One of the purposes of Callundan's interview with Berner, and the Waterhouse report, was to reverse Berner's original testimony. If Berner stood by her original testimony, then the as-yet-unrevealed Waterhouse report, and the Jordan and Hopkins statement that Mrs. Stanford died a natural death, were false.[11]

Jules Callundan left Honolulu saying that he would come to a conclusion about the solution of the mystery in San Francisco; it didn't take him long to reach one. On disembarking, he told reporters that they could decide the cause of death once the police released the interviews conducted in Hawaii, but he did not think the cause of death was murder or suicide. Callundan's final written report, if there was one, and the full transcripts of his interviews in Honolulu, have vanished. But on the same day the *Alameda* arrived, the police department gave reporters excerpts from his interviews with Berner, May Hunt, and Dr. Humphris, as well as Callundan's reasons for concluding that there was no evidence of poisoning.[12]

Reporters quickly noted that the interview with Berner differed dramatically from her testimony before the coroner's jury. Both her statements could not be true. Callundan's interview implied that Berner had lied under oath in her original testimony, but was telling the truth to him.[13]

Callundan attacked Dr. Humphris directly. Callundan argued that the circumstances of Mrs. Stanford's death were incompatible with the spasms brought on by strychnine, and that Dr. Humphris's testimony was riddled with mistakes and contradictions.[14]

The attack on Humphris floundered because Humphris's testimony contained neither mistakes nor contradictions. Callundan accused Humphris of making a false statement when he testified that Mrs. Stanford died in bed when, in fact, she died in a chair. Because she died in the chair, Callundan concluded that Mrs. Stanford could not have experienced strychnine spasms, which would have thrown her from the chair. But the false statements belonged to Callundan. Humphris testified that Jane Stanford died in the chair, and only when he and Dr. Day failed to detect a pulse did they move her body to the bed. The record of the coroner's jury showed that Dr. Humphris, Dr. Murray, Bertha Berner, and May Hunt all testified to the reality of the spasms, and the victim herself proclaimed their onset. Callundan, faced with witnesses who described spasms that did not throw the victim to the floor, simply denied that the spasms occurred. The witnesses could believe him or their lying eyes.

Callundan gave the reporters a seemingly plausible argument: a violent spasm would have overturned the pan of water Bertha Berner had placed on Mrs. Stanford's lap to warm her hands as well as the basin of water at her feet. But Callundan neglected to show that the basins of water were present when the spasms came on. Dr. Humphris took a glass from her hand when the final spasm came on, which would indicate her hands were free and not in a basin of water. Dr. H. V. Murray, who saw her just before the fatal spasm, mentioned neither a basin of water on Mrs. Stanford's lap nor one at her feet. May Hunt did mention putting Jane Stanford's hands and feet in warm water, but she did not say that the containers of hot water were still there when the last spasm occurred. Berner, too, mentioned the hot water, but did not say it was there before the last spasm. When Dr. Humphris returned to prepare a hypodermic and medicine, it seems likely that he would have removed the water before he tried to administer the medicine. The *San Francisco Call*, which quoted Berner's testimony, had Berner and May Hunt rubbing Mrs. Stanford's hands and feet prior to the last spasm. There was no mention of the water.[15]

Harry Reynolds said that in his opinion the death was the result of natural causes attributable to fat around Jane Stanford's heart. He said San Francisco doctors could decide. But if San Francisco doctors were to decide, why had he, a detective, rendered a medical conclusion that contradicted the autopsy? He did not mention the Waterhouse report.[16]

Jordan delivered the curtain speech. Not only did Jane Stanford die a natural death, but he insinuated that the Hawaiian authorities and doctors fabricated the evidence of the poisoning. Even though she denied it, he repeated the claim that Berner took the bicarbonate without bad effect. He now said that Berner took the soda before Mrs. Stanford and there was no strychnine in it.[17]

When an astonished reporter from the *Call* pressed Jordan on how he could disregard and discredit the work of the Hawaiian doctors, officials, and chemists, Jordan "made a remark of startling import." He said, "I know all about them and their work." The reporter pressed Jordan, asking if he was saying that they rendered a verdict of strychnine poisoning without evidence. How had the strychnine gotten in the bicarbonate? Had someone added it later? Jordan refused to reply. He said that he had reported to Mountford Wilson, and it was up to Wilson to release the details. He told the *Call* that in regard to the statement he and Hopkins issued in Honolulu, the public "may rest assured that we knew what we were talking about. . . ."[18]

The *Sacramento Bee* was incredulous. It quoted the coroner's jury transcript in which Berner said she refused Jane Stanford's suggestion that she too take some bicarbonate. The newspaper wondered why Berner would have withheld such important evidence, and why she refused to say that she had taken the bicarbonate. When asked by reporters why his mere opinion should convince the public when the evidence of the autopsy, the attending physicians, and the police all pointed in the opposite direction, Jordan gave a Jordanian answer. "I do not care what the people think or what the constables say, I am firm in my opinion."[19]

It was not just reporters who were skeptical. Unnamed trustees were supposedly saying that they regarded the Jordan and Hopkins statement as "based largely on presumptions and hypotheses." Wilson, while publicly proclaiming the greatest respect for Hopkins and Jordan, insisted that the investigation would go forward. The presence of strychnine in both Hawaii and San Francisco needed to be explained. After all, the certificate filed by the registrar of births, deaths, and marriages in Honolulu with the Board of Health that allowed Jane Stanford's body to be removed from Hawaii stated cause of death as strychnine poisoning.[20]

Late that evening of March 21, the police investigation into Jane Stanford's death in Honolulu abruptly ended. The same documents and reports by detectives that proved so unconvincing to reporters convinced Chief of Detectives Burnett, Harry Morse, and acting chief of police Spillane. At midnight, after reviewing the evidence, Spillane issued a statement that Mrs. Stanford died of natural causes. Detective Reynolds commented that "Jordan and Hopkins got the straight of it." Detective Gibson, giving up his pursuit of Ah Wing, said she "died of heart disease brought on by indigestion . . ." from the picnic lunch eaten earlier that day. They said there was strychnine in the bicarbonate of soda but not enough to kill her. They based their conclusions "on doctors not party to the case." They did not name those doctors nor did they mention the Waterhouse report. Chief of Detectives Burnett did believe that an attempt was made on Mrs. Stanford's life in San Francisco, and that investigation remained open. "There is what is called a preponderance of evidence that points that way."

The *Chronicle* reported that the police conclusion of a natural death met the wishes of the public, but "from the testimony whether it will be agreed to is a different matter." The police cited "over 150,000 words of stenographic testimony the pith of which has already been given to the public." The pith had not convinced reporters.[21]

THE ADVOCATES OF A NATURAL DEATH never provided the evidence for their case, but the *San Francisco Post* pointed out that to the police this mattered less than the very fact of Jordan's and Hopkins's insistence on a natural death. Their stubborn assertion lessened the likelihood that prosecutors would ever obtain a conviction. The *Chronicle* explained that if the district attorney indicted a suspect in either poisoning and failed to obtain a conviction, the defendant would inevitably sue the Stanford estate because of Callundan's and other Morse Agency detectives' roles in the service of the estate.[22] This provided another reason for the estate not to cooperate with official attempts to prosecute the case.

CHAPTER 45

THE FUNERAL

AT 1:00 IN THE AFTERNOON on March 24, 1905, carriages arrived at the Stanford home on San Francisquito Creek. Jane's nearest family—her brother Charles Lathrop, his second wife, and their children—gathered at the mansion. Covered in California violets, her coffin had rested in the drawing room of the Palo Alto mansion for the previous day and night, but a more fitting place would have been the small room that she had turned into a chapel.

Jane Stanford never gave up her flirtation with the Catholic Church. In the spring of 1904, she had told Crothers that she was receiving instruction from Fr. Sasia, a Jesuit, in San Jose and would join the Church. But there were problems. She wanted the Church to acknowledge the orthodoxy of her own religious views. It was hard to go from leading the Church of Jane to becoming just another Roman Catholic. She didn't, but for a Protestant, she became very Catholic. The small room contained a triptych, apparently of the Holy Family, and a carved stone found in an old adobe on the Stanford estate and given to her by a local priest. The chapel served as a confessional, where Bertha Berner listened as Jane Stanford "would unburden her heart of troubles and perplexities."[1]

Many more people wished to attend the funeral service than the church could contain. More than 7,000 mourners watched as the body entered the university's inner quadrangle through the West Arch on its way to the Memorial Church. Ten Harry Morse Agency detectives circulated among them, hunting for pickpockets. The honorary pallbearers received the casket inside the church. A privileged 2,700, including the faculty and student body who had received passes, heard the funeral service.[2]

The mourners in the church and the crowd gathered in the quadrangle later followed the casket on its journey to the mausoleum. The cortege passed the monuments of Stanford's Stone Age through a campus that was both a boast and a disguise. Praised for her selflessness, Jane Stanford had preserved her son, her husband, and herself in stone and metal so that, to one degree or another, everything at Stanford in 1905 commemorated the Stanfords.[3] Her spiritualism hid in plain sight from the uninitiated.

Jane Stanford regarded the Memorial Church as the "Koohinoor" (the largest diamond among the British crown jewels) of the university. The church differed from its present reincarnation. The facade gave God and Jane's deceased husband equal billing. Like a theater marquee, the inscription ran in large letters over the entrance: "Erected to the Glory of God and the Loving Memory of My Husband Leland Stanford."[4]

The Memorial Church was Romanesque, permeated by Italy, where Leland Jr. had died. It contained "an exact copy" in mosaic of the "Lord's supper" in the Sistine Chapel. Under mosaics of the Old Testament prophets in the apse there were statues of "the twelve apostles in Carrara marble, which are each copies of the Apostles in the Church of St. John Lateran in Rome." The carving on the front of the marble altar was "a copy of the famous picture by Ciecere, called the 'Entombment.'" It depicted "the figures of Mary, the beloved Mother, Mary, the Sister of Martha, and Mary the Magdelen [sic] at the head, and the body of our Saviour being carried by three of His Disciples."[5]

It was easy to miss the imagery that lay outside orthodox Christianity. The Gilded Age, so materialist and focused on business, also loved esoteric knowledge and ritual. Leland Stanford was a high-level Mason, and when Jane built the church she filled it with Masonic symbols and representations. The resemblance of Masonic and Christian iconography allowed them to be concealed in plain sight. Only those with the necessary knowledge would recognize the Masonic identity of the grapevines, corn, triangles, squares, anchors, scenes of the building of the temple, and particularly the God's Eye in the dome. Jane did the same with spiritualism. The church was rife with angels—particularly female angels. Spiritualists, who regularly consorted with angels, would recognize the significance. The first stained-glass window on the western wall showed angels carrying young Leland Jr. into heaven. They captured the viewer's attention. Christ was in the corner, not center stage.

In the inner courtyard across the quadrangle from the church there stood a statue Jane Stanford had commissioned from Larkin G. Mead, a prominent sculptor of public monuments. He worked from a miniature made by the Galli brothers of Florence in the 1880s. The statue shows Jane kneeling, looking adoringly at her son Leland Jr., who was flanked by his father, staring blankly into the distance. The period's dominant strain of feminism identified women with the home and family. It argued for an imperial version of the home that propelled women outward into society. Jane stooped to conquer. Her status as a mother gave her authority over the university: an *alma mater*. She commissioned the statue in 1890, but she designed its pedestal in 1901 and had it cast in bronze. She considered having the statue carved in marble but never did.[6]

The Memorial Arch formed the boundary of the inner quadrangle. Made of San Jose sandstone, and at more than one hundred feet tall second in size only to the Arc de Triomphe, the arch dwarfed the adjacent buildings, looking like some Babylonian eruption amid the neo-Mission architecture. It commemorated the progress of civilization. Jane Stanford suggested the general outline of the story of civilization, and she gave Leland and herself featured roles. August Saint-Gaudens, the country's most famous sculptor, took her suggestions and created a written description of the historical and allegorical figures who would embody the story. John Evans, an architect and designer in the famous office of Charles Coolidge of Boston, designed the frieze encircling the arch to tell the story, and Rupert Schmid, a German-born sculptor, supervised its carving.[7]

The Gilded Age was so enthusiastic about monuments that there was a whole journal devoted to the subject. *The Monumental News* ran a piece that deciphered the symbolic meaning of the 150 figures that carried the story of civilization. Most, but not all, of the symbolic figures in the arch were female. The historical figures were largely male. Civilization handed the torch to the Genius of Civilization, a young boy who gave the torch to Providence, who gave it to Columbus. Columbus tore the veil from America, who was female and "attired in a mantle typical of Mexico and Peru." The final phase of the frieze began with industrial America, depicting "Electricity, Steam, Science" as well as "Philosophy, Medicine, Metaphysics and Mathematics." It culminated with Minerva, representing California, with a grizzly bear by her side. The Titans held up the Sierras as the railroad entered the state. Leland Stanford, in a pith helmet, and Jane, one of the few female historical figures and riding sidesaddle, marked out a path for the railway. The article claimed that this supposedly represented an actual incident in which Leland and Jane rode over the mountains to demonstrate that a route was possible. There was never any such trip, which was as fitting a commentary on Jane's account of civilization as could be made. One critic said the arch was "so bad it made the horses blush when they passed it."[8]

Everything the mourners saw on the funeral route was what Jane wanted them to see, but she could no longer control what the mourners heard. Charles Lathrop was nominally in charge of the funeral arrangements, but university officials—Charles Branner, the acting university president while David Starr Jordan was in Hawaii, and a faculty committee headed by Professor C. A. Duniway, the son of the West Coast's most famous suffragist, Abigail Scott Duniway—took over the preparations. They orchestrated the route, chose the pallbearers—including Crothers, Jordan, and Hopkins—arranged the sermons, and selected the audience. Their goal was to make Jane Stanford's connection with the university so seamless that there was no distinguishing one from the other.[9]

Professors Branner and Duniway, and President Jordan, were very much concerned with what should *not* be heard at the funeral. This put the Reverend John W. Dinsmore of San Jose, who agreed to give the sermon, in a difficult position.[10]

Reverend Dinsmore often preached in the Stanford Memorial Chapel, and had, in effect, auditioned for his role at the funeral by officiating at a memorial service for Jane Stanford on March 5. He sounded the notes Jordan would later appropriate, praising Jane Stanford as "a good woman. That is the best thing that can be said of anyone." She was noble, a queen with "high ideals, fixed principles, and unfaltering perseverance." She was a worthy steward of great wealth. The Stanfords had passed away, but their legacy would live in the university.[11]

Duniway made it clear to Dinsmore that the university wanted no mention of the circumstances of her death. Dinsmore understood that his words would need to be "sober, judicious and discreet." This was particularly necessary given the tumult in the press. The *San Francisco Call*'s coverage of his March 5 sermon was surrounded with the kinds of headlines Jordan very much wanted to avoid: "Secretary Said to Be a Medium," "Poison in the Capsules Given Mrs. Stanford," "Doctors Find Death Caused by Strychnine," "Her Statements Conflicting," "Will Ignores Senator's Kin," and more. Dinsmore tiptoed around this. "What fiend from the pit would want to murder her or put her in distress?" This was, all things considered, good enough for Acting President Branner. Dinsmore agreed to an interview with Branner the Monday before the Friday funeral. He left Branner his telephone number—Blue 1772—should further contact be necessary.[12]

Branner and the faculty committee kept a tight rein. They allotted Dinsmore fifteen minutes. There would be other clergy—including a rabbi—reading scripture and offering prayers. They seem to have worried less about the Reverend Charles R. Brown, who was to speak at the mausoleum. Brown considered David Starr Jordan "the greatest man" that it had ever been his privilege to know intimately. He could be trusted, but there were problems with having him give the main funeral sermon. Just before her death, Jane Stanford wrote Horace Davis that she "did not consider him [Brown] a high-class, cultivated, spiritual man." She made her brother Charles Lathrop promise "that if the Rev. Mr. Brown's name is presented for employment in any capacity at the University, that you disapprove of the same." Lathrop was not to be counted upon. There was Brown to send her off into eternity.[13]

Duniway also told Brown to avoid mention of the manner of Mrs. Stanford's death. He added that "the newspapers have invested the matter with circumstance of horror but . . . we should treat the death as not having these unusual circumstances."[14]

Dinsmore's sermon was as inward as the church in which he delivered it. He made no direct reference to the circumstances of Jane Stanford's death, but either from obtuseness or a desire to sabotage the university's effort to suppress the murder, virtually everything he mentioned brought the horrors of her death to mind. He talked of the mysterious ways of God, who filled the world with a "millionfold and merciless perversities and poisons, with invincible ministries of suffering and with tremendous dynamics of suffering and death." He created a human race with an "awful talent for rapacity, treachery, cruelty and crime." Dinsmore preached that "events unexpected and unwelcome confront us at every turn." Dinsmore said that "[o]ur lives may be said to be a series of surprises, punctuated at frequent intervals with shocks—startling and often terrific shocks. . . . Such a shock—great, sudden, startling, stunning—has come to this university . . . in the mysterious departure out of this world of the noble woman whose body now lies here. . . . Of her sudden and sorrowful taking off, with its puzzles and problems, it does not become me to say one word. All that I must leave to others."[15] References to poison, treachery, suffering, and mysterious departures were exactly what Jordan hoped to avoid.

The funeral procession from the church stretched for nearly a mile to the mausoleum. Directly behind the casket came Charles G. Lathrop and his family. Behind the Lathrops were May Hunt and Bertha Berner, who was escorted by her brother. The *San Francisco Call* reported that "[s]he was deathly pale, and it was apparent that but for the firm support her brother offered her it would have been impossible for her to keep her feet." Following them were the servants, among them Ah Wing. He was "plainly, almost poorly dressed in black . . . [carrying] in his hand a black soft felt hat with a heavy band of crape [*sic*] about it—." Jordan and Hopkins were at the head of the university delegation.[16] If someone had wished to make a macabre joke, they could not have done better. Leading her procession to the grave were people suspected of her murder, people who covered it up, and those she despised and wished to fire. Reverend Brown, a man she loathed, awaited to deliver the last words.

Morticians embalmed her body, but the body was only a shell. Doctors had already hollowed her out.[17] The eulogists acted as morticians of memory, embalming her life and legacy, covering her blemishes. At the mausoleum the Reverend Charles Brown praised "this noble woman [who] came forth with a tender, gracious interest in all the boys and girls who in years to come would gather here upon her own estate and within these goodly buildings to receive training and equipment for that life of useful service which she would have chosen for her own son." After the Episcopal burial service and a hymn—"Nearer, My God, to Thee"—the Stanford choir sang the school's alma mater. The pallbearers placed the casket into the steel chest inside the mausoleum. The next day the chest was placed in the sarcophagus—in between her husband and son—which was then sealed.[18]

The funeral ended with a prayer for the university, but in a sense the university's prayer was already answered. Jane Stanford was dead. Her money would go to Leland Stanford Junior University. The only challenge to her will came the next year from Annie Stanford, the widow of Leland Stanford's brother Asa, who accused Jane Stanford of fraud for failing to fulfill a contract made between the two brothers. The court rejected her suit. She had filed too late.[19]

Jane Stanford's death may have saved Stanford University. It certainly saved David Starr Jordan's job. Jordan never mastered Jane Stanford while she lived, but death made her malleable. He refashioned Jane Stanford and reduced her down to her "one great purpose," Stanford University. She was a "lone sad figure," devoted to fulfilling her husband's legacy, and acting as an agent of "God's providence."[20] He eulogized her as the most devoted of wives, a woman without a trace of selfishness or egotism. He praised her as a model of self-sacrifice, whose only desires were to make the university "effective for wisdom and righteousness." He linked her to a string of adjectives—"wise, devoted, steadfast, prudent, patient and just"—and he could have gone on since "every good word we can use was hers by right." She was the "wisest as well as the most generous friend of learning in our time."[21]

For all practical purposes Julius Goebel's career at Stanford was buried along with Jane Stanford, his ally in the controversy with Jordan. Jordan took the first steps to dismiss Goebel in February of 1905 while Jane Stanford was still very much alive in Hawaii, but he finished the job when he returned with her body. As was his habit, he made sure the news of Goebel's termination would not be released until he left Palo Alto that summer. Jordan's handpicked advisory board ratified the decision while giving reasons for the dismissal that were either vague or ridiculous, such as that Goebel had not returned library books on time. The trustees backed Jordan, on the grounds that they lacked, despite their continuing efforts, authority to challenge Jordan's right to hire and fire.[22]

Crothers and Davis thought Goebel had spoken so harshly of Jordan that he could not remain. They hoped inducements could be offered for Goebel to go quietly without "another eruption." They made sure Goebel got a year's sabbatical and vouched for him at Harvard and elsewhere. Harvard's Charles Eliot, all too familiar with the circus at Stanford, gave Goebel a temporary position, which the newspapers saw as an implicit criticism of Jordan. Crothers's and Davis's aid to Goebel may not have been a payoff, but Goebel, like Crothers, initially said nothing.[23]

And here David Starr Jordan wanted the story to end. Someone had murdered Jane Stanford, and someone walked away free, as most murderers do. They go on with their lives, quite able to keep their own secrets.

David Starr Jordan not only let a murderer escape; he covered up the murder itself because it was much better for those who mattered—most of her Lathrop relatives, Stanford University, David Starr Jordan, Mountford Wilson, and the Stanford faculty—that she died a natural death. The Morse detectives had been hired to secure such an outcome. The San Francisco police had other things to worry about.

But this was not the end of the story.

CHAPTER 46

COVERING UP
THE COVER-UP

COVERING UP JANE STANFORD'S murder eventually required covering up the cover-up. David Starr Jordan succeeded in halting the investigation without either discovering new and compelling evidence to discredit the conclusion of the coroner's jury or producing evidence for a natural death. The Waterhouse "testimony" was so weak he did not dare release it. Jordan only made assertions, which convinced neither the press nor the Hawaiian police.

The San Francisco Police Department and the executors of the Stanford estate were not interested in questioning Jordan's story. Once Jordan publicly announced that Jane Stanford's death was from natural causes, neither the detectives nor their superiors had any desire to investigate Tay Wang's claims.

If Jane Stanford had died a natural death, then further investigation of the earlier Poland Spring Water poisoning seemed profitless. It could only underline the presence of strychnine not once but twice in Jane Stanford's waters and medicine. This would not benefit the estate, the university, or the San Francisco police.

Bertha Berner became the sympathetic center of the drama. She was an attractive woman approaching middle age who had spent much of her life tending to the care of a demanding and rich employer. She was devoted to her own mother. Newspaper accounts emphasized that she mourned more obviously and seemingly more deeply than Stanford's own family. The repeated claim of no motive for a murder warded off the real motives she had for wanting Jane Stanford to die. No one explored her past mercurial relationship with Jane Stanford, or the trips that forced her to choose between her own sick mother and Mrs. Stanford. To leave Mrs. Stanford was to lose her job and risk her inheritance in Mrs. Stanford's will.

Jordan linked himself to Berner in a marriage of convenience. He protected her from accusations of murder by claiming there was no murder. She helped him argue that there was no murder by reversing her testimony before the coroner's jury. She understandably preferred perjury to a trial for murder. He wanted to avoid any trial that could bare his and the university's secrets and bring challenges to the will and endowments.

The problem with Berner's purchase of bicarbonate still lingered, and in the days before Jane Stanford's funeral, Jordan told two different stories about it—one publicly, the other privately.

On March 22, Jordan explained that the packet of bicarbonate found in Jane Stanford's luggage could not be the packet purchased by Berner in Palo Alto or the source of the bicarbonate in the bottle. A bottle of cologne had overturned and saturated the soda purchased in Palo Alto. He did not explain how he knew this. He did not explain why neither Berner nor the maids mentioned the cologne incident. If his own source was Berner, then it was yet another change in her story.[1]

The next day Jordan wrote to Mountford Wilson with a second story. His letter to Wilson clearly picks up on a previous discussion. It begins, "As to the matter of the bottle of bicarbonate which had gone stale . . ." The source of the story of the stale bicarbonate was Annie Mary Lathrop, Charles's wife, who was, like Bertha Berner, the child of German immigrants. If Mrs. Lathrop had told Jordan the story, their conversation must have taken place between March 21, when Jordan returned from Hawaii to San Francisco, and March 23 when he wrote Wilson. It could not have been earlier because the news of the new bicarbonate purchase in Palo Alto broke on March 4 when he was departing for Hawaii. He could have consulted with Mrs. Lathrop only after he returned. Jordan told Wilson that Mrs. Lathrop overheard a conversation—with whom it is unclear since an inkblot mars the letter—that led her to understand that Mrs. Stanford took some of the stale bicarbonate at the Hotel Vendome in San Jose. Mrs. Stanford said "she ought not to have done so because it came out of the house in the City and it was stale. She said she would throw it out and get some fresh." Jordan stressed the bicarbonate was stale and not bitter because bitterness would have indicated the presence of strychnine. Jordan told Wilson that "I think that it could be shown that Mrs. Stanford had this bottle with her in San Jose and took a dose from it." Finding it stale, she bought new bicarbonate in Palo Alto but then spilled cologne on it and took the bottle with the stale bicarbonate to Hawaii. "I am coming to be more and more convinced," he wrote, "that the bottle was tampered with on the night of Mrs. Stanford's death."[2]

The story concerns less what Mrs. Lathrop heard than Jordan's interpretation of it, his surmises, and his desired conclusions. He writes that "Mrs. Lathrop understood," "I think that it could be shown," "I am coming to be more and more convinced." Berner, too, he wrote, remembers "something of that kind."

If the strychnine was introduced that evening, Bertha Berner would seem to be the most likely suspect. If she did not do it, who did? The next day Jordan wrote Carl Smith accusing Dr. Humphris of placing the poison in the bicarbonate after her death.[3] As in Callundan's story of the Poland Spring Water, someone poisoned the soda after the fact.

The shadow of the bottle of bicarbonate would linger for years. George Crothers, whose memory of the events around Jane Stanford's death became less exact with time, said that "one person who was close to her asked [when told that Mrs. Stanford had died] whether it was the bicarbonate of soda?" He did not name the person, but from the context it seems to have been Mrs. Lathrop. She must have possessed some reason to suspect the new soda in the old bottle.[4]

Crothers also said that Jane Stanford consulted with Judge Leib during her stay in San Jose after the Poland Spring Water incident. The judge suggested she replace all her medicines. Crothers said she replaced all the medicines except the bicarbonate of soda, which she kept in an old-fashioned widemouthed bottle unusual at the time that allowed her to take out the soda with a spoon. Crothers then incorrectly claimed that Berner said that this bottle, clearly labeled Adelaide, Australia, was bought in India during their long 1903–1904 trip. He thought it possible that it was never used.[5]

But these were an old man's memories of distant conversations. They are muddled. All that remains is the suspicion that the travels of the bottle contained the key to Jane Stanford's death.

BERTHA BERNER APPRECIATED Jordan's efforts to protect her. On March 28 she wrote to him "expressing my Mother's, brother's, and my own deep gratitude for all your having gone to Honolulu means to us. I realize the sky is not clear yet, but feel the knowledge I possess of having done no wrong to my dear Mrs. Stanford must prevail."[6] Jordan, for his part, replied, "To my mind, so far as criticism of your conduct is concerned, the sky is not clearing, but is wholly cleared."[7]

Berner's protestation of innocence was oddly equivocal. Saying that she knew that she had done no wrong to Jane Stanford was not the same as saying she had done nothing to Jane Stanford. Her wording in the letter to Leib thanking him for his support was equally oblique. She appreciated his "expression of confidence in me at a time when it was so much needed, for my mother was on the verge of breaking down. I realize the sad and horrible problem before us has not been solved, but I base my trust for final vindication upon the knowledge that I have not done anything to my dear Mrs. Stanford for which I need to reproach myself."[8] But why had her mother been on the verge of breaking down on receiving news of the first, Poland Spring Water, poisoning? What did she know or suspect? Why did Leib's support ease her mother's fears? And why the intimation of some act for which others might reproach her?

With murder eliminated, any attempt to pursue the other suspects in the Poland Spring Water incident—Ah Wing, Elizabeth Richmond, and Albert Beverly—would only draw Berner back into the case, which was dangerous for everyone concerned. Later there would be accusations that Elizabeth Richmond had a bad opium habit, and opium habits led back to Chinatown. The story was probably not true. In any case, the police did not investigate.[9] Better to let sleeping dogs lie.

Dr. Humphris was not ready to let the Stanford murder case drop. Having seen Jordan's denunciation of him in the *Honolulu Bulletin*, he wrote Jordan on March 20 demanding to know if "it is true that you made this statement." He also wanted to know the basis for Jordan's declaration that Mrs. Stanford did not die of strychnine. Jordan replied after Jane Stanford's funeral. He denied having said anything like what was attributed to him in the *Bulletin*. And for the first time, he revealed the existence of the Waterhouse report. He said he based his conclusions on the "very careful cross examination of Miss Berner and Miss Hunt by one of the best-informed physicians in Honolulu," and on the "judgments of various others" who examined the evidence. He regretted that the paragraph in the *Bulletin* should have been published.[10]

Jordan lied to Humphris. He regretted nothing, and he repeated the published assertions he made in the paper in private correspondence. The day before writing Humphris he amplified them. Jane Stanford, he wrote, "had an attack of neuralgia of the heart." The diagnosis of strychnine poisoning arose from "an incompetent and dishonest physician, and a still more incompetent but less dishonest coroner's jury." There was not a single symptom of strychnine poisoning; the trace in the chemist's report arose from the cascara capsule. The bicarbonate bottle "had been in the hands of people of doubtful character and sensational tendencies and may have been contaminated by associations." Mrs. Stanford, the man who was her adversary and enemy wrote, "had no enemies."[11]

He also solicited support for his slander of Humphris. He asked Wilson to "[k]indly remind Mr. Callundan that Dr. Humphris himself was the first to accuse the bottle of carbonate of soda." Jordan claimed that after Humphris tasted it "or pretending to do so, he declared that 'there was enough strychnine in it to kill ten men.' Perhaps when he read up the symptoms a little he found it necessary to bolster his case by having the bottle made to correspond with his diagnosis." Not only did Humphris say no such thing that I can find in the record, but Jordan had no way of knowing what he said. Neither he nor Callundan was even in Hawaii at the time Humphris tasted the bicarbonate. Berner and May Hunt were in the room at the time, but they never claimed Humphris said what Jordan contended.[12]

Jordan, as was his wont, escalated the accusations from incompetence to fraud and extortion. The bottle of bicarbonate "had been tampered with on the night of Mrs. Stanford's death." Jordan was "morally certain" that Humphris put the poison in the bottle. Humphris then spread the rumor of strychnine poisoning "without the slightest evidence of any kind." His motive was the supposedly "higher fee that would come from a murder case than a case of heart disease." Jordan continued to insist that Jane Stanford had no enemy in the world, and that no one was more beloved in California.[13]

In mid-April, Dr. Day deduced that Waterhouse must be the physician Jordan referred to as discrediting the attending physicians. Day saw Waterhouse and Jordan dining at the University Club the night before

Jordan's departure and connected the dots. He and Dr. Humphris asked to see the report.[14] Carl Smith, the Hawaiian ex-judge and legislator who was acting as Jordan's "attorney and representative," refused to reveal the "testimony." Smith asserted that since Waterhouse was "substantially paid" for his opinion, the reports were Jordan's proprietary information and could not be released without Jordan's permission.[15]

The outraged doctors confronted Waterhouse and demanded to know why he had not consulted them. Waterhouse seemed confused. He said that he had not thought of it. Waterhouse told them that he believed Jane Stanford never had a convulsion. He based this on "what he had heard and read."[16]

Jordan tried to buck up Waterhouse, telling him that his writing the report was justified since "there could be no case in the world of greater importance than this, or one touching on the interests of so many people." But if this were so, why should Waterhouse, Jordan, and Mountford Wilson refuse to release the report unless they feared an examination of what it contained? Jordan, characteristically, shifted the responsibility elsewhere. He said the report—paid for by the executors of the estate—was the property of the estate, and he would need their permission to release it.[17]

Smelling blood, the doctors intensified their attack, criticizing Jordan for trying to discredit "up-to-date and well equipped medical men" on the basis of a medical education he received twenty years previously. Jordan held firm. He knew releasing the Waterhouse report would only damage the case for a natural death and open Bertha Berner up to renewed examination.[18]

Carl Smith, having proved so helpful to Jordan in Hawaii, reminded the president of the law school appointment that Jordan had dangled before him. There was no position. Stanford was staffing the law school cut-rate with young men at half the salary mentioned to Smith.[19]

Jordan did receive some support from Dr. Shorey, one of the chemists who tested for strychnine. He disassociated himself from the letter published by Humphris and the other physicians on the grounds that he was a chemist, not a physician, and unqualified to make a clinical diagnosis of any kind. Jordan thanked him and assured him that the death was natural and that Jane Stanford "had not an enemy in the world, and there is no one who could possibly have gained anything by her death." He said that the evidence of the doctors disappeared under cross-examination by Callundan and Reynolds, and that the distortion of the limbs was congenital and not the result of strychnine poisoning.[20]

———

JORDAN COULD HAVE left well enough alone. No matter how much the Hawaiian doctors, the Hawaiian police, and the newspapers insisted there had been a murder, the San Francisco police put the case to rest. But Jordan's lies always seemed to require new lies. The more dubious his actions, the more he insisted on their rectitude and demanded that others vouch for them.

Jordan told Smith that influential doctors were scrutinizing the evidence and supported Waterhouse's conclusions, but he did not name the doctors. Examining the heart should have been relatively straightforward, but in early May the doctors were still at work.[21]

Then, on May 25, 1905, the *San Francisco Examiner* reported that a nephew of Leland Stanford, Welton Stanford, was offering a $1,000 reward to find and convict the murderer of his aunt. He was frustrated at the abandonment of the case by the San Francisco police.[22] Mountford Wilson expressed astonishment, since Welton Stanford was not a blood relative of Jane Stanford but rather the son of one of Leland's brothers and could not gain from any contest of the will. A contest was exactly what Wilson most feared.[23]

The next day a story appeared in the *Examiner* proclaiming that a "final report" showed that no poison was found and Jane Stanford died of natural causes. "Experts" had spent weeks in analyzing "the internal organs of the body" brought back to San Francisco. The newspaper story relied on more than the toxicological report since it validated Jordan's conclusion that "she ate food which caused indigestion and heart failure." The point of the story was as clear as its source was murky. "Under the circumstances there will be no necessity for further inducements for the apprehension of any person for the murder of the late lamented benefactress as offered by Welton Stanford of Schenectady, N.Y."[24]

It was fitting that a university founder who sought the advice of ghosts should be the subject of what became a ghost report—often heard from but never seen. Dr. William Ophuls, the head of pathology at Cooper Medical College, led the team of doctors who reexamined Jane Stanford's heart.

Ophuls faced a conflict of interest. David Starr Jordan was considering making Cooper Medical College part of Stanford University, and thus Ophuls, who would become the first dean of the Stanford Medical School, was agreeing to do sensitive work for a man who would be his future employer. The estate remunerated Ophuls and the other doctors on his team very well. A year after Jane Stanford's death, the estate paid $1,000 each to Ophuls, Dr. Charles Morgan, and H. A. L. Ryfklgel for the "inquiry to the cause of death of decd." In December of 1907, nearly three years after Jane Stanford's death, Jordan claimed that he had not yet seen "a final" report from the San Francisco doctors, even though beginning in May of 1905 he was quoting such a report. Both the failure to ever reveal the report, and the long delay in payment, raises doubts about it.[25]

Neither I nor anyone else has ever found a copy of the report. It was either well hidden or destroyed. It survives only in the account Bertha Berner gave of it in her memoir, and in a masterful analysis of that account by Dr. Stanley Cutler. The report remained secret because it did not say what Jordan and Berner wanted it to say. Berner claimed that Mrs. Stanford died of a ruptured artery in the first edition of her memoir, and if this was the report's conclusion then it was everything Jordan could have wished. But Berner dropped that claim in the second edition of her memoir. The best Dr. Ophuls could do was to say what the autopsy already revealed: Jane Stanford had chronic myocarditis, which at the time referred to patchy areas of scarring in the heart, sometimes with infiltration of fatty deposits. Such scarring was common in the elderly, but without symptoms of angina pectoris—which is to say chest pain—the significance of such scarring for a pathologist was unclear. It did not mean the patient died of a heart attack.[26]

Ophuls did say myocarditis was "the most probable cause of death," but this was not sustained by his own research. Ophuls studied cardiovascular disease and concluded in previous publications that the scars represented healed myocarditis, which "occurs more commonly than is generally acknowledged." He found such evidence of myocarditis to be virtually universal in women of Stanford's age during that period. It would have been far more surprising if he did not find "chronic myocarditis."[27]

Ophuls's conclusions about strychnine also proved disappointing to Jordan. Ophuls thought that Stanford's "death was due to the effect of a dose of strychnine, in itself not lethal, but determined in the direction of a fatal result of age and disease." The report concluded, "There is no postmortem evidence that Mrs. Stanford died of strychnine poisoning."[28]

The doctors had a narrow view of "postmortem evidence." They did not comment on or consider the strychnine found in the bicarbonate of soda and the reports of the attending physicians because they did not consider them as postmortem evidence. They ignored the Hawaiian autopsy, which did indicate the kind of rigidity of muscles characteristic of strychnine poisoning, as did the fading purple color test. Add them in and strychnine poisoning seemed the likely diagnosis. By "postmortem evidence" they meant only their own examination of the organs. As Cutler points out, though, given the organs at their disposal, the San Francisco doctors' own chemical tests could only be inconclusive. The only way that they could say there was no rigidity was by relying on the Waterhouse report.[29]

Ophuls wisely steered clear of death by indigestion, the cause initially advanced by Jordan. Berner buttressed that theory on her own in her memoir, where she tells a story of undercooked and soggy gingerbread at the picnic lunch the day of Mrs. Stanford's death. This, plus the chocolates she ate, supposedly alarmed Berner "for as a rule she [Jane Stanford] ate so carefully" and the doctor forbade sweets. Even in 1905 death by gingerbread was a zany diagnosis.[30]

Releasing the equivocal Ophuls report would have led back to the Waterhouse report and brought new attention to Berner's contradictions. This would not help Jordan's or Wilson's case. Jordan characteristically referred to the Ophuls report for years without actually producing it. He was probably the source of the *Examiner* story in May of 1905. In 1921 he wrote a letter to then President Lyman Wilbur of Stanford explaining that he had decided not to talk about Jane Stanford's death in his autobiography but wished to provide a record for the university. He replicated the language Berner used in her memoir and then eliminated. He said, "Dr. William Ophuls and a committee of surgeons of the Cooper Medical College staff . . . reported the rupture of the coronary, as expected by Dr. Waterhouse." Jordan said that he always regretted, for Bertha Berner's sake, that the board decided not to publish the Ophuls report, but he thought there was no point in reopening these questions now, sixteen years after Stanford's death.[31]

JORDAN REMAINED AT STANFORD until the end of the school year, but he was preparing to leave for a planned six-month vacation in Europe to recover from the strain brought on by Jane Stanford's death. For some reason, his wife, Jessie, initially refused to go with him. He would travel with his eldest daughter by his first marriage, who never regarded Jessie Jordan as her mother. In the end, his wife relented and joined him.[32]

Before departing, Jordan presided over the commencement exercises at Stanford University. On May 24, 1905, Jordan gave the "final words" to the 250 men and women receiving degrees from Stanford. Everything they had learned, he told them, "should be an impulse to action."

> If you have planned somewhat, then carry out your
> plans. If you have learned the nature of something, then
> turn your knowledge into execution. If you have gained
> aspirations these count for nothing except as you try to
> make them good. . . . There is no virtue in knowledge, in
> training, in emotion, or in aspiration except as you use
> them in the conduct of life.
>
> And the conduct of life is not a negative thing—to
> commit no crimes, to keep out of jail and to wait until
> things come to you. This is not righteousness. To do
> nothing wrong is not to live aright. For living is a most
> positive matter, moving things, changing things, using
> man and matter to accomplish the results which seem
> to you worth while.[33]

He may not have meant the speech to sound like a justification of his own actions in the Stanford case, but it did. He had taken command of events; he moved things, changed things, and used "man and matter to accomplish the results that to him seemed worth while." He may have done things that were wrong, but, by his standards, he lived aright.

And he had stayed out of jail.

CHAPTER 47

ALMOST AN ACT
OF JUST RETRIBUTION

JANE STANFORD LONGED to bring Harvard professor William James to Stanford, and on February 23, 1905, the *San Jose Mercury* announced that he was coming for a semester. James was the country's foremost philosopher and psychologist, but his interest in spiritualism attracted Jane Stanford. He was the chair of the American branch of the Society for Psychical Research. Less than a week after the announcement, Jane Stanford was dead.[1]

The long wake of her death still lingered when James arrived at Stanford in January of 1906. In the summer of 1905 Julius Goebel renewed his attacks on Jordan, and the Hawaiian doctors continued to denounce him, causing Jordan to cut short his European trip. Horace Davis, having done what he could for Goebel, continued his efforts to get the Board of Trustees to strip Jordan of the power to dismiss faculty, arguing that it made professors dependent, destroyed academic freedom, and prevented the university from recruiting "a competent faculty."[2]

Under assault on many fronts and with embarrassing stories filling the press, Jordan lied, contradicted himself, and then launched an assault of his own. At the end of December, while in Denver, Jordan gave a newspaper interview to a reporter from the *San Francisco Bulletin*. He promised revelations from yet another unseen report that would show that the story of the Honolulu poisoning was the result of a "dastardly plot" by Hawaiian officials "to secure big fees." He said no strychnine was found in Mrs.

Stanford's room, and again referring to the Ophuls report, said a second examination of her heart established beyond doubt that "the aorta had been ruptured. Moreover, the San Francisco poisoning was the work of disaffected servants who sought to discredit Bertha Berner and deprive her of her inheritance."[3]

This quickly backfired. High Sheriff Henry indignantly denied Jordan's accusations and defied Jordan and the Stanford estate to give "an honest report of all the facts in their knowledge." The alliance of convenience that joined Charles Lathrop and David Starr Jordan in defense of the will and trusts now frayed. Lathrop, who never liked Jordan, told reporters that Jordan had done all the talking and he would have to answer all the questions. Callundan, apparently irritated, said he had no idea what Jordan was talking about. Jordan never saw the reports Callundan submitted and was in no position to describe them. If the police possessed the evidence incriminating Hawaiian officials, as Jordan suggested, they would have made arrests. Callundan considered the Honolulu bills modest for the amount of time doctors put into the case. Callundan suggested Jordan had been misquoted. He did not know why Jordan brought the matter up since "doctors" had decided that she died of a heart attack.[4]

Jordan quickly backtracked and disavowed the Denver report as "a jumble of blunder and invention." But there was little in it that he was not saying privately. He had already accused the doctors in Hawaii of falsifying evidence. He repeatedly claimed definitive evidence of a heart attack.[5]

High Sheriff Henry scoffed at Jordan's claim that he was misquoted. Reporters, Henry said, made mistakes but "they don't make a story out of whole cloth." He insinuated that Jordan was complicit in the murder and guided the cover-up. Henry said that he learned that Stanford University was nearly bankrupt and in urgent need of money. He said Jordan and Hopkins came to Honolulu for the sole purpose of making it seem "that Mrs. Stanford died from natural causes and was not murdered." He predicted rich people would not leave large sums to universities "when they think they thereby risk having the term of their natural days shortened for the purpose of getting at the money left in their wills."[6]

Even if the authorities never charged her, Bertha Berner remained under popular suspicion. A supposed "final" report by the Morse Agency claimed Ah Wing had accused her, but Mrs. Stanford did not believe him. A woman named Laura Todd clipped stories from the *Bulletin* and sent them to Governor Carter in Hawaii. "Fancy Dr. Jordan talking like he does, if reports are true, he favors Miss Berner." After her return from Hawaii, Berner remained largely confined to her home in Menlo Park, caring for her mother, who died on July 22, 1905. The papers reported that the house was a gift to Bertha from Jane Stanford, but this was not true. It belonged to her mother, who then left it to Bertha and her brother. The two old women who had shaped and constrained her life were now gone. She received inheritances from both of them and lived quietly. The *Call* did report that Berner told friends that she had been accused of everything—murdering Jane Stanford and desiring her millions. She wanted an investigation that would give the actual facts to the public. She loved Mrs. Stanford "and did everything I could for her."[7]

IN JANUARY OF 1906, William James arrived at Stanford at the height of his fame. Nearly sixty-four, he was an old man for the time, conscious of the toll lecturing took and ready to retire. His intellectual foundation, as he put it to Gertrude Stein, was never to "reject anything. Nothing has been proved. If you reject anything, that is the beginning of the end as an intellectual." James had more than an academic interest in spiritualism. He, too, had lost a child, an infant named Hermann. In attending séances and consulting psychics, he encountered fraud after fraud, but he held open the possibility of what he called a white crow—the exception that upended the regularity and predictability of the world. "When that which is *you* passes out of the body," he wrote his sister Alice, who died in 1892, "I am sure there will be an explosion of liberated force until then eclipsed and kept down." Alice, who didn't believe any such thing, replied, "When I am gone, pray don't think of me simply as a creature that might have been something else." She wrote in her diary, concerning a medium frequented and studied by her brother, that "I hope the dreadful Mrs. Piper isn't set loose upon my defenseless soul." But if one Alice James scorned spiritualism, another Alice, William's wife, was, like Jane Stanford, a spiritualist.[8]

James was attracted to Stanford University by an easterner's fascination with California, but mostly he came for the money. "If I can only get through these next 4 months and pocket the $5,000 I shall be the happiest man alive."[9] James's only class, a history of philosophy, was large— 300 enrolled students plus 150 visitors—and his lectures went over the students' heads. They did not understand "what 'hypothesis,' 'analogy,' 'percept,' 'concept,' and other such words, as 'abstract,' 'concrete,' etc." meant. He found it hard, he wrote, "to aim too low!" He dreaded the grind of teaching that drained his dwindling energies, which he wanted to go toward finishing a long-postponed book.[10] During his time at the university, one of his few mentions of Jane Stanford's death was to give thanks that the university holiday commemorating her demise allowed him to cancel a class.[11]

He brought conflicting opinions about the university and California with him, and he did not so much resolve them as change between them like suits of clothes. Some of his views were clichés, others were astute, and still others were the ignorant certitudes of a stranger to a place.[12]

California did not disappoint him—"so simple the life, so benign the elements." James praised the "classic landscape, the perfection of climate," but after his wife joined him, it rained nearly every day for three weeks. Still, following a storm California was glorious, reminding James of what Oliver Wendell Holmes Sr. once told him of a similar day: "it looked as if God had just spit on his sleeve and polished up the Universe till you could see your face reflected in it." As the weather improved and the gout that plagued him receded, James thought California exquisite—"If I were younger I would fall in love with this state."[13]

He wrote that Stanford provided "the simplest life, no one rich, the sexes on an equality, yet all the essential needs of the soul provided for in amplest measure." After a couple of months his letters contained plenty of contrary evidence. He thought "the only drawback was the social insipidity." In a phrase he would repeat with variations over the course of his stay, he wrote of "the great human vacuum round about, the lonely nature. The historic silence fairly rings in one's ears as one listens." But all in all, he could not imagine a better place to live or work, as long as he could spend a quarter of the year away. A person needed the money to travel to the east and abroad to visit "the centres of corruption, with historic backgrounds. . . ."[14]

James initially believed the university flush with possibility. Stanford could be "first-rate" if the "authorities" would spend the necessary money, but he didn't think they possessed "imagination enough to see their chance or good sense enough to be advised by others." The university needed to attract "really first-rate men . . . paying them for what they sacrifice in coming—what their wives sacrifice chiefly." But neither the president nor the trustees aspired to be much more than "a second-rate teaching college."[15]

He personally found Jordan pleasant, and he repeated the denunciations of Goebel by Jordan's friends, but he later regretted being drawn into the quarrel between them. Jordan could not have been pleased when James addressed the local YWCA on "spiritism."[16]

James seemed frankest, as faculty members often are, in giving advice to a colleague offered a position at Stanford. He told the philosopher Ralph Barton Perry that the advantages of Stanford were the "splendid climate," the opportunity for undistracted work, "the excellent wholesome, earnest, though relatively to Harvard somewhat immature tone of the students," and a relatively young and superior faculty. Because the institution was still new, there was an opportunity to shape it.

But the cons could not be ignored. The salaries were so small that "a bad grumbling habit has set in, which is demoralizing to the tone of the teaching." Wives paid a higher price than their husbands: "hired help being so hard to get, the wives suffer from too much housework." The cost of living was high, the social life stultifying. Perry should not believe what Jordan told him. "He means well, but is vague, talks impulsively, and can't live up to his intentions." Things might turn out well, but Perry could not count on it.[17]

James told him to "*come* by all means," but Perry chose to pay more attention to the body of the letter rather than to the conclusion. Perry refused the offer. James said he made the right decision.[18]

By early April, with "every lecture a dead weight," William James was longing for the semester to end. At 5:13 a.m. on April 18, 1906, the great San Francisco earthquake liberated him. His "room was shaken like a rat by a terrier." The wooden houses remained intact, but virtually all the chimneys came down, and the earthquake left "the higher University buildings largely piles of ruins." He accompanied a colleague to San Francisco to search for her sister. He was glad he did, "for the spectacle was memorable, of a whole population in the streets with what baggage they could rescue from their houses about to burn, while the flames and the explosions were steadily advancing and making everyone move farther. The fires most beautiful in the effulgent sunshine."[19]

The university sustained substantial damage—although not as much as initially feared—with the greatest loss affecting what was dearest to Jane Stanford: Jane Stanford's monuments to her family. It demolished the

Memorial Arch, leaving only the base of the two columns that anchored it. Both remain today with only air between them. The brick wings of the museum collapsed and would never be replaced. The tower of the Memorial Church fell, and the north wall exploded out into the quadrangle. The university reconstructed it without the original tower and steeple.[20] Except for the mausoleum, isolated in a corner of the campus, the university's connection to the Stanfords became a series of absences.

Annie Stanford, the widow of Leland Stanford's brother Asa, took grim satisfaction. She remembered Jane telling her old and sick husband, "When your brother died, our relations were severed. I don't know you." She regarded the destruction of the arch "almost an act of just retribution" for Jane's cruelty, pitilessness, and vengefulness.[21]

AFTER THE EARTHQUAKE, William James quickly left California, but before leaving he wrote to Horace Davis. The two intended to meet and discuss the university but had not done so. James did not mince words. The physical ruin of the university now matched its intellectual impoverishment. Well before the earthquake, the faculty was demoralized: "there is an amount of disbelief in the wisdom of the governing powers of the University that threatens to ruin everything." The faculty regarded the university as an ordinary American college where the administration aimed to hire staff "at the lowest market price they can severally be got for." Much of the faculty was ready to depart at the first invitation. The university administration was secretive, and, so the faculty believed, prone to favoritism and false promises. There was some affection for the president but contempt and mistrust of the institution. Mrs. Stanford's death provided the opportunity for a radical new departure, but nothing happened. He recommended that only the buildings needed for instruction should be repaired, the rest should be stabilized and left as ruins "standing as monuments to the earthquake and the eventual appeals to donors." The money raised should be invested in faculty. This would advertise the belief that the primary function of a university was intellectual. Without a radically new policy, Stanford would be a failure.[22]

Jordan assured Davis that the views conveyed by William James were not those of "the responsible members of the faculty."[23]

IN THE WAKE OF THE EARTHQUAKE, David Starr Jordan finished his reconstruction of Jane Stanford. The elements of what became a small book—*The Story of a Good Woman*—had been in circulation since her death, and he pulled them together in an address at Founders Day, March 9, 1909. He said it was neither a character study nor an appreciation, and he made no reference to her "personal peculiarities whether of strength or weakness." Stanford was a university founded on love, the love of a mother for her child, her husband, and ultimately all the children of humanity. That mother, he said, died in Honolulu of a "rupture of the coronary artery."

Jordan actually spoke more about Leland Stanford than his wife. When he turned to Jane Stanford, he mostly talked about her money. He praised her "friends and advisors, Samuel F. Leib, Timothy Hopkins, Francis E. Spencer and Russell Wilson, as well as . . . her faithful secretary, Miss Bertha Berner."

Jordan quoted Jane Stanford as saying, "I will never concern myself with the religion, the politics, or the love affairs of any professor in Stanford University." He said she religiously kept this resolution.[24]

Jordan's wife, Jessie Jordan, offered her own remembrance of Jane Stanford more than twenty years after the founder's death. Jane Stanford would have "given her life, if necessary, to save the university." She thought her death in Honolulu was a gift, since even Mrs. Stanford's "great spirit would have broken under the tragedy of the earthquake of 1906." Then "she would have felt forsaken if not betrayed by God."[25] Jessie Jordan may have been right. The collapse of her monuments to herself and her family might have crushed her. Someone spared her the pain. Willingly or not, Jane Stanford probably gave her life to save the university.

Fremont Older was one of the few who did not forget the abandonment of the Stanford murder investigation. Older helped send Ruef to prison, but then he turned and fought for his pardon. He became aware of the good in bad people and the bad in the good. In the fight against Ruef, he and other "reformers and the lawyers, and the officers of the court, and the detectives, the courts and the law had to do whatever it seemed necessary to do to win. I realized that we had to get down once or twice to Ruef's level to prove him guilty and get him into the penitentiary." Older

286 WHO KILLED JANE STANFORD?

became more and more uncomfortable that the newspapers fighting Ruef were themselves on the take and condoned some crimes to prevent other crimes.[26] Older, Green, Ruef, Callundan—even Phelan—swam in the same murky San Francisco waters.

But there was a difference in the corruption around Ruef and the corruption around the Stanford case. Ruef went to prison. His crimes, which did not include murder, were not covered up. Whoever killed Jane Stanford walked, the authorities in San Francisco denied there was a crime, and David Starr Jordan never voiced any regrets.

The earthquake destroyed not only the monuments to the Stanfords but presumably also the records of the investigation, which have never been found. San Francisco had far more important things to think about. Stanford did not become a church school for boys; it was a university, although admittedly until after World War II a sleepy, mediocre university overshadowed by Berkeley. The school's most illustrious alumnus, Herbert Hoover, became a trustee and would, in 1913, execute George Crothers's plan and kick Jordan upstairs with the honorific title of chancellor.

The early days of the university became an anodyne tale told in official histories, pious memoirs, and campus tours.

But the story does not end here. Somebody killed Jane Stanford.

WHO KILLED HER?

HISTORIANS GO FOR THE BIG PICTURE. We map the forest, not the trees. My initial interest in Jane Stanford's death was less about who committed the crime than on the erasure of the crime itself. I cared less about an individual murderer than about the Gilded Age world that produced the murderer, created motives for murder, and allowed that murderer to get away. I am satisfied that I got the big picture—how and why the cover-up took place and how David Starr Jordan could execute it.

But I can see why historians might drive detectives crazy. They operate on a different scale. A good modern detective would doggedly ask one simple question: Who killed Jane Stanford? I have not yet answered this question, but I will.

In 1951 Josephine Tey published a mystery, *The Daughter of Time*, which still sells briskly. Its plot involves Alan Grant, a police detective incapacitated with a broken leg, who from boredom becomes interested in King Richard III and his supposed murder of his nephews—the little princes—in the Tower of London to secure his throne. Grant hates historians. They do not pay attention to details. In their search for the forest—the big picture—they neglect the trees. "A man who is interested in what makes people tick doesn't write history. He writes novels, or becomes an alienist, or a magistrate . . . Or a confidence man. Or a fortune-teller. A man who understands about people hasn't any yen to write history. History is toy soldiers." Or—Tey does not have to add—he becomes a detective.

Detectives are all about the trees. Grant sets out to dismantle the case against Richard by focusing on the details. He ultimately discovers that historians had already undermined the tale but that it lived on anyway. This becomes another reason for him to dismiss historians. They are ineffectual.[1]

Tey and her detective Grant are both wildly ahistorical and pretend that forests and trees demand the same questions. They think that no matter the time or place, a historian is a historian; a detective is a detective. But modern detectives have protocols that those a century ago did not have. The detectives in the Stanford case act like Grant's make-believe historians: they seem to neglect evidence, float implausible theories, and show little curiosity about possible motives.

Having mapped my forest, I was in the spring, summer, and fall of 2020—the first year of Covid—dissatisfied. I understood who covered up the crime, how they did it, and why. I knew how one very peculiar university worked, and traced the networks of corruption in San Francisco. And although I suspected who killed Jane Stanford, I could not demonstrate it even to my own satisfaction. This grated on me.

I spent considerable time talking with my brother, Stephen, about Jane Stanford's death. Stephen writes crime fiction, which is different from being a mystery writer. As my mother told my son, Jesse, when he was still a child, "Your uncle writes real books, not like your father. People read them."

Stephen's books grew darker over time, but his protagonists, even as they became intertwined with the crimes at the centers of his stories, remained sympathetic. They really wanted to find out what happened. The reader ultimately knows who killed whom and why. But then, Stephen can make things up when he needs a solution. He can invent the necessary evidence and establish connections. He only has to make his connections plausible.

I can't invent, and I can't go back in time and make my detectives actually want to arrest the murderer; still, my brother has a lot to teach me. The lessons I fail to absorb are my fault, not his.

I also know that I am pushing history beyond its usual capacities when, more than a century after Jane Stanford's murder, I try to identify her murderer.

When I write a history at a granular scale, the people I write about become more alive to me than those I encounter every day. Like Jane Stanford, I talk to dead people. This no longer scares my wife.

If my characters were here, they would have a lot to explain, and I have come to know them well enough to be pretty sure how they would react. David Starr Jordan would lie and defame me; Ah Wing would go silent and pretend he does not understand what he understands all too well. Albert Beverly would grow irritated, point out he was nowhere near the site of either poisoning, and that of course Lathrop accused him: rich people, particularly rich people like Charles Lathrop, always kick down and kiss up. The rich do not like those they cannot control and whom they suspect, rightly in Beverly's case, despise them. Elizabeth Richmond would talk, and talk, and talk, never giving a fully satisfying answer, contradicting herself, but also never providing the evidence necessary to overcome her physical distance from the second poisoning and absence from the mansion as Jane Stanford prepared to leave for Hawaii. Crothers would tell me, "Yes, she was murdered." But he would not tell me much more beyond hinting that I should keep my eye on the prize. The university was saved, successful challenges to the will and trusts averted, and that is what matters. Mountford Wilson would not talk at all. Callundan would watch me and smile.

And Bertha Berner? I am not sure. Would she be the Berner in the garden with Lord Kitchener? Or the Berner, bereaved and sympathetic, telling me that she knew things looked bad, but did I really believe she was capable of murder?

I tell Stephen that at 3:00 in the morning, an hour when I am often awake, I keep coming back to the pure strychnine placed in the bicarbonate in Hawaii. Anyone could get the rat poison placed in the Poland Spring Water in San Francisco, but pure strychnine was neither common nor readily available. Buying it involved having the purchase recorded in a poison book.

Stephen walks me through what amounts to a police procedural, common to both actual detectives and crime writers. Detectives need to establish means, motive, and opportunity. In every case, he says, there are choke points—the opportunity—where the murderer or his or her agents have to be present, and at that moment they need the means and the motive to commit the crime. If they cannot be connected to these tight confluences that disparate people and evidence squeeze through on their way to the murder, then they must be eliminated as suspects.

There are, we both agree, two obvious choke points in the Stanford case. The first is the night in January 1905 when Jane Stanford drank the Poland Spring Water. The cast of suspects is large: Bertha Berner and the servants, Elizabeth Richmond, Ah Wing, and his nephew. More tangentially, there are the butler Albert Beverly because of his connections with Richmond and Berner, and David Starr Jordan, who—perhaps too coincidentally—was in San Francisco that evening and encountered Berner and Jane Stanford the next morning and talked of strychnine. This choke point is particularly bad for Bertha Berner, because without Berner's intervention, Jane Stanford should not even have been in the mansion the night of the poisoning. She should have been in Palo Alto. Bertha Berner persuaded her to stay. But the detectives did not pursue this clue. They contended she had no motive to kill.

The second choke point is much narrower. Only one person present at the San Francisco poisoning was present in Hawaii when Jane Stanford died, and that was Bertha Berner. Two poisonings, two doses of strychnine, Berner the only person present both times, plus her purchase of the bicarbonate that later contained the poison: all this spells trouble for Bertha Berner.

But there are other possibilities. The San Francisco police did not collect fingerprints in 1905; someone could have placed the poison in the bottle in San Francisco without leaving a trace and waited for Jane Stanford to die far away. This could have been Berner. It could have been Ah Wing, but it could not have been Beverly or Richmond. Both left Jane Stanford's service well before her departure for Japan.

I go through my suspects. There is no clear motive for Beverly or Richmond. Richmond may have been eccentric, and she certainly changed her stories, but there never was a clear reason for her to put rat poison in Jane Stanford's Poland Spring Water. If she wanted to get Berner dismissed—and there is no evidence she did—then why not just tell Jane Stanford that Berner had been sleeping with Beverly, and that the two of them had been raking off money from the household accounts for years? Berner insisted that Jane Stanford already knew of her role in the rake-offs, but she said this only under duress after Mrs. Stanford's death. Grace Gilmore told a similar story of Beverly's rake-offs during the 1903–1904 Pacific trip, but she did not mention Berner. Nor did she mention Berner's likely affair with Beverly.

Beverly, according to the "bad" letter Callundan confiscated, was angry with Berner, but beyond accusing her of a betrayal, we do not know why. Maybe she told Stanford of the rake-offs; maybe he knew she was now sleeping with P. J. Schwab, the mysterious pharmacist. I do not know.

But even if he was angry at Berner, why poison Jane Stanford? A role in the first poisoning was possible, if unlikely, but the second? He did not have access to the bottle of bicarbonate. It is hard not to agree with the butler. Lathrop hated Beverly and entwined him in the investigation.

And David Starr Jordan? He certainly had a motive, one everyone but Julius Goebel was interested in disguising: Jane Stanford was going to fire him when she returned from her trip. In the winter of 1905, he was sick, worried, and distraught. The walls were closing in on him.

And there are incriminating circumstances. He was in San Francisco and in contact with Berner and Jane Stanford the weekend of the first poisoning. This could have been a coincidence, and so could the alacrity with which he identified the substance put in the water as strychnine. And there is a possibility that he and Berner already had a partnership. It seems likely that Berner was informing him of the correspondence between Goebel and Jane Stanford. And there is his suspicious firing of Goebel. Jane Stanford died on the last day of February 1905, but in between her departure for Hawaii and her death, Jordan took his first steps to dismiss Goebel, as if he knew she would soon pose no danger to him. The panicked reaction of Maria Berner to whatever her daughter told her immediately following the first poisoning, her supposed statement of a collaboration between a man—presumed to be Ah Wing but perhaps Beverly or Jordan—and the household staff, and August Berner's equal panic and his attempt to meet with Jordan before he left for Hawaii, all are compatible with some kind of understanding between Berner and Jordan. Jordan knew of Mrs. Soule's recent suicide in which she swallowed rat poison. She was the wife of a Stanford employee, and he wrote a letter of condolence. Rat poison in the water might look like a suicide and not a murder.

But this is where Jordan's complicity in the actual murder falls apart. For him, a death by suicide would be as dangerous as murder. It would open up the possibility of a challenge to Jane Stanford's will and trusts and endanger the university that Jordan was trying to control. Jordan was ruthless, often reckless, but he was not self-destructive. Even if he was capable of such a thing, the attempt would be out of character precisely because it was unlikely to achieve his ends.

The second, successful attempt—precisely the right amount of strychnine placed at the top of the bottle—was, for the opposite reason, outside Jordan's usual modus operandi. He relied on authority, brute force, and intimidation. Look at the Ross Affair, the Gilbert Affair, the Pease Affair, and the cover-up. All were clumsy exercises in power and influence.

Ah Wing? I think Detective Edward Gibson set him up to take the fall, which is not to say that he was unworthy of suspicion. Ah Wing had a motive. The Stanfords and Lathrops betrayed him. He knew there was a bequest for him in Jane Stanford's will. With Berner in the mansion, he felt his own authority undermined. He quarreled with her. His family awaited him in China. He had reason to want Jane Stanford to die soon. Berner kept insinuating his guilt. He, like Richmond, kept changing his stories.

And strychnine? He could have obtained strychnine in Chinatown. One of the episodes of the war between the See Yups and the Chinese Educational Society involved the attempt by Ah Sow—dubbed a Mongolian Lucretia Borgia by the press—to poison her husband Fong Ling, who took shelter in the Chinese Educational Society headquarters after turning against the See Yups. She brought him a bowl of turnip soup, but Fong Ling was suspicious of his wife's sudden solicitude. They were living separately since his flight. She had asked for a divorce and taken a lover, who was a See Yup fighting man. When Fong Ling asked his wife to taste the soup, she did so, but then she surreptitiously tried to spit it out. Seeing this, his friends warned him not to drink it. Fong Ling had the soup tested. The newspapers initially reported that it was laced with arsenic, but then said the poison was strychnine. His wife was thrown in jail.[2]

I cannot clear Ah Wing, but neither can I convict him. I cannot place him alone in the room where the bicarbonate was packed, even if I can also not exclude him.

But everything that makes Ah Wing a suspect multiplies when attached to Bertha Berner. The constant refrain citing her long service with Jane Stanford as a reason not to suspect her becomes a cause for suspicion when the rifts, quarrels, and frustrations of the relationship emerge. Her admission under interrogation in Hawaii that she could not bear to travel alone with Jane Stanford underlined her fears about more trips. If the first poisoning was intended to prevent another trip to Europe in the spring, it backfired. It only precipitated the Pacific voyage. She needed more than May Hunt's presence to endure that.[3] But Berner not only feared the strains of another trip with an irascible and demanding woman who denied her control over her body and her time, she also resented Jane

Stanford's demand that Berner leave her own sick mother in order to care for her. It grated. And given Berner's claim that Stanford used her money to get her way, it is hard not to think she feared being cut out of Jane Stanford's will.

I am hardly the first to suspect Berner—my own students in the first class I taught on the Stanford poisoning suspected her—but I am the first, I think, to bare her troubled and turbulent past with Jane Stanford, the absences and contradictions of her stories, and the burdens Mrs. Stanford forced her to bear. And if Berner herself was a medium, easing Stanford into the next life would not seem like murder. She only granted Stanford's own wish to reunite with her husband and son. On the Pacific voyage, she urged Mrs. Stanford to turn back, but it was to no avail. No more than Stanford would Berner have expected death to be so hard. Her shock and dismay at the death were probably quite honest.

Berner possessed a motive, but did she have the means? Before clapping the handcuffs on her, there is the strychnine—the pure strychnine—that killed Jane Stanford. If Berner committed the murder, how did she graduate so quickly from rat poison in copious amounts to pure strychnine at nearly precisely the dose necessary to kill? It is possible that she was not the first poisoner, but even if the first poisoner and the second poisoner were different people—which I do not believe—Berner alone was present at the second poisoning, and the question remains, where did the poison come from? Pure strychnine is hard to obtain, even if newspaper stories indicate that the rule of entering purchases in the poison book may have been obeyed in the breach.

Only three of the central figures in my story could have gotten pure strychnine easily. The first is Jules Callundan. During the Poland Spring Water investigation, he and other Morse detectives supposedly spent nearly a month scouring San Francisco and the Bay Area for pharmacies that sold strychnine. This was very peculiar since the chemist's report stated clearly that rat poison—easily available—had been placed in the Poland Spring Water. Why go looking for pure strychnine? This is clairvoyant detective work. They were looking for the weapon used in a murder that had yet to take place.

The second is David Starr Jordan, who professed, rightly or wrongly, a familiarity with strychnine. The university's chemistry building must have contained strychnine, but I was unable to confirm this—the records

294 WHO KILLED JANE STANFORD?

of what was in the laboratories at Stanford in 1905 no longer exist, or at least I could not find them.

And finally, and most intriguingly, there is the druggist, P. J. Schwab. Although he appears only glancingly toward the end of the story, he becomes for me the key to the whole mystery. Insert him into the narrative and things begin to click into place. He worked in one of the Palo Alto pharmacies and was friendly with Berner. Accused of embezzlement, he was clearly a man willing to take chances, and he could have gotten her the poison without leaving a record.[4]

Although no one at the time credited the San Francisco police with investigative skills, I think during much of the research for the book I underestimated them. There was the seemingly meaningless detail in a small newspaper story: the police had interviewed James Guilfoy, the owner of a factory in San Francisco, who claimed to have information on Schwab. The interview seems to have been the end of their interest. Schwab was not mentioned again in connection to the investigation.

Stephen flags this. Schwab is too important to ignore. Bertha Berner returned to California in the spring of 1904 to find a sick mother and Albert Beverly returning to his wife. Maybe she just met Schwab that spring—a recently divorced man who, like her, spoke German. Their friendship could have been the treachery that Beverly denounced in the "bad" letter he sent Berner, which she gave to Callundan. Jane Stanford's decision to travel threatened both her ability to take care of her mother and, perhaps, her friendship with Schwab. Mrs. Soule's suicide in December could have provided the inspiration for using rat poison to send Jane Stanford off to meet her relatives. Jane Stanford was old, eager to see her dead husband and son. Suicide would be a plausible explanation for her death.

When the first poisoning failed and hastened the extended travel Berner feared, Schwab became the solution. Schwab could get her pure strychnine. He, wittingly or not, did so. She hoped not to use it; she wanted to persuade Stanford to return to California, but she failed. She stiffened her resolve and put poison in the bicarbonate in Honolulu before Stanford could leave for Japan. With news of Jane Stanford's murder, Schwab recognized his liability. The detectives were looking for him, and he fled.

Stephen points out the problems with this theory. I know Schwab went bankrupt in Mountain View. He was selling insurance, working as a druggist, and living in a hotel and then, apparently, in a boardinghouse in San Francisco. He seemed to have needed money and tried to embezzle it, but he failed. He did not have the resources to disappear. And if he did, even if he had changed his name, why didn't he return once the police decided Jane Stanford died a natural death? The threat was gone. But he never returned. A man whom I can easily track over the previous ten years vanishes.

I look for Schwab, but find only false leads. I begin to doubt that Schwab had just moved on and started a new life. There was something strange about the police search before he disappeared. The *Examiner* reported two addresses for Schwab, one in San Francisco and one in Oakland, but I can find no evidence that anyone looked for him at either address.

I check out the first address—1114 Washington Street in Oakland. It was the "mammoth" store of the Kahn Brothers. They were dry goods merchants, and although they appear to have sublet some space for commercial purpose—Dr. M. M. Carter, a "hair physician," listed his address as the Kahn building—there is no evidence that anyone lived there.[5]

The second address at 220 Waller in San Francisco was supposedly a mailing address. In 1904 that was the residence of Anna Brandt, a widow. She apparently took in boarders, for Jean Detjean, a painter, lived there. It is possible that the *Examiner*, which got so many details wrong, reversed the addresses. Schwab lived at 220 Waller, but then why give the Washington Street address in Oakland, a place where neither he nor anyone else lived? He might not have given it. The *Examiner* again could have mistaken a San Francisco address for one in Oakland, just across the bay.[6]

I try to make some sense of Schwab's movements in 1904–1905. He was married and lived in Mountain View, but his wife, Katie Schwab, filed for divorce in the Superior Court of San Francisco, where Superior Court Judge John Hunt granted it in July of 1904 when Berner was back in Palo Alto.[7] Why go to another county to divorce your husband? San Francisco's divorce records vanished in the earthquake, but the newspapers listed divorces. In recording the divorce, the *Chronicle* reported that the Schwabs married in Mountain View in Santa Clara County in 1900. I look for the marriage record to get his ex-wife's maiden name. A search of the available records for P. J. Schwab yields nothing, but in the *San Jose Herald*'s marriage listings for July 14, 1900, there is one for a P. J. Schway and Katherine E. Doyle of Mountain View.[8] People seemed to have had a hard time getting Schwab's name right.

A little searching reveals that Katherine (Katie) Doyle of Mountain

View was most likely Katherine (Katie) Doyle of San Francisco before her marriage.[9] This would explain why she filed for divorce in San Francisco. In 1910 she was single and living on Washington Street in San Francisco, the same street that the *Examiner* listed as Schwab's residence in Oakland in 1905.[10] It is plausible that Schwab lived at 220 Waller, and his ex-wife who lived on Washington Street kept his mail.[11]

And Guilfoy? He entered the story because he claimed to know something. The police needed to know what he knew, but how and why would he know anything about a druggist who worked in small towns south of San Francisco? Katie Doyle, Schwab's ex-wife, might provide the answer. Her parents still lived in the city, and her father, Richard Doyle, was a blacksmith and iron worker.[12] James Guilfoy owned a cornice factory and employed metal workers. I have no evidence that Doyle worked with or for Guilfoy, but both were Irish, both were metal workers, and from other accounts, Guilfoy talked a lot. It is possible that Doyle told Guilfoy of his daughter's troubles and of her ex-husband's friendship with Bertha Berner. When the news came of Jane Stanford's death by strychnine, Guilfoy or someone else connected the druggist, the strychnine, and Berner, and went to the police. The police found a garrulous Irishman, but all he had was supposition and gossip—"mere conjecture," as the *Examiner* reported. There are no further records of a search for Schwab. The logical next step would be for detectives or reporters to talk to his ex-wife, who now lived in San Francisco. Or they could have asked Berner about him. They did not, as far as I can discover, do either of these things.

There were four police detectives assigned to the case. One, Harry Reynolds, specialized in escorting prisoners; he accompanied Jordan to Hawaii. Edward Gibson concentrated on Chinatown. That left Jerimiah Dinan and Ed Wren, and they were most likely the detectives who interviewed Guilfoy. Both detectives were corrupt; neither was stupid.

Dinan, with his ties to Mayor Schmitz, was a man on the rise; Ed Wren was his ally. Kid Sullivan also rose with Dinan and served the same function as Big Cheung did in Chinatown. He collected money from brothels, pimps, gamblers, liquor store owners, and anyone else seeking to avoid police raids, and funneled it upward. In the spring of 1905, following the conclusion of the Stanford investigation, Dinan became San Francisco's chief of police.[13]

I begin to think that Dinan and Wren are one step ahead of me. The police didn't look for Schwab because they had already found him. Dinan and Wren, or perhaps Kid Sullivan and his gang, may have paid Schwab a visit. They knew he no longer had anything to say.

In Gilded Age San Francisco it was hardly out of the question for a druggist who knew too much to meet an untimely end or be persuaded to disappear. It was hardly even notable. In May of 1907 Ruef pleaded guilty to extortion. That July a jury also convicted Mayor Schmitz, although the conviction would be overturned on appeal. Prosecutors also arraigned Dinan on charges of corruption. He was acquitted when the witnesses against him failed to appear, but he was removed as chief. He retained support within the department, where he remained first as a corporal and then as a detective. He advocated for Wren as his successor, but William Biggy got the job. An angry Dinan threatened to have the police stand aside while Kid Sullivan "[tore] up the town" to hurt the reform mayor who replaced Schmitz.[14]

Dinan in his corruption was a fair sample of the San Francisco police, and his fall did not change things. A muckraking piece in *McClure's Magazine* said that by the end of 1906 the department was "so demoralized and so corrupt that it might almost be said to constitute a distinct criminal class." In 1908 Francis Heney, the special prosecutor who brought down Schmitz and Ruef, arraigned Ruef on additional counts of bribery. During the trial in November, an assassin, Morris Haas, put a pistol near Heney's ear and pulled the trigger. Heney miraculously survived. Haas did not. While under police guard, he committed suicide in his cell. Somehow he had obtained a derringer. The district attorney's office and the Citizens' League of Justice accused Chief Biggy of being complicit in Haas's death. With Ruef's trial still underway, Biggy disappeared from a police launch in San Francisco Bay. The only man with him on the launch could not explain how he vanished. Biggy's body was found floating in the bay two weeks later.[15]

All of this influences how I think about P. J. Schwab. In San Francisco in the early twentieth century, a murder in Chinatown cost $300. Newspaper editors needed bodyguards. Fremont Older had a contract taken out on his life; the man prosecuting the Ruef machine was shot in a courtroom; his assassin somehow obtained the pistol he needed to commit suicide in the city jail; and the chief of police disappeared into the bay. In the battle over the Fair estate that involved both George Crothers and Mountford Wilson, litigants attempted murder and bought a California Supreme Court justice. Considering all this, the disappearance of a potential key witness and possible accessory to murder in the Stanford case raises possibilities that in another time and place might seem implausible, but here seem almost predictable. The bounds of the possible stretched beyond the furthest imaginable horizons in Gilded Age San Francisco.

I think Schwab supplied Berner with the strychnine. They were friends in 1904. *Friend* was as elastic a word in the early twentieth century as it is in the twenty-first. Maybe the relationship deepened when it became clear to Berner that Albert Beverly was not leaving his wife. Something happened between Berner and Beverly that made him write the "bad" letter to her before her departure to Hawaii with Jane Stanford. The treachery Beverly condemned might have involved Berner's new friend. This is a leap. The Morse detectives kept the letter. They knew things about Berner that Berner preferred be kept quiet. The detectives said the letter revealed nothing about Jane Stanford's murder. If it mentioned Schwab, they might have retained it as insurance that Berner remained quiet.

The things I do know—the Palo Alto purchase of the bicarbonate of soda and her original denial of it, her proximity at both poisonings, her changing stories, her motives for wishing Jane Stanford dead—seem damning for Berner. She bought the bicarbonate; she lied about it; and then the packet appeared in Hawaii. Jordan recognized it was incriminatory and made up a story about perfume spilling on it. He never explained the quite uncontaminated packet of bicarbonate found by the Hawaiian police.

I think the police knew that Schwab provided the final piece of the puzzle. The druggist gave Berner access not only to the strychnine but also to information on how to use it. He would have known the minimum fatal dose and how, if placed on the surface of the bicarbonate, it would not mix. If all went according to plan, the victim would swallow the strychnine and leave pure bicarbonate behind. Berner was the one who took the spoonful of bicarbonate and strychnine from the bottle. Jane Stanford would have tasted the strychnine when she swallowed it, but by then she was alone and it was too late. She said she had been poisoned. She had.

Berner and Schwab were both in the right place at the right time for the bicarbonate and the strychnine to converge. Schwab was in Palo Alto when Berner and Stanford purchased the bicarbonate. Berner was in Palo Alto and San Francisco in early February when Schwab may have obtained the strychnine.

There is a final problem. Why, if the first poisoning was inspired by Mrs. Soule's suicide, did Berner insist in Hawaii that Mrs. Stanford would never commit suicide? Because by then she was in conversation with representatives of the estate, who certainly told her of the dangers suicide would present for the will and her inheritance. When Jordan arrived and pressed for a natural death, he persuaded Berner that a natural death was more in her interest than suicide. She told him and Callundan what they wanted to hear, and they incorporated it in the Waterhouse report.

The circumstantial evidence is damning, and the failure of the detectives, the police, and the estate to pursue it—at least publicly—makes it more damning still. Berner might have been a suspect in the eyes of the press, and even the Honolulu police, but not in the eyes of Callundan, the Stanford estate, or the San Francisco police. It is hard not to be suspicious that the investigation shut down so quickly not because there was no murder but because those in charge of the investigation knew who the murderer was and that a trial would do no one any good.

Jordan saved Berner because he had to in order to save himself, the will, the trust documents, and ultimately the university. He as much as Berner benefited from Jane Stanford's death. Berner knew too much about Jordan, the university, and Jane Stanford for a trial in which she testified to be anything but a disaster for Jordan, the estate, and the university. Jane Stanford's natural death ruled out murder and suicide. It vitiated challenges to the will and grants that threatened the university and existing legatees. No one could indict Berner if there was no crime. And so Callundan had Berner contradict her testimony before the coroner's jury, and Jordan had Waterhouse write a report denying the poisoning. Everyone convinced Bertha Berner to shut up, and so she largely would for more than a quarter of a century.

And P. J. Schwab? He disappeared.

The cover-up orchestrated by Jordan and Wilson never convinced everyone, but it did not have to; it only needed to convince the corrupt and distracted San Francisco Police Department.

The evidence is circumstantial, but it is persuasive. Josephine Tey and her fictional detective misunderstood both historians and detectives. Detectives are products of their time and place. They do not always seek to solve crimes. And sometimes historians notice details detectives choose to ignore. Bertha Berner killed Jane Stanford, and David Starr Jordan covered up the crime. Jordan was an accessory after the fact.

And Berner's book, her memoir of Jane Stanford, written so long after her death? It is less a lie, though it contains lies, less a deception, though it contains deception, and less an erasure, though key events vanish, than it is an account of what might have been. If only Jane Stanford let Berner love whom she wished when she wished. If only her mother was not sick. If only they had not stopped in Palo Alto on the way to San Francisco from San Jose to buy the bicarbonate. If only Beverly did not have a wife. If only she could have revealed the name of the man who placed the "Green Stone" necklace under her plate in New Zealand. If only she had not taken kickbacks. If only there was no rat poison in the Poland Spring Water. If only she did not know Schwab. If only Jane Stanford had died peacefully in the fullness of her years. If only . . .

Berner constructed a memory where the if-onlys vanished. Then she wrote it down.

Bertha Berner and her brother lived in their Menlo Park home until they sold it in the 1920s, when they moved into the refurbished carriage house behind it. August Berner died in November of 1943; Bertha Berner on March 11, 1945. The son of the family who bought the house said that suspicion continued to circulate around her. "The loyalty attributed to Miss Berner was later disputed by acquaintances, who suggested that she may have helped Jane Stanford accelerate her demise while in Hawaii."[16]

Stephen, who creates characters for a living, thinks she was a hard woman: selfish, manipulative, clever, and adept at turning things to her advantage. I think she was a murderer, but up until the moment of the murder, I can't help sympathizing with her.

———

IN 2019 THE STANFORD ADMINISTRATION removed David Starr Jordan's name from Jordan Hall because of his writings on eugenics. They renamed the road in front of the Quad Jane Stanford Way.

ACKNOWLEDGMENTS

MY INTEREST IN JANE STANFORD'S DEATH originated in two classes that I taught at Stanford University. My first set of students were a particular delight. I set out to teach them, and they, and Natalie Johnson, my teaching assistant, taught me. Their questions and research helped shape the book.

The second class was one I taught with Jake Warga, who supervised the students' work in creating a podcast. I benefited as much as the students from Jake's ability to craft a story out of a dismaying array of characters and details. The class spurred me to write this book. As I worked through the last draft, Jake sent me a case of Poland Spring Water. He is a funny man and a fine writer.

As I get older, my books become family affairs. This one involved long conversations with my brother Stephen, who writes crime fiction. He taught me how to think about a mystery, how to unravel it, and how to recognize clues worth pursuing. His fingerprints are all over *Who Killed Jane Stanford?*

One advantage of a long academic career is that you accumulate friends and ex-students (often the same people) who know about life in universities past and present, about writing, and who do not hesitate to become exasperated with you. Jen Seltz, Rachel St. John, Marni Sandweiss, and Virginia Scharff all gave early drafts of this a thorough reading and were generous in telling me what was wrong with it and, occasionally, what was right. They helped me find a way to tell a story about an event in which most people involved wanted to disguise and bury what had happened. Their advice saved readers of this book considerable suffering. I am grateful.

Archivists are the hidden heroes of historical research. The archivists at Stanford University helped me find material where I had not thought to look, and when they, like me, could not explain where documents that once existed had gone, it reassured me that more than my own ineptitude was involved. Maggie Kimball retired as the research for this book was just beginning, but she was always ready to offer me advice on where to look next. Daniel Hartwig, who succeeded her, was an immense help with both the class and my research.

Other scholars were generous with help on particular problems. Julie Cain and Laura Jones were both always ready to share their knowledge of Stanford University. Kathryn Gin Lum helped me with the literature on spiritualism. Tom Mullaney, Tamara Venit Shelton, Alastair Su, Gordon Chang, and Beth Lew Williams all helped with the mysterious Tay Wang letter. Lulu Miller, whose book I relied on in my treatment of David Starr Jordan, shared with me some of Jordan's writings that I would otherwise have missed. Jenny Pegg's work on spiritualism and Thomas Welton Stanford aided me greatly.

Shirley Buchanan did valuable research for me in Hawaii, when Covid made it impossible to travel there, and Chad Frazier did equal service in getting materials from the Goebel Papers in the Library of Congress.

I have worked with my agent Georges Borchardt for years, but in this book he went beyond his usual services to make a suggestion on the structure of this book that improved it immensely. My editor Steve Forman at W. W. Norton spent many days with this manuscript, and his suggestions went well beyond the usual editorial fine-tuning. He helped me shape the book, condense it, and surrender details without sacrificing historical context. He made me explain to him—and myself—why I was doing what I was doing. His aid was valuable beyond saying, and I am grateful.

My wife Beverly's illness prevented her from taking as active a role in this book as she had in others. Her death before the publication of this book plunged me into a grief that seems to have no bottom. I experienced sorrow and woe similar to the emotions that launched the story I tell.

NOTES

ABBREVIATIONS

Throughout the Notes, the abbreviated form of San Francisco newspaper names is used (*Examiner, Bulletin*, etc.), omitting the name of the city. All other newspaper names use the full name including city.

In notes that cite collections of papers (Stanford Papers, Crothers Papers, Gardner Collection, etc.), an abbreviated system is used for each specific location: "S." stands for "series," "b." stands for "box," and "f." stands for "folder."

PREFACE

1 "Tomb Awaits Remains," *Call*, March 16, 1905, 2; "Poison Kills Mrs. Stanford in Hawaii," *New York Commercial Advertiser*, March 1, 1905, Clippings, 23: 27.

2 Jane Stanford to Mrs. Jordan, Aug. 31, 1900, Stanford Papers, S. 1, b. 2, f. 3.

3 Address delivered at the Dedication Service, Jan. 25, 1903, by Reverend D. Charles Gardner, Gardner Collection, b. 1.

4 Jean H. Baker, *Mary Todd Lincoln: A Biography* (New York: W. W. Norton, 1987), 217–22. The literature on spiritualism is immense. Martin Halliwell and Joel D. S. Rasmussen, *William James and the Transatlantic Conversation: Pragmatism, Pluralism, and Philosophy of Religion* (New York: Oxford University Press, 2014), 31–64; Ann Braude, *Radical Spirits: Spiritualism and Women's Rights in Nineteenth-Century America* (Boston: Beacon Press, 1989); Molly McGarry, *Ghosts of Futures Past: Spiritualism and the Cultural Politics of Nineteenth-Century America* (Berkeley: University of California Press, 2008); R. Laurence Moore, *In Search of White Crows: Spiritualism, Parapsychology, and American Culture* (New York: Oxford University Press, 1977), 55–57, 60, 65–67.

5 Jane Stanford to Andrew D. White, 1902, Stanford Papers, S. 1, b. 2, f. 7; Jane Stanford to Andrew D. White, March 11, 1903, Stanford Papers, S. 1, b. 2, f. 8.

6 Memorial Church Inscriptions, Stanford Office of Religious Life, https://religiouslife .stanford.edu/memorial-church/memorial-church-inscriptions; "Address of Jane Lathrop

Stanford Upon Her Inauguration as President of the Board of Trustees of The Leland Stanford Junior University" (July 6, 1903), 18.

7   Robert W. P. Cutler, *The Mysterious Death of Jane Stanford* (Palo Alto, CA: Stanford University Press, 2003).

8   Dashiell Hammett, *The Maltese Falcon* in *Complete Novels*, ed. Steven Marcus (New York: Library of America, 1999), 392.

CHAPTER 1: THE FIRST POISONING

1   Diana Strazdes, "The Millionaire's Palace: Leland Stanford's Commission for Pottier & Stymus in San Francisco," *Winterthur Portfolio* 36, no. 4 (Winter 2001): 213–16, 220. Bertha Berner, *Mrs. Leland Stanford: An Intimate Account* (Stanford, CA: Stanford University Press, 1935), 19–20. The mansion consisted of a ground floor, a first floor, a second floor, and a third floor. The first floor was thus on the second story and so on.

2   Strazdes, "The Millionaire's Palace," 213–16, 220. Jane Stanford to Mary Miller, Sept. 10, 1904, Stanford Papers, S. 1, b. 2, f. 9.

3   A census entry under her father's name, August Berner, has her born in 1863. Her passport gave her date of birth as 1865. National Archives and Records Administration (NARA); Washington, DC; Roll #: 555; Volume #: Roll 555 – 07 Jun 1900 – 11 Jun 1900. U.S. Passport Applications, 1795–1925 [database online]. "Miss Bertha Berner, Stanford Residence" written on back. Series, Biographical Photographs, SHPC Photo ID 1338, Department of Special Collections and University Archives, b. 2, f. Berner, Bertha.

4   "Miss Berner's Story of Poison Last January," *Examiner*, March 22, 1905, Clippings, 25: 179.

5   "Mrs. Stanford's Views on Communion with the Dead," *Pacific Commercial Advertiser*, March 11, 1905, 6.

6   David L. Richards, *Poland Spring: A Tale of the Gilded Age* (Lebanon, NH: University Press of New England, 2005), 5, 79, 111–12, 120–23, 130–33.

7   "Miss Richmond Talks Quite Freely," *Examiner*, March 4, 1905, 5.

8   "Secretary Is Tangled Among Contradictions," *Examiner*, March 4, 1905, 2; "Miss Berner's Story of Poison Last January," *Examiner*, March 22, 1905, Clippings, 25: 179.

9   "Miss Berner's Story of Poison Last January," *Examiner*, March 22, 1905, Clippings, 25: 179.

10   "Mystery Still Shrouds Motive of Poisoning," *Chronicle*, Feb. 21, 1905, 16; "Suspected Girl Declares That an Attempt Was Made to Murder Mrs Stanford," *Bulletin*, Feb. 19, 1905, Clippings, 23: 2.

11   "Criticised [*sic*] Her Strange Manner," *Bulletin*, March 7, 1905, Clippings, 25: 25.

12   "Important Admissions Are Made by Woman," *Bulletin*, March 8, 1905, Clippings, 25: 54.

13   "Maids Give Accounts That Conflict," *Examiner*, Feb. 20, 1905; "Suspected Girl Declares," *Bulletin*, Feb. 19, 1905, Clippings, 23: 2.

14   "Criticised [*sic*] Her Strange Manner," *Bulletin*, March 7, 1905, Clippings, 25: 25.

15   "Search for Motive in Stanford Poison Case," *Examiner*, Feb. 20, 1905, 1–2; "Large Corps of Sleuths at Work," *Examiner*, March 4, 1905, 6.

16   "Miss Berner's Story of Poison Last January," *Examiner*, March 22, 1905, Clippings, 25: 179.

17   "Miss Berner's Story of Poison Last January," *Examiner*, March 22, 1905, Clippings, 25: 179; "Lay Stress on Soda Find," *Chronicle*, March 11, 1905.

18   "Miss Berner's Story of Poison Last January," *Examiner*, March 22, 1905, Clippings, 25: 179.

19   Berner, *Mrs. Leland Stanford*, 201.

20 Berner, *Mrs. Leland Stanford*, 201; Crothers to Mrs. Fremont Older, Jan. 30, 1947, Crothers Papers, Correspondence, b. 4.
21 "Criticised [*sic*] Her Strange Manner," *Bulletin*, March 7, 1905, Clippings, 25: 25.
22 Berner, *Mrs. Leland Stanford*, 201; "Miss Berner's Story of Poison Last January," *Examiner*, March 22, 1905, Clippings, 25: 179.
23 "Criticised [*sic*] Her Strange Manner," *Bulletin*, March 7, 1905, Clippings, 25: 25; Berner, *Mrs. Leland Stanford*, 201; "Train Schedule" *Call*, Jan. 6, 1905, 14.
24 "Explains His Work for the Poor," *Call*, Jan. 15, 1905.
25 "President Jordan Scouts the Idea of Her Suicide," *Call*, March 3, 1905; "Criticised [*sic*] Her Strange Manner," *Bulletin*, March 7, 1905, Clippings, 25: 25.
26 "No Attempt to Poison Mrs. Stanford," *Mercury*, Feb. 20, 1905, Clippings, 23: 5; "Poisoning Story Is Not True," *Berkeley Gazette*, Feb. 20, 1905, Clippings, 23: 5.
27 W. K. B. Fowler to Jordan, Jan. 20, 1905, Jordan Papers, S. 1-A, b. 43–434.
28 Jordan to Fowler, Jan. 25, 1905, Jordan Papers, S. 1-B, b. 26: 55.
29 Jordan to Ray Lyman Wilbur, May 18, 1921, Stanford Papers, S. 4, b. 1, f. 11.
30 Jordan to Ray Lyman Wilbur, May 18, 1921, Stanford Papers, S. 4, b. 1, f. 11; "President Jordan Scouts the Idea of Her Suicide," *Call*, March 3, 1905.

CHAPTER 2: STRYCHNINE
1 "Not Looking for Poisoner," *Call*, Feb. 22, 1905, Clippings, 23: 6.
2 *Sacramento Bee*, Jan. 21, 1905, Clippings, 22: 219; *Examiner*, Jan. 21, 1905, Clippings, 2: 220; Sally Sharp, "The Smart Set," *Call*, Jan. 18, 1905, 8, Jan. 21, 1905, 8.
3 Re: "Wilson," Crothers Papers, b. 20, f. 1; "T. Hopkins," Crothers Papers, b. 20, f. 3.
4 "Old Friends Say Mrs. Stanford Had No Hallucinations," *Call*, March 3, 1905, 1; "Not Looking for Poisoner," *Call*, Feb. 22, 1905, Clippings, 23: 6.
5 Elizabeth Richmond, "Suspected Girl Declares," *Bulletin*, Feb. 19, 1905.
6 "Poison Found Was Not Chemically Pure," *Chronicle*, March 4, 1905, 2.
7 "Suspected Girl Declares," *Bulletin*, Feb. 19, 1905.
8 John Boessenecker, *Lawman: The Life and Times of Harry Morse, 1835–1912* (Norman: University of Oklahoma Press, 1998), 5–227. For perjury and evidence, 224–25.
9 "Poison Was Dissolved in the Water," *Bulletin*, Feb. 19, 1905; "Strychnine Placed in Mineral Water," *Examiner*, Feb. 19, 1905, 1; "Not Looking for Poisoner," *Call*, Feb. 21, 1905; "Maids Give Accounts That Conflict," *Examiner*, Feb. 20, 1905, 1.
10 Boessenecker, *Lawman*, 226–27.
11 "Hayes Dies of His Injuries," *Call*, March 25, 1903; "Mrs. O'Connell His Companion," *Chronicle*, March 26, 1903, 14; "Jury Says Hayes Died by Accident," *Chronicle*, March 28, 1903, 16.
12 Poison Was Dissolved in the Water," *Bulletin*, Feb. 19, 1905; "Strychnine Placed in Mineral Water," *Examiner*, Feb. 19, 1905; "Not Looking for Poisoner," *Call*, Feb. 21, 1905; "Maids Give Accounts That Conflict," *Examiner*, Feb. 20, 1905, 1; "Attempt Made to Poison Mrs. Stanford," *Mercury*, Feb. 19, 1905, mentions story broke Feb. 18.
13 "Suspected Girl Declares," *Bulletin*, Feb. 19, 1905; "Dr. Boericke Gives Opinion," *Call*, March 3, 1905, 2.

CHAPTER 3: WATCHING THE DETECTIVES
1 "Thinks Report Misleading," *Call*, Dec. 31, 1905, 1; "Jordan Alleges Attempt to Loot Stanford," *Call*, Dec. 31, 1905, 1.
2 "Mrs. Stanford's Maid," "Suspected Girl Declares," *Bulletin*, Feb. 19, 1905, Clippings, 23: 2; "Important Admissions Are Made by Woman," *Bulletin*, March 8, 1905, Clippings, 25: 54; "Important Admissions Are Made by Woman," *Bulletin*, March 8, 1905, Clippings, 25: 54.

3 "Mrs. Stanford's Maid," "Suspected Girl Declares," *Bulletin*, Feb. 19, 1905, Clippings, 23: 2; "Important Admissions Are Made by Woman," *Bulletin*, March 8, 1905, Clippings, 25: 54; "Poison Was Dissolved in the Water," *Bulletin*, Feb. 19, 1905.

4 "Suspected Girl Declares," *Bulletin*, Feb. 19, 1905, Clippings, 23: 2; "Maid Saw Deadly Poison in Bottle," *Bulletin*, Feb. 20, 1905, Clippings, 23: 7.

5 "Not Looking for Poisoner," *Call*, Feb. 22, 1905, Clippings, 23: 6.

6 "Important Admissions Are Made by Woman," *Bulletin*, March 8, 1905, 25: 54.

7 "Arrests Likely Any Time," *Call*, March 12, 1905, 28; "Miss Richmond Talks Quite Freely," *Examiner*, March 4, 1905, 5.

8 "Thinks Report Misleading," *Call*, Dec. 31, 1905, 1; "Not Looking for Poisoner," *Call*, Feb. 21, 1905, 14; "Mrs. Stanford Is Told of Stories Published," *Bulletin*, Feb. 22, 1905, Clippings, 23: 8; "Mystery Still Shrouds Motive of Poisoning," *Chronicle*, Feb. 21, 1905, Clippings, 23: 9.

9 "Maid Saw Deadly Poison in Bottle," *Bulletin*, Feb. 20, 1905; "Mystery Still Shrouds Motive of Poisoning," *Chronicle*, Feb. 21, 1905.

10 "Mystery Still Shrouds Motive of Poisoning," *Chronicle*, Feb. 21, 1905, 16; *P-W-R Manual, Power-Weightman-Rosengarten Co., Manufacturing Chemists* (Philadelphia, 1924), 356, 358; Cutler, *Mysterious Death*, 38–40; John Harris Trestrail III, *Chemical Poisoning: Criminal Poisoning, Investigational Guide for Law Enforcement, Forensic Scientists, and Attorneys*, 2d ed. (Totowa, NJ: Humana Press, 2007), 122; "Stanford Servant," *Examiner*, Feb. 20, 1905, 2; "Positive Denial Is Made by the Police," *Chronicle*, March 8, 1905, 2.

11 "Police and Brother of Wife Seek Stanford Poison Plot Motive," *Los Angeles Examiner*, Feb. 20, 1905, Clippings, 23: 8.

CHAPTER 4: AH WING AND WONG TOY WONG

1 Dashiell Hammett, "Dead Yellow Women," in *Crime Stories and Other Writings* (New York: Library of America, 2001), 409.

2 "Mrs. Stanford Was Frequently Threatened by Chinese," *Mercury*, March 8, 1905, 1.

3 "Crazy Wong Toy Wong Threatened the Life of Mrs. Jane Stanford," no newspaper listed, March 12, 1905, Clippings, 25: 96; Wong Toy Wong, no. 2128, Mendocino State Hospital, California State Hospital Records, 1856–1923, Commitment Registers, Book 5–07, 1903–1909, MF8:11, 6 volumes, Dept. of Mental Hygiene—Hospitals, California State Archives, Sacramento, California.

4 "Crazy Wong Toy Wong Threatened," no newspaper listed, March 12, 1905, Clippings, 25: 96; Wong Toy Wong, no. 2128, Mendocino State Hospital, California State Hospital Records, 1856–1923, Commitment Registers, Book 5–07, 1903–1909, MF8:11, 6 volumes, Dept. of Mental Hygiene—Hospitals, California State Archives, Sacramento, California.

5 "Crazy Wong Toy Wong Threatened," no newspaper listed, March 12, 1905, Clippings, 25: 96.

6 Mae Ngai, *The Chinese Question: The Gold Rushes and Global Politics* (New York: W. W. Norton, 2021), 16, 54–55.

7 Ngai, *The Chinese Question*, 60, 76–77.

8 "Ah Wing Account," http://quake06.stanford.edu/centennial/gallery/documents/ahwing.html; Holograph Copy of Jane Stanford's Will, 1899, Stanford Papers; S. 4, b. 1, f. 5; Lani Ah Tye Farkas, *Bury My Bones in America: The Saga of a Chinese Family in California, 1852–1996* (Nevada City, CA: Carl Mautz Publishing, 1998), 8. The See Yups fragmented into several *huigans*, but it does not appear that Ah Wing would have been part of any of the breakaway groups. Lawrence Douglas Taylor Hansen, "The Chinese Six Companies of San Francisco and the Smuggling of Chinese Immigrants

Across the U.S.-Mexico Border, 1882–1930," *Journal of the Southwest* 48, no. 1 (Spring 2006): 37–61.

9 Ngai, *The Chinese Question*, 78–79, 90–91; Jingyi Song, *Denver's Chinatown, 1875–1900: Gone But Not Forgotten* (Boston: Brill, 2020), 72–74.

10 "Why He Was Murdered," *Call*, Jan. 24, 1897, 1.

11 Little Pete (Fun Jing Toy, Fong Ching), Ship Passengers: 1846–1899, The Maritime Heritage Project, San Francisco, https://www.maritimeheritage.org/news/Chinese-Little-Pete.html. Fong Ching, Guardians of the City, Sheriff's Department, https://www.guardiansofthecity.org/sheriff/inmates/little_pete.html; *People v. Fong Ching* (No. 20, 448), Supreme Court of California, Jan. 28, 1889; *Pacific Reporter* 20 (St. Paul: West Publishing Company, 1889): 396–99; Thomas Libby, "Hindsight: 114 Years Ago," *Daily Journal: California Lawyer*, Jan. 1, 2011; "Little Pete's Career," *Call*, Jan. 24, 1897, 1, 8; Morgan Gerard Boyd, "The Gold Mountain Theater Riots: A Social History of Chinese Theater Riots in San Francisco during the 1870s and 1880s," San Jose State University SJSU ScholarWorks Master's Theses and Graduate Research, Fall 2012, 75; "Cunning Little Pete," *Call*, Dec. 24, 1895, 14; "Little Pete on a Wheel," *Call*, Feb. 16, 1896, 8. There is a lengthy account of Little Pete of dubious reliability in John P. Young, *San Francisco: A History of the Pacific Coast Metropolis*, vol. 2 (Chicago: S.J. Clarke Publishing Company, 1912), 816–18; Julia Flynn Siler, *The White Devil's Daughters: The Women Who Fought Slavery in San Francisco's Chinatown* (New York: Alfred A. Knopf, 2019), 79–82, 103, 107; Ngai, *The Chinese Question*, 76.

12 "Police Patrol," *Call*, Nov. 2, 1895; "The Rival Jockey Clubs," *Call*, June 7, 1895, 10; "Pacific Coast Jockey Club Meeting," *Call*, Nov. 27, 1895, 9.

13 "Why He Was Murdered," *Call*, Jan. 24, 1897; "Foul Murder at San Francisco," *Sacramento Daily Union*, Jan. 24, 1897, 5; "Testimony of Lieutenant William Price," *Reports of the Industrial Commission on Immigration*, vol. 15 (Washington, DC: Government Printing Office, 1901), 777; "Chief Crowley's Views," *Call*, Jan. 26, 1897, 5; Siler, *The White Devil's Daughters*, 106–8.

14 "Says Little Pete Raced to the End," *Call*, Jan. 28, 1897, 1; "Richmond Has Good Prospects," *Call*, May 29, 1896, 9.

15 "Long Winded Search," *Call*, April 7, 1892, 3; "An Opium Factory," *Call*, June 30, 1892, 6; "Chinese Tricks," *Call*, Sept. 16, 1893, 7; "Little Pete's Career," *Call*, Jan. 24, 1897, 1; Boyd, "The Gold Mountain Theater Riots," 75; Commissioner Jesse B. Cook, "San Francisco's Old Chinatown," *San Francisco Police and Peace Officers' Journal*, June 1931, https://www.city-sightseeing.us/en/chinatown-information; *Reports of the Industrial Commission on Immigration*, vol. 15 of the Commission Reports (Washington, DC: Government Printing Office, 1901), 777–78; "Jordan and Hopkins," no newspaper listed, March 11, 1905, Clippings, 25.

16 "Why He Was Murdered," *Call*, Jan. 24, 1897, 1; "Foul Murder at San Francisco," *Sacramento Daily Union*, Jan. 24, 1897, 5; "Testimony of Lieutenant William Price," *Reports of the Industrial Commission*, 777; "Chief Crowley's Views," *Call*, Jan. 26, 1897; Siler, *The White Devil's Daughters*, 106–8.

17 "Foul Murder at San Francisco," *Sacramento Daily Union*, Jan. 24, 1897, 5; "Little Pete Murdered by His Enemies," *Call*, Jan. 24, 1897.

CHAPTER 5: THE WAY TO SAN JOSE

1 The most recent and most insightful book on David Starr Jordan is Lulu Miller, *Why Fish Don't Exist: A Story of Loss, Love, and the Hidden Order of Life* (New York: Simon & Schuster, 2020); David Starr Jordan, *The Days of a Man: Being Memories of a Naturalist, Teacher and Minor Prophet of Democracy* (Arkose Press, 2015).

2 Berner, *Mrs. Leland Stanford*, 202.

3 Jane Stanford to Horace Davis, Jan. 28, 1905, Stanford Papers, S. 1, b. 2, f. 10; Jordan to Sloss, Jan. 25, 1905, Jordan Papers, S. 1-AA, b. 13, v. 26.

4 Jane Stanford to Board of Trustees, Feb. 1, 1905, Davis Papers, b. 1, f. 14; Jane Stanford to Horace Davis, Jan. 28, 1905, Stanford Papers, S. 1, b. 2, f. 10.

5 Jane Stanford to Board of Trustees, Feb. 1, 1905, Davis Papers, b. 1, f. 14; Jane Stanford to Horace Davis, Jan. 28, 1905, Stanford Papers, S. 1, b. 2, f. 10.

6 Leib to D. S. Jordan, Feb. 10, 1905, Leib to Crothers, Feb. 18, 1905, Leib Papers, b. 2, f. 4.

7 Jane Stanford to Board of Trustees, Feb. 1, 1905, Davis Papers, b. 1, f. 14; Jane Stanford to Horace Davis, Jan. 28, 1905, Stanford Papers, S. 1, b. 2, f. 10.

8 Jane Stanford to Jordan, Feb. 5, 1905, Stanford Papers, b. 2, f. 30; Jane Stanford to May Hopkins, Sept. 10, 1900, Stanford Papers, S. 1, b. 2, f. 3.

9 Leib to Jordan, Feb. 13, 1905, Jordan Papers, S. 1-A, b. 43–436; Leib to Jordan, Feb. 15, 1905, Jordan Papers, S. 1-A, b. 43–438.

10 Ray Lyman Wilbur to Jordan, Feb. 4, 1905, Jordan Papers, S. 1-A, b. 43–436; Jordan to Richard D. Harlan, Feb. 4, 1905, Jordan Papers, b. 13, v. 26: 159; Jordan to Wilbur, Feb. 6, 1905, Jordan Papers, S. 1-AA, b. 13, v. 26: 181.

11 "Dr. Boericke Gives Opinion," *Call*, March 3, 1905.

12 Jane Stanford to Board of Trustees, Feb. 13, 1905, Minutes, Meeting Feb. 22, 1905, Board of Trustees, b. 38, pp. 94–96.

13 "Arrests to Come Soon in the Stanford Case," *Chronicle*, March 4, 1905, 1, 3; "Tells Story of Buying the Soda," *Examiner*, March 4, 1905, Clippings, 23.

14 Tells Story of Buying the Soda," *Examiner*, March 4, 1905, Clippings, 23.

15 "Suspected Poisoner May Soon Be Behind Bars," *Call*, March 3, 1905, 2; "What Do the Berners Know of the Case?" *Mercury*, March 4, 1905, Clippings, 24: 59; "Chemical Bought in Palo Alto," *Examiner*, March 3, 1905, 2; "Dies at Her Home in Menlo Park," *Chronicle*, July 23, 1905, 40.

16 "What Do the Berners Know of the Case?" *Mercury*, March 4, 1905, Clippings, 24: 59.

17 "What Do the Berners Know of the Case?" *Mercury*, March 4, 1905, Clippings, 24: 59.

18 Memorandum, Crothers Papers, b. 20, f. 2; "Rough Draft," Crothers Papers, b. 20, f. 2, p. 2; Crothers to Elliott, Feb. 11, 1937, Elliott Papers, b. 3, f. 27; for hotel, Jane Stanford to May Hopkins, Feb. 15, 1905, Stanford Papers, S. 1, b. 2, f. 10; "Police Inquire into the Details of the Case," *Call*, March 6, 1905, 1.

19 Testimony of May Hunt, Coroner's Inquest, 15–23.

20 Memorandum, Crothers Papers, SC0130, b. 20, f. 2; "Rough Draft," Crothers Papers, b. 20, f. 2, p. 2; Crothers to Elliott, Feb. 11, 1937, Elliott Papers, b. 3, f. 27. She also told Jennie Lathrop, Jennie Watson to Ray Lyman Wilbur, Jan. 1932, Wilbur Papers, b. 86, f. Watson.

21 "Rough Draft," Crothers Papers, S. 3, b. 20, f. 2, pp. 2, 4, 7; "Distinguished People Sail on Liner Korea," *Call*, Feb. 16, 1905.

22 Jane Stanford to George Crothers, Feb. 15, 1905; enclosure with Crothers to Elliott, Feb. 7, 1937, Elliott Papers, b. 3, f. 7.

23 Jane Stanford to George Crothers, Feb. 15, 1905; enclosure with Crothers to Elliott, Feb. 7, 1937, Elliott Papers, b. 3, f. 7.

24 Memorandum, Crothers Papers, b. 20, f. 2; "Rough Draft," Crothers Papers, b. 20, f. 2, p. 2; Crothers to Elliott, Feb. 7, 1937, Elliott Papers, b. 3, f. 7; "Lost Stanford Letter Reappears," *San Jose Mercury News*, March 11, 1937.

25 Memorandum, Crothers Papers, b. 20, f. 2; "Rough Draft," Crothers Papers, b. 20, f. 2, p. 2; Crothers to Elliott, Feb. 11, 1937, Elliott Papers, b. 3, f. 27; Jane Stanford to May

Hopkins, Feb. 15, 1905, Stanford Papers, S. 1, b. 2, f. 10; Jennie Watson to Ray Lyman Wilbur, Jan. 1932, Wilbur Papers, b. 86, Watson Papers, b. 86, f. Watson.

26 George Crothers to S. F. Leib, Feb. 15, 1905, Leib Papers, b. 1, f. 4.

CHAPTER 6: BERTHA BERNER WRITES A LIFE

1 Bertha Berner, *Mrs. Leland Stanford*, 1–2.

2 Crothers to Elliott, March 25, 1935, Elliott Papers, b. 3, f. 4; Jennie Lathrop Watson to Wilbur, Feb. 14, 1932, April 22, 1932, Wilbur Papers, b. 86, f. Watson; Wilbur to Crothers, Dec. 29, 1934, Elliott Papers, b. 3, f. 4.

3 Orrin Leslie Elliott, *Stanford University: The First 25 Years* (Stanford: Stanford University Press, 1937), x, 464–65; Crothers to Elliott, Oct. 2, 1931, Elliott Papers, b. 3, f. 5. He also expressed doubts about her account to the widow of Fremont Older. Crothers to Mrs. Fremont Older, Jan. 30, 1947, Crothers Papers, Correspondence, S. I, Outgoing b. 3, Memoranda, Chapter 17, enclosed with Crothers to Frederick Rogers, June 24, 1947; Crothers Papers, S. VII, General Memoranda, b. 21, f. 45. Mrs. Fremont Older wrote a largely innocuous account that repeated both Older's and Berner's mistakes and added new ones. Mrs. Fremont Older, *San Francisco: Magic City* (New York: Longmans, Green, 1961), 53–54.

4 Berner, *Mrs. Leland Stanford*, 202.

5 Testimony of Bertha Berner, March 6, 1905, Coroner's Inquest, 10.

6 Berner, *Mrs. Leland Stanford*, 202.

7 Berner, *Mrs. Leland Stanford*, 202.

8 Memorandum, Crothers Papers, S. 6, b. 20, f. 2; "Rough Draft," Crothers Papers, S. 6, b. 20, f. 2, p. 2; Crothers to Elliott, Feb. 11, 1937, Elliott Papers, b. 3, f. 27; Jane Stanford to May Hopkins, Feb. 15, 1905, Stanford Papers, S. 1, b. 2, f. 10.

9 Berner, *Mrs. Leland Stanford*, 125–26.

CHAPTER 7: LELAND STANFORD JR.

1 Sarah B. Cooper to Jane Stanford, March 3, 1896, Stanford Papers, S. 1, b. 3, f. 23.

2 Herbert C. Nash, "Biographical Sketch," in *In Memoriam: Leland Stanford, Jr.* (San Francisco? c. 1884).

3 Nash, "Biographical Sketch," 17–19, 32–34, 37; "Bequest to Ariel Lathrop Revives Story of a Quarrel," *Call*, March 5, 1905, 40.

4 "Bequest to Ariel Lathrop Revives Story of a Quarrel," *Call*, March 5, 1905, 40.

5 Jane Stanford to Russell Wilson, June 1, 1897, Stanford Papers, S. 1, b. 13, f. 1; Jane Stanford to David Starr Jordan, Nov. 22, 1897, Stanford Papers, S. 1, b. 2, f. 20.

6 Jane Stanford to Russell Wilson, June 1, 1897, Stanford Papers, S. 1, b. 13, f. 1; Jane Stanford to David Starr Jordan, Nov. 22, 1897, Stanford Papers, S. 1, b. 2, f. 20.

7 Nash, "Biographical Sketch," 25–27, 29.

8 "Ghost Builder of University," *London (Ontario) Advertiser*, Jan. 11, 1905 (?), Clippings, 22: 105.

9 "Spirit of Son Made Request," *San Diego Call*, March 3, 1905, Clippings, 24: 69; "Story of Birth of a University," *Baltimore American*, March 3, 1905, Clippings, 24: 71; "Spiritualism Is Belief of Church Says Rector," *New York American*, Dec. 23, 1904, Clippings, 22: 143.

10 "Senator Stanford's Dream," *The WASP*, March 11, 1905, Clippings, 24: 103.

11 Jane Stanford, Note, July 19, 1892, Stanford Papers, S. 1, b. 13.

12 Jane Stanford, Aix-Les Bains, Sept. 4, 1892, Stanford Papers, S. 1, b. 13.

13 Jane Stanford, Note, July 19, 1892, Stanford Papers, S. 1, b. 13.

14 Roland De Wolk, *American Disruptor: The Scandalous Life of Leland Stanford* (Berkeley: University of California Press, 2019), 22; Berner, *Mrs. Leland Stanford*, 47.

CHAPTER 8: GHOSTS AND MONEY

1 "Mystery Lies Thick About Two Poison Cases," *Chronicle*, March 2, 1905, 1.

2 The cathedral was destroyed in the earthquake and fire of 1906.

3 The Berner genealogy is complicated. There is a record of August's death in 1879, but he was quite alive in 1880. Death record, Find a Grave, https://search.ancestry.com /cgi-bin/sse.dll?dbid=60525&h=52675715&indiv=try&o_vc=Record:OtherRecord&rh Source=6742,

4 Minnesota State Census, 1885 State Census, Census ID: 516571, Minneapolis, Hennepin County, Minnesota, United States, Schedule 71, 13, volume p. no. 460; "Miss Berner a Kansan," *Chronicle*, March 8, 1905, 2; Berner, *Mrs. Leland Stanford*, 38; "There Was Poison in the House," *Chronicle*, March 19, 1905, 33; Census Place: Manitowoc Ward 1, Manitowoc, Wisconsin; Roll: M593_1723; Page: 191A; 1870 United States Federal Census population schedules, 1900; Census Place: San Francisco, San Francisco, California, Page: 7; Enumeration District: 0263; United States, Bureau of the Census, Twelfth Census of the United States, 1900.

5 *Harpers Weekly*, Dec. 27, 1884, 853; "Leland Stanford Jr.," *Examiner*, Nov. 29, 1884, 3.

6 Berner, *Mrs. Leland Stanford*, 37–38; "San Francisco: They Shame Them into Decency," *The American Israelite*, Feb. 6, 1885, 5; "The Stanford Obsequies," *Chronicle*, Dec. 1, 1884, 2; "In Memoriam," *Daily Alta California*, Dec. 1, 1884.

7 Berner, *Mrs. Leland Stanford*, 38.

8 Berner, *Mrs. Leland Stanford*, 35–36; *Daily Alta California*, Nov. 29, 1884.

9 Jordan to H. C. Nash, July 27, 1901, Jordan Papers, S. 1A, b. 52, f. 274.

10 "Bishop John Newman Dead," *New York Times*, July 6, 1899, 7; "A Stanford Church: Rev. Dr. Newman," *Chronicle*, Feb. 13, 1885, 2; "The Stanford Obsequies," *Chronicle*, Dec. 2, 1884, 5; Kenneth Rowe, "Building Monumental Methodist Cathedrals in America's Capital City, 1850–1950," *Methodist History* 50, no. 3 (April 2012): 2; *New York Times*, Jan. 16, 1882, 8; Alfred Emanuel Smith, "Francis Walton," *New Outlook* 29 (Jan. 1916): 278.

11 "Bishop John Newman Dead," *New York Times*, July 6, 1899, 7; Smith, "Francis Walton," 278.

12 Berner, *Mrs. Leland Stanford*, 36–37.

13 "San Francisco: They Shame Them into Decency," *The American Israelite*, Feb. 6, 1885, 5; "California Astonished," *Chicago Daily Tribune,* Jan. 2, 1885, 3; "The Stanford Obsequies," *Chronicle*, Dec. 1, 1884, 2; "In Memoriam," *Daily Alta California*, Dec. 1, 1884; Berner, *Mrs. Leland Stanford*, 37–38.

14 Berner, *Mrs. Leland Stanford*, 38–39; "Miss Berner's Story of Poison Last January," *Examiner*, March 22, 1905, Clippings, 25.

15 Jane Stanford to Wales L. Palmer, Oct. 3, 1904, Stanford Papers, S. 1, b. 2, f. 9; A. E. Newman to Jane Stanford, Dec. 23, 1884, Stanford Papers, S. 1, b. 7, f. 35; "J.P. Newman in San Francisco," *New York Times,* Feb. 24, 1885, 3.

16 "J.P. Newman in San Francisco," *New York Times*, Feb. 24, 1885, 3; "Rev. Dr. Newman," *Chronicle*, March 2, 1885, 2; "Dr. Newman and Spiritualism," *Washington Post*, March 13, 1885, 2.

17 "In Memoriam," *Daily Alta California*, Dec. 1, 1884, 8.

18 Berner, *Mrs. Leland Stanford*, 42–43; "Miss Berner Is Said to Be a Spiritualist Medium," *Call*, March 6, 1905; "Mrs. Stanford Refused to Take Butler Beverly to Islands," *Bulletin*, March 6, 1905, Clippings, 25: 3; "J.P. Newman in San Francisco," *New York Times*, Feb. 24, 1885, 3; "Rev. Dr. Newman," *Chronicle*, March 2, 1885, 2; "Dr. Newman and Spiritualism," *Washington Post*, March 13, 1885, 2.

19 Berner, *Mrs. Leland Stanford*, 42–43; Mrs. J. P. Newman, with an introduction by Bishop

John P. Newman, *Golden Links in the Chain that Connects Mother, Home, and Heaven: The Literature of Many Ages and Many Climes on the Three Dearest Names to Mortal Given* (St. Louis and New York: N.D. Thompson Publishing Company, 1890), ii.

20   "Rev. Dr. Newman," *Chronicle*, March 2, 1885, 2; "Dr. Newman and Spiritualism," *Washington Post*, March 13, 1885, 2; Richard White, *Railroaded: The Transcontinentals and the Making of Modern America* (New York: W. W. Norton, 2011), 254–55.

21   Newman to Jane Stanford, July 12, 1894, A. E. Newman, March 19, 1893, Stanford Papers, S. 1, b. 7, f. 35; Berner, *Mrs. Leland Stanford*, 43–44.

22   E. Daniel Potts, "Stanford, Thomas Welton (1832–1918)," *Australian Dictionary of Biography, National Centre of Biography*, Australian National University.

23   Object # AM–00–359, Object Collection, https://purl.stanford.edu/my452hw6791.

24   For a nineteenth-century account, Chung Ling Soo, *Spirit Slate Writing and Kindred Phenomena* (New York: Munn & Co., 1898).

25   Object # AM–00–359, Object Collection, https://purl.stanford.edu/vp035dn0656.

26   Leland Stanford Jr. 2–12, T.W. Stanford Apports, Arch-AM–00–359; Leland Stanford Jr. 2–10, T.W. Stanford Apports, Arch-AM–00–359, SC1048, both in Objects Collection, b. 2.

27   Leland Stanford Jr. slate, 2–2, T.W. Stanford Apports, Arch-AM–00–359, Objects Collection, b. 2.

28   Leland Stanford Jr. slate, 2–10, T.W. Stanford Apports, Arch-AM–00–359, Leland Stanford Jr. slate, 2–12, T.W. Stanford Apports, Arch-AM–00–359, SC1048, both in Objects Collection, b. 2.

29   Objects Collection, http://www.oac.cdlib.org/findaid/ark:/13030/kt2b69r8fw.

30   Object # AM–00–359, Stanford University, Objects Collection, https://purl.stanford.edu/mw415vq7774.

CHAPTER 9: LELAND STANFORD JUNIOR UNIVERSITY

1   White, *Railroaded*, 255.

2   De Wolk, *American Disruptor*, 39–40, 47–48, 51.

3   De Wolk, *American Disruptor*, 61–62, 68–69.

4   Benjamin Madley, *An American Genocide* (New Haven: Yale University Press, 2016), 2–3, 301–2, 316–17, 350; De Wolk, *American Disruptor*, 14–23, 43, 49, 56, 69.

5   White, *Railroaded*, 99.

6   White, *Railroaded*, 255, 262.

7   White, *Railroaded*, 99.

8   White, *Railroaded*, 262–64.

9   Jordan, *Days of a Man*, 1: 118, 354–55; De Wolk, *American Disruptor*, 179–80; Bertha Berner Interviews, Dec. 12, 1927, Clark Papers, b. 2, Notebook 1927–29; Bertha Berner Interviews, March 13, 1929, Sept. 5, 1929, Clark Papers, b. 2, Notebook 1927–29.

10   George Crothers to Mrs. Fremont Older, Jan. 30, 1947, Crothers Papers, S. 1, b. 11.

11   Cole Manley, "Stanford, Rockefeller, and Carnegie: Redefining the Classical University in the Gilded Age," Honors Thesis, History Department, Stanford University, 2015, gives a nice account of Stanford's educational ambitions. Jordan, *Days of a Man*, 1: 118, 354–55; De Wolk, *American Disruptor*, 179–80.

12   Andrew Carnegie, *The Gospel of Wealth and Other Timely Essays* (Garden City, NY: Doubleday, Doran, and Company, 1933), 16, 21–22, 5, 13.

13   Ambrose Bierce, *The Devil's Dictionary* (Cleveland, OH: World Publishing Company, 1911), 290.

14   David Starr Jordan to Charles Eliot, Nov. 14, 1894, Records of the President, Harvard, file David S. Jordan, 1894, 1900–1901.

15 De Wolk, *American Disruptor*, 179–80.

16 Horace Davis to Charles Eliot, Dec. 10, 1906, Records of the President, Harvard, b. 123, file Stanford University, 1906–1908.

17 The Act of the Legislature, the Enabling Act, and the Grant of Endowment are all in *The Leland Stanford Jr. University, Circular 1*, 5–22; George Crothers, "Outline of the History of the Founding of Leland Stanford Junior University," reprint from the Fortieth Anniversary Number of the *Stanford Illustrated Review*, published by the Stanford Alumni Association, vol. XXXIII, no. 1; "Withdrawal of Illegal, Impossible, and Undesirable Provisions," Crothers Papers, b. 20, f. 20; "Notes Concerning: by GEC, The Stanford Charter," Crothers Papers, b. 20, f. 25; Crothers to Leib, Jan. 20, 1900, Leib Papers, b. 1, f. 4; Memorandum on Titles, Crothers Papers, S. 6, b. 20.

18 The Act of the Legislature, the Enabling Act, and the Grant of Endowment, are both in *The Leland Stanford Jr. University, Circular 1*, 5–22; Crothers, "Outline of the History"; "Withdrawal of Illegal, Impossible, and Undesirable Provisions," Crothers Papers, b. 20, f. 20; "Notes Concerning: by GEC, The Stanford Charter," Crothers Papers, b. 20, f. 25; Crothers to Leib, Jan. 20, 1900, Leib Papers, b. 1, f. 4; Memorandum on Titles, Crothers Papers, S. 6, b. 20; Elliott, *Stanford University*, 25.

CHAPTER 10: DAVID STARR JORDAN

1 Jordan, *Days of a Man*, 1: 219–20; Elliott, *Stanford University*, 159.

2 De Wolk, *American Disruptor*, 179–80; Elliott, *Stanford University*, 19–21, 41.

3 Elliott, *Stanford University*, 41; "Prof. Moss on Trial," *New York Times*, Dec. 21, 1884, 1; Jordan, *Days of a Man*, 1: 289–93, 297, 299–300.

4 Jordan, *Days of a Man*, 1: 145–46; Miller, *Why Fish Don't Exist*, 21–29.

5 Jordan, *Days of a Man*, 1: 149–53, 185–86, 219–20.

6 Miller, *Why Fish Don't Exist*, 48.

7 Miller, *Why Fish Don't Exist*, 52–53; Jordan, *Days of a Man*, 1: 302, 325–27.

8 Jordan, *Days of a Man*, 1: 289–93, 297, 299–300, 353–55.

9 Jordan, *Days of a Man*, 1: 118, 354–55.

10 "The University's Financial Status," Crothers Memoranda, Crothers Papers, S. 3, b. 20, f. 3.

11 Crothers, "Outline of the History"; "Hazards of Volition Escaped," Crothers Papers, S. 3, b. 20, f. 1; "University's Financial Status," Crothers Papers, S. 3, b. 20, f. 3, 5; Real Estate Owned by Estate of Leland Stanford, Deceased. Taxes were $6983; revenue was $6606; Founding of Stanford University, Crothers Papers, S. 3, b. 20, f. 3, 5–6; Elliott, *Stanford University*, 254; Crothers, "Outline of the History"; David Starr Jordan to Charles Eliot, Oct. 30, 1894, Records of the President, Harvard, b. 49, file David S. Jordan, 1894, 1900–1901.

12 Elliott, *Stanford University*, 50–64, 98, 103.

13 University's Financial Status, Crothers Papers, S. 3, b. 20, f. 3, 5–6; White, *Railroaded*, 398–413; David Starr Jordan to Charles Eliot, Oct. 30, 1894, Records of the President, Harvard, b. 49, file David S. Jordan, 1894, 1900–1901; "Stanford's Will," *Call*, July 1, 1893, 8.

14 David C. Frederick, *Rugged Justice: The Ninth Circuit Court of Appeals and the American West, 1891–1941* (Berkeley: University of California Press, 1994), 34–51; Financial Status, Crothers Papers, S. 3, b. 20, f. 3, 5–6; Elliott, *Stanford University*, 258–71; Crothers, "Outline of the History."

15 David Starr Jordan to Charles Eliot, Oct. 30, 1894, Records of the President, Harvard, b. 49, file David S. Jordan, 1894, 1900–1901.

16 Frederick, *Rugged Justice*, 34–51.

17 "Stanford's Will," *Call*, July 1, 1893, 8; Crothers, "Outline of the History"; "Re: Wilson," Crothers Papers, S. 3, b. 20, f. 1; Joseph Choate to Jane Stanford, Feb. 9, 1896, Stanford Papers, S. 1, b. 3, f. 21; "Rough Draft," Crothers Papers, S. 3, b. 20, f. 2, 6.
18 Crothers to Considine, June 21, 1948, 7–8, Crothers Papers, S. 1, b. 11.

CHAPTER 11: INDEPENDENCE

1 Joanne J. Meyerowitz, *Women Adrift: Independent Wage Earners in Chicago, 1880–1930* (Chicago: University of Chicago Press, 1987).
2 Richard White, *The Republic for Which It Stands: The United States During Reconstruction and the Gilded Age, 1865–1896* (New York: Oxford University Press, 2017), 731–35, 738; John D'Emilio and Estelle Freedman, *Intimate Matters: A History of Sexuality in America* (New York: Harper & Row, 1988), 191–94.
3 Charlotte Perkins Gilman, *The Living of Charlotte Perkins Gilman: An Autobiography* (New York: Harper Colophon Books, 1975, original edition, 1972), 171.
4 *San Francisco, California Directories, 1889–91* [database on-line] (San Francisco, CA: Painter and Co. Publishing, 1890).
5 "Mrs. Stanford Refused," *Bulletin*, March 6, 1905, Clippings, 25: 3. "Beverly Not Wanted on Voyage," *Examiner*, March 7, 1905, Clippings, 25: 24; "Interview with Bertha Berner, March 13, 1929," Bertha Berner Interviews, Clark Papers, b. 2, Notebook 1927–29.
6 "Interview with Bertha Berner, March 13, 1929," Bertha Berner Interviews, Clark Papers, b. 2, Notebook 1927–29; "Senator Stanford's Mammoth Stable," *Washington Evening Star*, Aug. 7, 1886, 8.
7 De Wolk, *American Disruptor,* 176–77; Bertha Berner to David Starr Jordan, March 11, 1912, Jordan Papers, S. 1-A, b. 78, f. 727.
8 Jordan, *Days of a Man*, 1: 355; "Miss Berner's Story of Poison Last January," *Examiner*, March 22, 1905, Clippings, 25: 179; Bertha Berner Interviews, Dec. 12, 1927, Clark Papers, b. 2, Notebook 1927–29.
9 "Librarian Nash of Stanford Dead," *Chronicle*, June 8, 1902, 3.
10 Virginia A. McConnell, *Sympathy for the Devil: The Emmanuel Baptist Murders of Old San Francisco* (Lincoln: University of Nebraska Press, 2005).
11 McConnell, *Sympathy for the Devil*, 195, 210, 236–37, 241, 245, 250.
12 McConnell, *Sympathy for the Devil*, 214–15; Boessenecker, *Lawman*, 277–84; McConnell, *Sympathy for the Devil*, 214–15.
13 Berner, *Mrs. Leland Stanford*, 39, 56, 59ff; Berner to Jordan, March 11, 1912, Jordan Papers, S. 1-A, b. 78, f. 727; George Clark Interview with Bertha Berner, Sept. 5, 1929, Clark Papers, b. 2, Notebook 1927–29; *San Francisco, California, City Directory, 1898*, 261; *San Francisco, California City Directory, 1896*, 206.

CHAPTER 12: SURROGATES

1 Elliott, *Stanford University*, 326–37; Samuels, "The Firing of E. A. Ross from Stanford University," 183–90, quote 188; Ross Affair, Notebook, 5; Mrs. Stanford's Address of June 1, 1897, *Stanford University: The Founding Grant with Amendments, Legislation, and Court Decrees*, Stanford University (Published by the University, 1987), 12–13; "Address of Jane Lathrop Stanford Upon Her Inauguration as President of the Board of Trustees of the Leland Stanford Junior University" (July 6, 1903), 6.
2 Jane Stanford to Archbishop Riordan, March 4, 1902, Stanford Papers, S. 1, b. 2, f. 7; Stanford to J.L., n.d., Stanford Papers, S. 1, b. 2, f. 11; Herbert C. Nash, *In Memoriam: Leland Stanford, Jr.* (San Francisco?: no publisher, c. 1884); Jane Stanford to David Starr Jordan, April 28, 1900, Stanford Papers, S. 1, b. 2, f. 24; Stanford to Jordan, Aug. 9, 1900, Stanford Papers, S. 1, b. 2, f. 25.

3 Jordan to Charles Brown, Sept. 1, 1899, Jordan Papers, S. 1-B, b. 52, f. 266; George H. Hepworth, *They Met in Heaven* (New York: E. P. Dutton & Company, 1894), 149, 159; Jordan to Leib, June 5, 1900, Leib Papers, b. 1, f. 7.

4 Laurence R. Veysey, *The Emergence of the American University* (Chicago: University of Chicago Press, 1965), 401; Walter P. Metzger, *Academic Freedom in the Age of the University* (New York: Columbia University Press), 163, fn. 87.

5 Jane Stanford to Jordan, Sept. 5, 1899, Stanford Papers, S. 1, b. 2, f. 23; Jane Stanford to Jordan, May 9, 1900, Stanford Collection, S. 1, b. 2, f. 24.

6 *Address to the Trustees by Jane L. Stanford, Feb. 11, 1897* (Published by the University, Stanford, CA, 1897), 6; "Enabling Act," Section 11, in *The Founding Grant with Amendments, Legislation, and Court Decrees*, Stanford University (Published by the University, 1987), 34; "Stanford Charter," Crothers Papers, S. 3, b. 20, f. 25, 16; Jane Stanford to Andrew D. White, 1902, Stanford Papers, S. 1, b. 2, f. 7.

7 "Enabling Act," Section 11, 34; "Notes Re: GEC, Stanford Charter," Crothers Papers, S. 3, b. 20, f. 25, 15.

8 "Amendments of Mrs. Stanford," Fragmentary Memoranda, Crothers Papers, S. 3, b. 21, f. 12.

9 "Mrs. Stanford's Views," *Pacific Commercial Advertiser*, March 11, 1905, 6.

10 Jane Stanford to Jordan, Oct. 23, 1896, Stanford Papers, S. 1, b. 2, f. 18; Elliott, *Stanford University*, 327.

11 Jane Stanford to Mrs. Jordan, March 25, 1899, Stanford Papers, S. 1, b. 13, f. 1.

12 Gabriel Rosenberg, "No Scrubs: Livestock Breeding, Race, and State Power in the Early Twentieth-Century United States," *Journal of American History* 107, no. 2 (Sept. 2020): 362–87.

13 David Starr Jordan, *The Human Harvest: A Study of the Decay of Races Through the Survival of the Unfit* (Boston: American Unitarian Association, 1912, copyright 1907), 13–16, 31, 33, 35; Edward McNall Burns, *David Starr Jordan, Prophet of Freedom* (Stanford: Stanford University Press, 1953), 61.

14 Jordan, *The Human Harvest*, 40–41; Frank Covey, "Palo Alto Stock Farm," appendix to Berner, *Mrs. Leland Stanford*, 225, 29.

15 David Starr Jordan, "The Moral of the Sympsychograph," *Popular Science Monthly*, Sept. 1896, 597–602; Jordan, *Days of a Man*, 599–600.

16 Jane Stanford, Transcript, Aix-les Bains, Sept. 4, 1892, Stanford Papers, S. 1, Transcripts, b. 13, 4.

17 George Crothers to Mrs. Fremont Older, Jan. 30, 1947, Crothers Papers, S. 1, b. 11; Crothers to O.L. Elliott, Sept. 16, 1931, Elliott Papers, b. 3, f. 5.

18 Memorandum, n.d., Crothers Papers, S. 3, b. 20, f. 2; Crothers, "Outline of the History," 19; "Memoranda dictated immediately before the visit of Mrs. G.O. Wilson editor of the *Stanford Illustrated Review*, June 17, 1930," Crothers Papers, S. 3, b. 20, f. 9, 3–4.

19 Crothers, "Outline of the History," 19; "Memoranda dictated immediately before the visit of Mrs. G.O. Wilson editor of the *Stanford Illustrated Review*, June 17, 1930," Crothers Papers, S. 3, b. 20, f. 9, 3–4.

20 Crothers, "Outline of the History," 4; "Re: Wilson," Crothers Papers, S. 3, b. 20.

21 "Notes Concerning the Stanford Charter," Crothers Papers, b. 20, f. 25; George Crothers to S. F. Leib, Dec. 20, 1900, Leib Papers, b. 1, f. 4; George Crothers to David Jordan, Jan. 20, 1900, Leib Papers, b. 1, f. 4.

22 George Crothers to Mrs. Fremont Older, Jan. 30, 1947, Crothers Papers, S. 1, b. 11; Crothers to O.L. Elliott, March 15, 1935, Elliott Papers, b. 3, f. 4; "Withdrawal of Illegal, Impossible, and Undesirable Provisions," Crothers Papers, S. 3, b. 20, f. 20; "Notes

Concerning: by GEC, The Stanford Charter," Crothers Papers, S. 3, b. 20, f. 25; Crothers to Leib, Jan. 20, 1900, Leib Papers, b. 1, f. 4.

23 Crothers, "Outline of the History."

24 Crothers, "Outline of the History."

25 Crothers, "Outline of the History"; "The California Constitutional Amendment Campaigns: A Fragmentary Memorandum," Crothers Papers, S. 3, b. 20, f. 9, 1–7.

CHAPTER 13: FOLLOW THE MONEY

1 Oscar Tully Shuck, ed., *History of the Bar and Bench of California* (n.p. Commercial Printing House, 1901), 337–45.

2 Elliott, *Stanford University*, 282; Crothers, "Outline of the History," 18.

3 "Re: Wilson," Crothers Papers, S. 6, b. 20, p. 5; University's Financial Status, Crothers Papers, S. 6, b. 20, f. 3, pp. 5–6.

4 Elliott, *Stanford University*, 271; "Legacies Must Be Paid in Cash," *Chronicle*, Sept. 25, 1897, 9; Jane Stanford to Russell Wilson, June 1, 1897, Jane Stanford to David Starr Jordan, Aug. 30, 1897, both in Stanford Papers, S. 1, b. 13, f. 1; Fragmentary Memoranda, Crothers Papers, S. 7, b. 21, f. 14.

5 Crothers, "Outline of the History"; "Rough Draft," Crothers Papers, S. 6, b. 20, f. 2, p. 6; Crothers to Leib, July 29, 1902, Leib Papers, b. 1, f. 4.

6 Elliott, *Stanford University*, 271; *Chronicle*, Sept. 25, 1897, Stanford Papers, S. 7, b. 2, Clippings, f. 1; Jane Stanford to Russell Wilson, June 1, 1897; Jane Stanford to David Starr Jordan, Aug. 30, 1897, both in Stanford Papers, S. 1, b. 13, f. 1; Fragmentary Memoranda, Crothers Papers, b. 21, f. 14.

7 Jane Stanford to David Starr Jordan, Nov. 22, 1897, Stanford Papers, b. 2, f. 20.

8 David Lavender, *The Great Persuader: A Biography of Collis P. Huntington* (Boulder: University of Colorado Press, 1998, original edition, 1969), 374.

9 Elliott, *Stanford University*, 282; Daggett Stuart, *Chapters on the History of the Southern Pacific* (New York: The Ronald Press Company, 1922), 412–24.

10 Crothers, "Outline of the History," 18; "Huntington in Control," *Bulletin*, Nov. 15, 1899, Stanford Papers, S. 7, b. 1, f. 5; "Control of the Espee Passes to the Speyers," *Examiner*, Dec. 5, 1899, 2.

11 Elliott, *Stanford University*, 282; "Founding of Stanford University," Crothers Papers, S. 6, b. 20, f. 3, pp. 7–8; "Memoranda Re: Stanford University, Stanford, Jane, Actions Taken By," Crothers Papers, S. 7, b. 21, f. 45. Crothers's estimates of the loss increased over the years. By the 1940s he put it at $2 million a year in income and $100 million in value to the endowment. Crothers to Considine, July 21, 1948, and "Stanford Crises" (Memo handed to Mr. Considine 6/21/48), Crothers Papers, Memoranda Regarding Stanford University, S. 6, b. 20; "Mrs. Stanford in Mobile," *Call*, March 9, 1900.

12 "Withdrawal of Illegal, Impossible, and Undesirable Provisions," Crothers Papers, S. 6, b. 20, f. 20; Crothers, "Outline of the History"; "Rough Draft," n.d., Crothers Papers, S. 6, b. 20, f. 2, p. 3; "A Few Striking Chronological Events Regarding Stanford," Crothers Papers, S. 6, b. 20, f. 3; "The California Constitutional Amendment Campaigns: A Fragmentary Memorandum," June 30, 1930, Crothers Papers, S. 6, b. 20, f. 9; Crothers Memorandum, typewritten, Crothers Papers, S. 7, b. 21, f. 12.

13 Estimates of the value of the property transferred understandably varies since much of it did not have a clear market value. Elliott, *Stanford University*, 282. Crothers later put it at $25 million. "Memoranda dictated immediately before the visit of Mrs. G.O. Wilson editor of the *Stanford Illustrated Review*, June 17, 1930," Crothers Papers, S. 6, b. 20, f. 9,

pp. 3–4; "A Few Striking Chronological Events Regarding Stanford," Crothers Papers, S. 6, b. 20, f. 3; University's Financial Status, f. 3, p. 8.

14 "Withdrawal of Illegal, Impossible and Undesirable Provisions," Crothers Papers, S. 6, b. 20, f. 20, p. 25; "Re: Wilson," Crothers Papers, S. 6, b. 20, pp. 1–3; "Hazards of Volition Escaped," Crothers Papers, S. 6, b. 20, f. 1, pp. 6–7.

15 "Withdrawal of Illegal, Impossible and Undesirable Provisions," Crothers Papers, S. 6, b. 20, f. 20, p. 25. "Re: Wilson," Crothers Papers, S. 6, b. 20, pp. 1–3; "Hazards of Volition Escaped," Crothers Papers, S. 6, b. 20, f. 1, pp. 6–7.

16 "Re: Wilson," Crothers Papers, S. 6, b. 20, pp. 1–3; "Rough Draft," Crothers Papers, S. 6, b. 20, f. 2, p. 7; "Stanford Crises," Crothers Papers, S. 7, b. 21, Fragmentary Memorandum, f. 14; Jennie Watson (nee Lathrop) to Wilbur, March 18, 1932, Wilbur Papers, b. 86, file Watson; Crothers to Elliott, March 18, 1935, Elliott Papers, b. 3, f. 4, p. 6; "Founding of Stanford University," Crothers Papers, b. 20, f. 3.

17 "Rough Draft," n.d., Crothers Papers, S. 1, b. 20, f. 2, p. 3; "A Few Striking Chronological Events Regarding Stanford," Crothers Papers, S. 6, b. 20, f. 3; "The California Constitutional Amendment Campaigns: A Fragmentary Memorandum," June 30, 1930, "Memoranda Re: Stanford University, Stanford, Jane, Actions Taken By," Crothers Papers, S. 7, b. 21, f. 9; Fragmentary Memorandum, f. 14; "Stanford Crises," Crothers Papers, S. 6, b. 20, p. 3.

18 "Hazards of Volition Escaped," "Withdrawal of Illegal, Impossible and Undesirable Provisions," Crothers Papers, S. 3, b. 20, f. 20, pp. 15–16; "Stanford Charter," Crothers Papers, S. 3, b. 20, f. 25, p. 17; Crothers to Jordan, Dec. 27, 1899, Leib Papers, b. 1, f. 4; "Stanford Charter," Crothers Papers, S. 6, b. 20, f. 25, p. 17; S. F. Leib to Jane Stanford, Dec. 12, 1901, Stanford Papers, S. 1, b. 7, f. 1.

CHAPTER 14: COMINGS AND GOINGS

1 "Expected to Make a Tour of Japan," *Chronicle*, March 12, 1905, 18; Berner, *Mrs. Leland Stanford*, 114–15.

2 Berner, *Mrs. Leland Stanford*, 115–17.

3 Berner, *Mrs. Leland Stanford*, 117.

4 Berner, *Mrs. Leland Stanford*, facing 128. Eighteen years would mean she hired Berner in 1882, two years before Leland Jr.'s death.

5 Julia Grant to Stanford, May 8, 1900, Stanford Papers, S. 1, b. 5, f. 10; Berner, *Mrs. Leland Stanford*, 126.

6 Twelfth Census of the United States, 1900, Schedule One, Population, San Francisco, Assembly District 43, Precinct 13, Sheet Number 9, 36–01, p. 9; Enumeration District: 0281, NARA.

7 "Mrs. Stanford's Secretary," *Seattle Times*, March 8, 1905, Clippings, 25: 44. Lula Rice does not appear to have become Mrs. E. D. Benson. Nor, presuming Mrs. E. D. Benson had been single when she worked for Jane Stanford, can I find any record of her maiden name.

8 Twelfth Census of the United States, Schedule One, Population, San Francisco, Enumeration District 263, Assembly District 43, Sheet Number 7, 36–01, NARA.

9 Berner to Jordan, March 11, 1912, Jordan Papers, S. 1-A, b. 78, f. 727.

10 National Archives and Records Administration (NARA); Washington, DC; Roll #: 555; Volume #: Roll 555 - 07 Jun 1900–11 Jun 1900, Volume #: Roll 555 - 07 Jun 1900–11 Jun 1900; Ancestry.com. U.S. Passport Applications, 1795–1925.

11 "Local Police Are Puzzled," *Chronicle*, March 6, 1905, 2; CPI Inflation Calculator, https://www.in2013dollars.com/us/inflation/1905?amount=10000. For alternate calculations, see Measuring Worth.com.

12 Berner, *Mrs. Leland Stanford*, 213.

13 "Sues Stanford Estate for a Million," *Examiner*, June 5, 1906, 2; "Rich Relatives Let Him Die in Abject Poverty," *Examiner*, June 7, 1906, 3.

14 *Call*, March 25, 1905; "Ah Wing Account," http://quake06.stanford.edu/centennial /gallery/documents/ahwing.html.

15 "Former Servants Tell Police About Rake-off," *Chronicle*, March 9, 1905, 2; "Death of a Brother of Mrs. Stanford," *Call*, April 4, 1899, 4; "Henry C. Lathrop's Estate," *Call*, June 17, 1899, 5; "Lathrop's Will," *Call*, April 15, 1899, 4.

16 "Former Servants Tell Police About Rake-off," *Chronicle*, March 9, 1905, 2; "Death of a Brother of Mrs. Stanford," *Call*, April 4, 1899, 4; "Henry C. Lathrop's Estate," *Call*, June 17, 1899, 5; "Lathrop's Will," *Call*, April 15, 1899, 9; "Police Question Servants Sharply," *Examiner*, March 4, 1905, 4; Charles Lathrop to Jane Stanford, May 1, 1902, Stanford Papers, S. 1, b. 7, f. 6.

17 Jane L. Stanford, Census Place: San Francisco, San Francisco, California; Page: 9; Enumeration District: 0281; United States of America, Bureau of the Census, Twelfth Census of the United States, 1900.

18 Charles Lathrop to Jane Stanford, May 1, 1902, Stanford Papers, S. 1, b. 7, f. 6; "Police Question Servants Sharply," *Examiner*, March 4, 1905, 4; "Miss Berner's Story of Poison Last January," *Examiner*, March 22, 1905, 3.

19 Jane Stanford to Jordan, Jan. 22, 1902, Stanford Papers, S. 1, b. 13, f. 2; Jane Stanford to Mrs. Jordan, Feb. 3, 1902, Stanford Papers, S. 1, b. 2, f. 6; Berner, *Mrs. Leland Stanford*, 149–51. She dates the trip to the fall of 1901, but from Stanford's correspondence, she was mistaken; Charles Lathrop to Jane Stanford, May 8, 1902, Stanford Papers, S. 1, b. 7, f. 6; "Ah Wing Account," http://quake06.stanford.edu/centennial/gallery/documents /ahwing.html.

CHAPTER 15: EDWARD ROSS

1 Edward Alsworth Ross, *Seventy Years of It: An Autobiography* (New York: D. Appleton-Century Company, 1936), 45–55; Elliott, *Stanford University*, 331.

2 Ross, *Seventy Years of It*, 51; Elliott, *Stanford University*, 331–33; Crothers to Elliott, April 2, 1932, Elliott Papers, b. 3, f. 2.

3 Jordan to Ross, Nov. 17, 1900, Ross Papers, r. 3; George Crothers, Re: Ross Removal, 3, Crothers Papers, S. 6, b. 21; Jordan, "Memorandum in re: Dr. Ross," c. 1901, Jordan Papers, S. 1-B, b. 49, f. 217.

4 Edward Ross, Specific Demands of the Farmer, Class Notes 1895, 57, Ross Papers, r. 3.

5 Elliott, *Stanford University*, 331.

6 H.B. Lathrop to Ross, c. Nov. 1900, Ross Papers, r. 3; Crothers to Elliott, April 2, 1932, Elliott Papers, b. 3, f. 2.

7 Edward Ross to Mother, Oct. 17, 1896, Ross Papers, r. 2; Ross, *Seventy Years*, 66; E.A. Ross to Taussig, March 2, 1901, Records of the President, Harvard, b. 62, file Edward A Ross.

8 Charles Kerr to Ross, Sept. 26, 1896; F.A. Adams to Dear Sir, Sept. 26, 1896; William H. Alford to Ross, Nov. 2, 1896; Charles Reed to Ross, July 16, 1896, Ross Papers, r. 2.

9 Edward Ross to Mother, Oct. 17, 1896; William H. Alford to Edward Ross, Oct. 13, 1896; Democratic National Committee to Ross, Oct. 5, 1896; Charles Kerr to Ross, Sept. 26, 1896, Ross Papers, r. 2.

10 David Starr Jordan to E.A. Ross, Oct. 20, 1896, Ross Papers, r. 2; Copy of draft letter, Jordan to Ross, Oct. 1896, Ross Affair Notebook, 27; Elliott, *Stanford University*, 335–39.

11 Edward Ross to Mother, Oct. 17, 1896, Ross Papers, r. 2.

12 Ross Affair Notebook, 4, 5; Jordan, "Memorandum in re: Dr. Ross," c. 1901, Jordan

Papers, S. I-B, b. 49, f. 217; Elliott, *Stanford University*, 334; Jordan to Stanford, May 21, 1900, Ross Affair Notebook, 29–30; E.A. Ross to Taussig, March 2, 1901, Records of the President, Harvard, b. 62, file Edward A. Ross.

13 Jane Stanford to Jordan, Jan. 18, 1897, Stanford Papers, b. 2, f. 19; "Memorandum in re: Dr. Ross," c. 1901, Jordan Papers, S. 1-B, b. 49, f. 217.

14 Ross Affair Notebook, 5; *Stanford University: The Founding Grant with Amendments, Legislation, and Court Decrees*, Stanford University (Published by the University, 1987); "Memo of Conference Between Geo. C. Crothers, and O.L. Elliott," Sept. 25, 1931, Crothers Papers, S. 7, b. 21, f. 11; "Grant of Endowment," Leland Stanford Jr. University Circular 1 (Palo Alto, Stanford University, 1891, reprint), section IV, no. 14, p. 14.

15 Stanford Publications, Trustees, Series, Issues 12–18, Stanford University, 1904, 39; Appendix G, The Ross Case, Jordan Papers, S. 5, b. 7, f. 7, p. 2; "Copy of Questions and Mr. Crothers' Penciled Answers," Feb. 1, 1931, Q 9, Elliott Papers, b. 3, f. 2.

16 Elliott, *Stanford University*, 331–37; Samuels, "The Firing of E. A. Ross from Stanford University," 183–90, quote 188. Ross Affair, Notebook, 5; Mrs. Stanford's Address of June 1, 1897, *Stanford University: The Founding Grant with Amendments, Legislation, and Court Decrees*, Stanford University (Published by the University, 1987), 12–13.

17 Jane Stanford to Jordan, March 23, 1899, Stanford Papers, S. 1, b. 1, f. 32; "Comments on University News," *The Bachelor of Arts* 2 (Feb. 1896): 383–84; *Harpers Weekly*, Jan. 4, 1896, vol. XL, 18.

18 Jane Stanford to Jordan, March 23, 1899, Stanford Papers, S. 1, b. 1, f. 32; "Comments on University News," *The Bachelor of Arts* 2 (Feb. 1896): 383–84. *Harpers Weekly*, Jan. 4, 1896, vol. XL, 18.

19 Jane Stanford to Jordan, March 23, 1899, Stanford Papers, S. 1, b. 1, f. 32.

20 "Control of the Espee Passes to the Speyers," *Examiner*, Dec. 5, 1899, 2; Jordan draft of letter to Jane Stanford, n.d., c. March 1899, Jordan Papers, b. 52, f. 277. There is a second similar draft, undated, in Jordan Papers, S. 1-B, f. 51–277.

21 Jordan draft of letter to Jane Stanford, n.d., c. March 1899, Jordan Papers, S. 1-B, b. 52, f. 277.

22 Jane Stanford to Jordan, March 23, 1899, S. I, b. 1, f. 32.

23 "Re: Ross Dismissal," 3–4, Crothers Papers, S. 6, b. 20.

CHAPTER 16: THE ROSS AFFAIR

1 Ross to Mother, Dec. 15, 1899, Ross Papers, r. 2; Ross, *Seventy Years of It*, 58; Edward Maples to Orrin Elliott, Jan. 20, 1933, Elliott Papers, b. 2, f. 22; Jordan to Ross, May 9, 1900, Ross Papers, r. 2.

2 Ross Affair, Notebook, 6; "Re: Ross Removal," 3–4, Crothers Papers, S. 6, b. 21; Elliott, *Stanford University*, 340–41; "Warning Against Coolie 'Natives' and Japanese," *Call*, May 8, 1900, 12.

3 *Call*, May 8, 1900; Elliott, *Stanford University*, 340–41; Ross to Mother, Sept. 9, 1900, Ross Papers, r. 2; Jordan to Charles W. Eliot, Oct. 1, 1900, Jordan Papers, S. I-B, b. 49, f. 215; Burns, *David Starr Jordan*, 61–66; Gordon H. Chang, "The Chinese and the Stanfords: Nineteenth-Century America's Fraught Relationship with the China Men," in *The Chinese and the Iron Road: Building the Transcontinental Railroad*, eds. Gordon H. Chang and Shelley Fisher Fishkin (Stanford: Stanford University Press, 2019), 346–64, particularly 354–57.

4 *Call*, May 8, 1900; "EXHIBIT 'M': Report of Address of Dr. Ross," Ross Affair Notebook, 28; Elliott, *Stanford University*, 340–41; Jordan to Jane Stanford, May 21, 1900, Ross Affair Notebook, 29–34; "Re: Ross Removal," Crothers Papers, S. 7, b. 21.

5 Jane Stanford to David Starr Jordan, May 17, 1900, Stanford Papers, b. 2, f. 25; Jordan,

"Memorandum in re: Dr. Ross," c. 1901, Jordan Papers, S. 1-B, b. 49, f. 217; Jordan to Charles W. Eliot, Oct. 1, 1900, Jordan Papers, S. I-B, b. 49, f. 215.

6 Jane Stanford to Jordan, May 17, 1900, Stanford Papers, S. 1, b. 2, f. 25; Jordan, "Memorandum in re: Dr. Ross," c. 1901, Jordan Papers, S. 1-B, b. 49, f. 217.

7 Jordan to Jane Stanford, May 21, 1900, Ross Affair Notebook, 29–32; Ross to Stanford, May 21, 1900, Ross Papers, r. 2; Jordan to Leib, June 5, 1900, Leib Papers, b. 1, f. 7.

8 Jordan to Stanford, May 21, 1900, Ross Affair, Notebook, 33; Ross to Stanford, May 21, 1900, Ross Papers, r. 2; Elliott, *Stanford University*, 344–45.

9 Richard Hofstadter and Walter P. Metzger, *The Development of Academic Freedom in the United States* (New York: Columbia University Press, 1955), 326–444.

10 Ross to Stanford, May 19, 1900, Ross Affair Notebook, 35–41. The letter in the Notebook is dated March 19, apparently a typo; Elliott, *Stanford University*, 341; Jordan, "Memorandum in re: Dr. Ross," c. 1901, Jordan Papers, S. I-B, b. 49, f. 217.

11 Jane Stanford to Jordan, May 28, 1900, Ross Affair Notebook, 17; H.B. Lathrop to Ross, c. Nov. 1900, Ross Papers, r. 3.

12 Elliott, *Stanford University*, 346–47; Jordan to Stanford, May 21, 1900, Ross Affair Notebook, 29–34.

13 Elliott, *Stanford University*, 344–45; H.B. Lathrop to Ross, c. Nov. 1900, Feb. 14, 1901, Ross Papers, r. 3; "Hazards of Volition Escaped," 8–9, Crothers Memoranda, Crothers Papers, S. 6, b. 20.

14 Jordan to Ross, June 15, 1900, Ross Papers, r. 2; Elliott, *Stanford University*, 348–49; Jordan to Ross, June 15, 1900, Jordan Papers, S. 1-B, b. 48, f. 212.

15 Jordan to Ross, June 15, 1900, Ross Papers, r. 2; Elliott, *Stanford University*, 348–49.

16 Ross to Jordan, June 5, 1900, Jordan Papers, S. 1-B, b. 48, f. 212; "Report of the Committee of Economists on the Dismissal of Edward A. Ross from Leland Stanford Jr. University," Ross Affair Notebook, 51; Ross to Mother, Sept. 9, 1900, Ross Papers, r. 2.

17 "Report of the Committee of Economists on the Dismissal of Edward A. Ross from Leland Stanford Jr. University," 1–3; Elliott, *Stanford University*, 346–48, 351–53; Jordan to Mrs. Stanford, May 26, 1900, Ross Affair Notebook, 16; Stanford to Jordan, May 28, 1900, Ross Affair Notebook, 17; Harry Pratt Judson to Jordan, May 28, 1900, Ross Papers, r. 2; David Starr Jordan to Charles Kendall Adams, May 29, 1900, Jordan Papers, S. I-B, b. 48, f. 214.

18 David Starr Jordan to Charles Eliot, Oct. 1, 1900, Albion Small to David Starr Jordan, June 28, 1901, Records of the President, Harvard, b. 49, file Jordan; Charles Eliot to Jordan, Oct. 10, 1900, Jordan to Charles W. Eliot, Oct. 1, 1900, Jordan Papers, S. I-B, b. 49, f. 215.

CHAPTER 17: ROSS STRIKES BACK

1 Quoted in Miller, *Why Fish Don't Exist*, 69; "Sudden Death of Barbara Jordan," *Call*, Sept. 14, 1900, 4.

2 Inscribed copy of Ernest Warburton Shurtleff, *The Shadow of the Angel* (Boston: L. Prang & Company, 1895); Jane Stanford to Mrs. Jordan, Dec. 6, 1901, Stanford Papers, S. 1, b. 2, f. 6.

3 David Starr Jordan, "The Education of the Neminist," *Popular Science Monthly* 56 (Dec. 1899): 176–86.

4 Jordan to Ross, Nov. 11, 1900, Ross Papers, r. 3; "Report of the Committee of Economists on the Dismissal of Edward A. Ross from Leland Stanford Jr. University," 1–3; Elliott, *Stanford University*, 351–53; "Sudden Death of Barbara Jordan," *Call*, Sept. 14, 1900.

5 Mayor Phelan to Ross, Nov. 11, 1900, Ross to Mother, Dec. 18, 1900, Ross Papers, r. 3; "Memoranda dictated immediately before visit of Mrs. G.O. Wilson editor of the

Stanford Illustrated Review, June 17, 1930," Crothers Papers, S. 6, b. 20, f. 9; Article IX, California Constitution of 1879, with Amendments, Section 10, amended Nov. 6, 1900.

6 Ross to *San Francisco Chronicle*, Nov. 14, 1900, Ross Affair Notebook, 21–22; "Dr. Edward Ross Forced Out," *Chronicle*, Nov. 14, 1900, 1; Edward Maples to Orrin Elliott, Jan. 20, 1933, Elliott Papers, b. 2, f. 22.

7 Ross to Mother, Dec. 18, 1900, Jan. 15, 1901, Ross Papers, r. 3; E.R. Seligman to Ross, Nov. 25, 1900, Ross Papers, r. 3.

8 Ross Affair Notebook, 9; Elliott, *Stanford University*, 352–53; Jordan to Ross, Nov. 14, 1900, Ross Papers, r. 3; Jordan to Ross, Nov. 17, 1900, Ross Papers, r. 3; Jordan to Ross, Nov. 18, 1900, Ross Papers, r. 3; H.B. Lathrop to Ross, May 2, 1900, Ross Papers, r. 3; Jordan to Ross, Nov.? 1900, Ross Papers, r. 3.

9 Ross to Clark, about Nov. 19 or 20, 1900, Jordan Papers, b. 48, f. 212.

10 George Howard to Ross, Jan. 27, 1901, George Howard to Seligman, Feb. 15, 1901, both in Ross Papers, r. 3; Statement to Class, n.d., 1901, George Howard to Jordan, Nov. 17, 1900, George Howard to Jordan, Jan. 12, 1901, Jordan Papers, b. 48, f. 213.

11 George Howard to Ross, Jan. 27, 1901, George Howard to Seligman, Feb. 15, 1901, Ross Papers, r. 3; Jane Stanford to S.F. Leib, April 10, 1900, Stanford Papers, S. 1, b. 2, f. 2; Frederick Rogers to Judge Crothers, Aug. 31, 1946, S. 1, b. 3; George Howard to Ross, Jan. 27, 1901, George Howard to Seligman, Feb. 15, 1901, Ross Papers, r. 3.

12 Howard to Seligman, Feb. 15, 1901, Ross Papers, r. 3.

13 "The Resignation of Dr. Ross," Proposed Statement, Dec. 3, 1900, not made, Jordan Papers, S. I-B, b. 49, f. 217.

14 Jane Stanford to David Starr Jordan, May 17, 1900, Stanford Papers, S. 1, b. 2, f. 25; Jane Stanford to David Starr Jordan, May 9, 1900, Stanford Papers, S. 1, b. 2, f. 24; Jane Stanford to David Starr Jordan, March 23, 1899, Stanford Papers, S. 1, b. 2, f. 22; Frederick Rand Rogers to Crothers, Aug. 31, 1946, Crothers Papers, S. 1, b. 3, 1–3.

15 David Starr Jordan to Jane Stanford, Nov. 21, 1900, Jordan to Stanford, Dec. 10, 1900, Stanford Papers, S. 1, b. 6, f. 30; Jane Stanford to David Starr Jordan, Dec. 14, 1900, Stanford Papers, S. 1, b. 2, f. 25; Jane Stanford to David Starr Jordan, Jan. 30, 1901, Stanford Papers, S. 1, b. 2, f. 26.

16 David Starr Jordan to George E. Howard, Jan. 9, 1901, Jordan Papers, S. I-B, b. 49, f. 216; Elliott, *Stanford University*, 360–64; George Howard to Jordan, Jan. 12, 1901, Jordan Papers, S. 1-B, b. 48, f. 213.

17 Morton Aldrich to Jordan, Nov. 19, 1900, Jordan Papers, S. I-B, b. 48, f. 214; "Leland Stanford Jr. University," *Science* 13 (Jan. 25, 1901): 143; Lucile Eaves to Ross, Jan. 16, 1901, Ross Papers, r. 3; George Howard to Ross, Feb. 11, 1901, George Howard to Seligman, Feb. 25, 1901, Ross Papers, r. 3.

18 Jane Stanford to Jordan, Jan. 30, 1901, Stanford Papers, S. 1, b. 2, f. 26; Jane Stanford to Jordan, March 25, 1901, Stanford Papers, S. 1, b. 2, f. 26; George Howard to G.A. Clark, June 11, 1901, Ross Affair Notebook, 45.

19 Frank Fetter to Jordan, Feb. 15, 1901, Fetter to Jordan, Feb. 25, 1901, Jordan to Charles W. Eliot, Oct. 1, 1900, Jordan Papers, S. I-B, b. 49, f. 215; Frank Fetter to Ely, Feb. 8, 1901, Fetter to Ross, April 21, 1901, Ross Papers, r. 3; H.B. Lathrop to Ross, March 5, 1901, H.B. Lathrop to Ross, Nov. 1900? (but could be 1901), Ross Papers, r. 3; Horace Davis, "Some Radical Needs at Stanford," *The Stanford Sequoia* 17, no. 7 (March 1906): 196.

20 Clyde Duniway to Jordan, Dec. 16, 1900, Jordan to Clark, Jan. 16, 1901, Jordan Papers, S. I-B, b. 49, f. 216; Julius Goebel to David Starr Jordan, Nov. 18, 1900, Jordan Papers, S. 1-B, b. 49, f. 216.

21   Jordan to Clark, Jan. 16, 1901, Jordan Papers, S. I-B, b. 49, f. 216; Elliott, *Stanford University*, 364.
22   Walter Rose to Jordan, Dec. 20, 1900, Jordan Papers, S. 1-B, b. 49, f. 217; Anthony Suzzalo to Jordan, Feb. 26, 1901, Jordan Papers, b. 49, f. 217; "Hazards of Volition Escaped," Crothers Papers, S. 7, b. 20, f. 1; Crothers, Fragmentary Memoranda, pink sheets, 1–2, Crothers Papers, S. 7, b. 21, f. 12.
23   "Six of Seven of Stanford's Faculty Are for McKinley and Hobart and Prosperity," *Chronicle*, Sept. 27, 1896, Elliott Papers, b. 2, f. 21; Stanford University Alumni Association of San Francisco, "Report of Special Committee Appointed to Investigate Causes Leading to the Forced Resignation of Dr. E.A. Ross," Report Presented and Adopted, Jan. 26, 1901, Ross Papers, r. 3, Subject Files; Anthony Suzallo, Feb. 8, 1901, Jordan Papers, S. 1-B, b. 49, f. 217; Hofstadter and Metzger, *The Development of Academic Freedom*, 401–12.
24   Stanford University Alumni Association of San Francisco, "Report of Special Committee," Ross Papers, r. 30.
25   Stanford Hazards Escaped, Notes by G. E. Crothers, March 23, 1932, 4, Elliott Papers, b. 2, f. 24.
26   C.N. Little to Ross, Feb. 23, 1901, Ross Papers, r. 3; H.B. Lathrop to Ross, Feb. 14, 1901, Ross to Wife, Feb. 6, 1901; Seligman to Ross, March 3, 1901, Ross Papers, r. 3.
27   Jordan to Phillips, Dec. 3, 1900, Jordan Papers, S. I-B, b. 49, f, 21; J.W. Osborne to Ross, Jan. 1–5, 1900, Ross Papers, r. 3; Jordan to Lamont, Managing Editor of *New York World*, Dec. 10, 1900, W.H. Hudson? to Ross, Feb. 5, 1901, Ross Papers, r. 3.
28   Ross to Mother, Dec. 18, 1900, Ross Papers, r. 3; Frank Fetter to Jordan, Jan. 5, 1901, Jordan to Charles W. Eliot, Oct. 1, 1900, David Starr Jordan Papers, S. I-B, b. 49, f. 215; Seligman to Ross, Feb. 19, 1901, Ross Papers, r. 3. There is a notation of April? at the top. This is mistaken.
29   "Report of the Committee of Economists on the Dismissal of Edward A. Ross from Leland Stanford Jr. University," Feb. 20, 1901, copy in Ross Affair Notebook.
30   Jordan to Edwin Seligman, Henry Farnam, and Henry Gardner, Feb. 7, 1901, Jordan Papers, S. 1-B, b. 49, f. 217; C.N. Little to Ross, Feb. 25, 1901, Ross Papers, r. 3.
31   H.B. Lathrop to Ross, March 5, 1901, Ross Papers, r. 3; J.G. Banner, "Freedom of Speech in University Circles," Feb. 23, 1901, Jordan Papers, S. 1-B, b. 48, f. 213; Veysey, *The Emergence of the American University*, 416–17; Branner to Jordan, Feb. 26, 1901, Jordan Papers, S. 1-B, b. 48, f. 278; Branner to Jordan, March 15, 1901, Jordan Papers, b. 48, f. 214.
32   David Starr Jordan to Charles Eliot, June 21, 1901, Records of the President, Harvard, b. 49, file Jordan.

CHAPTER 18: "HE TOLD IT NICE"
1   Hammett, *The Maltese Falcon*, 436.
2   Mayor Phelan to Ross, Nov. 11, 1900, Ross to Mother, Dec. 18, 1900, Ross Papers, r. 3; Philip Ethington, *The Public City: The Political Construction of Urban Life in San Francisco, 1850–1890: Politics, Power, and Urban Development* (Berkeley: University of California Press, 2001), 345–46, 377–98.
3   Fremont Older, *My Own Story* (New York: Macmillan, 1926), 19–21, 36–38.
4   Older, *My Own Story*, 23–31.
5   Boessenecker, *Lawman*, 289–90; "Policemen New and Old," *Chronicle*, Jan. 5, 1900, 5.
6   Richard White, *It's Your Misfortune and None of My Own: A New History of the American West* (Norman: University of Oklahoma Press, 1991), 260; Boessenecker, *Lawman*, 287–89; Richard White, *Railroaded*, 412–13.
7   Boessenecker, *Lawman*, 287–89; Drew Isenberg, *Wyatt Earp* (New York: Hill and Wang, 2013), 184.

8   Boessenecker, *Lawman*, 287–89; White, *Railroaded*, 410–11; Older, *My Own Story*, 40–41, 77–81, 127–36.
9   Boessenecker, *Lawman*, 287–89; Isenberg, *Wyatt Earp*, 181–87.
10 White, *Railroaded*, 410–13.
11 Boessenecker, *Lawman*, 289–90.
12 White, *Railroaded*, 410–13.
13 "Conspiracy to Betray City to Criminals," *Call*, Jan. 13, 1900; "Mayor Phelan Guilty of a Felony," *Call*, Jan. 16, 1900.
14 William B. Secrest, *Dark and Tangled Threads of Crime: San Francisco's Famous Police Detective Isaiah W. Lees* (San Francisco: Quill Driver Books, 2004), 304–5.
15 "Released All Claim on Him," *Call*, June 18, 1891; "A Patrolman's Bride," *Chronicle*, June 9, 1893, 4; "How Congressman Helps His Son-In-Law," *Examiner*, Oct. 18, 1902, 2.

CHAPTER 19: THE DESPOT

1   Frank Fetter to Ross, April 21, 1901, Ross Papers, r. 3; C.N. Little to Ross, Feb. 23, 1901, Ross Papers, r. 3.
2   E.R. Seligman to Ross, Feb. 24, 1901, Ross Papers, r. 3.
3   Charles Eliot to Jordan, June 4, 1901, Jordan Papers, S. 1-B, b. 49, f. 215.
4   Charles Eliot to Jordan, June 4, 1901, Jordan Papers, S. 1-B, b. 49, f. 215.
5   Jordan to Horace Davis, May 16, Jordan Papers, S. 1-B, b. 48, f. 209.
6   H.B. Lathrop to Ross, May 2, 1901, Ross Papers, r. 3; *The Stanford Daily*, April 26, 1901; Horace Davis to Charles Eliot, Sept. 17, 1908, Records of the President, Harvard, b. 123, file Stanford University; Goebel to Jane Stanford, n.d., Goebel to H. Davis, n.d., Goebel Papers, b. 1; Charles Gilbert to Jordan, Jan. 19, 1901, Jordan Papers, b. 28, f. 275; Goebel to H. Davis, n.d., Goebel Papers, b. 3, f. Gilbert.
7   Goebel to Stanford, n.d., Goebel Papers, b. 1.
8   Schmidt to Jane Stanford, Sept. 24, 1901, Goebel Papers, b. 3, f. Gilbert; Goebel draft letter, Goebel Papers, b. 3, f. Gilbert; Editors of Sequoia, "U.S., School Yearbooks, 1880–2012," Yearbook Title: *Quad*, 1904.
9   Schmidt to Stanford, Sept. 24, 1901, Goebel Papers, b. 3, f. Gilbert.
10 Branner Memorandum, June 1, 1901, David Starr Jordan to Mr. Clark, June 14, 1901, Jordan Papers, S. I-B, b. 47–194; Branner to Jordan, June 9, 1901, Jordan Papers, b. 29, f. 286; "Professor's Life Crossed by Girl Graduate," *Examiner*, June 3, 1901, 1; Schmidt to Stanford, Sept. 24, 1901, Goebel Papers, b. 3, f. Gilbert; Branner to Jordan, Jordan Papers, S. 1-AA, b. 29, f. 286.
11 Gilbert to Jordan, June 18, 1901, Jordan Papers, S. 1-AA, b. 29, f. 286; Jordan to Jane Stanford, Nov. 5, 1902, Stanford Papers, S. 1, b. 6, f. 34.
12 Branner to Jordan, June 9, 1901, Jordan Papers, S. 1-AA, b. 29, f. 286; Jordan to Stanford, Dec. 12, 1901, Stanford Papers, S. 1, b. 6, f. 31.
13 David Starr Jordan to Mr. Clark, June 14, 1901, Jordan Papers, S. I-B, b. 47–194; Goebel to Jane Stanford, n.d., Goebel Papers, b. 4, f. Removal; "Board of Trustees Elect John Nourse," *Daily Palo Alto*, Feb. 11, 1920.
14 Schmidt to Stanford, Sept. 24, 1901, Goebel Papers, b. 3, f. Gilbert; Babine to Jordan, July 20, 1901, Jordan Papers, S. 1-B, b. 50–239.
15 Schmidt to Stanford, Sept. 24, 1901, Schmidt to Goebel, June 20, 1905, Goebel Papers, b. 3, f. Gilbert; W.B. Carnochan, "The Case of Julius Goebel, Stanford, 1905," *The American Scholar* 72, no. 3 (Summer 2003): 95–108.
16 Schmidt to Stanford, Sept. 24, 1901, Goebel Papers, b. 3, f. Gilbert.
17 Goebel draft letter, Goebel Papers, b. 3, f. Gilbert.
18 Goebel draft letter, Goebel to Jane Stanford, n.d. (c. 1904), Goebel to Davis, 1905, all

in Goebel Papers, b. 3, f. Gilbert. The university now owns a copy of Krafft-Ebing, but it was apparently bought in the 1920s or 1930s.

19 Jordan to Stanford, Dec. 12, 1901, Stanford Papers, S. 1, b. 6, f. 31; William James to Alice James, Jan. 9, 1906, 2332, James Papers; *Report of the Library*, Stanford University, 1902, 4, Jordan Papers, 1-B, b. 50–237.

20 Pease to Jordan, Sept. 25, 1900, Jordan to Pease, Sept. 25, 1900, H.R. Fairclough to Jordan, Jan. 8, 1902, Jordan Papers, S. I-B, b. 48, f. 208.

21 Jordan to Pease, Feb. 3, 1900, Jordan to Stanford, Jan. 11, 1902, Stanford Papers, S. 1, b. 6, f. 32; Pease to Jordan, April 22, 1901, Pease to Jordan, May 25, 1902, Memo to Mrs. S., March 6, 1902, Jordan to Clark, May 8, 1902, Jordan to Lathrop, n.d. (c. 1902), Jordan Papers, S. I-B, b. 48, f. 208; "The Case of Professor Pease," Jordan Papers, S. I-B, b. 48, f. 209; Elliott, *Stanford University*, 58; Pease file, Correspondence with Pease's comments, n.d. (c. 1902), Jordan Papers, S. I-B, b. 35–344.

22 Martin Singer, "Autocracy in an American University: The Cause of the Stanford Troubles," unpublished manuscript, n.d. (c. July 1905), Goebel Papers, b. 3, f. Removal; Jordan to Hopkins, May 16, 1902, Jordan Papers, S. I-B, b. 48, f. 209; Pease to Jordan, May 23, 1902, Jordan Papers, S. 1-A, b. 32–319; Pease file, Correspondence with Pease's comments, n.d. (c. 1902), Jordan Papers, S. I-B, b. 35–344, 31–32; Timothy Hopkins to Jordan, June 2, 1902, Jordan Papers, S. I-B, b. 33–321.

23 Jordan to Prof. xxx, May 13, 1902, Timothy Hopkins, with enclosure, to Jordan, May 15, 1903, Jordan Papers, S. I-B, b. 48, f. 208; Jordan to Clark, May 8, 1902, Jordan Papers, S. I-B, b. 48, f. 209; E.L. Campbell to Nathan Abbot, May 2, 1902, enclosure with Campbell to Jordan, May 3, 1902, Jordan Papers, S. I-A, b. 32–317.

24 Jane Stanford to Jordan, Jan. 30, 1901, Stanford Papers, S. 1, b. 2, f. 26; Jane Stanford to David Starr Jordan, May 17, 1900, Stanford Papers, S. 1, b. 2, f. 25; "Professor Pease Is Dismissed," *Call*, May 25, 1902, 27; Pease to Jordan, May 23, 1902, Jordan Papers, S. I-B, b. 48, f. 209; Pease file, Correspondence with Pease's comments, n.d. (c. 1902), Jordan Papers, S. I-B, b. 35–344, pp. 31–32.

25 Pease to Stanford, April 17, 1903, Pease to Goebel, Oct. 30, 1903, Goebel Papers, b. 3, f. Removal 1903–04.

26 Pease to Stanford, April 17, 1903, Pease to Goebel, Oct. 30, 1903, Goebel Papers, b. 3, f. Removal 1903–04.

27 Pease to Goebel, Oct. 30, 1903, Goebel Papers, b. 3, f. Removal 1903–04.

28 Charles Lathrop to Jane Stanford, May 16, 1902, Stanford Papers, S. 1, b. 7, f. 6.

29 Horace Davis to S.F. Leib, July 10, 1901, Horace Davis to S.F. Leib, May 15, 1902, S.F. Leib Papers, b. 1, f. 5; Davis to Jordan, May 20, 1902, Jordan Papers, S. 1-B, b. 60, f. 310; Davis to Jordan, June 6, 1902, Jordan Papers, S. 1-B, b. 60, f. 310.

30 Horace Davis to Charles Eliot, Dec. 10, 1906, Records of the President, Harvard, b. 123, file Stanford University, 1906–08.

CHAPTER 20: THE BREACH

1 "Hazards of Volition Escaped," Crothers Papers, S. 6, b. 20, f. 1, pp. 9–10; "Notes RE: GEC, Withdrawal of Invalid and Unworkable Amendments," Crothers Papers, S. 6, b. 20, f. 20 and f. 25, pp. 21–22; Jane Stanford to Leib, April 9, 1903, Leib Papers, b. 2.

2 Charles Lathrop to Jane Stanford, May 16, 1902, Stanford Papers, S. 1, b. 7, f. 6; Charles Lathrop to Jane Stanford, May 8, 1901, Stanford Papers, S. 1, b. 7, f. 6.

3 Jane Stanford to David Starr Jordan, June 12, 1903, Stanford Papers, S. 1, b. 2, f. 28.

4 David Starr Jordan to Jane Stanford, Feb. 1, 1902, Jordan Papers, S. 1-B, b. 52, f. 277.

5 Jane Stanford to David Starr Jordan, May 20, 1903, Stanford Papers, S. 1, b. 2, f. 28.

6 Jane Stanford to B.C. Blodgett, June 16, 1904, Stanford Papers, S.1, b. 2, f. 9.

7 Jane Stanford to Andrew D. White, March 11, 1903, Stanford Papers, S. 1, b. 2, f. 8; "Evolution of Religion," *New York Times*, Jan. 17, 1898, 10; Jane Stanford to Trustees, c. June 1, 1903, Elliott Papers, b. 2, f. 2.

8 R. Heber Newton, Misc. Notes, Newton Papers, b. 4; Lee Irwin, *Reincarnation in America: An Esoteric History* (Washington, DC: Lexington Books, 2017), 197.

9 Jane Stanford to Rev. Dr. Gardner, Sept. 30, 1902, Stanford Papers, b. 2, f. 7; "Dr. Heber Newton a Spiritualist," *Examiner*, Jan. 17, 1905, Clippings, 22: 179; "Evolution of Religion," *New York Times*, Jan. 17, 1898, 10.

10 "Resolution Adopted by the Warders and Vestry of All Souls Church Memorial on the Retirement of Reverend R. Heber Newton, D.D. as Rector," Newton Collection, Notebooks, 1902.

11 Jane Stanford to Trustees, c. June 1, 1903, Heber Newton to Jane Stanford, Feb. 19, 1903, Elliott Papers, b. 2, f. 2; Heber Newton to Jane Stanford, May 25, 1903, Gardner Collection, f. 9; R. Heber Newton to Jordan, Sept. 20, 1902, Jordan Papers, S. 1-B, b. 33–326.

12 R. Heber Newton, *The Mysticism of Music* (New York: G. P. Putnam's Sons, 1915), 17, 19, 39, 71, 76.

13 George Crothers, "The Dismissal of Heber Newton," Crothers Papers, S. 6, b. 20, f. 20; Heber Newton to Jane Stanford, May 25, 1903, Gardner Collection, b. 1, f. 9.

14 "Rough Draft," Crothers Papers, S. 6, b. 20, f. 2, pp. 8–9; Crothers to S.F. Leib, May 6, 1903, Leib Papers, b. 1, f. 4.

15 Heber Newton to Jane Stanford, c. Feb. 1903, Jane Stanford to Heber Newton, March 9, 1903, Elliott Papers, b. 2, f. 2.

16 Jane Stanford to S.F. Leib, March 25, 1903, Elliott Papers, b. 2, f. 2.

17 Jane Stanford to S.F. Leib, March 25, 1903, Elliott Papers, b. 2, f. 2.

18 Jane Stanford to R. Heber Newton, April 19, 1903, Jane Stanford to Charles Lathrop, March 31, 1903, Elliott Papers, b. 2, f. 2.

19 Heber Newton to Jane Stanford, May 25, 1903, Gardner Collection, b. 1, f. 9.

20 Jordan to Crothers, n.d. 1903, Jordan to Crothers, May 16, 1903, Jordan to Whitelaw Reid, n.d., Jordan Papers, S. 1-B, b. 50–242; Jordan to John M. Whiton?, Sept. 12, 1903, Jordan Papers, S. 1-B, b. 50–242; "Religious Life in America" by Dr. J. M. Whiton, clipping *London Daily Mail*, Whitelaw Reid to Jordan, Aug. 28, 1903, Jordan Papers, S. 1-B, b. 50–242.

21 Horace Davis to S.F. Leib, May 6, 1903, May 8, 1903, Leib Papers, b. 1, f. 5; Jane Stanford to Leib, April 9, 1903, Leib Papers, b. 2, f. 4; Jane Stanford to C.G. Lathrop, May 28, 1903, Stanford Papers, S. 1, b. 2, f. 8; S.F. Leib to Jane Stanford, Oct. 21, 1903, Stanford Papers, S. 1, b.7, f. 7.

22 "Hazards of Volition Escaped," Crothers Papers, S. 6, b. 20, f. 1, pp. 10–11; Stanford to Jordan, Dec. 4, 1904, Stanford Papers, b. 13, typescript copies.

CHAPTER 21: THE SURROGATE SON

1 Crothers, "Memoranda: Chapter 17," enclosed in letter from George Crothers to Frederick Rogers, June 24, 1947, Crothers Papers, S. 7, b. 21, f. 45.

2 "Hazards of Volition Escaped," Crothers Papers, S. 6, b. 20, f. 1, pp. 6–7; The California Constitutional Amendment Campaigns: A Fragmentary Memorandum," June 30, 1930, Crothers Papers, S. 6, b. 20, f. 9, pp. 5–6; "Defines Future Policy of Stanford University," *Chronicle*, Oct. 4, 1902, 9; Crothers to Stanford, March 21, 1902, Stanford Papers, S. 1, Incoming Correspondence, b. 3, f. 27.

3 "Hazards of Volition Escaped," Crothers Papers, S. 6, b. 20, f. 1, pp. 3–5, 9, 12–15; "Rough Draft," Crothers Papers, S. 6, b. 20, f. 2, p. 5; "Notes RE: GEC, Stanford Charter," Crothers Papers, S. 6, b. 20, f. 25, pp. 21–23.

4 "Rough Draft," Crothers Papers, S. 6, b. 20, f. 2, p. 5; "Hazards of Volition Escaped,"

Crothers Papers, S. 6, b. 20, f. 1, pp. 9, 12–16; "Resignation of Surviving Founder," Crothers Papers, S. 6, b. 20, f. 20, pp. 21–22.

5 "Hazards of Volition Escaped," Crothers Papers, b. 20, f. 1, pp. 11, 14–16; "Resignation of Surviving Founder," Crothers Papers, S. 6, b. 20, f. 20, pp. 21–22; "Notes RE: GEC, Withdrawal of Invalid and Unworkable Amendments," Crothers Papers, S. 6, b. 20, f. 20 and f. 25, p. 21. Crothers to Elliott, July 20, 1935, Elliott Papers, b. 3, f. 4.

6 "Hazards of Volition Escaped," Crothers Papers, b. 20, f. 1, p. 12; Memorandum, n.d., Crothers Papers, S. 6, b. 20, f. 2; "Resignation of Surviving Founder," Crothers Papers, S. 6, b. 20, f. 20, pp. 21–22; "Notes RE: GEC, Withdrawal of Invalid and Unworkable Amendments," S. 6, b. 20, f. 20 and f. 25.

7 "Hazards of Volition Escaped," Crothers Papers, S. 6, b. 20, f. 1, p. 5; "Notes RE: GEC, Withdrawal of Invalid and Unworkable Amendments," Crothers Papers, S. 6, b. 20, f. 20 and f. 25, pp. 7–8, 10; Crothers to S.F. Leib, Feb. 28, 1902, Leib Papers, b. 1, f. 4; "Pious Fund to Be Submitted for Decision," *Examiner*, Dec. 29, 1901, 7.

8 "Hazards of Volition Escaped," Crothers Papers, S. 6, b. 20, f. 1, pp. 5–7; "A Few Striking Chronological Events Re Stanford," Crothers Papers, S. 6, b. 20, f. 3, p. 4; "Withdrawal of Illegal, Impossible, and Undesirable Provisions," Crothers Papers, S. 6, b. 20, f. 20, pp. 12–14; Crothers to Leib, July 29, 1902, Leib Papers, b. 1, f. 4.

9 "The University's Financial Status," Crothers Papers, S. 6, b. 20, f. 20, p. 9; "Notes RE: GEC, The Stanford Charter," Crothers Papers, S. 6, b. 20, f. 25, pp. 16–17; *Chronicle*, Dec. 10, 1901, 12.

10 Jane Stanford, Will, 1902, Crothers Papers, S. 9, b. 22, f. 16.

11 "Mrs. Stanford's Will," Crothers Papers, S. 6, b. 20, f. 20, p. 27; "Notes RE: GEC, Withdrawal of Invalid and Unworkable Amendments," Crothers Papers, S. 6, b. 20, f. 20 and f. 25.

12 "Hazards of Volition Escaped," Crothers Papers, S. 6, b. 20, f. 1, p. 7; Jennie Lathrop to Wilbur, Dec. 1930, Jennie Watson to Wilbur, Jan. 1932, Jennie Lathrop to Wilbur, Jan. 28, 1932, March 18, 1932, April 22, 1932, all in Wilbur Papers, b. 86, f. Watson.

13 Crothers to S.F. Leib, July 29, 1902, Leib Papers, SC 116, b. 1, f. 4.

14 "Re: Wilson," Crothers Papers, S. 6, b. 20, f. 1; "Notes Concerning Stanford Charter by GEC," S. 6, b. 20, f. 25, p. 21; "Mrs. Stanford's Will," Crothers Papers, S. 6, b. 20, f. 25, p. 28; "Rough Draft," Crothers Papers, S. 6, b. 20, f. 2, p. 5; *Daily Palo Alto*, March 6, 1905; "Notes RE: GEC, Withdrawal of Invalid and Unworkable Amendments," Crothers Papers, S. 6, b. 20, f. 20 and f. 25, pp. 26–28.

15 "The University's Financial Status," Crothers Papers, S. 6, b. 20, f. 3, p. 8; "Hazards of Volition Escaped," Crothers Papers, S. 6, b. 20, f. 1, pp. 9–10.

16 "Resignation of Surviving Founder," Crothers Papers, S. 6, b. 20, f. 20, p. 22; "The Founding of Stanford University," Crothers Papers, S. 6, b. 20, f. 20, pp. 2–5; "Notes RE: GEC, Withdrawal of Invalid and Unworkable Amendments," Crothers Papers, S. 6, b. 20, f. 20 and f. 25, pp. 22–23.

17 "Women Students," Crothers Papers, S. 6, b. 20, f. 20, p. 24; "Notes RE: GEC, Withdrawal of Invalid and Unworkable Amendments," Crothers Papers, S. 6, b. 20, f. 20 and f. 25, pp. 24–25; Copy of "Stanford Crises," Crothers Papers, b. 21; "The Educational Ideals of Jane Lathrop Stanford" (Reprint from *San Jose Mercury*, 1933), 17; Crothers to S.F. Leib, May 30, 1903, Leib Papers, b. 1, f. 4.

18 "Women Students," Crothers Papers, S. 6, b. 20, f. 20, p. 24; "Notes RE: GEC, Withdrawal of Invalid and Unworkable Amendments," Crothers Papers, S. 6, b. 20, f. 20 and f. 25, pp. 24–25; Copy of "Stanford Crises," Crothers Papers, b. 21; "The Educational Ideals of Jane Lathrop Stanford" (Reprint from *San Jose Mercury*, 1933), 17; Crothers to S.F. Leib, May 30, 1903, Leib Papers, b. 1, f. 4.

19 Jane Stanford to Mrs. Mills, July 14, 1904, Stanford Papers, S. 1, b. 2, f. 9.
20 "The Founding of Stanford University," Crothers Papers, S. 6, b. 20, f. 20, pp. 2–4; Crothers to S.F. Leib, Dec. 26, 1902, Leib Papers, b. 1, f. 4.
21 Superior Court, County of Santa Clara, State of California. In the matter of the petition . . . for the ascertainment of the existence and terms of, and for the determination of the validity and legal effect of grants or other instruments, creating, changing or affecting trusts and estates for the founding, endowment and maintenance of the Leland Stanford Junior University. Petition . . . 1903, copy in Hathitrust; "The University's Financial Status," Crothers Papers, S. 6, b. 20, f. 3, p. 8; "The Founding of Stanford University," Crothers Papers, S. 6, b. 20, f. 20, pp. 2–7; "Special Proceeding"; "Fragmentary Memoranda," Crothers Papers, S. 7, b. 21, f. 13.
22 "Original Sources," Crothers Papers, S. 6, b. 20, f. 20, pp. 29–30.

CHAPTER 22: MY MAN BEVERLY

1 "Passengers Arriving," *Hawaiian Star*, June 21, 1902, 2; Jane Stanford to Mary Mille, Sept. 10, 1904, Stanford Papers, S. 1, b. 2, f. 9. The newspapers sometimes referred to him as Alfred Beverly. "Mystery Still Shrouds Motive of Poisoning," *Chronicle*, Feb. 21, 1905; Albert Beverly, Township 3, Lassen, California; Page: 9; Enumeration District: 0050, Register 5, Precinct 40, 1900 United States Federal Census.
2 Laura Beatty, *Lillie Langtry: Manners, Masks, and Morals* (London: Chatto & Windus, 1999), 127–258, quote 252; Helen Rocca Goss, "Lillie Langtry and Her California Ranch," *Historical Society of Southern California Quarterly* 37, no. 2 (June 1955): 161–76.
3 Township 3, Lassen, California; Page: 9; Enumeration District: 0050, 1900 United States Federal Census [database online]; "Henry Butters, Famous Man of Millions Dies," *Call*, Oct. 27, 1908; Register 5, Precinct 40, Great Register Years: *1896 District 40, Voter Registers, 1866–1898* [database online]. Original data: Great Registers, 1866–1898. Microfilm, 185 rolls. California State Library, Sacramento, California.
4 Bertha Berner, *Mrs. Leland Stanford*, 153–55; "Rough Draft," Crothers Papers, S. 6, b. 20, f. 2, p. 8. "Suspected Girl Declares," *Bulletin*, Feb. 19, 1902, Clippings, 23; "Mystery Still Shrouds Motive of Poisoning," *Chronicle*, Feb. 21, 1905; Berner, *Mrs. Leland Stanford*, 201.
5 "Mrs. Stanford Coming Home," *Examiner*, Feb. 17, 1902, 3; Jane Stanford to Leib, Jan. 22, 1902, Leib Papers, b. 2, f. 4.
6 "Will Get to the Bottom of the Mystery," *Chronicle*, March 9, 1903.
7 Berner's mother's will, and the actions of her brother and mother in 1902, contradict the story that Jane Stanford bought the house for Bertha. "Bertha Berner Not Talkative," *Call*, Dec. 31, 1905, 30; "Special Sale . . . 440 Acres in Menlo Park. . . May 11," Maurice Dore and Company, Auctioneers, Book 4, Misc. Records, Decree of Distribution, Jan. 21, 1907, v. 132, 563, Recorders Office, San Mateo County.
8 Berner to Jordan, March 11, 1912, Jordan Papers, S. 1-A, b. 78, f. 727.
9 "Dead Woman Victim of Graft," *Chronicle*, March 9, 1905, 1; "Miss Berner Tells of the Graft," *Chronicle*, March 22, 1905, 2.
10 "Miss Berner Tells of the Graft," *Chronicle*, March 22, 1905, 2; "Beverly Tells Tales of Graft," *Chronicle*, March 8, 1905, 3.
11 "Miss Berner Tells of the Graft," *Chronicle*, March 22, 1905, 2.
12 "Interview with Bertha Berner, March 13, 1929," Bertha Berner Interviews, George T. Clark Papers, b. 2, Notebook 1927–29.
13 Jane Stanford to Mary Miller, Sept. 10, 1904, Stanford Papers, S. 1, b. 2, f. 9.
14 Berner, *Mrs. Leland Stanford*, 165.

CHAPTER 23: THOMAS WELTON STANFORD

1 Elliott, *Stanford University*, 259; "Ventura Sails Today," *Call*, Aug. 6, 1903, 10.

2 Lewis Terman, "Thomas Welton Stanford," Stanford Family Papers, b. 8, f. 2, p. 3.

3 Moore, *In Search of White Crows*, 34, 36–37, 56–60; McGarry, *Ghosts of Futures Past*, 17–28.

4 Thomas W. Stanford to Caldwell, May 25, 1911, Board of Trustees Records, Supplementary Materials, b. 7, f. 4.

5 Berner, *Mrs. Leland Stanford*, 165–67.

6 Berner, *Mrs. Leland Stanford*, 167–68.

7 "Babylonian Stones Come from the Sky," *Santa Cruz Sentinel*, Oct. 27, 1903, 1.

8 "Believed in the Gifted Mystic," *Examiner*, Aug. 6, 1905, Clippings, 26: 101.

9 Jane Stanford to May Hopkins, Jan. 4, 1904, Stanford Papers, S. 1, b. 2, f. 9.

10 Thomas W. Stanford to Jane Stanford, Sept. 14, 1904, Stanford Papers, S. 1, b. 13, f. 2.

11 Thomas W. Stanford to Jane Stanford, Sept. 14, 1904, Stanford Papers, S. 1, b. 13, f. 2.

12 Jane Stanford to Wales L. Palmer, Oct. 3, 1904, Stanford Papers, S. 1, b. 2, f. 9.

13 Address to the Board of Trustees of Leland Stanford Junior University, Crothers Papers, S. 3, b. 13.

14 Elliott, *Stanford University*, 159; John Edgar Coover, *Experiments in Psychical Research at Leland Stanford Junior University*, psychical research monograph, no. 1 (Stanford: Stanford University Press, 1917).

CHAPTER 24: HOMECOMING

1 Jane Stanford to Crothers, Jan. 4, 1904, Stanford Papers, S. 1, b. 2, f. 9; Jane Stanford to Jordan, Jan. 21, 1904, Stanford Papers, S. 1, b. 2, f. 29.

2 Crothers to Stanford, Dec. 20, 1903, Stanford Papers, S. 1, b. 3, f. 27; Crothers to O.L. Elliott, Aug. 22, 1932, Elliott Papers, b. 3, f. 2, p. 5; Crothers to Stanford, Dec. 28, 1903, Stanford Papers, S. 1, b. 3, f. 27.

3 Davis Papers, b. 1, f. 9, 10, 11; Crothers to O.L. Elliott, Aug. 22, 1932, Elliott Papers, b. 3, f. 2; Crothers to Jane Stanford, Dec. 20, 1903, Stanford Papers, S. 1, b. 3, f. 27.

4 Horace Davis to David Starr Jordan, Aug. 6, 1904, Leib Papers, b. 1, f. 5; David Starr Jordan to Horace Davis, Sept. 9, 1903, Nov. 9, 1903, Davis Papers, b. 1, f. 9; David Starr Jordan to Davis, Dec. 15, 1903, Nicholas Murray Butler to Horace Davis, Nov. 9, 1903, C.L. Elliott to Jordan, Dec. 16, 1903, Davis Papers, b. 1, f. 10; Davis to Jordan, Sept. 3, 1903, Jordan Papers, S. 1-B, b. 60, f. 310; Crothers to Stanford, Dec. 28, 1903, Stanford Papers, S. 1, Correspondence, b. 3, f. 27.

5 Jane Stanford to Crothers, Jan. 4, 1904, Stanford Papers, S. 1, b. 2, f. 9.

6 "Hazards of Volition Escaped," Crothers Memoranda, Crothers Papers, S. 6, b. 20, f. 1; Jane Stanford to Davis, July 14, 1904, Stanford Papers, S. 1, b. 2, f. 9; Jane Stanford to Mary Miller, Sept. 10, 1904, Stanford Papers, b. 2, f. 9; Crothers to Elliott, July 22, 1932, Elliott Papers, b. 3, f. 2; "Fragmentary Memorandum," n.d., Crothers Papers, S. 7, b. 21, f. 12.

7 Letter of July 6, 1904, included with Jane L. Stanford, Address to the Board of Trustees of Leland Stanford Junior University, July 23, 1904, https://purl.stanford.edu/dh007wm7556, original in Crothers Papers; Address to the Board of Trustees of Leland Stanford Junior University, July 23, 1904. Also letter from Jane Stanford, July 6, 1904, Elliott Papers, b. 3, f. 2, digital copy https://searchworks.stanford.edu/view/ys952fv7289; Edward Everett Hale, "Memories of a Hundred Years," *The Outlook* 72, no. 5 (Oct. 4, 1902): 306.

8 To the Trustees, July 6, 1904, Stanford Papers, S. 5, b. 1, f. 5; Address to the Board of

Trustees, July 23, 1904. Also letter from Jane Stanford, July 6, 1904, Elliott Papers, b. 3, f. 2.

9 Goebel to Jane Stanford, n.d., Goebel Papers, b. 3; Goebel, "Autocracy at Stanford," 10–11, Goebel to Board of Trustees, July 7, 1905, Goebel Papers, b. 4; "The small or weak departments of the University," n.d., Stanford Papers, S. 5, b. 1, f. 13.

10 "The small or weak departments of the University," n.d., Stanford Papers, S. 5, b. 1, f. 13.

11 "Autocracy at Stanford," 2–3, 8, 11–12, 18–19, Goebel Papers, b. 4; Goebel to H. Davis, n.d., Goebel Papers, b. 1. [Martin Singer?] "The Goebel Case at Stanford," n.d., Goebel Papers, b. 4; Davis to Jordan, Aug. 16, 1904, Leib Papers, b. 1, f. 5; George Crothers to O.L. Elliott, Nov. 17, 1931, Elliott Papers, b. 3, f. 2.

12 Original Address to the Board of Trustees of the Leland Stanford University by Mrs. Jane L. Stanford, dated July 23, 1904, Read to the Board of Trustees, Aug. 1, 1904, Stanford Papers, S. 5, b. 1, f. 5.

13 Jane L. Stanford, Address to the Board of Trustees of Leland Stanford Junior University, July 23, 1904, Stanford Papers, S. 5, b. 1, f. 5. This copy is the one at https://purl.stanford .edu/dh007wm7556; Address to the Board of Trustees of Leland Stanford Junior University, July 23, 1904, read Aug. 1, 1904, Elliott Papers, b. 3, f. 2; George Crothers to Jane Stanford, July 9, 1904, July 18, 1904, Crothers Papers, b. 3, f. 27; Crothers to Elliott, Nov. 17, 1931, Elliott Papers, b. 3, f. 2.

14 Minutes of the Board of Trustees, Aug. 1, 1904; Board of Trustees, S. 1, Subseries 2: Minutes, b. 38, p. 9.

15 Crothers to Leib, July 11, 1904, Leib Papers, b. 1, f. 4; Crothers to Elliott, March 18, 1935, Elliott Papers, b. 3, f. 4, p. 6; Crothers to Elliott, Nov. 17, 1931, Crothers to Elliott, Nov. 30, 1931, 4, Crothers to Robert Swain, July 23, 1932, Crothers to Elliott, July 22, 1932, Elliott Papers, b. 3, f. 2.

CHAPTER 25: DOWNSTAIRS

1 Julie Cain obtained this information on Ah Wing that comes from the Time Books for the Stanford estate. The National Archives at Washington, DC, *Customs Passenger Lists of Vessels Arriving at San Francisco*; NAI Number: *4478116*; *Records of the Immigration and Naturalization Service, 1787–2004*; Record Group Number: *85*, NARA Roll Number: *02*, frame *999*.

2 "Beverly Says His Feelings Were Friendly," *Call*, March 4, 1905, 2; "Former Butler and Maid Left Under a Cloud," *Examiner*, March 4, 1905, Clippings, 23: 140; "New Theory Advanced in Stanford Mystery," *Herald*, March 4, 1905, Clippings, 23: 130; "Police Question Servants Sharply," *Examiner*, March 4, 1905, Clippings, 23: 125; "Miss Richmond Made Appeal to Beverly," *Examiner*, March 4, 1905, Clippings, 23: 123.

3 "Butler Gets Angry and Talks," *Examiner*, March 4, 1905, Clippings, 23: 123; "Beverly Says His Feelings Were Friendly," *Call*, March 4, 1905, 2; "Arrests to Come Soon in the Stanford Case," *Chronicle*, March 4, 1905, 1, 3.

4 "Talk of Poisoned Water," *Bulletin*, Feb. 20, 1905, Clippings, 23: 7; "Mrs. Stanford Refused," *Bulletin*, March 6, 1905, Clippings, 25: 3; "Another Name Given Police," *Call*, March 14, 1905, 5.

5 Jane Stanford to Mary Miller, Sept. 10, 1904, Stanford Papers, S. 1, b. 2, f. 9.

6 Bertha Berner, *Mrs. Leland Stanford*, 195–99.

7 Jane Stanford to Charles William Eliot, Dec. 12, 1904, Records of the President, Harvard, b. 123, file Mrs. Leland Stanford; Jane Stanford to Jordan, Dec. 4, 1904, Stanford Papers, S. 1, b. 13, f. 2.

8 "Mrs. Stanford Is Very Enthusiastic," *Omaha News*, Dec. 15, 1904; https://www.smith sonianmag.com/history/the-high-priestess-of-fraudulent-finance–45/.

9 Berner, *Mrs. Leland Stanford*, 210–11.

10 "Mystery Still Shrouds Motive of Poisoning," *Chronicle*, Feb. 21, 1905, 16; Berner, *Mrs. Leland Stanford*, 201; "Poison Was Dissolved in the Water," *Bulletin*, Feb. 19, 1905; "Strychnine Placed in Mineral Water," *Examiner*, Feb. 19, 1905, 1; "Talk of Poisoned Water," *Chronicle*, Feb. 20, 1905, 9; "Miss Berner Tells of the Graft," *Chronicle*, March 22, 1905, 2.

11 Frederick Rand Rogers to Crothers, Aug. 31, 1946, Crothers Papers, Correspondence, S. 1, b. 11; "Maids Give Accounts That Conflict," *Examiner*, Feb. 20, 1905.

12 "Miss Berner Tells of Graft," *Chronicle*, March 22, 1905, 2.

13 Beverly, "Physicians Barely Save Her Life," *Bulletin*, Feb. 17, 1905, Clippings, 23: 1; "Mystery Still Shrouds Motive of Poisoning," *Chronicle*, Feb. 21, 1905; "Talk of Poisoned Water," *Chronicle*, Feb. 20, 1905, 9; "Poison Was Dissolved in the Water," *Bulletin*, Feb. 19, 1905; "Another Name Given Police," *Call*, March 14, 1905, 5; "Police Story of Stanford Household Entanglements," *Examiner*, March 4, 1905, 1.

CHAPTER 26: THE WALLS CLOSE IN

1 Crothers to Davis, Oct. 8, 1904, two letters, Nov. 8, 1904, Davis Papers, b. 1, f. 12; Minutes of the Board of Trustees, Aug. 31, 1904; Trustees' Records, S. I, Subseries 2: Minutes, b. 38, 19; Minutes of the Board of Trustees, Oct. 26, 1904; Trustees Records, S. I, Subseries 2: Minutes, b. 38, 31; Minutes of the Board of Trustees, Nov. 30, 1904; Trustees Records, S. I, Subseries 2: Minutes, b. 38, 40, 57; Minutes of the Board of Trustees, Dec. 28, 1904; Trustees Records, S. I, Subseries 2: Minutes, b. 38, 60.

2 Crothers to Davis, Nov. 10, 1904, Davis Papers, b. 1, f. 12; "Withdrawal of Illegal, Impossible, and Undesirable Provisions," Crothers Papers, S. 6, b. 20, p. 23; Copy of Questions and Mr. Crothers penciled answers, enclosure with Crothers to Elliott, Feb. 1, 1932, Elliott Papers, b. 3, f. 2; "Hazards of Volition Escaped," Crothers Papers, S. 6, b. 20, f. 1, p. 10.

3 Davis to Joseph D. Grant, Dec. 18, 1905, Elliott Papers, b. 3, f. 2; Davis to Jordan, Aug. 16, 1904, Jordan Papers, S. 1-B, b. 60, f. 311; Horace Davis to Jane Stanford, Aug. 16, 1904, Davis to Leib, n.d. c. 1904, Leib Papers, b. 1, f. 5.

4 Horace Davis to Jordan, Sept. 3, 1904, Jordan Papers, 1-B, b. 60, f. 311; David Starr Jordan to Jane Stanford, July 26, July 27, Sept. 11, 1904, Stanford Papers, b. 6, f. 35; Jordan to Davis, Dec. 16, 1903, Davis Papers, b. 1, f. 10; Jordan to Branner, April 26, 1904, Jordan Papers, S. I-AA, b. 11; Severance to Jordan, Aug. 26, 1903, Jordan Papers, S. 1-B, b. 55–292; David Starr Jordan to Jane Stanford, July 27, 1904, Jordan to John Stillman, July 29, 1904, Jordan Papers, S. I-AA, b. 11; "Autocracy at Stanford," Goebel Papers, b. 4.

5 David Starr Jordan to Crothers, July 15, 1904, Jordan Papers, S. I-AA, b. 11; Lulu Miller, *Why Fish Don't Exist*, 52–53.

6 David Starr Jordan to Sherrill Osborne, May 6, 1904, Jordan Papers, S. 1-AA, b. 11; *San Francisco Call* to Jordan, Aug. 5, 1904, Jordan Papers, S. 1-A, b. 41–407.

7 David Starr Jordan to Jane Stanford, May 7, 1904, Jordan Papers, S. I-AA, b. 11; David Starr Jordan to Jane Stanford, July 16, 1904, Jordan Papers, S. I-AA, b. 11; David Starr Jordan to Jane Stanford, July 27, 1904, Jordan Papers, S. I-AA, b. 11.

8 Jane Stanford to Jordan, Aug. 9, 1904, Stanford Papers, S. 1, b. 2, f. 29.

9 David Starr Jordan to Jane Stanford, May 7, 1904, Jordan Papers, S. I-AA, b. 11; David Starr Jordan to Jane Stanford, July 16, 1904, Jordan Papers, S. I-AA, b. 11; David Starr Jordan to Jane Stanford, July 27, 1904, Jordan Papers, S. I-AA, b. 11; Jane Stanford to Jordan, Aug. 9, 1904, Stanford Papers, S. 1, b. 2, f. 29; Jane Stanford to Jordan, Sept. 10, 1904, Stanford Papers, S. 1, b. 13, f. 2.

10 Jordan to Board of Trustees, Nov. 15, 1904, Faculty Records (President's Office), b. 2, f. 1.

11 Jordan to Board of Trustees, Nov. 15, 1904, Faculty Records (President's Office), b. 2, f. 1; Jordan to *New York World*, c. Aug. 1903, Jordan Papers, S. 1-B, b. 55–291.

12 Jordan to Leib, Oct. 25, 1904, Davis Papers, b. 1, f. 12; Jordan to Board of Trustees, Nov. 15, 1904, Faculty Records (President's Office), b. 2, f. 1.

13 Jane Stanford to Susan Mills, July 14, 1904, Stanford Papers, S. 1, b. 2, f. 9.

14 Jennie Watson to Wilbur, Jan. 1932, Wilbur Papers, b. 86, f. Watson; Crothers to Davis, Nov. 10, 1904, Nov. 22, 1904, Davis Papers, b. 1, f. 12.

15 Jordan to Leib, Oct. 25, 1904, Davis Papers, b. 1, f. 12.

16 Jane Stanford to Jordan, n.d. c. Dec. 1904, Stanford Papers, S. 1, b. 13, f. 2.

17 Crothers to Davis, Nov. 22, 1904, Davis Papers, b. 1, f. 12.

18 Crothers to Jane Stanford, Oct. 24, 1904, Davis Papers, b. 1; f. 12; "No More 'Queening' on Stanford Campus," *Stockton Mail*, Feb. 22, 1905, Clippings, 24: 38; "The Men and Women of Stanford Are Annoyed," *San Jose Herald*, Feb. 22, 1905, Clippings, 24: 38.

19 Jane Stanford to Jordan, Dec. 4, 1904, Stanford Papers, S. 1, b. 2, f. 30.

20 Crothers to Jordan, Dec. 22, 1904, Elliott Papers, b. 3, f. 6.

21 "Withdrawal of Illegal, Impossible and Undesirable Provisions," Crothers Papers, S. 6, b. 20, f. 20; Crothers to Davis, Oct. 8, 1904, two letters, Nov. 8, 1904, Davis Papers, b. 1, f. 12.

22 "Withdrawal of Illegal, Impossible and Undesirable Provisions," Crothers Papers, S. 6, b. 20, f. 20; Crothers to Davis, Oct. 8, 1904, two letters, Nov. 8, 1904, Davis Papers, b. 1, f. 12; Horace Davis to Joseph Grant, Dec. 18, 1904, Elliott Papers, b. 3, f. 2.

23 Frederick Rand Rogers to Crothers, Aug. 31, 1946, Crothers Papers, Correspondence, S. 1, b. 11, pp. 1–4; "T. Hopkins (designated by Mrs. Stanford as weak sister)," Crothers Papers, S. 6, b. 2, f. 3. Even Horace Davis profiteered in small ways. Crothers considered Lathrop honest, but he, too, would be accused of fraud. *Call*, May 13, 1906.

24 Crothers to O.L. Elliott, Jan. 24, 1932, Elliott Papers, b. 2, f. 24, p. 15; Crothers to O.L. Elliott, Aug. 22, 1932, Elliott Papers, b. 3, f. 2, p. 4; Fragmentary Memoranda, n.d., Crothers Papers, S. 7, b. 21, f. 12.

25 Walter Miller to Jane Stanford, July 18, 1893, Stanford Papers, S. 1, b. 7, f. 32.

26 Elliott Conversation with George Crothers, Jan. 24, 1932, 3–4, Elliott Papers, b. 2, f. 22; Jennie Lathrop to Wilbur, Dec. 1930, Jennie Watson to Wilbur, Jan. 1932, Jennie Watson to Wilbur, Jan. 28, 1932, March 18, 1932, April 22, 1932, all in Wilbur Papers, b. 86, f. Watson. The kindest possible description of these letters is loopy. She claimed to have numerous letters from her aunt and her father, and she quoted from them. These were supposedly donated to Stanford, but they have disappeared. Crothers to Elliott, March 25, 1935, Elliott papers, b. 3, f. 4; Wilbur to Crothers, Dec. 29, 1935, Elliott Papers, b. 3, f. 2; Crothers to O.L. Elliott, Aug. 17, 1932, Elliott Papers, b. 3, f. 2; "Hazards of Volition Escaped," Crothers Papers, S. 6, b. 20, f. 1, pp. 6–7; Talking with George E. Crothers, Jan. 24, 1932, Elliott Papers, b. 2, f. 24.

CHAPTER 27: RESURRECTIONS AND SUICIDES

1 T.L. McFadden to Goebel, Dec. 9, 1904, Goebel to H. Davis, n.d., both in Goebel Papers, b. 3, f. Gilbert.

2 Schmidt to Goebel, June 20, 1905, Goebel Papers, b. 3, f. Gilbert; Goebel to H. Davis, n.d. c. 1905, Goebel Papers, b. 3, f. Gilbert.

3 "Took Her Own Life While Demented," *San Jose News*, Dec. 2, 1904; "She Takes Poison to Get Rest She Craved," *Mercury*, Dec. 5, 1904, Clippings, 12: 113–14; Jane Stanford to Jordan, April 7, 1896, Stanford Papers, S. 2, b. 13, transcripts; Eugene Soule to Jordan, Dec. 8, 1904, Jordan Papers, S. 1-A, b. 42–426.

4 "Beats the Record of Suicides in a Year," *Examiner*, Aug. 2, 1904, 9.

5 For one of numerous stories, "Kisses His Children as Death Creeps upon Him," *Examiner*, June 24, 9.

CHAPTER 28: MOANA HOTEL

1 "Distinguished People Sail on Liner Korea," *Call*, Feb. 16, 1905, 7; "Korea Sails with Many Men of Prominence," *Examiner*, Feb. 16, 1905, 14.
2 "Chemists Say Berner Potion Had Poison," *American*, March 8, 1905, Clippings, 25: 46.
3 "Beverly Not Wanted on Voyage," *Examiner*, March 7, 1905, Clippings, 25: 24.
4 James Carter, *In the Wake of the Setting Sun* (London: Hurst, 1908), 70–73.
5 Testimony of May Hunt, Coroner's Inquest, 18–19; "Strychnine Was the Cause of Her Death," *Hawaiian Star*, March 1, 1905, Clippings, 24; "No Motive for Murder Appears," *Chronicle*, March 2, 1905, 1; "Enjoyed the Voyage," *Call*, March 5, 1905, 40; "Beverly Not Wanted on Voyage," *Examiner*, March 7, 1905, Clippings, 25: 24; "Bertha Berner Talks of the Voyage," *Call*, March 13, 1905, 2.
6 *Thirteenth Census of the United States Taken in the Year 1910, Statistics for Hawaii* (Washington, DC: Government Printing Office, 1913), 9.
7 Carl Smith to David Starr Jordan, Feb. 13, 1902, March 20, 1902, Jordan Papers, S. 1-A, b. 31–306.
8 Hotel and Travel Notes, *Brooklyn Eagle*, March 3, 1901, 13; Daniel Logan, *Hawaii: Its People, Climate and Resources* (Honolulu: Pioneer Advertising Company, 1903), 66.
9 Testimony of May Hunt, Coroner's Inquest, 18–19; "Enjoyed the Voyage," *Call*, March 5, 1905; "Bertha Berner Talks of the Voyage," *Call*, March 13, 1905, 2; "Mrs. Jane Stanford Visits Honolulu," Stanford Papers, S. 7, b. 2, f. 10.
10 Testimony of Bertha Berner, Testimony of Lallah S. Highton, Coroner's Inquest, 65–67; "Mrs. Jane Stanford Dies," *Pacific Commercial Advertiser*, March 1, 1905, 4; "Sheriff Says Maid Is Not Suspected," *Chronicle*, March 3, 1905, 1; "Light Thrown on Stanford Death," *Chicago Evening Post*, March 2, 1905, Stanford Papers, S. 7, b. 1, f. 10.
11 Jane Stanford to Board of Trustees, Feb. 1, 1905, Davis Papers, b. 1, f. 14. The minutes of the meetings are in Trustees Records, S. I, Subseries 2: Minutes, SC1010, b. 38; Minutes of the Board of Trustees, March 18, 1905, Trustees Records, S. I, Subseries 2: Minutes, b. 38, v. 2, p. 104.

CHAPTER 29: WHEN SHE MET DEATH, SHE CALLED IT BY NAME

1 Testimony of Bertha Berner, Testimony of May Hunt, Coroner's Inquest, 11, 19–20; "Strychnine the Cause of Her Death," *Hawaiian Star*, March 1, 1905, 1, 5, 8; "Two Witnesses Think Poison Killed Mrs. Stanford," *Chronicle*, March 7, 1905, 1.
2 Testimony of May Hunt, Coroner's Inquest, 18–19; "Mrs. Stanford Was Poisoned," *Hawaiian Star*, March 1, 1905, 1; "No Motive for Murder Appears," *Chronicle*, March 2, 1905, 1; "Enjoyed the Voyage," *Call*, March 5, 1905, 40; "Chemical Bought in Palo Alto," *Examiner*, March 3, 1905, 1–2; "Beverly Not Wanted on Voyage," *Examiner*, March 7, 1905, Clippings, 25: 24; "Bertha Berner Talks of the Voyage," *Call*, March 13, 1905, 2; "Mrs. Jane Stanford Visits Honolulu," *Daily Palo Alto*, Stanford Papers, S. 7, b. 2, f. 10.
3 Testimony of Bertha Berner, Testimony of May Hunt, Coroner's Inquest, 11, 19–20.
4 James C. Whorton, "The Phenolphthalein Follies: Purgation and the Pleasure Principle in the Early Twentieth Century," *Pharmacy in History* 35, no. 1 (1993): 9, fn. 16, 22; "Strychnine Was the Cause of Her Death," *Hawaiian Star*, March 1, 1905, 1, 5, 8.
5 Testimony of May Hunt, Coroner's Inquest, March 1, 1905, 20–21; "Strychnine Was the Cause of Her Death," *Hawaiian Star*, March 1, 1905, 1, 5, 8.
6 Testimony of Bertha Berner, Testimony of May Hunt, Coroner's Inquest, 20–23.
7 "Mrs. Stanford Dies in Hawaii's Capital," *Los Angeles Times*, March 2, 1905, 1; "Mrs.

Stanford Was Poisoned," *Hawaiian Star*, March 1, 1905, 1, 5, 8; "Mrs. Stanford Dead: Poison Plot Alleged," *New York Tribune*, March 2, 1905.

8   Testimony of Dr. Francis Howard Humphris, Coroner's Inquest, 54–55; Testimony of Bertha Berner, Coroner's Inquest, 12.

9   Testimony of Bertha Berner, Coroner's Inquest, 11–12.

10 Testimony of Bertha Berner, Coroner's Inquest, 12; "Fear of Poison Drove Her Away," *Examiner*, March 3, 1905, 3.

11 Ernest Warburton Shurtleff, *The Shadow of an Angel* (Boston: L. Prang & Company, 1895); Testimony of Dr. H.V. Murray, March 6, 1905, Coroner's Inquest, 25.

12 Testimony of Dr. Humphris, Coroner's Inquest, 56–57; Testimony of Dr. Francis Root Day, Coroner's Inquest, 30; Testimony of H.V. Murray, Coroner's Inquest, 25; Cutler, *Mysterious Death*, 88–89.

13 Jeffrey K. Lyons, "The Pacific Cable, Hawai'i, and Global Communication," *Hawaiian Journal of History* 39 (2005): 46; "Brother and Lawyer Think Death Natural," *New York American*, March 1, 1905, Clippings, 24.

14 John Spillane to District Attorney, Honolulu, March 1, 1905, Attorney General.

CHAPTER 30: GEORGE CROTHERS COMES HOME

1   Crothers to O.L. Elliott, Feb. 11, 1937, Elliott Papers, b. 3, f. 7.

2   Memorandum, Crothers Papers, S. 6, b. 20, f. 2; "Rough Draft," Crothers Papers, S. 6, b. 20, f. 2, p. 2; Crothers to Elliott, Feb. 7, 1937, Elliott Papers, b. 3, f. 7; Crothers to O.L. Elliott, Feb. 2, 1937, Elliott Papers, b. 3, f. 7; "Withdrawal of Illegal, Impossible, and Undesirable Provisions," Crothers Papers, S. 6, b. 20, f. 20, pp. 23–24; Fragmentary Memoranda, n.d., Crothers Papers, S. 7, b. 21, f. 14.

3   "Outline; Fragmentary Memoranda," Crothers Papers, S. 7, b. 21, f. 14; Crothers to Leib, April 2, 1905, Leib Papers, b. 1, f. 4; "Memoranda dictated immediately before the visit of Mrs. G.O. Wilson editor of the *Stanford Illustrated Review*, June 17, 1930," Crothers Papers, S. 6, b. 20, f. 9, pp. 4–5; "Notes Concerning Stanford Charter by GEC,—Two Threatened Contests," Crothers Papers, S. 6, b. 20, f. 25, pp. 23–24.

4   Crothers to O.L. Elliott, March 18, 1935, Elliott Papers, b. 3, f. 4; "Hazards of Volition Escaped," Crothers Papers, S. 6, b. 20, f. 1, p. 7.

5   Memorandum, Crothers Papers, S. 6, b. 20, f. 2; "Rough Draft," Crothers Papers, S. 6, b. 20, f. 2, p. 2.

6   "Have No Clew to Poisoner," *Chronicle*, March 14, 1905, 9; "George Crothers on the Stanford Mystery," *Chico Record*, March 15, 1905, 4.

CHAPTER 31: THE HIGH SHERIFF

1   "Mrs. Stanford's Death," *Honolulu Advertiser*, March 1, 1905, 4; "Mrs. Stanford Dead: Poison Plot Alleged," *New-York Tribune*, March 2, 1905.

2   Theodore Roosevelt to David Starr Jordan, March 12, 1902, Jordan Papers, S. 1-A, b. 31, p. 309; Carl Smith to David Starr Jordan, Feb. 4, 1902, Jordan Papers, b. 31, f. 305; *Hawaiian Star*, Oct. 22, 1904, 1–2; "Local and General News," *The Independent (Honolulu)*, Nov. 11, 1904, 3; Gov. George Carter to President Roosevelt, June 6, 1905, Carter Papers.

3   William T. Rawlins, *Men of Hawaii, Being a Biographical Reference Library*, published by Honolulu Star-Bulletin, Limited, Territory of Hawaii, 1917, 1: 219.

4   "Police," by High Sheriff William Henry, in Hawaii, *Report of the Governor of the Territory of Hawaii, 1905*, Elihu Root Collection of United States Documents: series A.-F, volume 9.

5   "What Decision of Cause of Death May Involve," *Hawaiian Star*, March 3, 1905, 1, 5;

"Mystery and Secretiveness," *Hawaiian Star*, March 4, 1905, 4; John Spillane to District Attorney, Honolulu, March 1, 1905, Correspondence of the Attorney General, Day Book, Entry, March 7, 1905.

6   Testimony of Dr. Clifford B. Wood, Coroner's Inquest, 35–36; Autopsy report, 38–41.

7   Testimony of Dr. Clifford B. Wood, Coroner's Inquest, 34–36; Autopsy report, 38–41.

8   Drs. Wood & Day, Autopsy on the Body of Mrs. Jane L. Stanford, March 1, 1905, 39–41.

9   Testimony of R.A. Duncan, Coroner's Inquest, Jan. 22, 1905, 42–47.

10 "What Decision of Cause of Death May Involve," *Hawaiian Star*, March 3, 1905, 1, 5.

11 "Mrs. Stanford Was Poisoned," *Hawaiian Star*, March 1, 1905, 1, 5, 8; "Mrs. Stanford's Jewelry," *Hawaiian Star*, March 2, 1905, Clippings, 1, 5; "Mystery and Secretiveness," *Hawaiian Star*, March 4, 1905, 4.

12 "Poison in Vial," *Portland Oregonian*, March 1, 1905; "Mrs. Stanford Is Dead at Honolulu," *Call*, March 2, 1905, Clippings, 23; "High Sheriff of Honolulu Is Reticent," *Call*, March 3, 1905, 1; "Sheriff Says Maid Is Not Suspected," *Chronicle*, March 3, 1905, 1, 3; "Chemical Bought in Palo Alto," *Examiner*, March 3, 1905, 1–2; Cutler, *Mysterious Death*, 27–28; "Was Henry's Cable Really Forged," *Hawaiian Star*, March 30, 1905, 3.

13 "Mrs. Stanford Was Poisoned," *Honolulu Star*, March 1, 1905, 1, 5, 8; "Mrs. Stanford's Jewelry," *Hawaiian Star*, March 2, 1905, 1, 5.

14 "Mrs. Stanford Is Dead," *Call*, March 1, 1905, 1–5; "Mrs. Stanford Dead: Poison Plot Alleged," *New-York Tribune*, March 2, 1905.

15 "Mrs. Stanford's Jewelry," *Hawaiian Star*, March 2, 1905, 1, 5; Edward Greaney, "Hawaii's Big Six: A Cyclical Saga" (Reprinted from *The Encyclopedia of Hawaii*, a 1976 Bicentennial Project), i.

16 "Honolulu Officials Reticent," *Call*, March 6, 1905, 1; "Doctors All Agree on Stanford Case in Deadly Strychnine," *Honolulu Evening Bulletin*, March 7, 1905, 3; "What Decision of Cause of Death May Involve," *Hawaiian Star*, March 3, 1905, 1, 5.

17 "What Decision of Cause of Death May Involve," *Hawaiian Star*, March 3, 1905, 1, 5; "Sheriff Says Maid Is Not Suspected," *Chronicle*, March 3, 1905, 1, 3; "Accuses the Chinese Cook of the Murder of Mrs. Leland Stanford," *Boston American*, March 3, 1905; "Chinese Cook Suspected of Poisoning Mrs. Stanford," *Call*, March 3, 1905, 1–2.

18 Victim Did Not Give Her Any Clue," *Los Angeles Examiner*, March 4, 1905, Clippings, 23: 1–2.

CHAPTER 32: THE CASE IN SAN FRANCISCO

1   "Mrs. Stanford," *New York American*, March 1, 1905, Clippings, 23: 28; "Old Friends Say Mrs. Stanford Had No Hallucinations," *Call*, March 3, 1905, 3.

2   "No Motive for Murder Appears," *Chronicle*, March 2, 1905, 1; "Mrs. Jane L. Stanford Dies in Honolulu from Effects of Strychnine Poisoning," *Examiner*, March 2, 1905, 1; Elliott Papers, b. 1, f. 1; "Former Attempt to Give Potion Stoutly Denied," *Call*, March 2, 1905, 4; "Old Friends Say Mrs. Stanford Had No Hallucinations," *Call*, March 3, 1905, 3.

3   "High Sheriff of Honolulu Is Reticent," *Call*, March 3, 1905, 1; "Detective Morse Says Case Eludes All Hypotheses," *Call*, March 3, 1905, 3; "Servants Are Closely Questioned by Police," *Examiner*, March 3, 1905, Clippings, 23: 88; "President Jordan Scouts the Idea of Her Suicide," *Call*, March 3, 1905, 3.

4   Board of Police Commissioners to George Wittman, Feb. 16, 1905, Police Commissioners.

5   For a typical report, see Superior Court Decision, Superior Court, San Francisco, Department 9, Probate, James V. Coffey, Judge, Estate of Bertha M. Dolbeer, Deceased—No. 18 (New Series), No. 30856 (Old Series), *The Recorder* (San Francisco), Nov. 30, 1906, 4.

6   Walton Bean, *Boss Ruef's San Francisco* (Berkeley: University of California Press, 1968), 12–39.
7   "Many Pickpockets Are Captured by Police," *Chronicle*, Sept. 11, 1900, 14; "'Doc' Lee Taken Into Custody," *Call*, June 3, 1901, 6; "Bunko Men Play the Same Old Game," *Examiner*, Dec. 20, 1902, 10; "Bunko Men Operate in City Unmolested by Police," *Examiner*, Nov. 25, 1905, 7; "The Knave," *Oakland Tribune*, Dec. 2, 1906, 1; "Hired Ruef to Protect Barbary Coast Deadfall," *Examiner*, Nov. 23, 1906, 2; Paul Dexler, "Joe 'Kid' Sullivan: King of the Pickpockets," *Examiner*, Aug. 6, 2007; Bean, *Boss Ruef's San Francisco*, 50, 157.
8   Bean, *Boss Ruef's San Francisco*, 49–55, 169–70, 179–81.
9   "Maids Give Accounts That Conflict," *Examiner*, Feb. 20, 1905, 1; "Police Fail to Find Clews," *Bulletin*, March 11, 1905, Clippings, 25: 57; "Baffled Police Waiting to Hear from Detectives Sent to Honolulu," *Examiner*, March 12, 1905, 3.

CHAPTER 33: THE MEDICINE BOTTLE

1   "Mrs. Stanford Was Poisoned," *Hawaiian Star*, March 1, 1905, 1, 5, 8; "Maid and Secretary Treated as Suspects," *Examiner*, March 3, 1905, 1.
2   "Story of Her Death Told by Secretary," *Examiner*, March 3, 1905, 2.
3   "Sheriff Says Maid Is Not Suspected," *Chronicle*, March 3, 1905, 1, 3; "Police Question Servants," *Examiner*, March 4, 1905, 4.
4   "Special Cable to the Call," *Call*, March 4, 1905, 3; "Mrs. Stanford's Enemy Hidden," *Boston Post*, March 4, 1905, Clippings, 23; "Seeking a Motive: Stanford Case Mystery Police Watching Servants," *New-York Tribune*, March 4, 1905; "Chinese Cook Suspected of Poisoning Mrs. Stanford," *Call*, March 3, 1905, 1, 2; "Police Question Servants Sharply," *Examiner*, March 4, 1905, 4; "Strain of Implied Suspicion Telling on Murdered Woman's Secretary," *Call*, March 4, 1905, 3; "Bertha Berner on Verge of Utter Collapse," *Examiner*, March 6, 1905, 1.
5   "Motive Is a Mystery," *Examiner*, March 3, 1905, 4; "No Motive for Murder Appears," *Chronicle*, March 2, 1905, 1; "Miss Richmond Talks Quite Freely," *Examiner*, March 4, 1905, 5.
6   "Seeking a Motive: Stanford Case Mystery Police Watching Servants," *New-York Tribune*, March 4, 1905, 9.
7   "Chemical Bought in Palo Alto," *Examiner*, March 3, 1905, 1.
8   "Chemical Bought in Palo Alto," *Examiner*, March 3, 1905, 1.
9   "Chemical Bought in Palo Alto," *Examiner*, March 3, 1905, 1, 2.
10 "Maid and Secretary Treated as Suspects," *Examiner*, March 3, 1905, 1; "Miss Berner Contradicts Herself Admits Purchasing Bicarbonate of Soda," *Examiner*, March 4, 1905, 1; "Arrests to Come Soon in the Stanford Case," *Chronicle*, March 4, 1905, 1, 3.
11 "Tells Story of Buying the Soda," "Miss Berner Wanted No Bottle," both in *Examiner*, March 4, 1905, 1; "Arrests to Come Soon in the Stanford Case," *Chronicle*, March 4, 1905, 1, 3.
12 Tells Story of Buying the Soda," "Miss Berner Wanted No Bottle," both in *Examiner*, March 4, 1905, 1; "Arrests to Come Soon in the Stanford Case," *Chronicle*, March 4, 1905, 3.
13 "Secretary Is Tangled Among Contradictions," *Examiner*, March 4, 1905, 2; "Guilfoy Says He Has Poor Memory," *Call*, Sept. 1, 1908, 16.
14 "Secretary Is Tangled Among Contradictions," *Examiner*, March 4, 1905, 2.
15 P.J. Schwab, *San Jose City Directory*, 1902, *San Jose City Directory*, 1903; "Mountain View Incorporates," *Examiner*, Nov. 2, 1902, 12; *The Druggists Circular and Chemical Gazette*, vol. XLVII 1903 (New York, William Allison, Sept. 1903), cx.

16   "Suits Begun by Unhappy Wives," *Chronicle*, July 8, 1904, 13; "Divorce Proceedings,"
      Chronicle, Sept. 29, 1904, 16; P.J. Schwab, *Palo Alto City Directory*, 1904; for cruelty,
      Robert Griswold, "Law, Sex, Cruelty, and Divorce in Victorian America, 1840–1900,"
      American Quarterly 38, no. 5 (Winter 1986): 721–45; for Schwab: Paul J. Schwab: United
      States of America, Bureau of the Census, Twelfth Census of the United States, 1900;
      Census Place: Fremont, Santa Clara, California; Page: 3; Enumeration District: 0048;
      FHL microfilm: 1240110.

CHAPTER 34: SUSPECTS

1   "Awaiting the Inquest," *San Francisco News*, March 3, 1905, Clippings, 23: 90.
2   "Detectives Hasten to Honolulu," *Post*, March 4, 1905, Clippings, 23: 125; "Chemical
     Bought in Palo Alto," *Examiner*, March 3, 1905, 1; "Rough Draft," Crothers Papers, b.
     20, f. 2, 7–8.
3   "Arrests to Come Soon in the Stanford Case," *Chronicle*, March 4, 1905, 1, 3; "Detectives
     Keep Three Under Watch," *Call*, March 4, 1905, 1.
4   "Secretary Is Tangled Among Contradictions," *Examiner*, March 4, 1905, 2.
5   "Police Question Servants Sharply," *Examiner*, March 4, 1905, Clippings, 23: 125.
6   "Arrests to Come Soon in the Stanford Case," *Chronicle*, March 4, 1905, 1, 3; "Suspected
     Poisoner May Soon Be Behind Bars," *Call*, March 3, 1905, 2; "What Do the Berners
     Know of the Case?" *Mercury*, March 4, 1905, Clippings, 24: 59; "Poison Bought in Palo
     Alto," *Examiner*, March 3, 1905, 2.
7   "Miss Berner Devoted to Mrs. Stanford," *Bulletin*, March 5, 1905, Elliott Papers, b. 1,
     f. 1.
8   "Arrests to Come Soon in the Stanford Case," *Chronicle*, March 4, 1905, 1, 3; "Chem-
     ical Bought in Palo Alto," *Examiner*, March 3, 1904, 1–2; "Police Question Servants
     Sharply," *Examiner*, March 4, 1905, 4; "Detectives and Lawyer Confer," *Examiner*,
     March 4, 1905, Clippings, 23: 123.
9   "Miss Richmond Talks Quite Freely," *Examiner*, March 4, 1905, 5; "New Theory
     Advanced in Stanford Mystery," *Herald*, March 4, 1905, Clippings, 23: 130; "Police
     Question Servants Sharply," *Examine*r, March 4, 1905, Clippings, 23: 125.
10   "Miss Richmond Talks Quite Freely," *Examiner*, March 4, 1905, 5; "Police Question Ser-
     vants Sharply," *Examiner*, March 4, 1905, 4; "Miss Richmond Made Appeal to Beverly,"
     Examiner, March 4, 1905, Clippings, 23: 123; "Beverly Says His Feelings Were Friendly,"
     Call, March 4, 1905, 2; "New Theory Advanced in Stanford Mystery," *Herald*, March 4,
     1903, Clippings, 23: 130; "Chemical Bought in Palo Alto," *Examiner*, March 3, 1905,
     1–2; Jane Stanford to Horace Davis, July 14, 1904, Jane Stanford to Mary Miller, Sept.
     10, 1904, Stanford Papers, b. 2, f. 9.
11   "Police Question Servants Sharply," *Examiner*, March 4, 1905, 4; "Servants in the Nob
     Hill Mansion Under Strict Surveillance," *Call*, March 4, 1905, 3.
12   "Butler Gets Angry and Talks," *Examiner*, March 4, 1905, Clippings, 23: 123.
13   "Beverly Says His Feelings Were Friendly," *Call*, March 4, 1905, 2; "Arrests to Come
     Soon in the Stanford Case," *Chronicle*, March 4, 1905, 1, 3.
14   "Search for Motive in Stanford Poison Case," *Examiner*, Feb. 20, 1905, 1; "Poisoner
     Is a Mystery," *Examiner*, March 3, 1905, Clippings, 23: 89; "Former Butler and Maid
     Being Watched," *Oakland Tribune*, March 3, 1905, 1, Clippings, 23: 96; "Police Ques-
     tion Servants Sharply," *Examiner*, March 4, 1905, 4; "Denies that Sister Was Poisoned,"
     Examiner, March 6, 1905, Clippings, 25: 6.
15   Butler Gets Angry and Talks," *Examiner*, March 4, 1905, Clippings, 23: 123; "Beverly
     Says His Feelings Were Friendly," *Call*, March 4, 1905, 2; "Miss Richmond Talks Quite
     Freely," *Examiner*, March 4, 1905, 5.

16 "Chemical Found in Palo Alto," *Examiner*, March 3, 1905, 1; "Butler Gets Angry and Talks," *Examiner*, March 4, 1905, Clippings, 23: 123.

17 "Arrests to Come Soon in the Stanford Case," *Chronicle*, March 4, 1905, 1, 3.

18 "Butler Gets Angry and Talks," *Examiner*, March 4, 1905, Clippings, 23: 123.

19 Arrests to Come Soon in the Stanford Case," *Chronicle*, March 4, 1905, 1, 3; "Police Call on Ex-Butler," *Chronicle*, March 5, 1905, 17; "Suspected Murder in City," "Action of Police," *San Francisco News*, March 6, 1905, Clippings, 25; "Miss Richmond Is Interrogated at Length," *Chronicle*, March 5, 1905, 18.

20 "Mrs. Stanford's Will," *New York American*, March 5, 1905, Clippings, 23; "Brother Hears Good News," *Call*, March 5, 1905, 40; "Bertha Berner on Verge of Utter Collapse," *Examiner*, March 6, 1905, 1.

21 "He Thinks Miss Berner Is Loyal," *Chronicle*, March 5, 1905, 18; "Was Suffering from an Attack of Influenza," *Mercury*, March 8, 1905, Clippings, 25; "Police Say They Possess No Tangible Evidence," *Call*, March 11, 1905, 2.

22 "Miss Berner Talks with Detectives," *Examiner*, March 11, 1905, 3.

23 "Chemical Bought in Palo Alto," *Examiner*, March 3, 1905, 1–2; "Butler Gets Angry and Talks," *Examiner*, March 4, 1905, Clippings, 23: 123; "Arrests to Come Soon in the Stanford Case," *Chronicle*, March 4, 1905, 1, 3; "Police Again 'Sweat' Stanford Employees," *Examiner*, March 8, 1905, 2, 3.

CHAPTER 35: JORDAN AND HOPKINS CROSS THE PACIFIC

1 This and the following paragraphs are from Timothy Hopkins to May Hopkins, March 4, 1905, and March 9, 1905, Hopkins Papers, b. 1, f. 2; "Alameda Arrives with Big Crowd," *Hawaiian Star*, March 10, 1905, 8; "Will Bring Remains Here," *Examiner*, March 4, 1905, 5; "Body Will Arrive on China," *Call*, March 6, 1905; Timothy Hopkins to May Hopkins, March 9, 1905, Hopkins Papers, b. 1, f. 2.

2 "Detectives Hasten to Honolulu for Evidence of Murder," *Post*, March 4, 1905, Clippings, 23; "Detectives to Depart for Honolulu," *Examiner*, March 5, 1905, 40; Legal Matters, Account Estate of Jane Stanford, Crothers Papers, S. 9, b. 22, f. 2.

3 "Police Baffled by Poison Case," *Los Angeles Express*, March 6, 1905, Clippings, 25; "Officials of University and Detectives Leave," *Call*, March 1905; George Clark to Mrs. C.T. Mills, March 4, 1905, Jordan Papers, S. 1-AA, b. 13, p. 500.

4 "Light Thrown on Stanford Death," *Chicago Evening Post*, March 2, 1905, Stanford Papers, S. 7, b. 1, f. 10.

5 "Strange Tale of Private Medium," *Examiner*, March 4, 1905, 6; Rose L. Bushnell, "Two Evenings with the Psychic Forms," *Light*, May 9, 1891, 219; "Experiences of Mrs. Whitney, a Californian Medium," *The Medium and Daybreak*, Oct. 9, 1885, 646.

6 "Light Thrown on Stanford Death," *Chicago Evening Post*, March 2, 1905, Stanford Papers, S. 7, b. 1, f. 10; "Strange Tale of Private Medium," *Examiner*, March 4, 1905, 6; Rose L. Bushnell, "Two Evenings with the Psychic Forms," *Light*, May 9, 1891, 219; "Experiences of Mrs. Whitney, a Californian Medium," *The Medium and Daybreak*, Oct. 9, 1885, 646; "Miss Berner Said to Be Spiritualist Medium," *Call*, March 6, 1905, 2; Charles Deitz, "A Tomb for the Living: An Analysis of Late 19th-Century Newspaper Reporting on the Insane Asylum," PhD dissertation, School of Journalism and Communication, University of Oregon, 2018, 121–22.

7 Timothy Hopkins to May Hopkins, March 9, 1905, Hopkins Papers, b. 1, f. 2; "Officials of University and Detectives Leave," *Call*, March 5, 1905, 40; "Detectives Go to Honolulu," *Oakland Enquirer*, March 4, 1905, Clippings, 23; George Clark to Mrs. C.T. Mills, March 4, 1905, Jordan Papers, S. 1-AA, b. 13, p. 500.

8   "Poison that Killed Mrs. Stanford Was Self-Administered," *Los Angeles Examiner*, March 8, 1905, Clippings, 25; "Would Show Possibility of Suicide," *Call*, March 8, 1905, 1.

9   "Detectives Arrive at Honolulu," *Call*, March 11, 1905, 1.

10   Timothy Hopkins to May Hopkins, March 9, 1905, Hopkins Papers, b. 1, f. 2.

11   Timothy Hopkins to May Hopkins, March 9, 1905, Hopkins Papers, b. 1, f. 2.

12   Timothy Hopkins to May Hopkins, March 9, 1905, Hopkins Papers, b. 1, f. 2.

13   "Jury Shatters Belief It Was Not Murder," *Call*, March 11, 1905, 2.

CHAPTER 36: THE CORONER'S JURY

1   "Doctors Find Death Caused by Strychnine," *Call*, March 7, 1905, 1.

2   "Bertha Berner on the Verge of Utter Collapse," *Examiner*, March 6, 1905, 1; "Sheriff Henry Denies Reports No Poison Has Been Found," "Miss Berner Said to Be Spiritualist Medium," *Call*, March 6, 1905, 2; "Police Call on the Ex-Butler," *Chronicle*, March 6, 1905; "Police Photograph Former Butler and Miss Richmond," March 7, 1905, Clippings, 25: 16.

3   "Miss Berner Testifies," *Hawaiian Star*, March 6, 1905, 1, 8; "Doctors Find Death Caused by Strychnine," *Call*, March 7, 1905, 1–2; "Two Witnesses Think Poison Killed Mrs. Stanford," *Chronicle*, March 7, 1905, 1–2.

4   "Mrs. Stanford Poisoned," *Pacific Commercial Advertiser*, March 7, 1905, 1; "Miss Berner Testifies," *Hawaiian Star*, March 6, 1905, 8.

5   "Miss Berner Testifies," *Hawaiian Star*, March 6, 1905, 8.

6   "Mrs. Stanford Poisoned," *Pacific Commercial Advertiser*, March 7, 1905, 1, 4, 7; "Mrs. Stanford Was Poisoned," *Hawaiian Gazette*, March 7, 1905, 1; Testimony of Bertha Berner, Coroner's Inquest, 10–13.

7   "Doctors Find Death Caused by Strychnine," *Call*, March 7, 1905, 1–2; Testimony of Bertha Berner, Coroner's Inquest, 15–17.

8   "Mrs. Stanford Poisoned," *Pacific Commercial Advertiser*, March 7, 1905, 1, 4, 7; Testimony of Bertha Berner, Coroner's Inquest, 11–13.

9   Cutler, *Mysterious Death*, 36, 41–42; "Strychnine Caused the Death of Mrs. Jane L. Stanford," *Pacific Commercial Advertiser*, March 8, 1905, 7.

10   "Doctors Find Death Caused by Strychnine," *Call*, March 7, 1905, 2; "Would Show Possibility of Suicide," *Call*, March 8, 1905, 1.

11   "Doctors Find Death Caused by Strychnine," *Call*, March 7, 1905, 1–2; Testimony of Bertha Berner, Coroner's Inquest, 13; "Telling Death Story to the Coroner's Jury," *Chronicle*, March 7, 1905, 2.

12   "Chemists Declare that Mrs. Stanford Was Poisoned," *Call*, March 6, 1905; "Found Strychnine in Stomach," *Hawaiian Star*, March 7, 1905, Clippings, 25: 18; Cutler, *Mysterious Death*, 27–28.

13   Thomas Price, "How Strychnine Is Made and Its Properties," *Examiner*, March 3, 1905, 2; Cutler, *Mysterious Death*, 39–43; Cutler, *Mysterious Death*, 39–43.

14   "Found Small Quantity of Poison," *Bulletin*, March 8, 1905, Clippings, 25: 41; Cutler, *Mysterious Death*, 41; "Stanford Chemists Tell Their Story," *Hawaiian Star*, March 8, 1905, Clippings, 25: 53.

15   Hobart Amory Hare et al., *The National Standard Dispensatory: . . . in Accordance with the Eighth Decennial Revision of the United States Pharmacopoeia, as Amended to 1907* (Philadelphia and New York: Lea Brothers & Company, 1907), 1467.

16   Cutler, *Mysterious Death*, 42.

17   "Little Strychnine Found in Body or Bottle," "Death Not Due to Strychnine," *Chronicle*, March 8, 1905, 1; "Only a Trace of Poison in Mrs. Stanford's Entire Body," "Two-Grain Dose Fatal," both in *Examiner*, March 8, 1902, 2; "Poison in Stomach, Soda, and Cap-

sules," "Chemists Tell of Unmistakable Strychnine Tests, But Fear to Express Opinion," *Call*, March 8, 1908, 1.

18 "Strychnine Caused the Death of Mrs. Jane L. Stanford," *Pacific Commercial Advertiser*, March 8, 1905, 1–3.

19 Entry, March 7, 1905, Day Book, "Work Done on Stanford Mystery," *Hawaiian Star*, March 8, 1905, Clippings, 25: 53; *Pacific Commercial Advertiser*, March 8, 1905, Clippings, 25: 51.

20 "Sheriff Strangely Delays Close of Inquest," *Chronicle*, March 9, 1905, 1; "Still Wait for Results of Inquest," *Call*, March 9, 1902, 2.

21 "Honolulu Officials Reticent," *Call*, March 6, 1905; "Criticised [*sic*] Her Strange Manner," *Bulletin*, March 7, 1905, Clippings, 25: 25; no newspaper listed, March 8, 1905, Clippings, 25: 50; "Detectives in Hope of Clew," *Call*, March 9, 1905, 2; "Those Unremembered May Contest for Share of the Estate," *Los Angeles Examiner*, March 7, 1905, Clippings, 25; "Insanity May Void Mrs. Stanford's Will," March 6, 1905, *Boston Traveler*, Clippings, 24: 87; W. Norwood East, "Suicide from the Medico-Legal Aspect," *British Medical Journal* 2, no. 3683 (Aug. 8, 1931): 242.

22 "A Mysterious Suspect," *San Francisco News*, March 9, 1905, Clippings, 25: 56.

23 Coroner's Inquest Verdict, 70; Alkaloid, "Natural Cause Theory Absurd," *Post*, March 17, 1905, Clippings, 25: 143.

24 "Stanford Jury Says Murder," *New York Evening World*, March 10, 1905, Clippings, 25; "Jury Finds Mrs. Stanford Was Murdered," *Examiner*, March 10, 1905, Clippings, 25: 72; "Inquest," *Pacific Commercial Advertiser*, March 10, 1905, Clippings, 25: 71.

25 "Mrs. Stanford Was Murdered," *Pacific Commercial Advertiser*, March 10, 1905, Clippings, 25: 71.

26 "Jury Shatters Belief It Was Not Murder," *Call*, March 11, 1905, 2; "Strange Story of Testament," *Post*, March 10, 1905, Clippings, 25; "The Ferry Boat Is Due Today," *Pacific Commercial Advertiser*, March 10, 1905, 9.

CHAPTER 37: PAST IS PROLOGUE

1 Crothers, "Outline of the History."
2 "Has the President Been Successful?" Crothers Papers, S. 6, b. 20, f. 13.

CHAPTER 38: EVERYONE WAS LYING

1 "Baffled Police Waiting to Hear from Detectives Sent to Honolulu," *Examiner*, March 12, 1905, 1.
2 "Dead Woman Victim of Graft," *Chronicle*, March 9, 1905, 1.
3 "Police Photograph Former Butler and Miss Richmond," *Examiner*, March 7, 1905, Clippings, 25: 16; "Police Story of Stanford Household Entanglements," *Examiner*, March 4, 1905, 1.
4 "Former Servants Tell Police About Rake-off," *Chronicle*, March 9, 1905, 2; "Beverly Also Awaits Call," *Call*, March 10, 1905, 2.
5 "Butler's Story Contradicts," *Call*, March 8, 1905, 2; "Beverly Tells Tales of Graft," *Chronicle*, March 8, 1905, 3; "Beverly Also Awaits Call," *Call*, March 10, 1905, 2.
6 Former Servants Tell Police About Rake-off," *Chronicle*, March 9, 1905, 2; "Miss Richmond Talks of Graft," *Los Angeles Herald*, March 9, 1905, Clippings, 25.
7 "Former Servants Tell Police About Rake-off," *Chronicle*, March 9, 1905, 2.
8 "Former Servants Tell Police About Rake-off," *Chronicle*, March 9, 1905, 2; "Miss Berner Tells of Graft," *Chronicle*, March 22, 1905, 2.
9 "Arrests Likely Any Time," *Call*, March 12, 1905, 28; "Crazy Wong Toy Wong Threatened," no newspaper listed, March 12, 1905, Clippings, 25: 96.

10   "Miss Richmond More Confused," *Chronicle*, March 9, 1905, 1.
11   "Lay Stress on Find of Soda," *Chronicle*, March 11, 1905, 1.
12   "Lay Stress on Find of Soda," *Chronicle*, March 11, 1905, 1.
13   "Arrests Likely at Any Time," *Call*, March 12, 1905, 28.
14   "Tablets Contain Poison," *Call*, March 13, 1905, 1.
15   "Arrests Likely Any Time," *Call*, March 12, 1905, 28.

CHAPTER 39: JULES CALLUNDAN AND HARRY REYNOLDS

 1   "High Sheriff Enters His Denial," *Examiner*, March 15, 1905, 2; "New Light on Stanford Case," *Honolulu Sunday Advertiser*, March 12, 1905, 1, 3.
 2   "Jordan and Hopkins," no newspaper listed, March 11, 1905, Clippings, 25; "High Sheriff Enters His Denial," *Examiner*, March 15, 1905, 2; "New Light on Stanford Case," *Honolulu Sunday Advertiser*, March 12, 1905, 1, 3; Jordan, *Days of a Man*, 1: 145–46; Lulu Miller, *Why Fish Don't Exist*, 21–29.
 3   "Secretary to Be Brought to San Francisco," *Chronicle*, March 4, 1905, 3; "Pler Played a Bold Game," *Chronicle*, Sept. 24, 1902, 14; "Selection Causes Criticism of the Chief," *Examiner*, April 24, 1904, 8; "Detective Returns with Photo of Meir," *Examiner*, Jan. 16, 1906, 4; "Asks Investigation of Meir's Death," *Chronicle*, Jan. 10, 1906, 16.
 4   Notes, Legal Matters, Account Estate of Jane Stanford, c. 1905–06, Crothers Papers, S. 9, b. 22, f. 2; "Baffled Police Waiting to Hear from Detectives Sent to Honolulu," *Examiner*, March 12, 1905, 3; "To Take Berner Back," *Hawaiian Star*, March 10, 1905, 10.
 5   "Miss Berner Talks with Detectives," *Examiner*, March 11, 1905, 3; "Jordan and Hopkins," March 11, no newspaper listed, Clippings, 25; "Are Now Convinced She Was Murdered," *Call*, March 13, 1905, 2; Jordan to Edmund Shorey, April 15, 1905, Jordan Papers, S. I-AA, b. 14, p. 7.
 6   "Detectives Take Rapid Tour in Chinatown Alleys," *Honolulu Evening Bulletin*, March 10, 1905, 1.
 7   "Lay Stress on Soda Find," *Chronicle*, March 11, 1905, 1; "Nothing Found by Men Sent to Island," *Chronicle*, March 13, 1904, 4.
 8   "Crazy Wong Toy Wong Threatened," no newspaper listed, March 12, 1905, Clippings, 25: 96; Testimony of May Hunt, Coroner's Inquest, 16.
 9   "High Sheriff Enters His Denial," *Examiner*, March 15, 1905, 2.
10   "Claim Facts Did Not Warrant Verdict," *Chronicle*, March 22, 1905, 1.
11   Cutler, *Mysterious Death*, 17, 68; Jordan to Waterhouse, May 4, 1905, Jordan Papers, S. I-AA, b. 14; "Claim Facts Did Not Warrant Verdict," *Chronicle*, March 22, 1905, 1.
12   Cutler, *Mysterious Death*, 13; "Claim Facts Did Not Warrant Verdict," *Chronicle*, March 22, 1905, 1; Engledue Prideaux, "Case of Strychnine Poisoning Treated Successfully with Bromide of Potassium and Chloral," *The Lancet*, Jan. 8, 1881, 52–53.
13   "Miss Berner Talks with Detectives," *Examiner*, March 11, 1905, 3.
14   "Full Review of Stanford Case Prepared for Relatives," *Call*, March 23, 1905, 2.
15   "Full Review of Stanford Case Prepared for Relatives," *Call*, March 23, 1905, 2.
16   "Miss Berner Tells of Graft," *Chronicle*, March 22, 1905, 2.
17   "Miss Berner Tells of Graft," *Chronicle*, March 22, 1905, 2; "Police Get Beverly Letter," *Call*, March 22, 1905, 2; "Prepare to Drop Stanford Case," *Chronicle*, March 23, 1905, 9.
18   "Rough Draft," Crothers Papers, b. 20, f. 2, p. 8.
19   "Mrs. Stanford Died from Natural Causes," *Examiner*, March 14, 1905, 3.
20   "Stanford Funeral," *Hawaiian Star*, March 15, 1905, 1, 5; "Mrs. Stanford's Funeral to Take Place Today," *Pacific Commercial Advertiser*, March 15, 1905, 1, 4.

21 "Nothing Found by Men Sent to Island," *Chronicle*, March 13, 1904, 4; "Jordan and Hopkins United in a Statement," *Hawaiian Star*, March 15, 1905, 1, 5; Mrs. Stanford's Remains on Way to This City," *Call*, March 16, 1905, 2; "Funeral of Mrs. Stanford," *Pacific Commercial Advertiser*, March 16, 1905, 3; "Gets a Report from Reynolds," "Hold to Poison Theory," both in *Call*, March 15, 1905, 4.

22 "Mrs. Stanford Died from Natural Causes," *Examiner*, March 14, 1905, 3; "Stanford Funeral," *Hawaiian Star*, March 15, 1905, 1, 5; "Mrs. Stanford's Funeral to Take Place Today," *Pacific Commercial Advertiser*, March 15, 1905, 1, 4.

CHAPTER 40: REFRAMING THE INVESTIGATION

1 "Poison Undoubtedly Cause of Death," *Call*, March 7, 1905, 2; "Honolulu Officials Reticent," *Call*, March 6, 1905; "Criticised [*sic*] Her Strange Manner," *Bulletin*, March 7, 1905, Clippings, 25: 25; no newspaper listed, March 8, 1905, Clippings, 25: 50.

2 "Agree on Suspects but Withhold Identity," *Examiner*, March 9, 1905, 1; "Edna Wallace Hopper Begins New Suit for Dunsmuir Millions," *Examiner*, Nov. 10, 1905, 12; "Local Attorney Scored in Hopper Case," *Examiner*, Dec. 15, 1903, 5; "Edna Wallace Hopper on the Stand," *Call*, Jan. 23, 1904, 3; "Mrs. Hemphill's Will Is Missing," *Chronicle*, April 8, 1905, 1–2.

3 "Asked That Analysis Be Thorough," *Chronicle*, March 8, 1905, Clippings, 25: 38.

4 "Wilson Talks But Says Nothing," paper unknown, March 8, 1905, Clippings, 25: 40.

5 "Replies to Criticism," *Call*, March 11, 1905, 1–2.

6 Older, *My Own Story*, vii, 1–4, 6–21, 23–31.

7 Older, *My Own Story*, 31–33; "Attempt to Conceal Stanford Murder by Natural Death Theory," *Bulletin*, March 6, 1905, Clippings, 25: 3.

8 "Strange Story of Testament," *Post*, March 10, 1905, Clippings, 25.

9 "Talk of the Town," *Town Talk*, *Call*, March 11, 1905, Clippings, 25.

10 "Unfounded Suspicions," *Post*, March 6, 1905, Clippings, 25; for Post, Older, *My Own Story*, 36–37.

11 "Police Fail to Find Clews," *Bulletin*, March 11, 1905, Clippings, 25: 57; "Mountford Wilson in Doubt About the Stanfords," *Bulletin*, March 11, 1905, Clippings, 25; "Baffled Police Waiting to Hear from Detectives Sent to Honolulu," *Examiner*, March 12, 1905, Clippings, 25.

12 "Not Convinced That It Was Murder," *Chronicle*, March 11, 1905, 2; "Lay Stress on Find of Soda," *Chronicle*, March 11, 1905, 2.

13 "Slows Up," *San Francisco News*, March 11, 1905, Clippings, 25: 82.

14 "Insist Poison Caused Death," *Hawaiian Star*, March 11, 1905, 5.

15 "He Does Not Believe Mrs. Jane Stanford Was Murdered," *Oakland Tribune*, March 11, 1905, Clippings, 25: 80.

16 "Dargie and His Newspaper Vehicle for Plundering Public in Alameda County," *Call*, Dec. 8, 1907, 25; "Where Calhoun and Dargie Met," *Call*, Oct. 15, 1907, 8.

17 "Why the Evidence of Murder Is Ignored by Detectives," *Bulletin*, March 13, 1905; "Let the Public Honor Her Return," *Bulletin*, March 13, 1905, both in Clippings, 25.

18 "Police to Drop Stanford Case," *San Francisco News*, March 14, 1905, Clippings, 25; "Robbers and Victim Arrested," *Chronicle*, March 13, 1901, 7; "Confidential Clerk Swindles Employees," *Call*, Nov. 16, 1907, 7; "Cleary Seeks Reinstatement," *Call*, Dec. 28, 1901, 4; "Miss Richmond, Mrs. Stanford's Maid, Admits New Point," *San Francisco News*, March 13, 1905, Clippings, 25.

19 Arthur McEwen, "Spiritualism and Stanford University," *Bulletin*, March 14, 1905, Clippings, 25: 10.

CHAPTER 41: JORDAN AND WATERHOUSE

1 Smith to Jordan, March 23, 1905, Jordan Papers, S. I-A, b. 44–444; Smith to Jordan, April 30, 1905, Jordan Papers, S. I-A, b. 44–450. Smith changed his name to Carlsmith in 1911. John W. Siddal, *Men of Hawaii, Being a Biographical Reference Library*, 1: 59; Jordan to Mountford Wilson, April 13, 1905, Jordan Papers, I-AA Letter Books, b. 14, b. 28, pp. 151–52; Cutler, *Mysterious Death*, 91–94; Jordan to Wilbur, May 18, 1921, Stanford Papers, S. 4, b. 1, f. 11; Jordan to Waterhouse, May 4, 1905, Jordan Papers, I-AA, b. 14.

2 William James, *Pragmatism: A New Name for Some Old Ways of Thinking* (New York: Longman's Green, and Company, 1909, first edition 1907), 58.

3 Testimony of Dr. Waterhouse, 1–4; Bertha Berner Testimony, Coroner's Inquest, 12.

4 Testimony of Dr. Waterhouse, 5.

5 Testimony of Dr. Waterhouse, 5.

6 David Starr Jordan to Mountford Wilson, April 13, 1905, Jordan Papers, S. I-AA, b. 14.

7 "Claim Facts Did Not Warrant Verdict," *Chronicle*, March 22, 1905, 1; "Mrs. Stanford Case a Matter of Comment," *Call*, Sept. 7, 1905, Clippings, 26: 161.

8 "Miss Berner's Statement," *Hawaiian Star*, March 1, 1905, 1, 5; "Claim Facts Did Not Warrant Verdict," *Chronicle*, March 22, 1905, 1; Testimony of Bertha Berner, Coroner's Inquest, 12–13.

9 Jordan to Mountford Wilson, April 13, 1905, Jordan Papers, S. I-AA, b. 14.

10 Cutler, *Mysterious Death*, 49–54.

11 Cutler, *Mysterious Death*, 53–54.

12 Testimony of Dr. Waterhouse, 2.

13 Testimony of Bertha Berner, Coroner's Inquest, 11–12.

14 Testimony of Dr. Humphris, 57, Testimony of Dr. Francis Root Day, 30, Testimony of H.V. Murray, 25, all in Coroner's Inquest.

15 "Mrs. Stanford Was Poisoned," *Hawaiian Star*, March 1, 1905, 1, 5, 8; Berner to Waterhouse, March 14, 1905, Jane Stanford Papers, S. 4, b. 1, f. 11; Cutler, *Mysterious Death*, 51–52.

16 Berner to Waterhouse, March 14, 1905, Jane Stanford Papers, S. 4, b. 1, f. 11.

17 Waterhouse to Jordan, March 14, 1905, Berner to Waterhouse, March 14, 1905, Stanford Papers, Death and Estate Papers, S. 4, b. 1, f. 11.

18 Waterhouse to Jordan, April 5, 1905, Jordan Papers, b. 44–446.

19 "Mrs. Stanford Was Poisoned," *Hawaiian Star*, March 1, 1905, 1, 5, 8; Berner to Waterhouse, March 14, 1905, Stanford Papers, Death and Estate Papers, S. 4, b. 1, f. 11; Cutler, *Mysterious Death*, 63–64.

20 Cutler, *Mysterious Death*, 54–55; Carl Smith to Jordan, March 23, 1905, Jordan Papers, S. I-A, b. 44–444; Jordan to Mountford Wilson, April 13, 1905, Jordan Papers, S. I-AA, b. 14; Waterhouse to Jordan, March 14, 1905, Stanford Papers, S. 4, b. 1, f. 11.

21 Peter Olson Geffen, Report of a Visit to the Plantations Belonging to La Zacualpa Rubber Plantation Company, San Francisco, 1905, Jordan Papers, S. I-B, b. 51–269; Cutler, *Mysterious Death*, 68, 92–94; Carl Smith to Jordan, March 31, 1905, Jordan Papers, S. I-A, b. 44–445; Jordan to Mountford Wilson, May 10, 1905, Jordan Papers, S. I-AA, b. 14.

CHAPTER 42: A MELODRAMATIC DETECTIVE STORY

1 "Body of Mrs. Stanford on Way Home," *Bulletin*, March 15, 1905, Clippings, 25: 129; "Stanford Funeral," *Hawaiian Star*, March 15, 1905; "Mrs. Stanford's Funeral to Take Place Today," *Pacific Commercial Advertiser*, March 15, 1905; "Funeral of Mrs. Stanford," *Pacific Commercial Advertiser*, March 16, 1905, 1.

2 "Jordan and Hopkins United in a Statement," *Hawaiian Star*, March 15, 1905, 1, 5; the draft of the statement is dated March 16, but given the publication in the newspapers

a day earlier, this is impossible. "Original Draft," Death of Jane Stanford, Stanford Papers, S. 4, b. 1, f. 18.

3   "Opinion Divided Among People of Honolulu Regarding Death," *Call*, March 22, 1905, 1; "San Francisco Party Departs for Home," *Chronicle*, March 16, 1905, 1; "Hold to Poison Theory," *Call*, March 15, 1905, 4.

4   "Hold to Poison Theory," *Call*, March 15, 1905, 4.

5   Philip Jones to David Starr Jordan, Jan. 23, 1905, Jordan Papers, S. I-A, b. 43–434.

6   "Dr. Jordan Scored Local Poison Theory," *Evening Bulletin*, March 15, 1905, enclosure with Dr. F.H. Humphris to Jordan, March 20, 1905, Jordan Papers, S. I-A, b. 44–443.

7   "Jordan Says Officially that Mrs. Stanford Died a Natural Death," *Examiner*, March 16, 1905, 1; "Hold to Poison Theory," *Call*, March 15, 1905, 4.

8   "San Francisco Party Departs for Home," *Chronicle*, March 16, 1905, 1.

9   "Jordan and Hopkins Unite in a Statement," *Hawaiian Star*, March 15, 1905, 1, 5; Carl Smith to Jordan, March 15, 1905, Jordan Papers, S. I-A, b. 44–442.

10 "Story of Her Death Told by Secretary," *Examiner*, March 3, 1905, 2.

11 Carl Smith to Jordan, March 15, 1905, Jordan Papers, S. I-A, b. 44–442; David Starr Jordan to Carl Smith, March 28, 1905, Jordan Papers, S. 1-AA, b. 13, v. 27.

12 "Jordan and Hopkins United in a Statement," *Hawaiian Star*, March 15, 1905, 1, 5; "Funeral of Mrs. Stanford," *Pacific Commercial Advertiser*, March 16, 1905, 1; "Jordan Says Officially that Mrs. Stanford Died a Natural Death," *Examiner*, March 16, 1905, 1; David Starr Jordan to Carl Smith, March 28, 1905, Jordan Papers, S. 1-AA, b. 13, v. 27.

13 "Have No Clew to Poisoner," *Chronicle*, March 14, 1905, 9; "Mrs. Stanford Died from Natural Causes," *Examiner*, March 14, 1905, Clippings, 25; "George Crothers on the Stanford Mystery," *Chico Record*, March 15, 1905, Clippings, 25.

14 Crothers to Horace Davis, March 10, 1905, and March 25, 1905, Davis Papers, b. 1, f. 14.

CHAPTER 43: TAY WANG AND CHIEF OF POLICE WITTMAN

1   "Arrests Likely at Any Time," *Call*, March 12, 1905, p. 28.

2   "Locate the Place Where Poison Was Sold," *Examiner*, March 9, 1905, 2.

3   Tay Wang to Jordan, March 15, 1905, Jordan Papers, b. 51–258.

4   Tay Wang to Jordan, March 15, 1905, Jordan Papers, b. 51–258. Tom Mullaney helped me try to decipher the Tay Wang letter.

5   I would like to thank Gordon Chang, Beth Lew-Williams, Alastair Su, and particularly Tamara Venit-Shelton who steered me to Yung Wing, for help on this. Yingxia Yao, "Exile in One's Homeland: Yung Wing and the Chinese Educational Mission," Master's Thesis in Interdisciplinary Studies, Oregon State University, 2014, p. 56.

6   Tay Wang to Jordan, March 15, 1905, Jordan Papers, b. 51–258; M. Bassett to Jordan, Nov. 13, 1894, Jordan Papers, S. 1-B, b. 51–258.

7   *San Francisco Municipal Reports for the Fiscal Year 1895–96* (San Francisco: Hinton, Printing Company, 1896), Appendix Board of Supervisors, San Francisco, 1895–96, 161; *San Francisco Municipal Reports for the Fiscal Year 1900–1901* (San Francisco: Hinton Printing Company, 1901), 576; "The Fire Record," *Chronicle*, Dec. 7, 1904, 7.

8   "Blackmailers Put to Rout," *Call*, March 23, 1910, 10.

9   "Bloody Reprisals Follow Tong Difficulties Among Chinamen," *Call*, Jan. 19, 1903, 10; "Dynamite and Revolvers in War Between Two High Binder Tongs," *Examiner*, Feb. 11, 1903, 9; "Chinese Educational Society Makes Denial," *Chronicle*, Jan. 8, 1899, 32.

10 "The Saunterer," *Town Talk*, Aug. 22, 1903, 8; *San Francisco Daily Times*, v. 12.

11 "Death Comes to Informer," *Chronicle*, May 9, 1903, 13. For the cross-cultural currents of Chinatown, see Tamara Venit Shelton, *Herbs and Roots: A History of Chinese Doctors in the American Medical Marketplace* (New Haven: Yale University Press, 2019). Barbara

Berglund, *Making San Francisco American: Cultural Frontiers in the Urban West, 1846–1906* (Lawrence: University of Kansas Press, 2007); Amy K. Delfalco Lippert, *Consuming Identities: Visual Culture in Nineteenth-Century San Francisco* (New York: Oxford University Press, 2018), 119, 149–52, 233–36.

12 "Chinese Substitution Frauds Involve Very Many Persons," *Call*, Sept. 13, 1903, 34; "Arrest Leaders of Three Tongs," *Call*, May 10, 1903, 18; "Chinamen Escape Fish Contractors," *Los Angeles Herald*, April 16, 1904, page no. obscured; Bean, *Boss Ruef's San Francisco*, 38; "Hutton Smiles on HighBinders," *Call*, May 12, 1903, 9; "Say Wittman Was Good Chief," *Chronicle*, March 14, 1906, 9; "Armed Men Rob a Fantan Game," *Call*, Nov. 28, 1905, 14; "Graft Inquiry Is Fizzling," *Chronicle*, Dec. 7, 1904, 9.

13 "The Saunterer," *Town Talk*, Aug. 22, 1903, 8; *San Francisco Daily Times*, v. 12; "Tells of Chinese Gambling Dens Suppressed," *Examiner*, July 2, 1903.

14 "The Saunterer," *Town Talk*, Aug. 22, 1903, 8; "Could Not Prove Conspiracy," *Call*, June 26, 1903, 14; "Place Charge of Bribery Against Edw. W. Gunther," *Call*, May 26, 1904, 5; "Nguen Lun's Case Continued," *Call*, May 29, 1904, 30; "Hom Tai Foon Declares He Testified to Order," *Call*, May 20, 1904, 7.

15 Older, *My Own Story*, 44–48.

16 Older, *My Own Story*, 44–48; "Big Chung Indicted for Murder of Tom Yick," *Chronicle*, Dec. 29, 1904, 7.

17 Special Meeting, Feb. 6, 1905, Police Commissioners; Regular Meeting, Feb. 15, 1905, Police Commissioners.

18 "Commissioners Are Told Protection Is Bought," *Chronicle*, Dec. 4, 1904, 48.

19 Special Meeting, Feb. 27, 1905, Police Commissioners.

20 "In the Matter of the Investigation of the Alleged Corrupt Conditions Existing in Chinatown," Regular Meeting, March 27, 1905, Police Commissioners.

21 "Commissioners Are Told Protection Is Bought," *Chronicle*, Dec. 4, 1904, 48; Special Meeting, Feb. 27, 1905, Police Commissioners; "In the Matter of the Investigation of the Alleged Corrupt Conditions Existing in Chinatown," Regular Meeting, March 27, 1905, Police Commissioners; "Police Commissioners Pass Blame to Chief Wittman," *Chronicle*, Dec. 20, 1904, 16.

22 Bean, *Boss Ruef's San Francisco*, 50–53.

CHAPTER 44: DEATH OF AN INVESTIGATION

1 "Mrs. Stanford's Body Arrives on the Alameda," *San Francisco News*, March 21, 1905, Clippings, 25: 351; "Miss Berner Accompanied by Detectives," *Post*, March 21, 1905, Clippings, 25: 171; "Ends Long Journey to Palo Alto," *Call*, March 22, 1905, 2.

2 "Stand by Poison Theory," *Pacific Commercial Advertiser*, March 17, 1905, 1; "Stand by Their Guns," *Hawaiian Star*, March 17, 1905, 7.

3 "Natural Cause Theory Absurd," *Post*, March 17, 1905, Clippings, 25: 143.

4 "Not Moved by Others' Opinions," *Post*, March 18, 1905, Clippings, 25: 154.

5 "Refutation of Dr. Jordan by Men Who Know the Facts," *Bulletin*, March 18, 1905, Clippings, v. 23?; "Says There Was Poison in the House," *Chronicle*, March 19, 1905, 1.

6 "Newspapers Assassins of Reputation," *San Francisco Star*, March 18, 1905, Clippings, 25: 153.

7 "Why Palo Alto Will Not Accept the Murder Theory," *Bulletin*, March 20, 1905, Clippings, 25: 351.

8 "Captain Burnett to Form His Own Conclusions," *Call*, March 18, 1905, 2; "Refute Dr. Jordan's Statement," *Bulletin*, March 17, 1905, 1, Clippings, 25: 140–41.

9 "Determined to Clear Up Poland Water Mystery," *Call*, March 18, 1905, 2; "Refute Dr. Jordan's Statement," *Bulletin*, March 17, 1905, 1, Clippings, 25: 140–41.

10 "City Chemist to Solve Doubt," *Chronicle*, March 20, 1905, 12; "Wait Patiently for the Alameda," no newspaper listed, March 19, 1905, Clippings, 25: c. 162.

11 "Secretary Gives No New Light," *Call*, March 22, 1905, 1.

12 "Claim Facts Did Not Warrant Verdict," *Chronicle*, March 22, 1905, 3; "Jordan Says Evidence Warrants Conclusion," *Call*, March 22, 1905, 2; "Detectives Get Details They Can Work Upon," *Examiner*, March 22, 1905, 2.

13 "Claim Facts Did Not Warrant Verdict," *Chronicle*, March 22, 1905, 3; "Mrs. Stanford's Remains Guarded at Home," *Tribune*, March 22, 1905, Clippings, 25: 188.

14 "Claim Facts Did Not Warrant Verdict," *Chronicle*, March 22, 1905, 3.

15 "Alameda Comes to Port from Honolulu with Remains of Mrs. Stanford," *Call*, March 22, 1905, 1; Testimony of Dr. Francis Howard Humphris, c. March 6, 1905, 56–57, Testimony of Dr. H.V. Murray, March 6, 1905, 25, Testimony of May Hunt, c. March 9, 1905, 22, Testimony of Bertha Berner, March 6, 1905, all in Coroner's Inquest; "Doctors Say Death Was by Strychnine and Nothing Else," *Call*, March 7, 1905, 2.

16 "Claim Facts Did Not Warrant Verdict," *Chronicle*, March 22, 1905, 1; "Jordan Says Evidence Warrants Conclusion," *Call*, March 22, 1905, 2.

17 "Claim Facts Did Not Warrant Verdict," *Chronicle*, March 22, 1905, 1; "Jordan Says Evidence Warrants Conclusion," *Call*, March 22, 1905, 2.

18 Cutler, *Mysterious Death*, 61; "Jordan Says Evidence Warrants Conclusion," *Call*, March 22, 1905, 2.

19 "Mrs. Stanford's Body Arrives on the Alameda," *San Francisco News*, March 21, 1905, Clippings, 25; "A Strange Circumstance in the Stanford Case," *Sacramento Bee*, March 22, 1905, Clippings, 25; "Miss Berner Accompanied by Detectives," *Post*, March 21, 1905, Clippings, 25: 171; "Claim Facts Did Not Warrant Verdict," *Chronicle*, March 22, 1905, 1, 2.

20 "Mrs. Stanford's Body Arrives on the Alameda," *San Francisco News*, March 21, 1905, Clippings, 25; "A Strange Circumstance in the Stanford Case," *Sacramento Bee*, March 22, 1905, Clippings, 25; "Miss Berner Accompanied by Detectives," *Post*, March 21, 1905, Clippings, 25: 171; "Claim Facts Did Not Warrant Verdict," *Chronicle*, March 22, 1905, 1, 2; "Miss Berner and Miss Hunt Tell Their Grim Stories," *Examiner*, March 22, 1905, 2.

21 "Claim Facts Did Not Warrant Verdict"; "Miss Berner Tells of Graft," *Chronicle*, March 22, 1905, 3.

22 "Expect to Drop Stanford Case," *Post*, March 22, 1905, Clippings, 25; "Prepare to Drop Stanford Case," *Chronicle*, March 23, 1905, 9.

CHAPTER 45: THE FUNERAL

1 "Memorandum: Religion," Crothers Papers, S. 6, b. 20, f. 2; "Notes Concerning Stanford Charter by GEC," S. 6, b. 20, f. 25, p. 21; Berner, *Mrs. Leland Stanford*, 214.

2 *Daily Palo Alto*, March 24, 1905; "Mrs. Stanford Laid to Rest," *Los Angeles Herald*, March 25, 1905; "Escort the Remains from Home to Chapel," *Call*, March 25, 1905, 3; "Lull in Investigations," *Call*, March 24, 1905, 2; "Mrs. Stanford Now Lies with Her Loved Ones," *Chronicle*, March 25, 1905, 1.

3 *Daily Palo Alto*, March 24, 1905.

4 Jane Stanford to Andrew D. White, May 19, 1901, Stanford Papers, S. 1, b. 2, f. 4.

5 Jane Stanford to Andrew D. White, May 19, 1901, Stanford Papers, S. 1, b. 2, f. 4.

6 Larkin G. Mead to Mrs. Leland Stanford, Dec. 26, 1890, Jan. 6, 1894, Dec. 20, 1901, Stanford Papers, S. 1, Correspondence, b. 7, f. 24; David Starr Jordan to George Derby, Feb. 15, 1905, Jordan Papers, S. 1-AA, b. 13, v. 26: 254.

7 https://quake06.stanford.edu/centennial/gallery/structures/memarch/index.html;

"Memorial Arch and Frieze, Stanford University," *The Monumental News: A Monthly Journal of Monumental Art* 13 (Chicago, Nov. 1901): 624–25.

8 "Memorial Arch and Frieze, Stanford University," *The Monumental News*, 624–25; Will Irwin to Jordan, Jan. 25, 1902, Jordan Papers, S. 1-A, b. 30, f. 304.

9 *Cornell Daily Sun*, April 7, 1897; *Daily Palo Alto*, Sept. 29, 1908; Clark to Jacob Voorsanger, March 8, 1905, Jordan Papers, S. 1-AA, b. 13, v. 27; List of Pallbearers, March 18, 1905, Jordan Papers, S. 1-AA, b. 13, v. 27.

10 Clark to Dinsmore, March 4, 1905, Jordan Papers, b. 13, v. 26: 497.

11 "College Deep in Mourning," *Call*, March 5, 1905, 40; "Rev. J.W. Dinsmore's Tribute to Worth of a Noble Character," *Call*, March 6, 1905, 1.

12 John Dinsmore to President Jordan, March 3, 1905; John W. Dinsmore to J.C. Branner, March 18, 1905, Stanford Papers, S. 4, b. 1, f. 16; Duniway to Dinsmore, March 20, 1905, Jordan Papers, v. 13, v. 27: 142; *Daily Palo Alto*, March 23, 1905; "College Deep in Mourning," *Call*, March 5, 1905, 40; "Rev. J.W. Dinsmore's Tribute to Worth of a Noble Character," *Call*, March 6, 1905, 1; Duniway to Brown, March 22, 1905, Jordan Papers, S. 1-AA, b. 13, v. 27, 201-A.

13 Jane Lathrop Stanford, Order of Exercises for the Funeral Service in the Memorial Church, Leland Stanford Jr. University, Friday the Twenty-fourth of March Nineteen and Five, Stanford Papers, University Matters digital copy, https://stacks.stanford.edu/image/iiif/yg162gq5117%252FSC0033B_s4_b01_f13_i001/full/1000,694/0/default.jpg; Charles Reynolds Brown, *My Own Yesterdays* (New York: The Century Company, 1931), 264; Charles Lathrop to S.F. Leib, March 16, 1908, Leib Papers, b. 2, f. 1; Jane Stanford to Horace Davis, Jan. 28, 1905, Stanford Papers, S. 1, b. 2, f. 10; Jane Stanford to Horace Davis, Jan. 28, 1905, Stanford Papers, S. 1, b. 2, f. 10.

14 Chairman of Committee to Rev. Charles W. Brown, March 22, 1905, Stanford Papers, S. 4, b. 1, f. 16.

15 *Daily Palo Alto*, March 24, 1905, 3, 8.

16 Jane Lathrop Stanford, Order of Exercises for the Funeral Service in the Memorial Church, Stanford Papers, University Matters 33b, digital copy; "Mrs. Stanford Laid to Rest," *Los Angeles Herald*, March 25, 1905, 1; "Tribute of Respect," *Call*, March 25, 1905, 3; S.F. Leib to Jennie Lawton (a different niece), March 6, 1905, Stanford Papers, S. 4, b. 1, f. 10; "Contents of Will Made Known," *Call*, March 5, 1905, 39.

17 "The Body of Mrs. Stanford Will Reach the University To-Morrow," *Daily Palo Alto*, March 20, 1905; Services in Honolulu," *Daily Palo Alto*, March 16, 1905; Cutler, *Mysterious Death*, 18–19.

18 "Tribute of Respect," *Call*, March 25, 1905, 3.

19 General Arrangements for the Funeral of Mrs. Jane Stanford, Funeral and Memorial Services, 1905, Stanford Papers, S. 5, b. 1; https://searchworks.stanford.edu/view/zc526gw6427; "Asa P. Stanford's Widow Sues Estate for a Million," *Examiner*, June 5, 1906, 1; "Court Ends Feud of Stanford Heirs," *Examiner*, April 7, 1908, 1.

20 *Call*, March 4, 1905, Clippings, 24: 59; Jordan, *The Story of a Good Woman*, Prefatory Note, 2.

21 *Call*, March 4, 1905, Clippings, 24: 59; Jordan, *The Story of a Good Woman*, Prefatory Note, 2; *Literary Digest*, March 11, 1905, Clippings, 24: 102; "Services in Honolulu," *Daily Palo Alto*, March 16, 1905; "Dr. Jordan's Tribute," *Tacoma Washington News*, March 1, 1905, Clippings, 23: 5, 23: 23.

22 Memorandum, Confidential to George Herbert Palmer, Sept. 28, 1905, Jordan Papers, S. 1-B, b. 47, f. 197. Goebel preserved his correspondence with Jordan, starting with Jordan to Goebel, Feb. 28, 1905, see that and following letters, also Goebel to Advisory Board, n.d., 1905, and "Autocracy at Stanford," in Goebel Papers, b. 4; "Dismissed from

Stanford by Jordan," *Mercury*, June 1, 1905, Clippings, 26; S. Clark to Stillman, March 28, 1905, Jordan to Stillman, n.d. 1905, Goebel Papers, b. 3, f. Gilbert Affair; "Professor Jordan Will Shorten European Tour," *San Jose News*, Aug. 4, 1905; "Dr. Goebel Loser in Fight with Dr. Jordan," *Examiner*, Aug. 4, 1905, both in Clippings, 26: 95; W.B. Carnochan, "The Case of Julius Goebel: Stanford, 1905," *American Scholar* 72, no. 3 (Summer 2003): 95–108.

23 Crothers to Davis, May 29, 1905, and June 9, 1905, Davis Papers, b. 1, f. 15; Carnochan, "The Case of Julius Goebel," 101–8; "Talking with Mr. George E. Crothers," Sept. 25, 1931, Goebel Affair, Elliott Papers, b. 2, f. 24.

CHAPTER 46: COVERING UP THE COVER-UP

1 "Cologne Spilled on Soda," *Chronicle*, March 22, 1905, 3.

2 Jordan to Mountford Wilson, March 23, 1905, Stanford Papers, S. 4, b. 1, f. 11.

3 David Starr Jordan to Carl Smith, March 24, 1905, Stanford Papers, S. 4, b. 1, f. 11.

4 "Rough Draft," Crothers Papers, S. 6, b. 20, f. 2, pp. 7–8; "Memoranda, Chapter 17 for Elliott Book," Crothers Papers, S. 7, b. 21, f. 45.

5 Crothers to Mrs. Older, Jan. 30, 1947, Crothers Papers, Correspondence, Outgoing, b. 3; Memoranda in George E. Crothers to Frederick Rogers, June 24, 1947, Crothers Papers, S. 7, b. 21, f. 45; Memoranda Re: Stanford University, S. 7, b. 21, f. 47.

6 Bertha Berner to Jordan, March 28, 1905, Jordan Papers, S. 1-A, b. 44–445.

7 Jordan to Berner, March 30, 1905, Jordan Papers, b. 13, v. 27: 375.

8 Bertha Berner to S.F. Leib, 1905, Leib Papers, b. 1, f. 1.

9 "New Stanford Poison Hunt," *New York Times*, Aug. 26, 1905, 1.

10 Francis H. Humphris to Jordan, March 20, 1905, Jordan Papers, S. 1-A, b. 44–443; Jordan to Francis H. Humphris, March 28, 1905, Jordan Papers, S. 1-A, b. 13, v. 27.

11 Jordan to Robert Shaw, March 27, 1905, Jordan Papers, S. I-AA, b. 13, v. 27: 332.

12 Jordan to M.S. Wilson, March 22, 1905, Stanford Papers, S. 4, b. 1, f. 11.

13 David Starr Jordan to Carl Smith, March 24, 1905, Stanford Papers, S. 4, b. 1, f. 11; David Starr Jordan to Montford Wilson, March 23, 1905, Stanford Papers, S. 4, b. 1, f. 11; David Starr Jordan to Prof. Keinasuke Otaki, April 13, 1905, Jordan Papers, S. I-AA, b. 14; David Starr Jordan to Carl S. Smith, March 24, 1905, Stanford Papers, S. 4, b. 1, f. 11.

14 Waterhouse to Jordan, April 23, 1905, Jordan Papers, S. I-A, b. 44–449; Smith to Jordan, April 15, 1905, S. 1-A, b. 44–447.

15 Smith to Jordan, April 15, 1905, Jordan Papers, S. I-A, b. 44–447.

16 "Mrs. Stanford Case Matter of Comment," *Call*, Sept. 7, 1905, 9.

17 Jordan to Waterhouse, May 4, 1905, Jordan Papers, S. 1-AA, b. 14.

18 Smith to Jordan, April 30, 1905, Jordan Papers, S. I-A, b. 44–450.

19 Jordan to Smith, April 13, 1905, Jordan Papers, S. I-AA, b. 14.

20 Edmund Shorey to David Starr Jordan, March 31, 1905, Jordan Papers, S. 1-AA, b. 44–445; David Starr Jordan to Edmund Shorey, April 13, 1905, Jordan Papers, S. I-AA, b. 14, 7.

21 Jordan to Smith, May 4, 1905, and May 10, 1905, both in Jordan Papers, S. I-AA, b. 14; Jordan to Lyman Wilbur, May 18, 1921, Stanford Papers, S. 4, b. 1, f. 11.

22 Cutler, *Mysterious Death*, 71; "Would Solve Stanford Tragedy," *Examiner*, May 25, 1905, 1; "Welton Stanford to Take Up Inquiry," *Examiner*, May 26, 1905, 1.

23 Cutler, *Mysterious Death*, 71; "Would Solve Stanford Tragedy," *Examiner*, May 25, 1905, 1; "Welton Stanford to Take Up Inquiry," *Examiner*, May 26, 1905, 1; "$1000 Reward in Stanford Mystery," *Los Angeles Examiner*, May 25, 1905, Clippings, 26: 2; "Stanford Case," *Palo Alto Citizen*, May 27, 1905, Clippings, 26: 8.

24 Jordan to Smith, May 4, 1905, and May 10, 1905, both in Jordan Papers, S. I-AA, b. 14;

Jordan Lyman Wilbur, May 18, 1905, Stanford Papers, S. 4, b. 1, f. 11; "No Poison in Body of Founder," *Examiner*, May 26, 1905, 1.

25 Cutler, *Mysterious Death*, 71; "Fragmentary Memoranda," Crothers Papers, S. 9, b. 22, f. 2, pp. 2, 3; Handwritten Accounting, Legal Matters, Settling Estate, Crothers Papers, S. 9, b. 22, f. 11; "Search Traces of Strychnine," *Hawaiian Star*, Dec. 4, 1907, 1.

26 Cutler, *Mysterious Death*, 73; Bertha Berner, *Incidents in the Life of Mrs. Leland Stanford* (Ann Arbor, MI: Edwards Brothers, 1934), 179–80; Berner, *Mrs. Leland Stanford*, 205.

27 Cutler, *Mysterious Death*, 73.

28 Berner, *Mrs. Leland Stanford*, 210.

29 Cutler, *Mysterious Death*, 71.

30 Berner, *Mrs. Leland Stanford*, 205.

31 Jordan to Wilbur, May 18, 1921, Stanford Papers, S. Death and Estate, b. 1, f. 11.

32 "President Jordan on Vacation," *San Francisco News*, May 27, 1905, Clippings, 26: 9.

33 "Jordan Talks to Graduates," *Santa Cruz Sentinel*, May 26, 1905, 3.

CHAPTER 47: ALMOST AN ACT OF JUST RETRIBUTION

1 "Accepted Position at Stanford University," *Mercury*, Feb. 23, 1905, Clippings, 24: 42; Linda Simon, "William James at Stanford," *California History* 69, no. 4 (Winter 1990/1991): 332–41; William James to Jordan, Sept. 1, 1904, Jordan Papers, S. 1-A, b. 41–411.

2 Draft letter, Goebel to Horace Davis, 1905, Goebel Papers, b. 1; "Dr. Goebel Loser in Fight with Dr. Jordan," *Examiner*, Aug. 4, 1905; "Professor Jordan Will Shorten European Tour," *San Jose News*, Aug. 4, 1905, Clippings, 26: 95; Horace Davis to Joseph Grant, Dec. 18, 1905, Elliott Papers, b 3, f. 2.

3 "Stanford Denials and Facts," *Hawaiian Star*, Sept. 4, 1905, Clippings, 1; "Dr. Jordan Alleges a Plot to Loot Stanford Estate," *Call*, Dec. 31, 1905, 1, 30; Laura Todd to Gov. George Carter, Jan. 4, 1906, with enclosures, folder: Carter Miscellaneous (not indexed), Gov. 2–10, Hawaii State Archives.

4 "Dr. Jordan Alleges a Plot to Loot Stanford Estate," *Call*, Dec. 31, 1905, 1, 30.

5 "Fears the Result: President Jordan Now Says He Has Been Misquoted," *Santa Rosa Press Democrat*, Jan. 2, 1906, 1; "Sensation Promised by David Starr Jordan," *Call*, Dec. 31, 1905, 30; Jordan to Smith, March 24, 1905, Stanford Papers, Death and Estate, S. 4, b. 1, f. 11; Jordan to Robert Shaw, March 27, 1905, Jordan Papers, S. I-AA, b. 13, v. 27, pp. 332–33.

6 "Dr. Jordan Connected by High Sheriff with the Stanford Case," *Hawaiian Evening Bulletin*, Jan. 2, 1906, 1.

7 "No Poison Was Found," *Oakland Tribune*, May 26, 1905, 9; "Dr. Jordan Alleges a Plot to Loot Stanford Estate," *Call*, Dec. 31, 1905, 1, 30; Laura Todd to Gov. George Carter, Jan. 4, 1906, with enclosures, folder: Carter Miscellaneous (not indexed), Gov. 2–10, Hawaii State Archives; Maria Margaretha Berner, U.S. Find a Grave Index, Ancestry. com; "Dies at Her Home in Menlo Park," *Chronicle*, July 23, 1905, 40.

8 Simon, "William James at Stanford," 332–41; William James to Jordan, Sept. 1, 1904, Jordan Papers, S. 1-A, b. 41–411; "Accepted Position at Stanford University," Feb. 23, 1905, Clippings, 24: 42; Alice James to Henry James, April 8, 1906, *Correspondence of William James*, vol. 11 (Charlottesville: University of Virginia Press, 2003), 2926; Emily Harnett, "William James and the Spiritualist's Phone," *Lapham's Quarterly*, Feb. 4, 2019; Moore, *In Search of White Crows*.

9 William James to Alice James, Jan. 17, 1906, *Correspondence of William James*, vol. 11, 148.

10 William James to George Holmes Howison, Jan. 23, 1906, William James to Alice

James, Jan. 24, 1906, *Correspondence of William James*, vol. 11, 152–53; Simon, "William James at Stanford," 336; William James to Henry James, Feb. 1, 1906, *Correspondence of William James*, vol. 11, 161, fn. 3.

11   William James to Alexander James, March 5, 1906, *Correspondence of William James*, vol. 11, 187.

12   William James to Katherine Rodgers, Jan. 4, 1906, William James Papers, 3587.

13   William James to Katherine Rodgers, Jan. 4, 1906, William James Papers, 3587; William James to Alexander James, March 5, 1906, *Correspondence of William James*, vol. 11, 187; William James to Alice James, Jan. 16, 1906, *Correspondence of William James*, vol. 11, 145–46; William James to George Bucknam Dorr, March 20, 1906, *Correspondence of William James*, vol. 11, 190–91.

14   William James to Katherine Rodgers, Jan. 4, 1906, William James Papers, 3587; William James to Alexander James, March 5, 1906, *Correspondence of William James*, vol. 11, 187; William James to Alice James, Jan. 16, 1906, *Correspondence of William James*, vol. 11, 145–46; William James to George Bucknam Dorr, March 20, 1906, *Correspondence of William James*, vol. 11, 190–91.

15   William James to Pauline Goldmark, Feb. 13, 1906, *Correspondence of William James*, vol. 11, 177–78; James to Charles William Eliot, Feb. 22, 1906, *Correspondence of William James*, vol. 11, 181–82.

16   William James to Alice James, Jan. 30, 1906, William James Papers, 2346; William James to Alice James, Jan. 9, 1906, William James Papers, Houghton Library, 2332.

17   William James to Ralph Barton Perry, Feb. 26, 1906, *Correspondence of William James*, vol. 11, 183–84.

18   William James to Ralph Barton Perry, Feb. 26, 1906, *Correspondence of William James*, vol. 11, 183–84; William James to Ralph Barton Perry, April 11, 1906, *Correspondence of William James*, vol. 11, 200.

19   William James to Margaret Mary James, April 8, 1906, *Correspondence of William James*, vol. 11, 199; William James to Miss Frances R. Morse, April 22, 1906, *The Letters of William James*, ed. Henry James, vol. 2 (Boston: Atlantic Monthly Press, 1920), 247–49.

20   Elliott, *Stanford University*, 146–48.

21   "Sues Stanford Estate for a Million," *Examiner*, June 5, 1906, 2; "Rich Relatives Let Him Die in Abject Poverty," *Examiner*, June 7, 1906, 3.

22   William James to Horace Davis, April 19, 1906, Davis Papers, b. 1, f. 19.

23   David Starr Jordan to Horace Davis, May 20, 1906, Davis Papers, b. 1, f. 19.

24   Jordan, *The Story of a Good Woman*.

25   Mrs. Jordan on Mrs. Stanford, Paper Read to the Palo Alto Chapter of the Daughters of the American Revolution (1927), Elliott Papers, b. 2, f. 6.

26   Older, *My Own Story*, vi–viii.

EPILOGUE: WHO KILLED HER?

1   Josephine Tey, *The Daughter of Time* (New York: Scribner, 2020, original edition, 1951), 201.

2   "Chinese Tells Who Makes Plans for 'Yellow Death,'" *Examiner*, May 18, 1904, 10; "Court Hears Perjury Plot," *Examiner*, May 19, 1904, 3; "Fong Ling Switches His Former Testimony," *Chronicle*, May 18, 1904, 20; "Wants Presidents Jailed," *Call*, May 19, 1904, 9. There were several variants of the basic story: "Ah Sow Offers Husband Bowl of Poisoned Soup," *Call*, July 16, 1904, 16; "Like Lucretia Borgia," *Los Angeles Herald*, July 16, 1904, 2; "A Mongolian Borgia Fails in Her Attempt," *Chronicle*, July 16, 1904, 14; "Ah Sow Denies Putting Poison in the Soup," *Examiner*, July 20, 1904, 12.

3   "Miss Berner Tells of Graft," *Chronicle*, March 22, 1905, 2.

4   "Secretary Is Tangled Among Contradictions," *Examiner*, March 4, 1905, 2.

5   "Dr. M.M. Carter," *Tribune*, Aug. 19, 1906, 26; "Cotton Carnival Is Now On," *Tribune*, July 20, 1905, 2.

6   *Crocker-Langley San Francisco Directory for the Year Commencing 1904* (San Francisco: H.S. Crocker Co., 1904), 326, 563.

7   "Suits Begun by Unhappy Wives," *Chronicle*, July 8, 1904, 13.

8   "Marriage Certificates," *San Jose Herald*, July 14, 1900, 8.

9   Richard Doyle, 1880; Census: San Francisco, San Francisco, California; Roll: 77; Page: 320A; Enumeration District: 170, 1880.

10 Katherine Doyle, San Francisco Assembly District 42, San Francisco, California, Thirteenth Census of the United States, 1910 (NARA microfilm publication T624, 1,178 rolls); Records of the Bureau of the Census, Record Group 29, National Archives, Washington, DC, Roll: T624_101; Page: 15A; Enumeration District: 0282.

11 *Crocker-Langley San Francisco Directory for the Year Commencing 1904*, 326, 563.

12 Richard Doyle, 1900; Census Place: San Francisco, San Francisco, California; Page: 9; Enumeration District: 0097; FHL microfilm: 1240102, United States of America, Bureau of the Census, Twelfth Census of the United States, 1900. Washington, DC: National Archives and Records Administration, 1900, T623.

13 Paul Dexler, "Joe 'Kid' Sullivan: King of the Pickpockets," *Examiner*, Aug. 6, 2007; Bean, *Boss Ruef's San Francisco*, 50.

14 "Dinan Tries Tricks of Tammany," *Call*, Oct. 18, 1907, 1, 8; Paul Dexler, "Joe 'Kid' Sullivan: King of the Pickpockets," *Examiner*, Aug. 6, 2007; William Issel and Robert W. Cherny, *San Francisco, 1865–1932: Politics, Power, and Urban Development* (Berkeley: University of California Press), 154–57, 172–73; Bean, *Boss Ruef's San Francisco*, 189, 212–13, 226–27, 268, 284.

15 George Kennan, "The Fight for Reform in San Francisco," *McClure's Magazine* 29 (Sept. 1907): 547–60, quote, 552; Kevin Starr, *Inventing the Dream: California Through the Progressive Era* (New York: Oxford University Press, 1986), 266–67; Bean, *Boss Ruef's San Francisco*, 284–85.

16 Death, Bertha Berner, Ancestry.com, California Death Index, 1940–1997; Original data: State of California, California Death Index, 1940–1997; Sacramento, CA, USA: State of California Department of Health Services, Center for Health Statistics; Death, August Berner, Ancestry.com, California Death Index, 1940–1997; Original data: State of California, California Death Index, 1940–1997; Sacramento, CA, USA: State of California Department of Health Services, Center for Health Statistics; Thomas N. Canning to the Editor, Sept. 20, 2000, *Almanac News*, http://www.almanacnews.com/morgue/2000/2000_09_20.letter20.html.

INDEX

wills and trusts, 48, 59–60, 76–77, 83,
131–35, 175–76, 185–86, 199, 202, 205,
229–31, 243, 266–70, 291, 292, 299
Stanford, Leland, Jr.
collections, 3, 39
death, 3, 37–40, 51
memorial service and funeral, 41–44, 148
and slate writing, 47
travels of body after death, 42–43, 51
Stanford, Leland, Sr., 38
allegations of illegitimate son, 249
early years, 49–51
and eugenics, 23, 68–69, 300
as governor of California, 50–51
grieving son's death, 39–40
illness, 39
as Mason, 262
as railroad associate, 49–51
ranches, 57
settlement of estate, 75–79
and Southern Pacific Railroad, 63, 107
speech to trustees, 89
as U.S. Senator, 51, 62
views on education, 51–52, 57
Stanford, Thomas Welton, 46–47, 69,
143–46
Stanford, Welton, 275
Stanford choir, 266
Stanford family, 195–96
Stanford Mausoleum, 284
Stanford Medical School, 276
Stanford Memorial Arch, 263, 283–84
Stanford Memorial Church, 7–8, 44, 89,
123–27, 153, 261–62, 264, 284
Stanford Museum, 132, 161
Stanford Pharmacy, 25, 189–90, 207
Stanford University
amendments to founding documents,
71–72
annual report (1905), 23
archives, 47, 69, 70, 144, 145, 150
Board of Trustees, 17, 23–25, 28, 54, 70,
89, 101, 103, 118–21, 129–30, 133,
141, 147–51, 156–63, 169, 176, 259,
267, 279
campus, 261–64
Enabling Act, 53–54, 67, 71, 133
endowment and funding, 51, 54, 57–60,
66, 70–72, 78–79, 131–35, 159, 280
faculty resignations, 102–3

founding, 36, 39–40, 51–54
Founding Grant, 53–54, 71–72, 88, 99,
134
governance, 23–24, 27, 66–68, 120–22,
131–35, 147–51, 156–61
Grant of Endowment, 88, 99
historical accounts, 33–34
Jane's domination of, 66–70
Jane Stanford Way, 300
library, 66, 116–17, 119, 143, 158, 181
museum, 31, 39, 123, 132, 141, 148,
161, 284
Professor of Personal Ethics, 66
Psychic Research fellowship, 146
publicity, 9
reputation, 186
and Ross Affair, 115
salaries, 24–25, 59, 123, 157
"Stone Age," 123, 261
tax exemption, 99
Stanford University Trust Bank, 18
Stanley, W. L., 181, 183, 189, 205, 207, 229
Stead, W. T., 100
Stein, Gertrude, 281
Stevenson, Robert Louis, 3
Stillman, J. M., 104
Story of a Good Woman, The (Jordan), 285
streetcars, 8
street railways, 93, 101, 108, 132
strychnine; *See also* bicarbonate of soda
(and container); Poland Spring Water
poisoning
as agent of suicide/murder, 163–64
in pure form, 289, 291–92
in rat poison, 13, 16, 34, 163, 196
symptoms of poisoning by, 235–38,
256–58, 273
Stryker, Miss, 202
Suey Ying tong, 249–50
Sullivan, Joe "Kid," 186–87, 296, 297
Sun Lee Lung, 250
Suzzallo, Anthony, 103

Taylor, William E., 222, 224
Tay Wang, 248–50, 253, 269
"Testimony of Dr. Waterhouse," 235–36; *See
also* Waterhouse, Ernest C.
Tey, Josephine, 287–88, 299
They Met in Heaven (Hepworth), 66–67
Todd, Laura, 280